SPIRITUAL EXERCISES FOR A SECULAR AGE

SPIRITUAL EXERCISES FOR A SECULAR AGE

DESMOND AND THE QUEST FOR GOD

RYAN G. DUNS, SJ

FOREWORD BY WILLIAM DESMOND

University of Notre Dame Press
Notre Dame, Indiana

University of Notre Dame Press
Notre Dame, Indiana 46556
undpress.nd.edu
All Rights Reserved

Published in the United States of America

"Primary Wonder" by Denise Levertov, from *Sands of the Well*,
copyright ©1994, 1995, 1996 by Denise Levertov.
Reprinted by permission of New Directions Publishing Corp.

Library of Congress Control Number: 2020911372

ISBN: 978-0-268-10813-7 (Hardback)
ISBN: 978-0-268-10816-8 (WebPDF)
ISBN: 978-0-268-10815-1 (Epub)

CONTENTS

FOREWORD

There is much of music in this book. Indeed, there is music in the book, music with a poetic, religious, and philosophical resonance. Ryan Duns is himself an adept at traditional Irish music, and I am heartened to hear something of Irish music in the words of this work. There is also something of the musical, in theological and philosophical senses, that resonates in this work. As with much music that touches one, one is tempted into variations on the theme.

The book's exploration is a return archaeologically to origins, and in the musical sense, namely, to the muses that are the endowers of human originality in diverse domains: the poetic, the theological, and the philosophical. I do not invoke the muses to set pagan against Christian, and I do indeed think that one line of Catholic genius has been to call forth an including family of inspiration. If God is the companioning power par excellence, the muses are companioning powers, coming to the aid of the endowment that enables the originating powers of the diverse arts, offering the gift of being mindful. I have myself contrasted thought thinking itself to thought not only thinking its other but to thought *singing* its other. The others for philosophy in this case are especially the religious and mediately the theological, and also the poetic, though this not aestheticized in a more secularized sense but as a vocation pursed in the light of its family relation to the sacred. There is the note of this singing in Ryan Duns's work.

Duns provides us with an illuminating map of the contemporary landscape of thought where especially the contested place of the religious and diverse attitudes toward metaphysics are outlined. Charles Taylor is a major figure in this landscape, but figures such as John Caputo,

Richard Kearney, and Merold Westphal also appear. He beats the bounds of this space, and I am glad Duns has praise for my own praise of metaphysics and the impossibility of ever avoiding its ever-recurrent perplexities—and their ever-recurrent relevance to the explorations of theology. I need not repeat his admirable account of my own demurral relative to claims about the end of metaphysics, or to claims that our age is now postmetaphysical. Among other things, the cul-de-sac of the Heideggerian *Holzweg* has long been evident to me, and I harbor the hope that others too will come to see this. Instead of boringly repetitive onslaughts on "onto-theology," far better to compose what I have called "metaphysical cantos" relative to the God of the between.

Of course, ways are crucial. We travel through a landscape, and if the terrain is terra incognita, a map is truly helpful. I have traveled the landscape, and I do think this book as a map will be very helpful. I myself have talked about crossing and crisscrossing the landscape of the between, and on different journeys different senses of being might well present themselves as the fitting way to word the between. In this regard Duns rightly calls on Pierre Hadot as recalling us to the older sense of philosophy as a way of life.

Our relation to this kind of journey is necessarily intimate, even if opening up to the universal. Early in my own work the image of the journey is crucially present and recurrent latter. I described *Desire, Dialectic and Otherness* as an "Augustinian odyssey, embarked on in the wake of Hegel." The itinerary tried to remain true to the double directionality suggested by Augustine: *ab exterioribus ad interiora, ab inferioribus ad superiora*—"from the exterior to the interior, from the inferior to the superior."[1] It also tried to remain true to Augustine's deep words that God is *interior intimo meo et superior summo meo*—"more interior (to me) than my most intimate intimacy and superior to my highest summit" (*Conf.* 3.6.11)

The itinerary more to the forefront in this book is somewhat more Ignatian than Augustinian. One need not see these two in discordance. The stress is on discernment, and *askesis*. Duns is discerning in stressing the itinerant way of the thought. I am thinking of my book *Philosophy and Its Other: Ways of Being and Mind*. Here too are ways. I should also say that although in that work I speak of philosophy as a "discipline of mindful thought," I intend a more ecumenical sense of being mindful, not unrelated to the possibility of consecrated thought.

Crossing the between: the later Heidegger crosses (out) being and one can see the point, though *qua* gesture, its power, once made, tends soon to fade. I had toyed with the gesture of crossing out the entirety of *God and the Between*, as a figure of the apophatic side of the journey, but no publisher would stand for that. I did settle on the analogy with those older passports that carried stamps of journeys and destinations, but now crossed out once the passport had seen its day. The passport is still a witness to the fact that journeys were undertaken. Journeys would still call to be undertaken by others. In matters religious, no one else can undertake the journey for us, but witnesses can encourage or guide or warn. Duns picks up deftly on the image of the passport with multiple stamps, stressing also that others must themselves undertake their own journey along ways and along the way. Along the way we can get lost, we try to get our bearings, we conserve, we sometimes pause and think and sing.

I am recalled to the sense of an Ignatian itinerary with reference to a Jesuit philosopher/theologian who was important early in my own coming to philosophy: Bernard Lonergan. Lonergan speaks of his book *Insight* as being written from "a moving standpoint." I endorse the point. The practice of thought has this moving character, and later thoughts in an unfolding are intimately related to earlier, either as modifications or reformulations or repudiations. This means that the one who tries to follow the path should enter into the moving activity of thinking, become engaged in a kind of peregrine reflection rather than be the collector of cut-and-dried propositions. Strong too was Lonergan's stress on self-appropriation, a matter that also entails that no one else can substitute for you in undertaking the adventure of self-knowing.

I mention another figure, Hegel, with whom I have wrestled, as also giving witness to the "moving standpoint" of a dialectical unfolding, particularly in his *Phenomenology of Spirit*. The great French Jesuit Gaston Fessard wrote a book entitled *La dialectique des "Exercices spirituels" de saint Ignace de Loyola*. Duns's book here is closer to the metaxology of the *Spiritual Exercises*. The "moving standpoint" has something to do with the intimate togetherness of form and matter in a philosophical reflection. The dynamism of the unfolding is not merely propaedeutic to the static presentation of determinate results. It is not a merely embellishing form added to a content or matter that otherwise can be represented. There is a seeking of fidelity to the dynamic nature of the matter itself as it unfolds itself and comes to fitting form.

These considerations are at work also in this book. There is here a kind of artistic principle, insofar as the form of art is always a forming and never a frozen structure. Forming awakens mindful movement in resonance with the dynamism of the enlivened form. One might see how a musical piece very much witnesses to such a sense of moving form. Once again, a kind of music is in the air.

I take this musical air to resonate with the relating of philosophy and theology at work here. Philosophy and theology encounter each other on a threshold where they can turn away from each other, they can touch each other, they can turn towards each other. There is a myriad of ways of turning towards and turning away, or touching. Generally, when the definition of philosophy in modernity stresses self-determining thought, a kind of turning away from theology can ensue, such as we can find in any number of thinkers. What then of the touching and being touched on the threshold? One need only note that, though given their difference by this threshold, they can also be held together by it. I find with metaxological philosophy that a companioning relation is possible between the philosophical and the religious/theological. I find this throughout this work.

What of it? A new receptivity can awaken a new porosity between them, if philosophy is metaxological, that is, as essentially defined by its offering a *logos* of the *metaxu* (the between). Then philosophy is what it is, not solely in relation to itself, but in relation to its significant others. In fact, throughout the long history of different practices of philosophy, our being religious and, mediately, our being theological have been the most significant of philosophy's others. The claim of self-determining philosophy is an essentially modern projection of its venture and is not metaxological in this relevant regard: there is to be nothing between such philosophy and theology, for philosophy would define itself as essentialy for itself and self-determining.

If the threshold is metaxological, both our being religious and philosophical are intimate others in a porous between wherein what is most original and ultimate is to be diversely engaged. I tend to think of the relation of philosophy and theology as a companioning one. One must note that companions can be themselves, and yet if they are bound together, they may need each other and yet not always out of need alone. If companions break bread together (*cum-panis*), it is their shared need of what is beyond them both that binds them together.

This companioning allows reflection on the togetherness of being religious and philosophical in a living sense, rather than on boundary questions between philosophy and theology in an academic sense. Our being is to be religious, and this in an ontological rather than academic sense. Companioning suggests we take the exigence as more primordial than the discipline. Of course, the exigence may require the discipline to be more fully understood. It may also mean that the discipline without the exigence can become an intellectual *technē* without animating soul. We have sounding brass and clanging cymbals rather than music that can be concordant, even in discordance. This music puts us in mind here of the difference between philosophy considered as *scientia* (science) and as *sapientia* (wisdom).

It is not too much to say that companioning is central to Duns's work. The metaxological sense of threshold and porosity comes into play here, and I think this book dwells on this threshold with admirable porosity to a plurality of philosophical and theological voices. I admire how attuned this work is to the promise of such a metaxological companionship, again in a space where many voices seek to be heard. Rightly also it gives witness to the fact that this is not just a matter of intellectual reflection, though it is that, but more intimately it is in a living participation out of which the faithful mindfulness comes.

To return to ways: there are old ways that sometimes are rejected because they are old, or perhaps because they do not take us to destinations we want to reach, or perhaps we cannot walk them because we lack the desire and the fitness. There are old and new ways, and sometimes the old ways need clearing and renovation, having been unused and become overgrown with brambles. There are pathways that, almost by divine magic, come to be in the very act of walking along them. Ways of thought and spirit are sometimes such ways in the sense that they ask for the fitting word to make their manifestation. They are not conjured from nothing by us, but most often have to be newly found, and not so much brought into being by us as discovered in the daring act of stepping into the mystery of the unknown and finding oneself in being upheld and now able to move forward. The companionship of philosophy and religion finds them together with the companioning power in the act of moving forward, into pathways newly to be found again or dared, as if for the first time.

I think here that the music of this daring brings us back to the muse of poetics, equally intimate to our being religious and to consecrated thought. I need not repeat how I conceive the relation of poetics and system, but I do want to acknowledge how finely Duns is attuned to the poetics of the matter. There is a sacral poetics, a poetics that is consecrated and consecrates.

Interestingly, poetics and *askesis* can be seen in their togetherness, in a sense quite other to the way Nietzsche counterposes the power of art to the sapping of potency by ascetical morality. At stake is not asceticism in the form that Nietzsche criticizes, which is a superimposition that potentially mutilates. It is a finding of the fitting form, finding in the fitting form the words that are proper to the thing itself. *Askesis* entails a kind of "no," yes, but if so, it is a "no" that reopens the porosity, and what pours through the porosity is entirely positive or affirmative.

One of the most important witnesses of the porosity can be connected with meditative prayer. Religious porosity is perhaps the most intimate awakening of this porosity of being. Prayer at heart is not something that we simply do; it is something that we find ourselves in, something that comes to us, as we find ourselves already opened to the divine as other to us and yet as in intimate communication with us. The moments of so being graced happen to us in the most intimate and exposed porosity. We often endeavor to fill the original openness with many determinate things, with desires, ambitions, aspirations, interpretations, and so forth. The disciplines of prayer, meditation, and contemplation can be forms of *askesis* that allow for the uncluttering of the original porosity. Perhaps today many of us have difficulty with prayer because we have a diminished feel for this more original porosity of being. I take this book as an aid in uncluttering. Such aid is in familial solidarity with the spiritual exercises.

On *askesis* one recalls the discipline of the athlete, indeed the image of the runner used by St. Paul. The point of the discipline is to be released into the energies that will carry one to the end. (In the *Cratylus*, Socrates refers to himself as a runner who does not always stick to the track.) I have myself described the perfect race as one in which one seems almost in a kind of dreamless sleep, yet with most intense and acute mindfulness. One might compare it to the form that the Buddhists say is emptiness. Mulling on this book, one might say that Ignatian *keno-*

sis also might be named as reopening the porosity through which music that is divine can stream.

Finding the fitting form again: this entails finesse—a word used richly by Pascal, another kind of Augustinian, and not always received as a companion by friends of Ignatius. Finesse and the spirit of discernment are siblings in the same family, if not secret twins. The embrace of Pascal and Ignatius can happen in the intimate universal.

Passing through and the dynamic of thinking: music again is when it sounds, and when it no longer sounds, there is silence. It does not simply vanish, but its not being sounded perhaps resounds in the deeper porosity of the soul of which we mostly lack self-knowledge. Duns stresses well the side of thinking as an enactment: there is no thought without the thinking. The wording of the enactive performance of thinking has a poetics. The poetics is not other than cultivating the sacred or being cultivated: *cultus* invokes the act of worship, but there is something mysterious. Think of the poem "The Given Note" by Seamus Heaney: the note is taken from the air, out of the night, as it comes off the wind of the mid-Atlantic, from nowhere, and composes itself into air, with the fiddler, who has gone alone into the island, in tune. But the air is giving.

One could say: singing is just breathing in a certain way. But what breath? There is breathing that is breathtaking. One thinks of the great singer, for instance, Joan Sutherland, *la Stupenda*, as she was called. *Askesis*: recall the breath that comes effortlessly to the properly trained athlete—or the music that passes into the porosity of the soul and is transmitted into communicative form by being played—or the breath being incarnated by a fleshed wording of the sacred between. Enactment is a being enacted.

What comes across in Duns's book also is a feel for the surprise of revelation. In tune with what we have just said, one recalls the disciples at Emmaus who were gifted with a second awakening, though they seemed already to be awake, a second awakening that was an awakening for the first time. Metaxology here asks for *metanoia*. Companioning thought can seed a metanoetics. The companionship of the stranger along the road to Emmaus startles the disciples with his surprising finesse for the sacred writing. They share bread, break bread, and when the moment of manifestation and recognition comes, there is a passing and a vanishing—and a passion that is an inspiring. They turn back to Jerusalem.

I am engaged in a double sense by this book: my thought being engaged, I myself am engaged by this. There is a musical *seisiún* (session) staged playfully by Duns at the end, and Charles Taylor and I sit together. Taylor is perhaps not improbably placed in this scene: if I am not mistaken, on his mother's side, he does have Irish ancestry. Having read the book, the real *seisiún*, however, is perhaps more with Duns than Taylor. As author of this book he plays, so to say, all the instruments.

This is a splendid book, deftly molded into an admirable work of philosophical and theological reflection, a work in which also there is wise porosity among the aesthetic, the ethical, and the religious. These thoughts are inspired (I breathe again) by this book. Needless to say, something of the more personal voice inevitably is to be heard in its sapiential orientation. The personal voice that resounds in the work communicates imaginatively, intelligently, lucidly, and with wise measure. Such a companion does not only break and share bread. He inherits and is vexed by Socrates's last dream just before departing on *slí na fírinne*, and seeks himself to make music.

WILLIAM DESMOND
David Cook Chair in Philosophy,
  Villanova University, USA
Thomas A. F. Kelly Visiting Chair in
  Philosophy, Maynooth University, Ireland
Professor of Philosophy Emeritus, Institute
  of Philosophy, KU Leuven, Belgium

ACKNOWLEDGMENTS

To my brother Jesuits: there are no words to express what it means to stand in your company. Thank you for giving me the resources to follow my passions and to use my talents to help build God's Kingdom. I pray that, when I meet the Lord, he will say, "Welcome home, Ryan." Over his shoulder, I hope St. Ignatius nods and invites me to take my place in the Company of so many Jesuits who have shown me how to be a Companion of Jesus.

To my friends in Irish music and dancing: you have helped to keep me grounded over these years. I love few things more than playing and praying for you as a community. It would be foolish to name everyone—living and deceased—to whom I owe much. But I want to say thank you to Tom Hastings for teaching me to be a musician and to Anne Hall and Liam Harney for being dear friends and travel companions. My time playing Irish music for dancers has blessed me in a special way with the grace of disappearance: the better I do my job as a musician, the more I recede, the more the dancer can emerge on the stage. I hope as a theologian and priest to get out of the way so that others can do what they are called to do.

Thanks to my parents, Bob and Michele, and my siblings and their spouses, Colin and Charity, Torrey and Brian, and my sisters Reilley and Hagan. You endured much over these years and, though you care little about Rahner or Desmond, you were generous in listening to me. To my aunts and uncles and cousins: we are at our best when we are together. When we gather, we make good on the legacy left to us by Billy and Mary Kay, Alice and Junior.

Dominic Doyle: thank you for guiding me through Taylor's oeuvre and teaching me how not to be a cranky Thomist. Richard Kearney: your *Wake of Imagination* was the book that enkindled my interest in philosophy, and your unparalleled ability to weave narrative and philosophy together in scintillating prose serves as the model I should most like to follow.

Special thanks to William Desmond for your friendship and willingness to write the foreword to this book. I have tried to avoid ventriloquizing through you, hoping instead to do my best to represent you and your thought as honestly and clearly as possible. If I have betrayed this desire, *mea culpa*! With your blessing, the follow-up book will do better.

Brian Robinette: From the day I met you in January 2013, I knew you were the one I had to work with. Your brilliance is matched only by your humanity and generosity. I must thank Krista for sharing her husband and Trevor and Austin for sharing their father with his students. Brian, I am very proud to call you my teacher and my mentor, and it is one of my heart's joys to call you a friend. I hope you see your influence on what follows.

Finally, I want to acknowledge Emma, Quinn, Con, Hugh, and Declan. I have loved each one of you from the moment I knew you were to be born. Thank you for the gift you have been to our family. My greatest hope for you is that you will each open yourselves to the blessing and burden that is the life of Christian discipleship. Let the question of God animate your life's quest.

INTRODUCTION

> It is essential that the vision of reality which poetry offers be
> transformative, more than just a printout of the given circumstances
> of its time and place. The poet who would be most the poet has to
> attempt an act of writing that outstrips the conditions even as it
> observes them. The truly creative writer, by interposing his or her
> perception and expression, will transfigure the conditions and effect
> what I have been calling "the redress of poetry." The world is
> different after it has been read by a Shakespeare or an Emily
> Dickinson or a Samuel Beckett because it has been augmented by
> their reading of it.
>
> —Seamus Heaney, *The Redress of Poetry*

We have no shortage of images to describe the spiritual landscape of our age. John of the Cross: the dark night of the soul. Louis Dupré: the "desert of modern atheism."[1] William Desmond: the "night of atheism."[2] Each metaphor articulates a shift in the possibility of religious belief today. Charles Taylor poses the question in his magisterial *A Secular Age*: "Why was it virtually impossible not to believe in God in, say, 1500 in our Western society while in 2000 many of us find this not only easy, but even inescapable?"[3] How has it come to pass that paths once reliably trod by our spiritual ancestors appear, today, increasingly incapable of conveying us toward, or leading us to ponder the question of, God?

   Across the plane of unbelief, a theologically trained ear cannot help but hear echoes of Karl Rahner's prophecy: "The devout Christian of the future will either be a 'mystic,' one who has experienced 'something,' or he will cease to be anything at all."[4] A theologian whose life spanned the long and bloody twentieth century, Rahner never surrendered his confidence that God could be encountered in one's life. His optimism about the possibility of experiencing the divine, however, was tempered by his recognition that naïve or taken-for-granted belief had become impotent to mediate such an encounter. "All the societal supports of religion are collapsing and dying out in this secularized and pluralistic society," he observed, and if one is to have an authentic Christian spirituality, it will only be "through an ultimate, immediate encounter of the individual with God."[5] In a Rahnerian spirit, Taylor muses: "Inevitably and rightly Christian life today will look for and discover new ways of moving beyond the present orders to God. One could say that we look for new and unprecedented itineraries. Understanding our time in Christian terms is partly to discern these new paths, opened by pioneers who have discovered a way through the particular labyrinthine landscape we live in, its thickets and trackless wastes, to God."[6] If the desert sands of secularism have eroded ancient paths, or if atheism's dark night appears to have eclipsed the light of faith, believers face a choice. Either choose to abandon the pilgrimage and become a permanent resident in the spiritual desert or find the courage to venture out again and chart new and innovative itineraries to the sacred.

This book records an effort to show how William Desmond's metaxological metaphysics offers a response to Taylor's call for "new paths." The reader's eyebrows raise: "Metaphysics? Today? Have we not finished with that?" I know, I know: many now think the code has been called on metaphysics. For did not David Hume, long before Heidegger announced metaphysics' overcoming, conclude his *Enquiry* with this call? "If we take in our hand any volume; of divinity or school metaphysics, for instance, let us ask, *Does it contain any abstract reasoning concerning quantity or number?* No. *Does it contain any experimental reasoning concerning matter of fact and existence?* No. Commit it then to the flames: for it can contain nothing but sophistry and illusion."[7]

If I risk singeing my hand by reaching into the flames to rescue Desmond's texts, it is because I believe his works are needed by philosophers and theologians. It will be my task to argue for the viability of Desmond's thought and to demonstrate how, properly interpreted, metaxology can transfigure the way we behold the world around us. Metaxology offers something akin to Heaney's "redress of poetry," a transformed vision allowing us to behold not a different reality but reality differently.

As will become clearer throughout this study, metaxology is not a philosophical "system" for one to read and master. It is neither an abstract schema nor a Procrustean bed of concepts. Metaxology, an account or discourse (a *logos*) of the between or middle space (*metaxu*) in which we find ourselves, is better likened to an undertaking or a passionate itinerary. The word "passion" finds its origin in the Latin *patior, pati, passus sum*, meaning "to suffer" or "to undergo." So taken, Desmond leads us to the shore of Arnold's Dover Beach:

> The Sea of Faith
> Was once, too, at the full, and round earth's shore
> Lay like the folds of a bright girdle furled.
> But now I only hear
> Its melancholy, long, withdrawing roar,
> Retreating, to the breath
> Of the night-wind, down the vast edges drear
> And naked shingles of the world.
>
> Ah, love, let us be true
> To one another! for the world, which seems
> To lie before us like a land of dreams
> So various, so beautiful, so new,
> Hath really neither joy, nor love, nor light
> Nor certitude, nor peace, nor help for pain;
> And we are here as on a darkling plain
> Swept with confused alarms of struggle and flight,
> Where ignorant armies clash by night.[8]

Desmond invites us to stand firm on the shore and discern within the "melancholy, long, withdrawing roar" not the end of belief but a silent prelude to a reawakened sense God's presence. He gives a way of dwelling on the "darkling plain," not in a forlorn spirit of resignation, but in receptive openness to or vigilant listening for the advent of the Holy One. This is not metaphysics as an abstract system of idle speculation but metaphysics as an *askesis*, a spiritual practice that is meant to be lived out. As odd as it may sound, I believe metaxology makes possible a way of life. For those today who find belief in the Transcendent vexing or exercising, I want to suggest undertaking Desmond's philosophy as a form of spiritual exercise, an *askesis*, with the potential of renewing our sense of God.

At the risk of hyperbole, page 755 of *A Secular Age* changed my life. On this page, as quoted above, Taylor issues a summons for new itineraries capable of directing seekers toward an encounter with God. I describe this, in chapter 1, as Taylor's "Narnian moment." Recall the conclusion of C. S. Lewis's *The Lion, the Witch and the Wardrobe* when the children discover the wardrobe no longer conveys them to Narnia. The closure of this route does not mean Narnia has disappeared; it requires, rather, the children to remain attentive to the disclosure of new routes. To his credit, Taylor offers several exemplars of figures who have attempted to uncover such routes: Charles Péguy, Ivan Illich, and Gerard Manley Hopkins. But Taylor's summons prompted me to ask: Do we need new routes or might it be possible to repristinate some old ones? Although our first response to Taylor may be to extend the borders of his map, I am of a mind that there are other approaches. What if, instead of looking for wholly new itineraries, we look at old routes anew? Rather than a pilgrimage into distant lands, why don't we undertake an archaeological expedition to excavate the old routes to see if they might once more direct us toward an encounter with God. Traversing these routes in a new way might then enable us to perceive our age in a transformed and transformative way.

I accept as a truism that a map should never be mistaken for its territory: even the most vivid depiction of a terrain cannot replace having to negotiate it for oneself. Talk about something—whether it be our age, a workout program, or work of literature—cannot substitute for undertaking the matter for oneself. In chapter 1, "Beating the Bounds of *A Secular Age*," I orient the reader to the nature and function of the map Taylor draws throughout *A Secular Age*. The goal of this chapter is to give readers a sense of why the question of the Transcendent, or God, became increasingly exercising or vexing in the West. Rather than rehearsing the whole of Taylor's argument, I begin by considering how the text "works" by implicating readers in the story he unfolds. Then, using three metaphors (the moral corral, the ethical field, and the untracked forest), I lay out the rough topography of Taylor's map. His map, though, is not with-out a significant shortcoming: Taylor seems to presume precisely what today is so often contested, namely, God's very existence. He fails, as Paul Janz notes, to offer any substantive argument for God's existence. If Janz is right, if Taylor's map is marred by this lacuna, then I will enlist Irish-born philosopher William Desmond as a reliable guide who can redress this shortcoming by uncovering the map's hidden depths and by tutoring us through a series of "spiritual exercises" attuning us once more to the presence of the divine.

If chapter 1 surveys the map of our age, chapters 2 through 4 suggest how Desmond's metaxological metaphysics allows us to dwell within the territory Taylor so vibrantly explores. The core of my study, these chap-ters unfold in three moments. First, in chapter 2, "A Crack in Every-thing," I introduce readers to Desmond. After a brief biographical sketch, I enter into a conversation with a series of thinkers—Martin Heidegger, John Caputo, Richard Kearney, and Merold Westphal—about the vi-ability of a theological engagement with metaphysics and, somewhat playfully, suggest a set of "five commandments" metaphysics must obey. The bulk of this chapter provides a general overview to the systematic nature of Desmond's thought and shows how he and Taylor, even though not engaged in identical projects, complement one another. This chapter will be of interest to those who have heard of metaphysics' "overcoming" and wonder whether, and how, any attempt at metaphysics may yet be viable in our secular age.

Chapter 2 offers a broad overview of and introduction to metax-ology, but it falls to chapters 3 and 4 to show how metaxology works. My argument: Desmond's philosophy is best approached as a form of spiri-tual exercise aimed not so much at *informing* readers as *forming* them to perceive reality anew. The reader will rightly detect the presence of Pierre Hadot beneath this claim. In chapter 3, "Poetics of the Between," I use Hadot's work to frame Desmond's project. Approaching metaxology as a form of spiritual exercise, I believe, can aid the willing reader in culti-vating an attitude in which the question of the Transcendent may be resurrected. I admit immediately: to my knowledge, Desmond does not regard his own work in this way. Indeed, nearly thirty years ago he wrote, "The philosopher undergoes the discipline, not of spiritual exercise, but of mindful thought."[9] Even if this counts as a protest against my interpretation—which I doubt—I am resolute in my conviction that Desmond's philosophy is best approached as something that must be practiced, undertaken, and undergone, as a practice. This chapter concludes by reading what Desmond in *God and the Between* calls the "return to zero" as a type of spiritual exercise capable of rekindling a sense of metaphysical mindfulness and attuning one to discern the presence of the divine disclosed in and through the mundane.

In chapter 4, "Exercising Transcendence," we construct a series of four "spiritual exercises" inspired by Desmond's *God and the Between*. Undertaking these exercises as an *askesis* or spiritual discipline can help to reawaken a sense of God encountered not apart from the world but as a part of it. The wager: when approached as spiritual exercises, Desmond's indirections can transform the way we behold the world around us. Thus, rather than trying to offer us a new map, metaxology leads us along an itinerary whereby we can come to encounter the divine in the day-to-day and perceive signs of the Transcendent in the mundane. Moreover, by undergoing these exercises, we begin to see how metaxology can overlap with and contribute to the task of theological reflection.

In chapter 5, "Epiphanic Attunement," I consider the effect these exercises can have on one who undertakes them. The fruit of metaxological *askesis* results in what I regard, to borrow a term from Edmund Husserl, as the cultivation of *orthoaesthesis* (right perception). Metaxology does not give us to see a different world but capacitates us to behold the world differently. This chapter is by far the most speculative and tentative; it issues a series of promissory theological notes I hope to redeem later. But, for those who have journeyed this far, I hope to give a sense of how Desmond's philosophy opens new vistas for theological reflection. To be sure, one can and may well approach metaxology as a form of natural theology—many of our exercises undertaken in chapter 4 lend themselves to this. Nevertheless, a metaxological approach to theology can help us to rethink issues pertinent to fundamental theology (revelation and grace), theological method, and theological anthropology. I hesitate to be too explicit here in the introduction: if the net gain of this project were able to be stated succinctly at the beginning, then there would be little need to write, or read, hundreds of pages. The nuggets brought forth in this final chapter need further refinement and purification. But there are nuggets to be found—of this I am convinced— and if Desmond's metaphysics directs us toward a rich lode of theological insight, I am willing to risk unearthing a lot of fool's gold if this ends in discovering a rich vein of insight.

I conclude with a brief recapitulation of our itinerary, a journey taking us from Taylor's Quebec to Desmond's Cork. There we will make our way to a pub where Taylor and Desmond can, at the day's gloaming, raise a pint and offer a toast to the Transcendent. If we have found Desmond a reliable guide through our secular age, if he has opened our eyes to look at what we normally look past, then our time in the pub will be one of celebration. As the sun sets and as the Irish music fills the pub, we begin to marvel as we consider how the eclipse of the Transcendent, the dark night of atheism, is not a fait accompli but more of a transitory phase. The question of God is not something we can idly pass over, but it, as Desmond has shown us, must be passed through. Even if our quest for God never ends, even if our return route extends endlessly before us, we retain confidence that this is a journey worth making. By the fireside with Desmond as our companion, we may experience our own awakening akin to the opening stanzas of Dante's *Divine Comedy*:

> Half way along the road we have to go,
> I found myself obscured in a great forest,
> Bewildered, and I knew I had lost the way.
> It is hard to say just what the forest was like,
> How wild and rough it was, how overpowering,
> Even to remember it makes me afraid.
> So bitter it is, death itself is hardly more so;
> Yet there was good there, and to make it clear
> I will speak of other things that I perceived.
> I cannot tell exactly how I got there,
> I was so full of sleep at that point of my journey
> When, somehow, I left the proper way.[10]

If our age has wandered from the "proper way" and become lost in crepuscular darkness, then we need someone to meet us "half way along the road we have to go" and guide us onward. As a fellow traveler and guide, Desmond charts a philosophical itinerary he describes as "a journeying—a crossing and crisscrossing in and of the between, and a venturing beyond the between."[11] Desmond does not offer abstract philosophical propositions but an invitation to "come and see" whether we might venture toward, and encounter once more, the living God. Desmond offers us a "passport" for a metaphysical odyssey, though it is our bodies and minds, and not its paper pages, that record this crisscrossing as we venture on this quest.

Allow me a word about method, scope, and limitation. Richard Kearney recounts how Paul Ricoeur began his 1977 seminar by asking *d'où parlez-vous?* ("where do you speak from?")[12] I speak from the stance of an Irish American, a Jesuit priest, an Irish musician and theologian. My sense of the Church and faith comes as much from being raised a Catholic as it does from talking about religion and faith at the end of the bar. My best homiletic lessons were learned teaching ninth to twelfth graders: if you can make something interesting to sleep-deprived, hormonally charged adolescents, you can make anything interesting. I write this as I tried to teach: I am not Moses come down from the mount, so I proceed tentatively, more inductively and intuitively than deductively. Or, said in a Pascalian spirit, I aim to write with *esprit de finesse* more than *esprit de géometrie*.

This plays out in two ways. First, I admit to being an allusive—though, I hope, not elusive—writer. I find it helpful to offer concrete examples and to draw connections between ideas. You will find this in my many advertences to narrative, poetry, and music. I do not do it to show off erudition—little have I to show—but to build bridges and make connections between Desmond and other thinkers. Desmond is not yet well known, and it seems needful to show, in an era skeptical of metaphysics, how engaging his thought can be, enriching and illuminating in a host of areas. Ultimately, my goal is to show how beholding the world with metaxological eyes allows for the revelation of too easily concealed depths and riches. There is more to reality, I hope to show, than meets the secular eye. Second, I am reluctant to carry on side conversations in the notes: if it is not worth including in the text, it is not worth including. Consequently, I try to reserve notes for citations and resist, as best I can, from carrying on subconversations. I am not always successful, but I try. I also refrain from an excessive use of jargon, and the tone of my writing can at times be jocular and playful. Here, more than anywhere else, the influence of my being an Irish musician is evident: traditional Irish music accompanies Irish dancers. It is meant to engage and inspire, to draw people in and set them free to dance. So, although I adhere to scholarly convention and try to write for the academy, I am sensitive that persons of flesh and blood have to wade through the text. There is no reason the heavy lifting that awaits us—it is, at times, quite heavy—should be undertaken without some fun.

Now a word about the scope. First, it is not my intent to offer a digest of the whole of Desmond's thinking. I do not engage much with his work on Hegel, aesthetics, or ethics. His writings on these topics are important, but they do not seem as vital for answering Taylor's solicitation for new itineraries. Furthermore, there have been developments in Desmond's philosophy over the course of his career, but his metaphysics has remained consistently coordinated by what he regards as the "fourfold sense of being." No doubt, one might dedicate an entire study to examining the developments in how this fourfold is understood. This is not that study. After his long career as an author and teacher, it would be shocking were his thought to have failed to develop. These developments, though, tend to have a "deepening" effect: concepts introduced earlier in his career do not disappear or change so much as deepen and mature. As a result, my reading and interpretation of his philosophy takes for granted a certain integrity to his metaphysical reflections.

Pierre Hadot was convinced that the goal of ancient philosophy was not so much to *inform* readers as it was to *form* them and the way they perceived the world around them. In this spirit, I hope this book occasions readers to make an imaginative return to Dover Beach where we can stand once more on the shore of the Sea of Faith, scan its surface, and allow the reality of our age to be present fully to us. If we allow Desmond to guide us to the shore and to help train our vision anew, we will find we have no reason to quake or quail: the surrounding darkness need not be seen, or experienced, as extinguishing the Transcendent or as vanquishing God. Desmond gives us resources to stand firm beneath the dark night, to endure the shattering of nihilism, and to open our eyes to see amidst the dust and rubble the hints and glimmers of a new dawn. By morning's light, the Sea of Faith is transformed. No longer does it rush away from the shore but comes back again with a surge.

Such, at least, I want to argue. We set out with Taylor and let him show us the shape and contours of the shore's map. When we meet Desmond, we will allow him to convince us to take off our shoes and wander the shoreline where, perhaps, we will experience as though for the first time the rush of the Sea of Faith's waters and feel it pool and swirl around our ankles. I do not want only to describe spiritual exercises. I want to show also how Desmond's philosophy can be approached as an *askesis* one must undertake.

I recall Paul Elie's observation about pilgrimage:

> A pilgrimage is a journey undertaken in the light of a story. A great event has happened; the pilgrim hears the reports and goes in search of the evidence, aspiring to be an eyewitness. The pilgrim seeks not only to confirm the experience of others firsthand but to be changed by the experience. Pilgrims often make the journey in company, but each must be changed individually, they must see for themselves, each with his or her own eyes. And as they return to ordinary life the pilgrims must tell others what they saw, recasting the story in their own terms.[13]

This book offers one such story, and if it convinces others to set out to experience firsthand for themselves what is reported here, then it will have achieved its purpose.

This work adheres to scholarly convention, and it will, I hope, inform the reader. But I hope it works on a deeper and more affective level to invite the reader, as Augustine heard so many years ago, to take up and read, *tolle lege*. My grandmother never tired of reminding us that "the proof of the pudding is in the tasting." I reckon it might take a bit of coaxing to get some readers to sample this metaxological pudding. Even if you do not abandon all other fare and take up a strictly metaphysical diet, I think you will find how well Desmond's metaphysics can accompany, and flavor, lots of ways of thinking. Come along, if not for the pudding, then to see some new sights and meet a thinker you might well never have heard of before. I hope we can have a laugh along the way, share some verse, and discern on the shore of Dover Beach how our era has come to experience God's eclipse and whether Desmond might open before us a new itinerary returning us to the sacred. Perhaps we will find that what to many eyes and hearts appears to be an eclipse is the turning point as a new age of faith begins to dawn. He has, I believe, found a way to help us see the world with renewed eyes. The world, as Heaney notes in our epigraph, is different because William Desmond has reflected on and written about it. This book invites readers to come and see and experience this difference for themselves.

ONE

Beating the Bounds of *A Secular Age*

> One way to put the question that I want to answer here is this one:
> why was it virtually impossible not to believe in God in, say, 1500 in
> our Western society, while in 2000 many of us find this not only easy,
> but even inescapable?
>
> —Charles Taylor, *A Secular Age*

"There is a generalized sense in our culture," the Canadian philosopher
Charles Taylor observes, "that with the eclipse of the transcendent,
something may have been lost."[1] He continues:

> I put it in the optative mood, because people react very differently
> to this; some endorse this idea of loss, and seek to define what it is.
> Others want to downplay it, and paint it as an optional reaction,
> something we are in for only as long as we allow ourselves to wallow
> in nostalgia. Still others, again, while standing as firmly on the side
> of disenchantment as the critics of nostalgia, nevertheless accept
> that this sense of loss is inevitable; it is the price we pay for moder-
> nity and rationality, but we must courageously accept this bargain,
> and lucidly opt for what we have inevitably become.[2]

1

That there has been a change in the West's attitude toward the question of the Transcendent, or the question of God, is hardly debatable. Seminars entitled "Theology in a Secular Age," declining rates of religious involvement,[3] and countless YouTube channels, radio interviews, essays, journal articles, and monographs leave little doubt: our sense of contact with something "beyond ourselves" has attenuated.[4] What is not entirely clear, though, is what this "loss" means. For some, Taylor's "eclipse of the transcendent" records atheism's triumph: "God is dead. God remains dead. And we have killed him."[5] Others, as Louis Dupré notes, refuse to be called atheist because "atheism is still 'an inverted act of faith.' The humanist must start not with the denial of God, but with the affirmation of the human, the sole source of meaning."[6] And some, such as Paul Crowley, perceive this eclipse as a chance to develop "a theology that unifies the *fides quae* with the *fides qua* in a deeper understanding (mystagogic task), thereby enabling Christian theology to function within and address a people of the church and of the world who are steeped in a secular milieu (the missionary task)."[7] The "eclipse" admits, clearly, a variety of interpretations. To borrow an expression used elsewhere by Taylor, it has "its boosters as well as its knockers"[8] and many who fall between.

In Taylor's work, we find a penetrating interpretation and analysis of the space between modernity's "boosters" and "knockers" wherein we can recognize both what "is admirable and much that is debased and frightening."[9] As we will see, this sense of *between* is as central for Taylor as it is for William Desmond, whose metaxological metaphysics (a *logos* of the *metaxu*, or "between") I treat in subsequent chapters. Both thinkers contest claims that the "eclipse of the transcendent" is a settled matter. Instead, each guides his reader beneath the eclipse where one can feel the stress and strain of what Taylor calls the "Jamesian open space" where "the winds blow, where one can feel the pull in both directions"[10] toward belief and unbelief. In their writings, both invite readers to experience what is lost, or gained, when the transcendent horizon is wiped out. They challenge us to question whether the eclipse is permanent or transitory, whether it is over and done or is but a purgative process to be undergone as a prelude to belief's new dawn. For neither philosopher is the question of God settled.

If this "eclipse" is the defining feature of our so-called secular age, we should get clear on what the word "secular" describes. Taylor identifies three senses of "secular," which I demarcate using subscripts:

- Secular$_1$—this might be considered a more "classical" view of secularity, wherein the sphere of the secular or earthly is separated from the sphere of the eternal. Public spaces are "emptied of God, or of any reference to ultimate reality."
- Secular$_2$—reflects a more "modern" view of secularity. Public space is regarded as neutral to religion and nonconfessional. Secularity, so viewed, consists in the "falling off of religious belief and practice, in people turning away from God, and no longer going to Church."
- Secular$_3$—focuses on the "conditions of belief." Belief in God has ceased to be axiomatic or presumed; belief *and* unbelief are contested options.[11]

In *A Secular Age*, Taylor is occupied chiefly with tracing the development and contours of Secular$_3$, the society in which belief in God has become one option among many. What distinguishes Secular$_3$ from the sense of previous ages is that "the eclipse of all goals beyond human flourishing becomes conceivable; or better, it falls within the range of an imaginable life for masses of people."[12] Ours is an age in which we need not refer our actions, or direct our lives, toward anything beyond the terrestrial order. We daily encounter myriad beliefs varying in commitment and intensity: fervent Muslims, milquetoast Christians, upright atheists, duplicitous agnostics. The title of Greg Epstein's book *Good without God* sees as possible what earlier in the Latin West would have been unthinkable.[13] Of course, the "eclipse" experienced in Secular$_3$ does not mean our age has been plunged into depravity or nihilism; it means, rather, that appeal to or belief in the Transcendent—an impersonal good, a personal God, a numinous divine force—has become one option among many: belief, unbelief, agnosticism, downright hostility, and so on. Belief and unbelief, each one a viable position within Secular$_3$.

Taylor's claim about the nature of Secular$_3$ may raise eyebrows. At least in Western Europe and North America, the question of belief in the Transcendent, or God, is settled—and, increasingly, not in God's favor. The sentiment among this population can be expressed as, "Well, we may have believed in such things back in the old days, but today we have outgrown superstition. The wheels of history keep turning, and we have left God in the dust." Many just presupposed that the inexorable advance of science and technology will eventually do away with the God question. God will be "subtracted" out of our cultural and spiritual picture. This sentiment, characteristic of Taylor's Secular$_2$, is hardly new and finds its most familiar articulation Max Weber's work. Weber uses the term "disenchantment" to describe how scientific progress had done away with any need to appeal to a deity. On this view, advances in technology lead inexorably to the desacralization of the world as the presence of God, or a sense of openness to a transcendent realm, is cut off. Within our world, Weber writes, "there are in principle no *mysterious, incalculable powers at work*, but rather that one could in principle master everything through *calculation*. But that means the disenchantment of the world. One need no longer have recourse to magic in order to control or implore the spirits, as did the savage for whom such powers existed. Technology and calculation achieve that, and this more than anything else means intellectualization as such."[14]

In a disenchanted world, science squeezes religious belief out of the picture. Faith and reason are, at best, regarded as mutually exclusive and, at worst, antagonistic. The narrative of Secular$_2$ is firmly ensconced in and perpetuated by the work of the so-called New Atheists, such as Richard Dawkins, Daniel Dennett, Jerry Coyne, Lawrence Krauss, and Sam Harris, who pit science against religious belief. Science, they maintain, exorcises religious belief, and we are all the better for it. The author of Ecclesiastes would, surely, note the irony of these *New* Atheists, for their new atheism is but a sloppy retreading of old, and usually more sophisticated, arguments. There is, indeed, "nothing new under the sun" (Eccles. 1:9).

In *A Secular Age*, Taylor maps the "spiritual shape of the present age"[15] in a manner intended to challenge the "subtraction stories" perpetuated by Secular$_2$. Those who approach the text hoping for a clear and straightforward narration of historical events, however, are in for a shock. For reasons that will become clear, Taylor avoids offering a linear narration. Without a doubt, the text is certainly informative. But, and more importantly, the text is performative. That is, as he narrates various shifts and transformations between the years 1500 and 2000, he implicates the reader in the story's unfolding. In this, the reader of the text can discover oneself "being read" by it. Taylor, then, does not tell *a* story but, by implicating and involving us in its telling, reveals *our* story. He wants us to feel how, with the eclipse, "our actions, goals, achievements, and the like, have a lack of weight, gravity, thickness, substance. There is a deeper resonance which they lack, which we feel should be there."[16] James K. A. Smith corroborates this point when he observes that Taylor's goal "isn't demonstration or proof; the point isn't to offer a syllogism that secures analytical truth. Instead, the appeal is to a 'sense,' a feel for things."[17]

To give us this *feel*, Taylor invites us to dwell within his narrative and experience what he calls the "malaises of immanence."[18] Without gainsaying modernity's gains, he is keen to get us to *feel* for ourselves what has been lost on account of the eclipse by inducing (1) the sense of the fragility of meaning, the search for an overarching significance; (2) the felt flatness of our attempts to solemnize the crucial moments of passage in our lives; (3) the utter flatness, emptiness of the ordinary.[19] To read *A Secular Age* properly, one cannot approach it as a spectator. To undertake the text, one must risk undergoing it. One must dare to ascend the karaoke stage, take the mic, and sing with Peggy Lee the eclipse's anthem: "Is that all there is?"[20] The weight of this refrain should give us pause as we survey the darkening plain beneath belief's waning light. Is life flat and empty and bereft of ultimate meaning? Is this all there is?

The answer to Peggy Lee is a resounding *no*: we need not resign ourselves to the "fragility of meaning" or the "emptiness of the ordinary." Indeed, my goal is to demonstrate how William Desmond's metaphysics, when read as a form of "spiritual exercise," can reignite the question of God and cultivate a mode of attentiveness attuned to disclosures of the divine. His philosophy can attune readers to intimations of God present in the immanent order, divine epiphanies that can transmute the ennui of the eclipse into a spiritual *élan*.

To make my case for Desmond's project, I feel it necessary to begin with a chapter on Taylor. I do this, first, because Taylor offers us an informative and influential narrative of the forces and pressures leading to the eclipse of the transcendent dimension of human existence. He furnishes us with a historical map tracing how and why the question of God has become such a contested question. Second, the style of argument Taylor uses throughout *A Secular Age* endows the text with its performative character. The text induces readers to experience the pressures and movements it narrates. My hope: by showing how Taylor's text "works," I will have a reference point and model for engaging Desmond. Third, Taylor is better known. Even well-read colleagues look quizzically at me when I mention Desmond—and, if they recognize the name, it needs to be disambiguated from the silent film star of the 1920s. Because I believe Desmond needs to be better known among scholars, putting him in conversation with Taylor and other well-established thinkers will show he can enter into and contribute to an array of philosophical and theological conversations.

I begin by offering a "key" to interpreting and experiencing the force of *A Secular Age*, for how Taylor argues is as important as what he argues. By examining his argumentative strategy, we get a sense of how the text "performs" to reorient our perception of history and ourselves. Then I use metaphors drawn from "Iris Murdoch and Moral Philosophy"[21] to guide us through key moments of *A Secular Age*. Rest assured: I offer no exhaustive summary of his project. Still, I try to provide a sense of transitions and developments that have made the question of God problematic. This stage of our journey will allow us to consider what made and continues to make Secular$_2$ so convincing to so many while showing how it leaves certain questions unanswered. If we can discover reasons for believing the story of Secular$_2$ to be insufficient, it may prompt us to look for another, better account. Next, and finally, I evaluate how Taylor has "beaten the bounds" of our age and offered us reasons for believing the question of God to be worth pursuing. Nevertheless, although I commend him for providing us a vibrant and compelling map, I identify a crucial weakness. To anticipate: Taylor's account appears to *presuppose* the existence of God. But, as Paul Janz notes, this is problematic. How can Taylor challenge us to uncover new itineraries to God when the question of God's existence is at issue? Taylor, Janz fears, gives no reason for thinking there is any God for us to find! This omission provides the opportunity to introduce Desmond and show how his metaphysics can help fill in this crucial lacuna in Taylor's map.

TAYLOR'S ARGUMENTATIVE STRATEGY

A common complaint about Taylor's writing bemoans his wandering prose and his unwillingness to advance a clear thesis that he argues from beginning to end.[22] Hence readers' plaint that he requires a better editor. Please permit me to offer a more charitable reading. The hermeneutical key to unlocking Taylor's method can be found in "Explanation and Practical Reason."[23] In this essay he develops an argumentative strategy he calls "reasoning through transitions." He employs this strategy throughout his works, not least in *A Secular Age* and *Sources of the Self*, but seldom adverts explicitly to it. If I am correct that operative beneath Taylor's texts is a specific sort of argumentation, his wending prose can be approached as part of an intentional strategy aimed at having a perlocutionary effect. Rather than unfolding linearly, his arguments have a zig-zag pattern that work to disorient the reader and bring about cognitive dissonance. The reader is thrown off balance, as what had hitherto appeared the stable firmament of history is revealed to be more akin to shifting sands. The text disorients in order to reorient.[24]

We can see how this works by considering Taylor's efforts to undermine a depiction of the self he deems untenable and deleterious.[25] Hubert Dreyfus and Taylor open their recent *Retrieving Realism* with Wittgenstein's aphorism "A picture held us captive" (*Ein Bild hielt uns gefangen*).[26] The "picture" they see holding our imaginations captive, Peter Gordon writes, depicts the self as "'punctual,' that is, atomistic, individualistic, and only contingently bound to its cultural or historical surroundings."[27] Taylor inveighs against this depiction of the disengaged subject. Yet this picture has become our de facto understanding of the self. This raises a rather nettlesome problem, for Taylor seeks to convince his interlocutors not that one or another aspect of this depiction is incorrect but that the whole picture is wrong. Herein the challenge of how to get an audience to look at and reconsider the very framework or "picture" they take for granted. He faces, consequently, a twofold task: he needs (1) to demonstrate the weakness or insufficiency of the predominant "picture," and (2) to advance an alternative option as a "better account" that offers a more coherent understanding of what it means to be a self.

Taylor's first task, getting us to look *at* the frameworks we look *through*, might be likened to taking your father to have his eyeglass prescription checked. Dad may, at first, balk at the suggestion, even though it is apparent to everyone that he is not seeing well. Should you cajole him into scheduling an appointment, it is unlikely that the optometrist will proclaim apodictically, "You need new glasses!" Instead, she will probably employ a series of tests and demonstrations to show how, with a new prescription, dad would see better. Her goal is to show the inadequacy of the old lenses and to suggest how transitioning to a new prescription will be a benefit. In a way, Taylor does this philosophically through "reasoning in transition." This process tries

> to establish, not that some position is correct absolutely, but rather that some position is superior to some other. [Reasoning in transition] is concerned, covertly or openly, implicitly or explicitly, with comparative propositions. We show one of these comparative claims to be well founded when we can show that the move from A to B constitutes gains epistemically. This is something we do when we show, for instance, that we get from A to B by identifying and resolving a contradiction in A or a confusion which A relied on, or by acknowledging the importance of some factor which A screened out, or something of the sort. The argument fixes on the nature of the transition from A to B. The nerve of the rational proof consists in showing that this transition is an error-reducing one. The argument turns on rival interpretations of possible transitions from A to B, or B to A.[28]

This passage contrasts two competing models of argument. The first, what Taylor calls the "apodictic" model, believes that there is one, and only one, correct answer or position. Contemporary U.S. politics seems to have adopted an apodictic, or all-or-nothing, approach within its discourse. Apodictic arguments promise to deliver the decisive and devastating blow to one's opponent. An apodictic approach to convincing dad that he needs his eyes examined: "Dad, we know you think your vision is fine, but this is the third time you've driven through the back of the garage because you can't see the wall clearly. We're going."

Taylor's second, preferred model, reasoning in transition, can also be described as an ad hominem approach.[29] By no means a pejorative, ad hominem arguments are rooted in biographical narrative and reflect how "we have lived a transition which we understand as error-reducing and hence as an epistemic gain."[30] This approach shows how a move or transition from one position to another should be counted as a net gain and a benefit. Rather than the all-or-nothing approach of apodictic argument, an ad hominem strategy illuminates why another position, though not the best, is better than one's current stance. Instead of seeking a decisive victory, this strategy goes "to the person" (ad hominem) to show how a transition from point A to point B would be error-reducing. So, if apodictic approaches admit only the superlative, the *best* answer, ad hominem approaches accent the comparative and seek a *better* way. In daily life, one can find this sort of approach in communal discernment processes, in contract negotiation, and in grading papers. And lest we forget dad, we can find in his visit to the optometrist a decent analogy. For as the doctor takes dad through a series of exams and tests, he demonstrates how a movement from his old lenses to new ones would be error-reducing and life-improving. Dad, literally and figuratively, can be helped through a series of transitions to see better.

To appreciate the distinction between apodictic and ad hominem approaches, the next two subsections consider and evaluate both. The reader may be chary: "Isn't this a bunch of throat-clearing? Get to the point!" My point, though, is that one cannot simply assert facts and walk away (apodictic error). What we need to see is how an argument, and in particular Taylor's narrative argument, can unsettle the sediment of our typical ways of thinking. Like a myopic parent, one cannot just be told things might be seen otherwise, but, often enough, one needs to be shown how they might be. What Taylor does throughout his work, and especially in *A Secular Age*, is to offer a counternarrative that acts like the optometrist's tests. By showing how his approach makes better sense and brings clarity to our lives and experiences, he hopes to coax us away from our old lenses and adopt the ones he offers. We shall begin with the "bad model" of apodictic reasoning, and then, after uncovering its limitations, assess whether Taylor's ad hominem approach offers the better strategy.

Apodictic Reasoning

Apodictic reasoning resonates with the "naturalist temper of modern thought."[31] This temperament has been a long-standing concern for Taylor, dating back to his early and polemical engagement with behaviorism.[32] Behaviorism's project, Nicholas Smith notes, is "to give a mechanistic account of behavior at the 'molar' level, that is, at the level of the gross movements of an organism and the organism's environment."[33] Behaviorism is modeled on scientific methods developed during the scientific revolution.[34] Behaviorist psychologists, for instance, try to explain human behavior as they would explain the behavior of any other animal without any appeal or recourse to thoughts or feelings, intentions or motivations. One model, described by Nicholas Smith as Stimulus-Response,[35] tries to map the connections between any given stimulus and the response it elicits. The belief: given enough time, one could predict, for human and nonhuman animals, all future actions and behaviors.

Taylor regards this disengaged depiction of human agency as grossly misrepresentative because there is no neutral "view from nowhere" or Archimedean point granting an unobstructed view of reality. As Ruth Abbey notes, apodictic reasoning is hampered by a category error inasmuch as it construes human reasoning as "proceeding from its independent starting ground and employing neutral procedures, it presses on to conclusions that are final and certain. But once again, he [Taylor] sees it as a category error to use or expect this sort of reasoning in normative debates. While this mode of reasoning might work in some parts of the natural sciences, it cannot be transplanted into areas where the disputes are primarily ethical in nature."[36] Where apodictic reasoning errs is in its taking as its canon a model of rationality arising in the seventeenth century that presumes reason "should be as disengaged as possible from our implicit commitments and understandings, as it is in natural science, and as it must be if we are not to be victims of the status quo with all its imperfections and injustices."[37] By no means does Taylor deny the importance or gains of the natural sciences; his objection is to the often unquestioned belief that this form of reasoning must act as the standard for all forms of inquiry.

The shortcomings of apodictic reasoning become apparent if we consider Taylor's argument in "What Is Human Agency?" where he seeks to ascertain what we can attribute to ourselves as human agents that we would not attribute to animals.[38] He begins by affirming Harry Frankfurt's distinction between first- and second-order desires, meaning humans "are not alone in having desires and motives, or in making choices. They share these things with members of certain other species, some of which even appear to engage in deliberation and to make decisions based on prior thought. It seems to be peculiarly characteristic of humans, however, that they are able to form what I shall call 'second-order desires' or 'desires of the second order.'"[39] The family dog, for instance, may strongly desire to eat the steak on the table but checks this desire, contenting itself with kibble, lest it get a whack on the nose; a little girl wants to fling a brussels sprout at her brother but checks her desire and eats it, lest she be denied dessert. Both have desires, but there is a difference between them: what is "distinctively human is the power to *evaluate* our desires, to regard some as desirable and others as undesirable."[40] The girl realizes that flinging food is not nice and that she should not hurt her brother; or, perhaps, her desire for an ice cream outweighs her desire to fling food. The dog can do no such thing. Its restraint comes, not from evaluating competing desires, but as a result of training and conditioning. The most sophisticated dog cannot do what a child can: account for its actions.

Next, Taylor draws a distinction within second-order desire itself. In day-to-day life, we are confronted with a host of options requiring us to order and prioritize an array of competing desires. Because all desires are not equal, Taylor distinguishes "weak evaluation" from "strong evaluation." Take his example of choosing between a vacation in the north or the south. Each is uniquely attractive: a more rugged northern vacation appeals to one's sense of adventure, a more tropical southern vacation promises relaxation. One recognizes a qualitative difference between the options but, ultimately, opts for the northern holiday simply because one feels like it.[41] For Taylor, "weak evaluation" involves a comparison between objects (two vacations) and choosing the one that promises to bring about the greatest satisfaction to the choosing agent. It is a choice made for no other reason than one "feels like" taking a northern holiday.

"Strong" evaluation, by contrast, takes account of the "quality of our motivation" and is concerned with "the qualitative *worth* of different desires."[42] Such evaluation records a linguistic shift away from expressing personal preferences toward an attempt to articulate how and why one judges one desire more estimable than another. The strong evaluator experiences an expansion and an enrichment of her language; she develops "a vocabulary of worth" in which she is able "to express the superiority of one alternative, the language of higher and lower, noble and base, courageous and cowardly, integrated and fragmented, and so on."[43] A strong evaluator's growth in articulacy cultivates ever-greater depths within the agent:

> Now we are reflecting about our desires in terms of the kind of being we are in having them or carrying them out. Whereas a reflection about what we feel like more, which is all a simple weigher

can do in assessing motivations, keeps us as it were at the periphery; a reflection on the kind of beings we are takes us to the center of our existence as agents. Strong evaluation is not just a condition of articulacy about preferences, but also about the quality of the kind of beings we are or want to be. It is in this sense deeper.[44]

Weak evaluators distinguish between *what* one wants, yet, on this level, not much reflection is demanded. The strong evaluator, on the other hand, must take a stand, commit oneself, and can provide a rationale for one's choice. Growth in articulacy, an ability to dialogue with others about *what* we have chosen and to give an account for *why* we did so, is not epiphenomenal to what it means to be human. On the contrary, it is constitutive of personhood: "Our capacity for strong evaluation is an essential feature of a person."[45] Riffing on Springsteen, we might say, "Baby, we were born to judge."

Our capacity to grow as strong evaluators proves a surd to "the recurring ambition of our rationalist civilization to turn practical reflection as much as possible into calculation, an ambition whose major expression has been the doctrine of utilitarianism."[46] Utilitarianism would restrict one's range of options by indexing them to a single axiom, such as "maximize the good for the greatest number." Growth in strong evaluation, by contrast, leads to a proliferation of choices because one can recognize and must discern between competing goods. Faced with a host of options, the strong evaluator must take a stand on who one is and who one desires to be: "The simple weigher may hesitate, as before the éclair and mille-feuilles, and his momentary preference may go back and forth. But we would not say that he envisages his situation of choice now one way, now another. With strong evaluation, however, there can be and often is a plurality of ways of envisaging my predicament, and the choice may not be just between what is clearly the higher and the lower, but between two incommensurable ways of looking at this choice."[47]

To illustrate this, consider the difference between Mr. Spock and Captain Kirk. In *Star Trek: Into Darkness*, Spock's logic that "the needs of the many outweigh the needs of the few" makes him willing to sacrifice his life rather than violate the Prime Directive.[48] Kirk contravenes Spock's decision, risking his life and violating the Prime Directive by rescuing Spock. On the surface, the two appear committed to incommensurable goods: Spock to the "needs of the many" and Kirk to "friendship." But is there parity? No one is willing, of course, "to challenge the view that, other things being equal, it is better that men's desires be fulfilled than that they be frustrated, that they be happy rather than miserable. Counter-utilitarians challenge rather whether the entire range of ethical issues can be put in these terms, whether there are not other goals which can conflict with happiness, whose claims have to be adjudicated together with utility."[49] Perhaps something is absent from Spock's moral calculus.

If Spock's apodictic reasoning reflects a utilitarian commitment, we might press him for greater specificity and clarity. What are the "needs" of the many? How is this "good" defined and enacted? Are his principles self-evident or are they based on unexamined premises? In short: To what canon does Spock appeal? The limits of Spock's reasoning become apparent when contrasted with Kirk's. Kirk's *in extremis* actions reveal his character as a strong evaluator and expose the narrowness of Spock, who, contrasted with the captain, appears "insensitive or brutish or morally perverse."[50] We can admire Kirk, not for his recklessness, but because in taking account of the goods of loyalty, courage, and fidelity, he shows the exiguousness of Spock's reasoning.

What limits apodictic reasoning—whether behaviorism, naturalism, utilitarianism, and so on—is that its reach exceeds its grasp. It may be appropriate in certain settings and modes of inquiry, but when applied to intricate human situations, it preserves its explanatory force only by distorting what it means to be human. It reduces the complexity of the human situation to some single, manageable term. Thus, Spock's cool and disengaged logic chills us because, compared to Kirk, he appears inhuman. We regard Kirk all the better because Spock serves as his foil: his inhumanity reveals Kirk's humanity. Gene Roddenberry wrote better than he knew: even in the final frontier of space, where traveling at light speed is commonplace, the depths of humanity have not been filled in or exhaustively explored.

An apodictic approach is attractive because it is heir to a model of reasoning remarkable in its explanatory power. Buttressed by the prestige of the natural sciences, it has been imbued with an aura of indisputability. In the work of Sam Harris[51] and Daniel Dennett[52] there continues to be an outright "hostility to the notion of strong evaluation" and an insistence that reason "be as disengaged as possible from our implicit commitments and understandings."[53] But when we subject it to scrutiny, a Procrustean bed of disengaged logic cannot accommodate the width and depth of human selfhood. It cannot fulfill its promise to resolve all dilemmas because it cannot account for reality's complexity. Consider this: Is there a logical moral calculus able to yield, remainder-free, a correct "decision" when confronted with Sophie's choice? Can an appeal to any utilitarian principle justify the inhuman prosperity subtending the city in Ursula LeGuin's "The Ones Who Walk away from Omelas"?

Aristotle knew well the limits of apodictic reasoning. In book 5, chapter 10 of the *Nichomachean Ethics*, he anticipated instances where "the law makes a universal pronouncement and a particular case arises that is contrary to the universal pronouncement." Aristotle's response, Taylor would observe, is not to surrender to "a half-despairing, half-complacent embracing of an equivocal ethical subjectivism."[54] His suggestion: to "pronounce what the legislator himself would have pronounced had he been present and would have put into his law had he known about the case." Here we have an instance of *phronesis*, "practical wisdom." He suggests adopting a more flexible standard akin to "the lead standard used in Lesbian building." For just as this standard "is not fixed but adapts itself to the shape of the stone," so too does a decree based on the original lawmaker's intent allow the law to conform to the needs of the moment. As we shall now consider, Taylor shows us how to cultivate this type of practical reasoning when he argues for ad hominem reasoning's superiority.

Taylor's Tactic: Ad Hominem Reasoning

Whereas apodictic reasoning relies on a belief that interlocutors can be brought to recognize a single neutral criterion to resolve disputes, ad hominem reasoning assumes otherwise. Again, by ad hominem Taylor is *not* indicating the logical fallacy that attacks one's opponent rather than her argument. By ad hominem he means an argument that goes "to the person" and assumes the interlocutor's point of view. Essentially, this type of argument begins from another's standpoint and, through dialogue, shows how adopting an alternative position would prove beneficial. Rather than trying to find neutral ground, it directly engages dialogue partner. The goal is not to win at all costs but to convince the other that modifying her position would be beneficial. Unlike apodictic reasoning, which strives for absolute certainty without appealing to human experience, the ad hominem strategy moves progressively through a series of biographical transitions toward a provisional "better account" able to make better sense of one's experience while remaining open to further modification.[55]

How would this type of argument resolve disagreements, especially when parties cannot agree on a neutral criterion? For Taylor, in the absence of "externally defined criteria,"[56] we have no choice but to engage in dialogue.[57] Each must assume at least that "my opponent already shares at least some of the fundamental positions toward good and right which guide me."[58] For example, take X and Y as representing two competing positions. On an apodictic approach, an argument succeeds by showing that "X is false and Y true, or X has probability n and Y has $2n$."[59] But assume there is no neutral canon capable of settling their disagreement. Are we doomed to skepticism or to "agreeing to disagree"? No, not if we engage in ad hominem reasoning with an openness to making some sort of modification to one's own position.[60] Taylor offers three examples to show how "reasoning in transition" can work:

(a) Y can be shown to make better sense of difficulties internal to X than X can.[61]
(b) Y can be shown to present a development that cannot be explained in X's terms.[62]
(c) Transition from X to Y is shown to be error-reducing through the removal of "a contradiction, or overcoming of a confusion, or the recognition of a hitherto ignored relevant factor."[63]

Reasoning in transition proceeds by initiating a dialogue through which an agent in position X might recognize the benefits and advantages of position Y (or vice versa). It is potentially therapeutic inasmuch as the agent in position X, through this dialogue, comes to see how position Y is in fact more desirable or error-reducing. The trajectory of the argument is toward making "better sense" of one's life or bringing greater coherence to one's experiences. Rather than a zero-sum game of winner and loser, these arguments facilitate growth in self-understanding. In option (c), for instance, the agent begins from position X and attempts to imagine her life *as if* she had transitioned to position Y by imaginatively weighing how this transition ameliorates otherwise intractable *aporiae*, makes better sense of her life, or promises to be somehow error-reducing and advantageous.

Of their nature, ad hominem arguments are irrefragably open-ended. They are ongoing and ambiguous, not cut-and-dried, because the claim "is not that Y is correct *simpliciter* but just that whatever is 'ultimately true,' Y is better than X. It is, one might say, less false. . . . Its message is: whatever else turns out to be true, you can improve your epistemic position by moving from X to Y; this step is a gain."[64] Further modifications to one's position are bound to occur since, Alasdair MacIntyre notes, "our beliefs about what the marks of 'a best account so far' are will themselves change in what are at present unpredictable ways."[65] Ad hominem arguments possess a limitless "growing edge" and are open to further innovation and change. In this pursuit, one does not intend to gain the unalloyed "truth" but to record an epistemic gain.

Jason Blakely reads *A Secular Age* as engaging in (a), "an attempt to give a better theory of what secularism in fact means in light of the anomalies plaguing traditional secularization theories."[66] Taylor, in other words, can be read as claiming there are issues left unresolved by theorists such as Weber, Marx, Nietzsche, or Freud that require an alternative narrative. If Blakely is correct—and I think he is—it follows that elements of (b) will also be present throughout *A Secular Age*. If traditional secularization theories purport to show how belief in God declines and recedes as a direct consequence of advances in human reasoning, then Taylor seems to be saying, "On your theory, the modern subject has found appeals to transcendence increasingly problematic. Yet, how does your theory explain the panoply of spiritual options that have arisen over the last few centuries? Sure, what we would regard as 'traditional' religious practices have waned and changed shape. But people continue to seek ways to fill what they experience as a spiritual void. Does your theory have the resources to explain this ongoing quest? Might another explanation, such as the one I offer, work better?"

The strategies of (a) and (b) are similar inasmuch as they are contrastive. They work by demonstrating how one position is better able to explain data or resolve difficulties. But if we want to understand how *A*

Secular Age performs, we need to dwell on option (c), which derives its force not by assuming Y to be *obviously* superior to X, but by engaging in dialogue. This dialogue intends not merely to tell about another position but to show, practically and concretely, the advantages to be had by shifting to Y from X. In *A Secular Age*, Taylor walks with the reader and tries to expose the weakness of traditional secularization accounts and to offer an alternative narrative. Instead of laying out a parallel story, his text serves as an exercise in shifting readers' positions. The text works to the extent it initiates and sustains a dialogue that presses readers to question whether the account he offers makes better sense of their lives and experiences.

What sets (c) apart is that it proceeds "not through comparison to a rival theory but by direct appeal to a specific individual's lived experiences, intuitions, or sense of what is true."[67] Through dialogue, we become aware of certain inconsistencies and contradictions present in our lives. One had once regarded position X as stable, but through the course of sustained interaction, it now begins to appear fragile and less compelling. One transitions from X toward Y because one sees in Y the possibility of a better form of life. We are given to imagine ourselves otherwise and, coming to see this as a better way, we reform our lives accordingly. If apodictic argument seeks to shoehorn participants into one form of reasoning, the ad hominem approach allows participants to try another on for size and imagine themselves within various forms of life.

Colin Jager perceives how this strategy works to implicate the reader in Taylor's own way and potentially to induce a transformation of the reader's way of thinking. He describes *A Secular Age* as a story to be "told, experienced, undergone, in order for its force to be felt."[68] Taylor, he suggests, uses "philosophic song" as a "mode of critical thought because it forces its readers to undergo the very thing it is describing."[69] I would say that Taylor sings to his readers and tries to sing with them. He challenges readers to surrender modernity's hymnal and to take up and sing from a new score. His hunch: readers will find his composition more capacious, accommodating, and truer to the depth and breadth of their experience. If we learn to sing from the hymnbook of Secular$_3$, we will find our range now includes "transcendent notes" unavailable to those singing from Secular$_2$'s score.

Let me conclude with what I take to be the key difference between apodictic and ad hominem arguments, a distinction that may help us to appreciate Taylor's texts and also Desmond's. To my eye, the goal of apodictic reasoning—whether in moral argument or in modernity's subtraction narratives—is to *incapacitate* an opponent. You either show a fundamental premise to be false, or the other's reasoning to be riddled with errors, and you dismiss his or her position as foolish, misguided, or woefully ignorant. The goal is to win at any cost. Ad hominem approaches intend, by contrast, to *capacitate* one's interlocutor through dialogue. The goal is not to score points, or achieve a takedown, but to facilitate a new way of thinking. It is a biographical argument initiated to assist one's interlocutor in making a salutary transition toward a better account of life and experience. I will refer to and develop further the distinction between incapacitating and capacitating arguments throughout this book.

TRANSITIONING TO A SECULAR AGE

In the final chapter of *A Secular Age*, Taylor considers figures who broke free from the "immanent frame" by undergoing a conversion.[70] He focuses especially on Ivan Illich, Gerard Manley Hopkins, and Charles Péguy. He sees them as exemplars who sought, each in his own way, a greater sense of fulfillment or flourishing than he found readily available. Each broke out and charted with his life a new pathway to an encounter with God and discovered along the way a new mode of life. Now, by "conversion" Taylor does not mean returning to "an earlier formula, inspiring as many of these will undoubtedly be; there will always be an element of imitation of earlier models, but inevitably and rightly Christian life today will look for and discover new ways of moving beyond the present orders to God. One could say that we look for new and unprecedented itineraries. Understanding our time in Christian terms is partly to discern these new paths, opened by pioneers who have discovered a way through the particular labyrinthine landscape we live in, its thickets and trackless wastes, to God."[71]

This, for me, is the book's most provocative claim. His solicitation is not for a repetition of old ways but for a renewal that takes shape by forging new itineraries. To the dismay of Nietzsche's madman, Taylor has heard the news of God's death but does not believe it. If our ancestors' routes are no longer reliable, we are not bereft of options. Some of us may, or cannot but, feel impelled to set out into the desert in search of new or innovative routes capable of returning us to God.

Given his call for "new itineraries," we must ask, Why is a return necessary? *A Secular Age* offers a lengthy response to his question: "Why was it virtually impossible not to believe in God in, say, 1500 in our Western society, while in 2000 many of us find this not only easy, but even inescapable?"[72] Taylor's narrative accounts for how belief in God went from being axiomatic to bitterly contested, it explains why one finds Karen Armstrong's *The Case for God* and A. C. Grayling's *The God Argument: The Case against Religion and for Humanism* sharing a bookshelf. In what follows, I allow Taylor to guide our inquiry into how the "eclipse" came to pass. He will guide us along a winding itinerary toward a "Jamesian open space" where we can experience for ourselves the push and pull between belief and unbelief. Rather than portraying one or the other as the sole option, his narrative invites us to understand how a plurality, or a nova, of options has become available. Belief and disbelief, in this third form of secularity, Secular$_3$, admits of a wide range of positions and none is immune from its pull.

Before we begin, I must flag a strategic decision made on my part. The road through *A Secular Age* is long, winding, and confusing. Taylor's account is so complex that one can easily become waylaid at one or another point. In order to assist our progress, I import three metaphors from "Iris Murdoch and Moral Philosophy" to partition our journey. These metaphors—*the moral corral, the ethical field*, and *the forest of the unconditional*—do not appear in *A Secular Age*. Nevertheless, I think they are very much in keeping with key historical transitions narrated by Taylor. As we make our way across the terrain of Secular$_3$, I use these as landmarks to indicate where we are heading and where we have come from. Our journey will be recorded, then, as a series of transitions from one metaphor to another.

I structure each section similarly, beginning by identifying the metaphor and describing what it communicates. Next, I consider how the metaphor encapsulates key historical transitions. Finally, I suggest how the metaphor functions descriptively and performatively. In this, I am inspired by Desmond: playing on the bivalence of the Greek *meta*, meaning "in the midst" and "beyond," I explore how each metaphor (*meta* +

pherein = to transfer) makes sense of the transitions by guiding us "in the midst" of history and showing how it can "carry us beyond" its limits.[73] If my argument about the performative character of Taylor's work succeeds, we will see how these metaphors work to open up vistas beyond the immanent order, openings capable of enticing us to set out in search of new routes leading toward God.

THE MORAL CORRAL

By the metaphor of "moral corral" Taylor denotes how Anglo-Saxon philosophy has artificially truncated the scope of its inquiry into morality. With Iris Murdoch, Taylor faults this tradition for focusing on "questions of what we ought to do" while failing to address "questions about what it is good to be or what it is good to love."[74] Their claim, basically, is that modern morality fixated on the question of what is "right" and neglected the "good." In this period arose the two dominant systems of normative ethics, utilitarianism and deontology. For utilitarianism, an action is right if it maximizes benevolence; for deontology, what is right is what adheres to justice and duty. Each offered a rationale for its being the best, not just better, approach to ethical deliberation by laying claim to a single criterion. An apodictic shadow falls long over the moral corral and its two signature ethical systems.

Just as a corral restrains animals, removing them from their natural environment and penning them in, so too does the moral corral communicate a sense of an agent having been penned in and deprived its natural environment. Lost is the premodern vision of the human as embedded within the cosmic order or within the Great Chain of Being. The effect of this can be seen in how we understand the word "theory." In modernity, theory becomes something of a neutral or disengaged description of a reality. A premodern understanding of theory, by contrast, construed it as a practical and contemplative activity. Theory was a *praxis*, and "one of the highest activities of man, one which brings him close to the divine."[75] Less calculation than contemplation, theory was a stance toward reality attentive to how "the complete good of human life as rational doesn't simply consist in ethical excellence; it also includes the excellence of science. And the fulfillment of these requires a grasp of the cosmic order. Attending to both orders is thus constitutive of the human good."[76] Modernity's moral corral, we shall see, pares away theory's contemplative dimension and leaves it an etiolated version of its premodern self.

The corral metaphor is allusive. On the one hand, it evokes the kind of creatures who inhabit such structures, leading us to wonder whether humans and livestock are equipollent. On the other hand, the structure of a corral reminds us not only that the corral is an intentional construction, but also that it serves as much to keep things within itself as to keep things out. Clearly, this is not a value-neutral metaphor and is meant to provoke. Let us follow Taylor, then, to get a sense of the corral's contours and reflect on why anyone would have been enticed into it.

The Moral Corral: Encapsulated History

A first enticement into the moral corral came from what appeared, especially in utilitarian reasoning, to be the inheritance of the West's Christian heritage: "If one objects to a utilitarian that one might legitimately put, say, one's own integrity before the obligation to do the act which has the highest utility consequences, one invites the retort that one is self-indulgent and not really single-mindedly committed to human happiness, as one ought to be."[77] We *ought to be*, for the utilitarian, willing to put the needs of the many over the needs of the few; we *ought to be* the Good Samaritan described in Jesus's parable. Yet such codification, Ivan Illich inveighs, corrupts Jesus's intent: Jesus summoned his listeners not to the perfection of a neutral norm but one found only through a transformed understanding of what it means to be a neighbor. Utilitarian ethics "fixes" in a code what had been Christianity's radical innovation. A code, and not charity, empowers and directs action. Codification degrades charity, reducing it from divine gift to an adjective affixed to bureaucratic agencies whose job it is to take care of those I leave unattended.[78] Charity no longer quickens the virtues, or converts the heart, or elicits a response to someone's need. What utilitarianism claimed as continuity with its Christian past was actually its perversion: *corruptio optimi pessima*, "the corruption of the best is the worst." Utilitarianism persuades by dissembling charity. Instead of entering a network of *agape* that overturns old conventions, it succeeded in domesticating the anarchic love of God.[79]

In its drive to universalize benevolence, utilitarian reasoning narrowed its vision to focus on fulfilling requirements stipulated by a code and lost sight of the Good Samaritan for whom charity was an empowering and, by the measure of its day, anarchic call. By narrowing the focus of moral reflection to questions of what it is "right to do," it lost sight of a deeper concern with "what it is good to be." It is not surprising that this form of reasoning ascended in popularity in tandem with the scientific revolution. A desire for universally applicable procedures prompted a search for the single criterion on which to ground moral reasoning. If we take as foundational a desire for universalized "maximal benevolence," it seems that we could develop a procedure capable of achieving this goal. The drawback, as we saw above, is that a single criterion is incapable of meeting the needs of human fulfillment. Only by stripping away what appears fuzzy—emotion, desire, a sense of call or vocation—can the calculus work.

Taylor's claim is not that at some point thinkers collectively sat down and decided that "when we undertake moral reasoning, let's cut out all appeals to God." It is more that within the last few centuries such appeals to God became obsolete because appeals to anything "higher" became unnecessary. We get a sense of this in his explication of the "affirmation of ordinary life." Gaining momentum during the Reformation, this affirmation "dethroned the supposedly higher activities of contemplation and the civic life and put the center of gravity of goodness in ordinary living, production, and the family."[80] For the Reformers, the "sanctification of ordinary life" meant, first, ordinary life became the "site for the highest forms of Christian life" and, second, entailed "an antielitist thrust."[81] A point shared in common by the Reformers "was their rejection of mediation. The medieval Church as they understood it, a corporate body in which some, more dedicated, members could win merit and salvation for others who were less so, was anathema to them. There could be no such thing as more devoted or less devoted Christians: the personal commitment must be total or it was worthless."[82]

A homology exists between this rejection and the commitment to practical benevolence, for both try to universalize what had previously been a summons discerned in the life of individual Christians. By universalizing the call to holiness and affirming ordinary life, one does away with the need for an ecclesial hierarchy or clergy who pray for, intercede on behalf of, or mediate an encounter with the divine. God's accessibility to all walks of life effaces any hierarchy of holiness and inculcates a sense of egalitarianism among believers: ditchdiggers and sheepshearers, women and men, merchants and pastors. None better, none worse, all called by God in equal measure. Or, quoting Joseph Hall, "God loveth adverbs; and care not how good, but how well."[83] It is not *what* one does but *how* one does it that matters.

The transition toward "practical benevolence" and the "affirmation of ordinary life" are moments within a larger cultural revolution. Yet there is no unalloyed gain, and we must be cognizant of what was lost in this transition. In their affirmation of ordinary life, the Reformers emphasized God's ubiquity: from pope to pauper, God was near to all. Hence the disallowance of any "higher" calling to the monastery or the convent because all women and men are called equally to holiness. We should laud the Reformers' democratization of access to God, but we must also own that this led to a certain type of divine domestication: the God who could be encountered within the everyday, apart from liturgical celebrations or saints' feast days, became an everyday God. Consequently, the image of God morphs from the Transcendent One met at privileged moments in the liturgy or during the liturgical year into a God of the everyday. The irony of the Reformers' accomplishment of democratizing access to God is that by closing the gap between the quotidian order and God's transcendence, by making the divine immanently accessible, they unintentionally expedited the decline from premodernity's robust theism to a weakened deism and, eventually, to an exclusive humanism.

To get at the burgeoning of exclusive humanism, we need to take account of four "anthropocentric shifts" severing us from our sense of, and our need to appeal to, God. No one of these was enough to foreclose an appeal to God, but combined they exacerbated a sense of alienation from our emplacement within Great Chain of Being. In the seventeenth and eighteenth centuries, Taylor cites four "eclipses":

1. The Eclipse of Further Purpose—we owe to God's providence only the achievement of our own good. We do not need to refer our lives to a Transcendent God or appeal to transcendence—anything beyond ourselves—to achieve flourishing. All we owe to God is

achieving our own good. We should focus, therefore, on actualizing our own potentials and serving one another; our focus should be on a terrestrial *telos*.

2.   The Eclipse of Grace—God's plan is manifest for those willing to see it. We need nothing extra in order to grasp God's providential ordering of creation. Endowed with reason, we need nothing more—no divine aid or assistance—to achieve our end. Indeed, it is in our best interest to use reason rightly, because God will reward or punish us for how we have used what we have been given.

3.   The Eclipse of Mystery—created order evacuated of mystery because (1) our good is inner-worldly and (2) we can, using reason, understand God's purposes. God's providential order possesses no remainder and the possibility of miracles or divine intervention is foreclosed.

4.   The Eclipse of Our End—we lose the sense that God has a final transformation in store for us; the idea of "theiosis" or divinization or becoming a partaker in the divine life evanesces. We practice religion not to give greater honor and glory to God (*Ad Majorem Dei Gloriam*) but to achieve our own flourishing (*Ad Majorem Mei Gloriam*). Religious practices such as prayer and fasting lose sight of their eschatological target and become more interested in self-improvement.[84]

Over time this fourfold eclipse led to an increased fixation on the importance of daily life. Long before the U.S. Army adopted it, the slogan arising from these shifts was "Be All You Can Be." A noble sentiment, but not without dire theological consequences:

> If God's purpose for us really is simply that we flourish, and we flourish by judicious use of industry and instrumental reason, then what possible use could he have for a Saint Francis, who in a great élan of love calls on his followers to dedicate themselves to a life of poverty? At best, this must lower GNP, by withdrawing these mendicants from the workforce; but worse, it can lower the morale of the productive. Better to accept the limitations of our nature as self-loving creatures, and make the best of it.[85]

Under the waning light of a fading God, the figure of St. Francis grows ever-more peculiar, ever-more unintelligible according to the canons of a terrestrial logic. The slackening of eschatological tension, which had allowed us to regard Francis as a compelling model of a radical "fool for Christ" (1 Cor. 4:10), renders him now more of a sentimental figure. Please note an irony: many people pay a lot of money to place a statue of the *Poverello* in well-manicured gardens without any regard to the life he lived. This garden-variety Francis is more apt for Disney than devotion, more a quaint bourgeois totem than a jarring call to personal conversion.

Nevertheless, these eclipses did not leave us in the dark. On the contrary, as the light of the Transcendent diminished, we lit candles and, eventually, created lightbulbs to illuminate our way. And, surely, a focus on the here-and-now bore estimable fruits. As we grew less concerned less with the world to come, we focused more on the needs of our neighbors. Thus, Taylor writes, a new spiritual outlook evolved that believed "our first concern ought to be to increase life, relieve suffering, foster prosperity."[86] Without question, laudable developments. The transition from a focus on the celestial to the terrestrial, however, came at a cost: lost was any need to appeal to the Transcendent. God was not miraculously going to pop in to save the day, so why waste time praying when one can roll up one's sleeves and set to work? These shifts, subtle and gradual, presage the publication of Greg Epstein's *Good without God*: we can pursue the good, and be good, and do good, without appealing to grace or God.

Albeit traced with rough lines, what I am trying to bring into relief is the transformation within what Taylor calls our "social imaginary." The social imaginary is the "largely unstructured and inarticulate understanding of our whole situation, within which particular features of our world show up for us in the sense they have. It can never be adequately expressed in the form of explicit doctrines because of its unlimited and indefinite nature."[87] We live and act against this background without ever giving much thought to it. It is conveyed in narratives, enshrined in monuments and institutions, and observed in the way our calendars are structured around civic holidays and observances. The social imaginary provides the shared know-how when it comes to cultural expectations, social interactions, interpersonal dynamics, and humor: the way sarcasm works, or a joke is taken, depends on an intricate background making such exchanges possible. In effect, the social imaginary is the "common understanding which makes possible common practices, and a widely shared sense of legitimacy."[88]

In hindsight, we can see how historical developments contributed to and affected our social imaginary. In an earlier age, we entertained a sense of porosity to God. Through holy days and liturgical observances, both time and space were suffused with the sacred. Over time, however, our "social imaginary" became buffered to the divine. Advances in science and technology made it less necessary to invoke God; instrumental reason, not intercessory prayer, became our go-to response. Collectively, our gaze shifted from an eschatological horizon and turned to the present where we focused not on what God would do in the future but how we could act now. A commitment to justice and benevolence need not rely on or appeal to divine charity, but it can invoke a single-term norm—utilitarianism or deontology—that is universally accessible to reason. Apodictic reasoning, emboldened by the success of scientific inquiry, dominates. Nevertheless, what must be counted a gain—a growing sense of universal human rights and advances in procedural justice—casts a shadow. For as the "social imaginary" is buffered against God and directed by the light of human rationality, more attention is paid to what is "right" according to these single-term systems and less attention is given to human flourishing or what it is "good" to be.

A second enticement into the corral might be attributed to the way modern epistemology affected the way we imagined human agency. One of Descartes's signal contributions was to develop a sense of disengaged reason. For Descartes, this meant "self-monitoring reason, reasoning which can turn on its own proceedings and examine them for accuracy and reliability," canons of accuracy and reliability enshrined in his *les idées claires et distinctes*.[89] Anyone who has read his *Meditations* knows Descartes denies that sense impressions are capable of conveying certain and indubitable knowledge; there is always a threat that one may be misled. So, if contact with the world cannot be the bearer of knowledge, how can one be certain of anything? His solution involves an inward turn. Says Taylor: "Of course, the theme that the sage has to turn away from merely current opinion, and make a more rigorous examination that leads him to science, is a very old one, going back at least to Socrates and Plato."[90] What sets Descartes apart from this older tradition "is the reflexive nature of his turn. The seeker after science is not directed away from shifting and uncertain opinion toward the order of the unchanging, as with Plato, but rather within, to the contents of his own mind."[91] After Descartes, one no longer needs to appeal to the cosmos or an external authority to secure knowledge. One needs only to turn away from the fleeting impressions of the flesh, to focus inwardly, and to ascertain for oneself what is, and is not, certain. Here we see the nascent formation of an ideal "disengaged perspective." Trust is placed in a neutral procedural method promising to arrive at truth. For disengaged reason, the *cogito* stands aloof from the vicissitudes of daily life; one need only follow procedural reasoning to achieve the certainty of knowledge. The Cartesian subject becomes the ruler and measurer of all reality. Protagoras *redivivus*: "Man the measure of all things."

Methodologically, Descartes catalyzed a shift away from the older, Aristotelian, model toward what became the ideal of disengaged reason. This model, though, comes at a cost: "In fact, we can say that the founding move of the modern dualist sorting, and of the mechanization of the world picture, was this Cartesian kind of disengagement, which disinvests the world of objects around us of any meaning, be it the ordinary everyday meanings that things have for us as embodied agents—being available or out of reach, pressing on us or open, attractive or repulsive, inviting or forbidden—or be it the intrinsic purposes defined by Ideas."[92]

Disengagement is an affected pose, deliberately bracketing the ordinary appearance of phenomena. When unreflectively assumed, it falsely suggests neutrality and objectivity. The claim to neutrality has, then, a shadow side. Dreyfus and Taylor identify two "deeper levels" of motivation, one rooted in power, the other in pride, beneath this purportedly neutral stance:

> At a deeper level, the stance of disengagement has also benefited from a powerful ethical charge. It is strongly valued insofar as it is seen as inseparable from freedom, responsibility, and the self-transparency which we gain by reflection on our own thinking. . . . But once we come to see the world as mechanism, a domain of efficient causation, but without inherent purpose, then we are free to treat it as a neutral field where our main concern is how to affect our own purposes. Instrumental reason becomes the only appropriate category, and knowledge can be seen as the basis of power.

Disengagement is not only a source of power; it is also the in-strument of disenchantment. The world ceases to be the locus of spirits and magic forces. . . . There is a sense of invulnerability, in re-lation to the immemorial sense of being at the mercy of spirits and forces—but also the intuition that this invulnerability was hard won. It required effort, and also courage, to face down the primor-dial fears, and abandon the sense of comfort in our niche that a meaningful cosmos offers. And this generates a feeling of pride.[93]

Here, Dreyfus and Taylor cast a critical eye at the claim of "value-neutrality." Indeed, they detect beneath its surface claim deep and ulte-rior motives. To be sure, they are not decrying Descartes's project as misguided or errant. What they are pointing to, though, are the motiva-tional dynamics at play in the stance of the disengaged knower. Knowl-edge, power, and pride: the disengaged stance is less a natural pose, a disinterested "seeing things as they are," than it is an achievement with dire ramifications.

One ramification is a hypertrophied "procedure envy" modeled on supposedly neutral scientific inquiry. The achievement of scientific rea-soning became the index of *all* applications of reason; science provided both the standard by which reason was measured and the procedure rea-soning had to follow. Our trust need not be in the fallibility of a world in flux but in the power of our reason to apply an operational procedure leading toward knowledge. Single-term moralities, symptomatic of "pro-cedure envy," prove irresistible to moral philosophers: "At last the fuzzy intuitions of common sense can be reduced to clarity. What is more, all incommensurabilities, and hence, difficult decisions, can be ironed out. Utilitarianism both satisfies demand for rigor and homogeneity and fits well with the disengaged stance of instrumental reason. . . . But Kantian-ism also gets a charge from being rigorous and homogenous."[94] If one could just ascertain the central term—either benevolence or duty—and articulate the procedure to follow, one could then demonstrate the su-periority of one model over the other. Consequently, moral reasoning became increasingly concerned with foundations, canons, and codes, and fell increasingly out of touch with humanity's depths.

The convergence of moral and epistemological temperaments helped to shift our understanding of the world and our role within it. Taylor identifies three traits marking the emergent modern subject:

The first is the picture of the subject as ideally disengaged, that is, as free and rational to the extent that he has fully distinguished himself from the natural and social worlds, so that his identity is no longer to be defined in terms of what is outside him in these worlds. The second, which flows from this, is a punctual view of the self, ideally ready as free and rational to treat these worlds—and even some of the features of his own character—instrumentally, as subject to change and reorganizing in order the better to secure the welfare of himself and others. The third is the social consequence of the first two: atomistic construal of society as constituted by, or ultimately to be explained in terms of, individual purposes.[95]

This subject is disengaged, rationally in control, self-directive, and resistant to heteronomous influences. Morality, for this agent, is "a matter of thinking clearly and then proceeding to outward dealings with other men."[96]

We have reason to be skeptical of this agent. As suggested, "disengaged" is not synonymous with "disinterested." It is an affected stance; simply scratch beneath the surface and find that purportedly "neutral ground" conceals less than disinterested motivations. The modern subject chants "neutrality, objectivity, valueless inquiry," but is this a proclamation or an incantation? Is it possible for the process of "disenchantment" to have worked its own enchantment? Might it be that the freedom promised by disenchantment has lured the unwitting modern subject into a cell? Perhaps it is the case that modernity's hero is, at the end of it all, little more than a member of a vast herd.

The Moral Corral: Function

So, how does the metaphor of the moral corral work to (1) carry us "amidst" history?; and (2) can it ferry us, or at least point us, beyond itself to something more?

The work of the metaphor, in response to (1), is to encapsulate *one* way of living within what Taylor calls "the immanent frame."[97] Of this he writes: "The buffered identity of the disciplined individual moves in a constructed social space, where instrumental rationality is a key value, and time is pervasively secular. All of this makes up what I want to call the 'immanent frame.' There remains to add just one background idea: that this frame constitutes a 'natural' order, to be contrasted to a supernatural one, an 'immanent' world, over against a possible 'transcendent' one."[98]

The corral metaphor conveys a sense of dwelling within a "Closed World Structure (CWS)."[99] If the West's social imaginary is that of "the immanent frame," then the CWS is a "spin" or interpretation that is "clouded or cramped by a powerful picture which prevents one seeing important aspects of reality."[100] The narrowness and restrictiveness of the corral gives us a feel for the CWS. Yet, and this is crucial, this is but *one* way of interpreting what it means to be a self; it is not the only way. In the very act of telling a story, of interpreting the history leading to the development of the "immanent frame" and the CWS, Taylor shows that the corral is not a settled matter. Because he can offer an interpretation or alternative narrative to "subtraction stories," he puts into play the possibility that there may be better accounts available.

Herein we see an answer to (2). By showing us what has been gained and what has been lost through the transitions encapsulated by the corral metaphor, Taylor invites us to weigh whether the corral sufficiently accounts for the needs of human beings. The metaphor works not only retrospectively to describe transitions but also, and more importantly, to carry us "beyond" itself by showing the corral's inability to account sufficiently for human life. If we find the corral inhospitable to a thicker description of human agency incapable of accommodating our constitutive natures as strong evaluators, then we need to move beyond its confines to an environment where this is possible. The metaphor is neither neutral nor static. It is not neutral because it does not envision the corral as fitting for human agents. It is not static because, by awakening us to its restrictive confines, it provides an impetus for us to move beyond its fence and to find our place on a wider and more welcoming terrain.

THE ETHICAL FIELD

With the metaphor of "ethical field," Taylor offers a broader take on what it means to be a modern subject. Human reasoning, he contends, is not sufficiently understood within the confines of the corral; its full potency, so restricted within its strictures, cannot be realized. We need wider expanses and broader vistas if we are to flourish. Again, this is not a value-neutral metaphor: we were "trapped in the corral of morality" and have been "liberated" to enter the wider field.[101] There is liberation in coming to recognize the insufficiency of one narrative (corral) and gain to be had in transitioning to another (field). Taylor is not telling us that this is so but, by engaging us in a protracted dialogue, inviting us to imagine how this transition makes "better sense" of our lives. Cage-free is an appellation suited as much to humans as to chickens! We are meant to roam free of stifling confines.

From a stance within the ethical field, we see more clearly the limitations of the corral, that it possesses an overly "narrow view of what morality is as a dimension of human life."[102] From the field we appreciate better the limitations of what Taylor calls "subtraction stories" as having played a role in luring us into, and keeping us penned in, the corral. James Smith, glossing Weber, describes subtraction stories as "tales of enlightenment and progress and maturation that see the emergence of modernity and 'the secular' as shucking the detritus of belief and superstition. Once upon a time, as these subtraction stories rehearse it, we believed in sprites and fairies and gods and demons. But as we became rational, and especially as we marshaled naturalist explanations for what we used to attribute to spirits and forces, the world became progressively disenchanted. Religion and belief withered with scientific exorcism of superstition."[103] A subtraction story of the CWS's evolution portrays it as an inevitability of modernity's advance and an indisputable gain. On such a telling, there is "no epistemic loss involved in the transition; we have just shucked off some false beliefs, some fears of imagined objects."[104] Jettisoning belief in God, according to these tales, is part of growing up.

Taylor disputes this story. In fact, by means of his counternarrative, he shows how modernity's subtraction story could have been different and can be narrated otherwise. In effect, *A Secular Age* works to disrupt common "subtraction stories" that purport to recount neutrally the natural progress of history. Subtraction narratives, those claiming that the eclipse of transcendence was inevitable, are frequently haloed by an aura of disengaged scientific inquiry. They claim to tell a story composed of neutral facts, one that chronicles from a distance those events that led to the eclipse. But can such stories claim neutrality? Taylor sees, with Paul Ricoeur, how in emplotting a narrative one cannot sever the telling of the story from ethics and politics. A story's narration, Ricoeur observes, does not neutrally tell "one thing after another" because, in crafting a plot, one invariably makes decisions about what to include and what to exclude. When we tell stories we draw connections to show causal connections and to demonstrate how one event happened because of another event.[105] How we tell a story, how we make these narrative connections, is an ethical and political act. Whenever we tell a story, we make decisions about what to include and what to exclude, and these decisions are not ethically neutral.

For Taylor, subtraction stories masquerade as objective "telling the facts" while concealing their ethical and political aims. The plotline of their narration is not, because it cannot be, neutral. Thus, he dissents from, and wants to expose as being anything but neutral, the "coming of age" stories depicting our loss of a sense of God, or of the possibility of transcendence, as an inevitable and unalloyed gain. This is a type of deconstruction in which, he says, "I am arguing that it is only within some understanding of agency, in which disengaged scientific enquiry is woven into a story of courageous adulthood, to be attained through a renunciation of the more 'childish' comforts of meaning and beatitude, that the death of God story appears obvious."[106]

Secularization narratives are as much a moral story as they are accounts of scientific progress, historical contingencies, and philosophical insights. By offering an alternative account, a refiguration of the events within a new narrative, Taylor exposes the subtraction narratives' lack of neutrality and sheds light on their commitments to a certain, limited understanding of human agency. Yet the only way to recognize these limitations is by daring to break through the corral's fence, to step out into the expanses of the field, and see for oneself if the field provides a more hospitable environment than the corral.

The Ethical Field: Encapsulated History

Taylor contends that the fatal flaw of the single-term morality is that it "perpetuates a drastic foreshortening of our moral world, by concentrating only on what we are obligated to do."[107] By excluding or ignoring "what it is good to be" we lose a broader sense of what it means to be human. Even though modern philosophy has focused on the *right* over the *good*, there is a sense in which the two can never be completely dis-associated: "The sense that such and such is an action we are obligated by justice to perform cannot be separated from a sense that being just is a good way to be. If we had the first without any hint of the second, we would be dealing with a compulsion, like the neurotic necessity to wash one's hands or to remove stones from the road."[108] This, perhaps, reaffirms our dis-ease with Mr. Spock who, in his application of logic, seems to separate "being" (a friend) from "doing" (impersonal logic).

By articulating a more robust or "thicker" anthropology, Taylor appeals to our need for "life goods" and "constitutive goods." Part I of *Sources of the Self* elaborates these in detail. For our purposes, it is enough to note that by "life good" he means what it is good for humans *to be*. The language of virtue, literary exemplars, and Christian hagiography all provide patterns for a person's life. But what motivates the person, anchoring and coordinating one's aspirations, Taylor calls the "constitutive good." This good is what moves us to act. A courageous soldier gives his life for love of state; a martyr suffers death for love of God. But homologous actions do not betray identical intentions: each can explain himself, can articulate why he acted in such a manner, through an appeal to motivational content, or the good, orienting his life.

There is an intertwining of "life good" and "constitutive good" such that *what* one wants is rooted in and articulated through appeals to *why* one reckons this good. This is our task as thick evaluators and it proves itself an exercise in humanity: we must examine our lives, what we desire to be, and discern the constitutive good that motivates us. This "good," however, is no product of the will but is that which transcends us and magnetically draws the will. Iris Murdoch observes: "The concept Good resists collapse into the selfish empirical consciousness. It is not a mere value tag of the choosing will, and function and casual uses of 'good' (a good knife, a good fellow) are not, as some philosophers have wished to argue, clues to the structure of the concept. The proper and serious use of the term refers us to a perfection which is perhaps never exemplified in the world we know ('There is no good in us') and which carries with it the ideas of hierarchy and transcendence."[109] Our life's quest for Murdoch's good, or Taylor's God, necessitates growing in recognizing the interval between who we are and who we desire to be as we journey toward the transcendent horizon. We are engaged, always, in a progressive and perfective quest for transcendent good, for God.

When we place the robust vision of human agency Taylor advocates against the etiolated depiction of the moral corral's agent, we see why the human drive to flourish requires more than a single-term morality. Within the corral, one need not consider either what it is good to be (life good) or what it is we love (constitutive good). In the corral, our concern is for what is right, not what is good. Moral life, within the corral, is limited to acting rightly and nothing more. This, for Taylor, is intolerable because it is "a drastic reduction to think that we can capture the moral by focusing only on obligated action, as though it were of no ethical moment what you are and what you love. These are the essence of ethical life."[110] Murdoch, concurring with Taylor, observes that the Good broadens our moral vision beyond the corral's confines. "How do we know that the very great are not the perfect? We see differences, we sense directions, and we know that the Good is still somewhere beyond. The self, the place where we live, is a place of illusion. Goodness is connected with the attempt to see the unself, to see and to respond to the real world in the light of a virtuous consciousness. . . . 'Good is a transcendent reality' means that virtue is the attempt to pierce the veil of selfish consciousness and join the world as it really is."[111] The Good pierces the slats of the corral and beckons to move from illusion to reality.

The transition from corral to the field also reflects Taylor's rejection of the "confused inarticulacy of modern naturalism."[112] A naturalist account of humans treats its subject as it would any other object in nature. Appeals to motivation, or intention, only "express the way we feel, not the way things are."[113] Naturalist-inspired approaches dismiss as fuzzy or unscientific any nonmeasurable property. So reduced, one seems able to calculate what it is right to do—the single criterion—and develop procedures to achieve it.

What Taylor sees is how naturalist approaches take as a premise a point in need of argument, namely, "that our accounts of man should be naturalistic in just this sense."[114] What supports this claim? Is it that "objectivity" is objective or that neutrality is neutral? This seems to beg the question, as the stance of "objectivity" reflects a value of a subject. In valuing "objectivity" the inquirer claims to remove anything "fuzzy" or subjective, but this performs its own contradiction: in valuing objectivity, the agent projects *value* upon the research field. Richard Lewontin admits as much: "It is not that the methods and institutions of science somehow compel us to accept a material explanation of the phenomenal world but, on the contrary, we are forced by our a priori allegiance to material causes to create an apparatus of investigation and a set of concepts that produce material explanations, no matter how counterintuitive, no matter how mystifying to the uninitiated. Moreover that materialism is absolute, for we cannot allow a divine foot in the door."[115]

Lewontin tips his hand. Scientific inquiry does have allegiances and commitments. His materialistic credo both decides in advance the questions the investigator can ask and sets the parameters for the answers a researcher can accept. An a priori subjective value—materialism—sets the inquiry's terms of engagement. A neutral investigation can lead where it will only so long as it follows the rules that, in Lewontin's case, come from the materialist playbook.

Discomfited by the corral's narrowness, "we are induced to burst the boundaries of the foreshortened world and recognize the relevance for this world of what we are and love, as well as what we do."[116] Note the verbs: *induced* and *recognize*. Taylor wants us to see that the subtraction stories cavalierly narrating God's death are *stories*. And there are other ways of telling this story, and *A Secular Age* offers such alternative account. His narrative functions as a protracted ad hominem argument to give readers a new way of interpreting history and experiencing for themselves whether or not his story provides a better account. Readers tour with him the interior of the corral and consider if its single-term story is sufficient. The question he poses is whether we can actualize all of our potencies within its suffocating space.

In raising the question of human flourishing, Taylor appeals to what naturalists dismiss. For Taylor, the moral agent is driven by a desire for fullness. Indeed, he regards it as "axiomatic that everyone, and hence all philosophical positions, accept some definition of greatness and fullness in human life."[117] He adds, "I believe there is no escaping some version of what I called in an earlier discussion 'fullness'; for any livable understanding of human life, there must be some way in which this life looks good, whole, proper, really being lived as it should."[118] Once we realize our yearning for fulfillment cannot be sated by the corral's thin gruel, we may move toward the field.

Driven out into the wider field by a desire for fulfillment, we feel the force of Taylor's "cross pressures." Moving from the corral's shelter and stepping into the field's expanses, we begin to experience

> a mutual fragilization of different religious positions, as well as of the outlooks both of belief and unbelief. The whole culture experiences cross pressures, between the draw of the narratives of closed immanence on one side, and the sense of their inadequacy on the other, strengthened by encounter with existing milieu of religious practice, or just by some intimations of the transcendence. The cross pressures are experienced more acutely by some people and in some milieu than others, but over the whole culture, we can see them reflected in a number of middle positions, which have been drawn from both sides.[119]

An exit from the corral proves vexing. As strong evaluators, it forces us to discern our desires and order our lives according to some sense of the good. Forsaking the security of the corral's entails great risk as one must now sift through and choose between many options. In the field we now have many choices, many paths, but find ourselves burdened with having to choose and commit ourselves. Pulled in many different directions, our liberation into the ethical field condemns us to freedom.

The freedom of the field places us at a remove from the security of the corral, rendering us vulnerable to forces beyond our control. What we gain in expanded horizons and greater opportunities for exploration we lose in a sense of certainty, security, and order. In the field, we must choose from a seemingly endless host of options; we are free to choose, yet destined to live the consequences of our choice tormented by the thought that we may have chosen poorly.

The field metaphor encapsulates an ambiguous gain: we attain an insight into the insufficiency of the corral, but the liberation into the wider expanses of the field burdens us with having to commit ourselves to something we can live for. If we are induced to break free from the corral, what we gain as freedom and a hope for fulfillment carries the price of having to negotiate a host of options. Exiting involves a gamble, a risk, and having to feel and discern a host of pressures. For the field is wide with many possible pathways stretching before us. Behind us, old friends cry out for us to return to the corral, but, in the distance, we see the silhouettes of others who have set out in pursuit of the good, perhaps the God, who calls them. Having recognized the corral's limitations, we strike out and begin to discern how to live an ethical life, a life where we can "know what to do but also know what we want to be, and more crucially makes us love the good."[120] Instead of a single code, we find many different ways of life. We are called to roll the dice, to pledge ourselves to the search for fulfillment. It is an encumbered gain, for we now face the nova of options that defines Secular$_3$ and must commit ourselves, among the panoply of goods before us, to the one that seems to hold out to us our desired fulfillment.

The Ethical Field: Function

How, then, does the metaphor carry us "amidst" history? Can it ferry us, or point us, beyond itself?

Obviously, in terms of spatial imagery, the metaphor is contrastive. The restricted domain of the corral contrasts with the wider range of inquiry made possible by the field. Taylor gave us a feel for the narrowness and limited scope of the corral and, by extension, of the broader CWS in which the corral is rooted. We have seen its limitations, confronted its hidden biases, and listened to Taylor's counternarrative. Having heard an account that made better sense of elements ignored or discounted within the corral, we ventured forward. Released into the field, we are exposed and vulnerable. Voices clamor for our attention, pressures exert themselves upon us. Pulled in many directions, we must eventually wager our lives and choose a path, for even not choosing is a choice.

In the field we are called upon to discover, as Thomas à Becket quips in the film *Becket*, "an object worthy of my freedom." Entering the field requires one to accept and exercise one's agency within history: we are not rudderless ships, listing in the sea of time, but agents capable of charting a course. What do we do when, buffeted by wind and blinded by rain, dragged by currents and threatened by rocks, it is hard to steer or find a clear course? There is no formula to guide us. We must discern, weigh competing voices and claims, and risk our very selves.

Turning to our second question, does the field direct us beyond itself? This is harder to answer because Taylor is coy. He says he desires to talk about "our *sense* of things. I'm not talking about what people believe."[121] Or, in analyzing the CWS, he claims that he "will not be arguing either for or against an open or closed reading."[122] Unlike the corral, there is no single way to abide within the field. Here there are many competing goods. Some will orient their lives to the common good or dedicate themselves to supporting universal human rights. Others will orient their lives to God or to a belief in the supernatural. Still others will pursue fulfillment by their own lights and by relying on themselves. The field is a land of many diverging, crisscrossing, and sometimes competing ways.

We might take the field metaphor as a deliberate indirection. Taylor resists telling readers how to choose, but he does show us the consequences of having a choice. He wants us to feel these pressures and to discern how best to respond. In the field, there is no small degree of uncertainty because every path chosen means many others will remain untrod. We can move forward, we can move backward, we might even try to stay squarely in place. With every moment, a choice. To what, then, shall we commit our freedom?

UNTRACKED FOREST

If Taylor succeeds in guiding his reader from the corral to the field, it remains to be seen whether one is compelled to venture into the "forest." A move toward the forest's edge, he admits, "is hard to talk about . . . clearly and in a recognized common language."[123] This is because the forest is "virtually untracked. Or, rather, there are old tracks; they appear on maps which have been handed down to us. But when you get in there, it is very hard to find them. So we need people to make new trails."[124] Old routes, laid down in a different time and rooted in a different social imaginary, seem increasingly incapable of guiding modern pilgrims toward an encounter with God. Let's call this Taylor's Narnian insight, for when returning from Narnia the children

> felt they really must explain to the Professor why four of the coats out of his wardrobe were missing. And the Professor, who was a

very remarkable man, didn't tell them not to be silly or not to tell lies, but believed the whole story. "No," he said, "I don't think it will be any good trying to go back through the wardrobe door to get the coats. You won't get into Narnia again by that route. Nor would the coats be much use by now if you did! Eh? What's that? Yes, of course you'll get back to Narnia again some day. Once a King in Narnia, always a King in Narnia. But don't go trying to use the same route twice."[125]

The Professor does not deny the existence of Narnia, nor does he see the "modern" world as prohibiting access to it. He is mindful, though, that the route that took the children there in the first place cannot do so again. There is no hint of nostalgia for what has been; rather, one must remain watchful and attentive for signs of new pathways.

The reason Taylor finds this "hard to talk about" is because entering the forest demands a response to a summons; there is no prepaid package capable of guiding an individual into the forest nor any offering a direct route toward what it is that "commands our fullest love."[126] To the contrary, entrance into the forest is perilous, for one risks losing oneself in the attempt to find oneself beneath the forest canopy: pathless paths, sudden pitfalls, uncharted depths all pose a threat. The metaphor of the forest functions as a cipher for a passionate itinerary animated by our deepest longing. Restless desire drives us to trek beneath the forest's canopy, and we navigate its depths and our own. In coming to name and know these depths, we are gradually tutored into a language not of our own devising, a language of divine pedagogy that promises and enacts within those open to it a "transformation" of our whole lives.[127]

Admittedly, not all who roam the ethical field are moved to leave it. As we consider below, some prefer to wander roads paved by Friedrich Nietzsche and Martha Nussbaum because they regard with suspicion the forest and the "sacred" it conceals. The field on its own, they believe, possesses sufficient resources to make possible a flourishing life. The "sacred forest" metaphor is, then, hardly neutral. There are boosters who encourage (Illich, Hopkins) and knockers who discourage (Nussbaum, Nietzsche) entering its depths. The latter sentiment seems to hold sway in our age. If we regard Taylor's narrative as performing what it describes, if it gives us to feel for ourselves the pressures for and against entering the forest, we must now probe the forces that would have us remain on the ethical field and those that would have us wager our lives by entering the forest.

The Untracked Forest: Encapsulated History

Entering the forest involves committing to three premises. First, "acknowledging that life is not the whole story," and admitting "the point of things is not exhausted by life."[128] Second, enacting a "radical decentering of the self."[129] And third, effecting a stance of "*agape/karuna*" through a willing renunciation of life that, in a paradoxical return, promises to bring about the flourishing of life. Committing oneself in such a way, though, is difficult because "we have moved from a world in which the place of fullness was understood as unproblematically outside of or 'beyond' human life, to a conflicted age in which this construal is challenged by others which place it (in a wide range of different ways) 'within' human life."[130] The question for many is not whether we desire human flourishing but where one will find fulfillment. Canvassing some of our fellow field dwellers, we find a range of sentiments in regard to the forest.

There are some, such as Gerard Manley Hopkins, Ivan Illich, and Taylor himself, who have no qualms about adducing God as requisite for human flourishing. They countenance forest expeditions. Others, such as Martha Nussbaum, urge caution before plunging headlong into the forest. For her, efforts to transcend humanity are risky and threaten mutilation.[131] Human fulfillment, she believes, can be found without appealing to an external transcendence or to God. We do not need, on her account, to appeal to any transcendent good or God in order to flourish. Instead, she appeals to a form of internal transcendence enacted through deeds of compassion and care for others. Our flourishing, in this manner, comes about by working for the flourishing of others. Against Nussbaum, some of Nietzsche's descendants begin to protest. A neo-Nietzschean spin rejects appeals to anything beyond the immanent frame (God) and challenges the sufficiency of Nussbaum's internal transcendence. For neo-Nietzscheans, the possibility of "untroubled happiness is not only a childish illusion, but also involves a truncation of human nature."[132] Finding ourselves in the company of these other plain-dwellers, we see various "spins" on what is necessary to attain flourishing: an appeal to

(a) external transcendence or God, (b) internal transcendence, and (c) no transcendence, just "will to power."

Options (b) and (c) agree, against (a), in at least one important respect: they hold that there is *nothing* beyond life. Taylor sketches out what he takes to be the climate of our era in which the appeal to transcendence beyond human life (a) meets resistance:

1. Life, flourishing, driving back the frontiers of death and suffering are of supreme value.
2. This was not always so; it was not so for our ancestors and for people in other earlier civilizations.
3. One of the things which stopped it being so in the past was precisely a sense, inculcated by religion, that there were "higher" goals.
4. We arrive at (1) by a critique and overcoming of (this kind) of religion.[133]

On this telling, it was the insidious role of religion in (3) that held us back from affirming the supreme value of human life. We can recognize this as a subtraction story explaining how, once we removed the obstacle of religion, the human situation improved. And, as Taylor sees it, this is a dominant, if not hegemonic, view among religion's knockers.

Against religion's knockers, those who appeal to God can point to the "continued disappointments of secular humanism"[134] in achieving its end. Tipping his hand, Taylor observes how the position of exclusive humanism "closes the transcendent window, as though there were nothing beyond. More, as though it weren't an irrepressible need of the human heart to open that window, and first look, then go beyond. As though feeling this need were the result of a mistake, an erroneous world-view, bad conditions, or worse, some pathology."[135]

So, again, the question arises: Which position gives the better account of our lives?

Standing in the crowd on the ethical plain, it seems "an *ultimate surd* that people find very different ways to God, or the Good, or Nirvana, ways that seem to involve incompatible assumptions."[136] Many of us know both exclusive humanists who live with charity and confessing Christians who are hostile to strangers. We know some who never raise the question of "God" but pour themselves out in service to others.

There are believers who do not belong, belongers struggling to believe, and everything in between. How, then, to choose?

In place of a logical proof or syllogism, Taylor offers exemplars as a form of incarnate testimony. In recounting the routes they traversed, he hopes to inspire us to follow their lead. These biographies do not impose but proposes examples of itineraries into the forest. In these exemplars we find the stories "we need to enlarge our palette of points of contact with fullness; there are those which involve a contemplative grasp of this fullness (Bede, Havel, epiphanies of Loyola, Jonathan Edwards); as well as visions of the negative absence of fullness: desolation, emptiness, and the like. And there are those which consist in life-changing moments, being 'surprised by love.' This distinction can be, of course, merely notional: that is, the same event may partake of both."[137]

By reflecting on the lives of the converted, in hearing their stories, we grasp how "they bring into view something beyond that frame, which at the same time changes the meaning of all elements of the frame."[138] We find in the examples of our forbearers an inspiration to respond to our longing for fulfillment.

The Untracked Forest: Function

Carrying us "amidst" history, the forest metaphor leads us to the field's edge. The dense ridge of trees spreads before us. For those who see no reason to sacrifice the light of day to walk beneath the canopy of trees, who have no desire to cut and hack their way through the brush, there is scant reason to enter. Some would question the desire to enter because all resources necessary for flourishing are already available in the field. Yet there are those who have heard a voice from the forest who decide to enter its depths without knowing where they are going or how they will get there. They set forth in search of fulfillment and, in the process, come to find their stories drawn into a larger account of those who have gone ahead of us to seek, those who have found, and those who have been surprised by, an encounter with the Holy One.

The forest is, like the field, an ambiguous metaphor. Forests can be foreboding—as Hansel and Gretel discovered—but also places of unexpected fulfilment. Fangorn Forest was reputed to be haunted, but in the *Lord of the Rings* the Ents became heroic allies of the Fellowship. In Faulkner's "The Bear," the adolescent Sam, keen to espy a legendary bear, willingly divests himself of gun, watch, and compass—tools of the modern hunter—before entering into the woods where, without mechanical direction or orientation, he encounters the one he seeks. Prone and vulnerable, Sam experiences an epiphany disclosed on the bear's terms:

> Then he saw the bear. It did not emerge, appear: it was just there, immobile, fixed in the green and windless noon's hot dappling, not as big as he had dreamed it but as big as he had expected, bigger, dimensionless against the dappled obscurity, looking at him. Then it moved. It crossed the glade without haste, walking for an instant into the sun's full glare and out of it, and stopped again and looked back at him across one shoulder. Then it was gone. It didn't walk into the woods. It faded, sank back into the wilderness without motion as he had watched a fish, a huge old bass, sink back into the dark depths of its pool and vanish without even any movement of its fins.[139]

Forests, though, are dangerous places: ask Hansel and Gretel. And Taylor observes that "religious faith can be dangerous. Opening to transcendence is fraught with peril."[140] Contact with God may tempt one toward a crusade intent on purifying the world of its ills; or, transformed by *agape*, to put one's life on the line for the neighbor.

Can the forest ferry us beyond the CWS? Yes, but not easily. Read along the grain of the subtraction narratives, the metaphor seems foolish: Why leave the field? But if we pause to think maybe, just maybe, there is more to our story than the affirmation of life in the immanent frame, that our hunger for fullness can be sated only by risking such a venture, then we might find sufficient motivation to enter the forest. We, like Faulkner's Sam, must be vulnerable as we enter the forest and face the peril and promise of being transformed by our journey.

TAYLOR'S MAP: HOW A ROAD FROM QUEBEC LEADS TO CORK

Let me draw together the strands of my argument. I will first recapitulate my general thesis that Taylor's story of our "secular age" is a performative text. Second, I will evaluate the nature of Taylor's map. Third, I

will begin my more explicit engagement with William Desmond's phi-
losophy. If Taylor has given us a sense for how and why the question of
the transcendent became exercising, my proposal is to consider how
Desmond enables us to exercise transcendence as a spiritual practice.
The transition recorded here follows the road from Taylor's Quebec to
Desmond's Cork.

Text as Performance

I have tried to demonstrate how Taylor's use of ad hominem reasoning
affected not only his approach to negotiating moral disagreements but
also influenced the narrative he unspools in *A Secular Age*. He rejects,
as insufficient to the thickness and depth of human life, recourse to
apodictic-style arguments. Such arguments appeal to an external, supposedly neutral, criterion as the canon by which one can resolve disputes.
The gist of this of argument is that if we could just get it right, if we
could establish the right procedure, we could resolve all disagreements.
Apodictic arguments are on the lookout for an unassailable and universal
principle, always and everywhere binding. More colloquially expressed,
this type of argument assumes one size fits all.

Subtraction stories textually instantiate this form of argument.
These stories recount how, in earlier times, constraints placed on humans
(superstitions, religion) worked against human flourishing. Once these
impediments were removed, however, things improved. These are stories
of addition by subtraction. By liberating ourselves "from certain earlier,
confining horizons, or illusions, or limitations of knowledge"[141] we come
of age as courageous, illusion-free, adults.[142] The loss of religion, the increased sense of autonomy or of the buffered self, these are taken as net
gains over the conditions of the past. All that was lost needed to be lost
in order for humans to flourish. At that time we were held back by religion and superstition, in the accursed "Dark Ages," but let us rejoice and
be glad as we now stand beneath reason's light. So the story goes.

Taylor's response is to tell a counternarrative that, he admits, could
and should have been longer. He does so because "we grasp our lives in
a narrative."[143] He challenges subtraction stories by inviting us directly,
through his ad hominem approach, to abide within his narrative to see
how it suits us. He offers, as I suggested earlier, a capacitating approach
meant to empower its hearer to make an ameliorating transition toward

a better form of life. In this approach, he has venerable forebears. The prophet Nathan[144] told a story of a terrible injustice that enflamed David's anger, but Nathan's story is about David. When he realizes the story implicates him, David is led to repentance. Walking to Emmaus, the stranger's retelling of events sparks a flame within the disciples. Their story is renarrated by their mysterious companion, who walks with them and opens the scriptures anew. With eyes opened at the breaking of the bread, they return to their companions, not to resume an old way of life, but capacitated to live as bearers of the news of Christ's triumph over death.[145]

The zigzag movement of Taylor's story unsettles the hegemony of the subtraction stories and, by exposing their shortcomings, makes possible a new understanding of our age. I tried to express the main movements and contrasting feel of his story by showing how his metaphors encapsulate history and express ways of dwelling in our age. By allowing ourselves to be implicated in his account, we are capacitated to see our lives, and our history, with new eyes. Like a skilled optometrist, he has tried to offer us a new framework or lens through which to see the world. With his assistance, we may now find that the sealed-off barriers and bulwarks against God may not be as solid as some of religion's knockers would have us believe. The "eclipse" may be less an inescapable feature of history than a temporary, and quite remediable, myopia.

A Taylor-Made Map: Is There Any *There* There?

A line from *Twin Peaks* (2017) expresses well Taylor's map: "This map is very old, but it is always current; it is a living thing." By narrating transitions from the corral to the field to the forest, Taylor sketches a map accounting for historical landmarks and developments as well as the existential forces that weigh upon, push, and pull those living in our age. He is less interested in erecting "Do Not Enter" signs than in showing how various routes or modes of life arose, were appealing, and continue to entice. He allows us to inhabit the map, to get a feel for its topography, and he gives us some avuncular advice and indications about how we might venture into the forest.

The map tells an old story, dating back centuries, but it is a story we cannot help but to find ourselves within. We recognize that shifts have taken place. In some settings, at least in the West, the name "Jesus" is less likely to occasion the tip of a hat, or a bend in the knee, than it is to raise eyebrows leery of proselytization. Taylor gives us a sense of how we got here and what this means for how we understand ourselves. He maps out a story with many twists and turns, remarkable convergences and co-incidences. And, by implicating the reader and offering a counternarrative of an alternative setting to the "facts" of history, he makes it possible for readers to choose for themselves the trajectory they will follow in the future.

What do the bounds of our age look like? The beating of the bounds, in earlier eras, "involved the whole parish, and could only be effective as a collective act of this whole."[146] As the parish redefined its boundaries, it interwove time with space, *kairos* and *topos*, as the parish redefined its boundaries. The act provided as much a sense of geographical co-ordinates as it did an existential terrain helping to define where, and to whom, parishioners belonged. So, if *A Secular Age* "beats the bounds" of our era, it does so by indicating the limits of Taylor's Secular$_2$ and tries to redraw the map according to Secular$_3$. What makes the bounds of Secular$_3$ distinct is a porosity to a source of fulfillment that is nei-ther mapped nor mappable; instead of closed borders, the edges of the map are open to the Transcendent. To the chagrin of those who advo-cate strict materialist reductionism or who delight in recounting tales of Secular$_2$, we cannot bracket out or ignore the stirring of the human heart. Taylor's claim, ultimately, is that an adequate picture of human life must account for the whole scope of human experience, even those stir-rings and longings we can neither measure nor manage. Taylor cannot compel us by logical argument to enter the sacred forest, but he does provide exemplars who have gone before us. By following their lead, we contribute to his map, which is a living thing that grows with each new itinerary taken.

Allow me, though, to raise a potentially scuttling objection. Put pithily, what if there isn't any *there* there? What if appeals to God are appeals to nothing? Taylor may be right that all humans feel drawn to attain human fulfillment. He may, moreover, be correct in giving a pow-erful account of what it is to live beneath the "eclipse." But what is to prevent this from being a snipe hunt? "Go out and pursue the snipe," we are told, but behind our backs it is whispered, "if one exists." Paul Janz seems to be making this critique: "The crux of the problem . . . stems from Taylor's continuous treatment of transcendence merely according to its linguistically or conceptually analytical definition as that which is 'beyond' the immanent (which effectively turns out to be the merely negative definition of transcendence as 'not the immanent')."[147] The issue is that, as Taylor uses it, "the term 'transcendence' is not yet an independent or 'ontological' *source* of anything; it is rather solely a *product* of logical thinking, and entirely abstract and negative one at that."[148] The critique: Taylor repeatedly gestures in God's direction, offers exemplars who claim to have encountered this divine "source," yet he has not demonstrated that God exists. A gap yawns between Taylor's logic and his ontology. "Set out to encounter God again! Wager your life and enter the forest," our well-meaning uncle tells us, and gives us a map. He assures us that the quest for new itineraries to God is possible because exemplars have forged new itineraries to God. But what reason do we have, apart from a yearning for fulfillment, for setting out in the first place? How do we know it is worth the risk?

Janz makes an important point. It would be helpful were Taylor to give an account "of *how* that which is transcendent announces itself uniquely and genuinely as a life-meaningful authority for questions of moral sources or human fullness."[149] If only obliquely, Taylor might be read as doing this with his exemplars. Conversion stories give us instances of embodied palimpsests that recount, in and through their lives, how God makes a new life possible. Janz, though, wants a more robust accounting for how God enters into human history. Indeed, the weight of his point must not be ignored. A reader who has accompanied Taylor through *A Secular Age* may feel a stir of desire to embark on a new itinerary to the sacred, may want to uncover a new route, yet may nevertheless pause. One hesitates due to a lack of confidence that what, or who, is sought in the forest abides there. At the moment, we are left to wonder whether our map is indeed a reliable guide, whether it reveals openings through which we might begin to approach God, or if what seems to be openings are actually spots where the ink of the map has been rubbed away and needs to be filled in. Perhaps the map is complete, its borders solid. Perhaps there are no openings and no return paths to God. In the background, Peggy Lee continues to croon "Is that all there is?" The worm of doubt stirs anew within our depths. Perhaps, after all, this is it.

Turning from Quebec to Cork

With Janz's question in mind, let me begin to pivot toward the work of William Desmond. Desmond distinguishes his project from that of Taylor's: "My emphasis is less on telling the story of modernity, offering hermeneutical narratives of the complex unfoldings of multifarious impulses, inspirations, trends, dreams, excesses, rational sobrieties, and so forth, defining the shaping of modernity. My interests have a certain metaphysical character to them."[150] It is in this metaphysical character of Desmond's thought that I believe we can find a necessary supplement to Taylor's map. Indeed, I want to argue that Desmond is a figure necessary for those who dwell on the plain, who yearn for a sense of fulfillment, but feel so exercised or vexed by the question of transcendence they can hardly assay all their options, let alone choose to commit themselves to any one of them.

Desmond can assist those who feel beset by the surfeit of choices. His philosophy, he writes, aims "to bring a developed habit of mindfulness to bear on what is at play in being, especially with regard to the basic presuppositions, sources, and orientations toward the 'to be' that mark our being in the midst of things."[151] My task is to understand both how Desmond enacts this goal and how his works can be approached in such a way that they aid in developing a "habit of mindfulness" attentive and responsive to God. I do this by approaching his thought in light of ancient spiritual exercises, defined by Pierre Hadot as "voluntary, personal practices intended to bring about a transformation of the individual."[152] Desmond's metaphysics needs to be undergone if they are to reignite metaphysical astonishment and open new pathways to God.

So, let us gather our belongings and bid adieu to Taylor. We tuck his map into our pockets, double-check to see that we have our philosophical passports in hand, and set out from Quebec to Cork, Ireland, and Desmond's home. Taylor has given us reason to believe that the stories of the impossibility of transcendence, or of God's death, may be false. There are, perhaps, still untrekked ways that can restore a sense of the divine. We shall bring Taylor's map to Desmond to see if his "Augustinian odyssey embarked upon in the wake of Hegel"[153] might uncover a new route or renew some old ones. Let us hope that lessons learned in

Cork can be offered, at the end of our journey, to Taylor both to preserve and advance his work. With Desmond's assistance, we can provide a compelling philosophical response to Janz's call for "some sort of critical or rationally demonstrative account, however indirect it might have to be, of what the meaningfully authoritative 'content' of the transcendent might be for human life."[154] We can advance and augment Taylor's map by forging, in Desmond's company, "new itineraries" capable of guiding seekers toward a horizon where we may behold the new dawn of belief in God in a secular age.

TWO

A Crack in Everything

Introducing William Desmond's Metaphysics

> Achilles is not quite invulnerable; the sacred waters did not wash the
> heel by which Thetis held him. Siegfried, in the Nibelungen, is not
> quite immortal, for a leaf fell on his back whilst he was bathing in the
> dragon's blood, and that spot which it covered is mortal. There is a
> crack in everything God has made.
>
> —Ralph Waldo Emerson, *"Compensation"*

This chapter introduces readers to William Desmond and his metaxological metaphysics. Born in Cork, Ireland, in 1951, Desmond describes
himself as having grown up in the Middle Ages, "an Irish Catholic, fostered on a sense of the mystery of God and God's ways, on a sympathy
for the rejected and the outside whom we cannot judge not to be God's
favored, fostered, too, on an esteem that God's creation, nature, was
good."[1] At an early age Desmond fell in love with poetry, especially
Wordsworth, and later took an interest in the works of Shakespeare.
After a year in the Dominican novitiate, he enrolled at University College Cork where he eventually focused his studies on English and phi-

losophy. Following an MA in philosophy, focusing on Collingwood's aesthetics, he moved to the United States, where he earned a PhD in philosophy at Penn State University. After doctoral studies, Desmond taught at St. Bonaventure for one year (1978–79) before returning to Ireland with the intention of making his home there. This was not to be: three years later, he returned to the United States to teach at Loyola University in Baltimore (1982–94). In 1994, he crossed the Atlantic once more to take a position at the Katholieke Universiteit Leuven, Belgium, where he taught until his retirement in 2017.

As befits one feted as "Ireland's most distinguished living philosopher,"[2] Desmond's work engages an array of thinkers—Heraclitus to Hegel, Plato to Nietzsche—and topics ranging from metaphysics to ethics to aesthetics to religion. His interlocutors include Richard Kearney, Cyril O'Regan, John Caputo, and a growing body of students who write appreciatively of his wisdom and generosity. Not least among these is Christopher Ben Simpson, whose work has gone a long way in making Desmond's thought more widely known.[3] Finally, three of his monographs have been extensively engaged in journals,[4] and two volumes of essays inspired by and in response to his thought are now available.[5]

In the introduction to *Between System and Poetics*, Anthony Kelly describes Desmond's ambition: "Desmond sees it as his task to find an adequate place for genuine alterity, the other which is nevertheless not alien, to revitalize the transcendent and to show its ineluctability for the ontological constitution of the human and of any understanding of the human which can lay claim to adequacy."[6] A daunting task, seeing as Desmond's philosophy is incorrigibly metaphysical in character and that, he admits, "metaphysics is a word not in good odor in some quarters today."[7] Yet, Richard Kearney observes, Desmond has always had a skeptical eye for "the fast and quick, for cheap notions of the destruction of metaphysics when not properly understood or when used as an excuse to ignore the rich complexity of the Western philosophy of Being, as if one could just sweep it aside and begin all over again from scratch, from the ground zero of our transcendental egos."[8]

Kearney aptly likens Desmond to the solitary marathoner, a thinker in for the long haul. This seems an apt description, especially given the request Desmond makes of would-be readers: "I do not ask for uncritical readers, but I do ask for disciplined readers—reader who have studied hard and long, who can take their time to think; readers who have not shunned solitude; readers suspicious of themselves before being suspicious of others; readers patient when demands are made on them; readers themselves adventurers; readers who ask for more than the rhetorics fashionable in academic philosophy, and who hate the substitution of 'relevant' ideology for the seriousness of truth."[9]

Desmond's philosophy, as will become apparent, offers no shortcuts and cannot be traversed quickly; it is a pilgrimage, not a jaunt. To take up his work requires, too, a willingness to risk being transformed as one reads. As I hope to show, Desmond's metaxology offers readers an invitation to undertake a philosophical *askesis*, or exercise, capable of cultivating a renewed mode of metaphysical attentiveness.

Those familiar with the mood of contemporary philosophy may be reluctant to accept this invitation. Desmond, in fact, anticipates skepticism: "I know that metaphysics is a word not in good odor in some quarters today, whether among some technical virtuosi of the analytical persuasion, or among the hermeneutical mandarins of the Continental persuasion, to say nothing of the dithyrambic textualists among the deconstructionists."[10] An "unrepentant" metaphysician, he insists we "need to ask the question of being; we need to ask the question of human being; we need to ask the question of the being of God."[11] One wonders, is this the wish of a philosopher too stubborn to accept metaphysics' overcoming? Clearly, Desmond has not yet read John Manoussakis's recent essay, which begins with the following observation: "William Desmond is arguably in our times the last metaphysician."[12]

The last metaphysician! A serious charge, not least for a book arguing for reading Desmond's metaphysics as a form of "spiritual exercise" capable of making us conscious once more of the transcendent dimension of human life, of raising again the question of God, and transforming the way we view the world. It stands to reason, then, that when a major philosopher of religion dubs the figure whose thought you promote as "the last metaphysician," you should be on alert. For even if Manoussakis does not wish for metaphysics or metaphysicians to go the way of the dodo, there are many scholars who regard metaphysics as a bankrupt enterprise and who are bemused, if not chuffed, to learn than metaphysicians are not yet extinct. Do we not live, as the titles of so many books proclaim, in a postmetaphysical age?[13]

To argue for the viability of metaphysics in general, and to advocate for Desmond's in particular, we need to get our bearings. To situate Desmond within the philosophical milieu, I propose to canvas the various critiques of metaphysics leveled by Martin Heidegger, John Caputo, Richard Kearney, and Merold Westphal. Of course, other figures could have been engaged: Jean-Luc Marion, Emmanuel Falque, and Kevin Hector have taken up the topic of metaphysics and its purported overcoming. Moreover, each of the authors I selected could be treated singly and at greater length. My choices owe as much to my competence (meager as this may be) as to biography: I spend more time reading these figures than I have others, and in the case of Westphal and Kearney, both were my teacher.

First, I employ Taylor's *ad hominem* strategy to engage Heidegger, Caputo, Kearney, and Westphal in a form of capacitating argument. Rather than showing how Critic X incapacitates all attempts at metaphysics, or how Desmond incapacitates Critic Y, I allow each critic to bring to light inconsistencies, contradictions, and missteps that have hampered earlier attempts at metaphysics. I try, in other words, to see how trenchant critiques made by smart thinkers might serve to capacitate a viable metaphysics. Each of our critics is right to level a "*justified refusal* of what is not to be affirmed," but though each "no" forecloses an earlier attempt at metaphysics, this does not necessarily mean any "no" has or can foreclose future efforts. Indeed, the salutary "no" of skepticism, for Desmond, "grows out of the presentiment that there is a norm or ideal that is short-changed or betrayed . . . the 'no' of genuine skepticism is the overt expression of something more deeply recessed—something not just a matter of negation."[14] An ad hominem or capacitating approach permits us to see how critique proves error-reducing and creates an opening for a renewed approach to metaphysical reflection. Paradoxically, the "no" of critique affirms by recognizing an absence in previous attempts; each critic identifies "something that is missing" in earlier practices. Conversation with these critics leads me to propose five "commandments" to be obeyed by thinkers interested not only in the viability of metaphysics but also by theologians who wish to draw on the tools of metaphysical reflection in their own work.

Next I offer a broad introduction to Desmond's systematic metaphysics. I stress *systematic* because, as he maintains, "one can reflect systematically without necessarily claiming possession of the system in the closed and totalizing sense."[15] Metaphysics needs to think with categories, but its task cannot be delimited by its categories; metaphysicians must remain "mindful of what exceeds system."[16] Hewing closely to Simpson's schema in *Religion, Metaphysics, and the Postmodern*, I orient the reader to Desmond's metaxological framework and the key concepts essential for understanding his project. Throughout this discussion, I draw attention to areas of overlap with Taylor.

Then I examine how Desmond's philosophy functions to inculcate a style of metaxological mindfulness. Metaphysics does not offer, at least as Desmond practices it, a disengaged description of being. We are implicated in the happening of being, and metaphysics reflects our effort to account for what it means "to be" while caught up in the midst of things. Desmond, like Taylor, tries to tell us our story in a way that gives us to perceive what it means "to be" anew. Here we see how Desmond complements and deepens Taylor's map by bringing to the surface otherwise recessed resources. Metaxology, so rendered, not only articulates a way of thinking philosophy but also makes possible a metaphysical way of life.

I conclude, first, by affirming my belief in Desmond's ability to preserve Taylor's project and explain how he advances it. Next, and more playfully, I offer a metaxological reading of Emerson's line from our chapter epitaph: "there is a crack in everything God has made." So read, the "crack" is no tragic flaw, but rather a graced opening allowing us to experience "the deepest ontological intimacy of our being."[17] This take on the line, finally, allows me to propose Desmond as the metaphysician of the "crack" and paves the way for my argument that metaxology lends itself to being approached as a form of spiritual exercise.

CONTESTING METAPHYSICS: BETWEEN THE KNOCKERS AND THE BOOSTERS

It is common coin among many philosophers and theologians that metaphysics and ontotheology are synonymous. Surely Iain Thomson is not alone in believing that "Heidegger's *Destruktion* of the metaphysical tradition leads him to the view that *all Western metaphysical systems* make foundational claims best understood as 'ontotheological.'"[18] Ontotheology, as used here, conflates ontology (the study of beings *qua* beings) with theology (the reflection on being's ultimate source). The result is ontotheology, a philosophical attempt to inscribe a god within a system of categories. God, for the ontotheologian, is not the source and sustainer of all being but, rather, *a* being within the system.

The adequation of metaphysics and ontotheology may, however, be unwarranted. John Betz, for instance, wonders whether Heidegger, in his account of how metaphysics became ontotheological, might have "forgotten or misremembered something."[19] Can one paint the whole history of metaphysics, from Aristotle to Hegel, with a single brush? For Betz, Heidegger seems to forget—intentionally or not—aspects of the Christian metaphysical tradition that do not reduce God into a being. Although there have been many practices of metaphysics, Betz writes, "under Heidegger's solvent influence, all these colors bleed into one."[20]

Each of the authors considered—Heidegger, Caputo, Kearney, and Westphal—harbor reservations about the nature and reach of metaphysics. I want to look at their critiques as an exercise in debris clearing. If we can get clear about how previous practices of metaphysics have erred, we can put safeguards into place to avoid future missteps. The "no" each author speaks to metaphysics can, I believe, lead eventually to a "yes." Although many more authors could be considered, I hope these four will give a sense of the attitudes scholars have toward metaphysics, ranging from outright knockers to tepid boosters and those who fall in between.

Martin Heidegger

We get to the heart of Heidegger's critique of metaphysics as ontotheology with his question, "How does the deity enter into philosophy?"[21] He answers: "Assuming that philosophy, as thinking, is the free and spontaneous self-involvement with beings as such, then the deity can come into philosophy only insofar *as philosophy, of its own accord and by its own nature, requires and determines that and how the deity enters into it.*"[22]

For Heidegger, the god of ontotheology does not irrupt freely into the human order. It is not the theophanic deity of the burning bush or the God disclosed at Jesus's baptism or in the Transfiguration. The god of metaphysics, rather, has been dragooned into philosophy and placed at its service. Philosophy, as it were, writes the job description and employs god in a narrowly circumscribed position. For Heidegger, this is a long-standing and irresistible temptation for metaphysics: "since its beginning with the Greeks has eminently been both ontology and theology. . . . For this reason my inaugural lecture *What Is Metaphysics?* (1929) defines metaphysics as the question about beings as such *and* as a whole. The wholeness of this whole is the unity of all beings that unifies as the generative ground."[23]

The final sentence reveals ontotheology's goal. As Merold Westphal writes, ontotheology tries to put its god "whether it be the Unmoved Mover, or Nature, or Spirit, or the Market to work as the keystone of a metaphysical theory designed to render the whole of reality intelligible to philosophical reflection."[24] This god enters metaphysics not through a divine epiphany, or a moment of dramatic revelation, but as the divine glue to subtend the wholeness of the whole and make the whole of being intelligible to human reason.

The god of metaphysics should be regarded as a functional god who acts as the "*causa prima* that corresponds to the reason-giving path back to the *ultima ratio*, the final accounting."[25] This god is inscribed within the conceptual system and placed at its service. Evoking Pascal's critique of the god of the philosophers, Heidegger claims *causa sui* is "the right name for the god of philosophy. Man can neither pray nor sacrifice to this god. Before the *causa sui*, man can neither fall to his knees in awe nor can he play music and dance before this god."[26] Even if ontotheology's god is the highest being within its system, it remains nevertheless within the system. Ironically, abandoning metaphysics and embracing a "godless thinking" may be more hospitable to the advent of the true God "than onto-theo-logic would like to admit."[27]

What Heidegger rejects, D. C. Schindler observes, is any "absorption of theology into philosophy."[28] Yet, Westphal notes, this critique does not hit *all* metaphysicians: "It is not always sufficiently noticed that his paradigms are Aristotle and Hegel and that the target of his analysis of 'the onto-theo-logical constitution of metaphysics' is a tradition that stretches from Anaximander to Nietzsche, which isn't quite the same as the tradition that stretches from Augustine to Kierkegaard."[29] Heidegger's atheism is less an outright denial of God's existence, such as we find in Dawkins or Dennett, than a methodological decision to dislodge the god co-opted by certain philosophers' overzealous and overreaching practices of metaphysics. In this, Heidegger repeats Kant's "I have found it necessary to deny knowledge in order to make room for faith."[30] One must reject the god indexed to human reason to make room for God's advent.

Accordingly, claims of Heidegger's "overcoming" of metaphysics require finesse. Certainly, he overcomes a *type* of metaphysics, one that incorporates a god into its system as an explanatory cause, a divine cog in the machine. Theologians, in fact, should applaud his efforts to raze the Temple of any and all conceptual idols. For the god of ontotheology, or any god indexed and subservient to human rationality and its quest to make the whole of reality intelligible, cannot be worshiped. Restricted by reason's constraints, such gods are but exsanguinated deities, drained of holiness and mystery. We should, consequently, adopt a healthy skepticism toward any metaphysics that claims to deliver "the system" guaranteed to make sense of the whole. But even if Heidegger justifiably refuses any metaphysics that would absorb theology into philosophy, or denude God of all mystery and holiness, this does not necessarily require abandoning all practices of metaphysics. His "no" may turn out to help us discern a practice to which theologians may say "yes."

Westphal succinctly and helpfully summarizes Heidegger's overall critique:

1. Onto-theology is calculative thinking
2. Onto-theology is representational thinking
3. Onto-theology is bad theology[31]

These share a common root: a "rationalist demand for total intelligibility."[32] Ontotheology turns the biblical God into a god, a being among beings, invoked only to hold the system together and to make sense of the whole. But it would be too hasty to interpret Heidegger's advocacy for a godless thinking as a summons to, or warrant for, outright atheism. Even if he demonstrates little personal interest in theology, his "overcoming" of metaphysics as ontotheology can be read as a salutary effort to chasten the pretense of human reason in its effort to corral the divine. Maybe Heidegger is not so radical, having as a forbear Augustine: *si comprehendis non est Deus* (if you understand, it is not God).

In light of this brief survey, let me offer a Heidegger-inspired first commandment for a theological engagement with metaphysics: *Thou shalt not index the divine to human reason.* Even if he is often interpreted as a hostile knocker, a nuanced reading of Heidegger recognizes that his critique does not apply universally to metaphysics. His "no" to ontotheology points to something recessed and in need of being drawn out by an adequate metaphysics. Thus, a metaphysics capable of interacting with theology (1) cannot set a priori terms for God's arrival and (2) cannot inscribe a god within its system to make sense of or render the whole transparent to human reason. It requires an epistemic humility and openness, a recognition of its own limits and a hospitality to the arrival of One who arrives not on our terms but its own.

John Caputo

Christopher Ben Simpson aptly summarizes Caputo's "problem" with metaphysics: Metaphysics is not faithful to life insofar as it is an abstract system "that privileges static unity in order to provide a stable foundation for life."[33] It is not faithful to life because it offers "eloquent assurances about Being and presence even as factical existence was being tossed about by *physis* and *kinesis*."[34] Elsewhere, Caputo sharpens this criticism, decrying metaphysics for providing a too-abstract "account of what is called 'mind-independent being,' that amounts to an account of the way things are *when we are not there*."[35] If metaphysics wants to study the "really real," then "physics is all the metaphysics we're ever going to get."[36] His advice to an aspiring metaphysician stings: "Brush up on your 'superstring field theory' or whatever will supersede superstrings next week."[37] Metaphysics has been supplanted by physics, so bone up on calculus and stop wasting time speculating about being and substance!

As an abstract system, Caputo continues, metaphysics privileges *static unity* and claims to provide a *stable foundation for life*. But for him, neither religion nor metaphysics can lay claim to a perspicuous viewpoint or unassailable foundation. Metaphysics and religion are both human practices and, as such, "always deconstructible in the light of the love of God, which is not deconstructible."[38] Although metaphysics promises to offer the all-encompassing "system" in which all things fit and in which the flux is controlled, it cannot possibly deliver. Indeed, in its attempt to make good on its empty promise, it succeeds only in betraying its practitioners by removing them from the flux, not capacitating them to deal with it.[39]

Finally, lest any doubt about his sentiment linger, Caputo writes, "I do not embrace a naturalist metaphysics, no more than I embrace a supernaturalist metaphysics. I resist every embrace of metaphysics. When it comes to embraces, I vastly prefer flesh and blood (which is my materialism)."[40] Having sworn off metaphysics, he offers instead a "radical hermeneutics." This approach, he avers, stays with the difficulty of life, avoids the "easy assurances of metaphysics," and "pushes itself to the brink and writes philosophy from the edge."[41]

The hot vehemence Caputo directs against metaphysics leads him to proffer what he calls a "cold hermeneutics" that does not believe in "'Truth'—it renounces all such capitalization—something hidden by and stored up in a tradition which is groaning to deliver it to us. It has lost its innocence about that and is tossed about by the flux, by the play, by the slippage. It understands that meaning is an effect. . . . Just when the metaphysics of presence is about to convince us that being clings to being, that truth is a well-rounded whole, a hermeneutical or eschatological circle, cold hermeneutics opens up an abyss."[42]

Caputo desires to remain faithful to the messiness of the quotidian, to remain in the flux rather than seeking a back door out of it. There is, moreover, a Heideggerian trace in his denial of a "Truth" that can be systematized or controlled. There exists no privileged access to, or possession of, the Truth; one cannot claim to possess any Archimedean point that affords an uninhibited or disengaged view. Caputo, clearly, is no Daedalus who offers us wings to soar above the flux.

We find in Caputo, furthermore, a link between his claim that "meaning is an effect" and his understanding of God: "The *meaning* of God is enacted in these multiple movements of love, but these movements are simply too multiple, too polyvalent, too irreducible, too uncontainable to identify, to define, or determine."[43] God is not "the Truth" arrived at through speculation, nor is God the object of privileged propositions guarded by magisterial authority. God, for Caputo, "is not only a name but an injunction, an invitation, a solicitation, to commend, to let all things be commended, to God."[44] The meaning of "God," for Caputo, is achieved through action; it is enacted in "openness to a future that I can neither master nor see coming."[45] True religion comes not from acquiring knowledge or infallible propositions but is lived as a "restlessness with the real that involves risking your neck."[46] God comes to us as a question, not an answer, and we enact religion as our response.

This suggests two Caputo-quickened commandments a viable metaphysics, whether on its own or intended for use by theologians, must observe. Second commandment: *Thou shalt not be faithless to the flux.* Third commandment: *Thou shalt not produce counterfeit gods.*

Second commandment: To allay Caputo's concerns, metaphysics must give a faithful account of the flux of the everyday. This means it must account for concrete lived reality while remaining attentive to the inherent fragility of existence. Within the quotidian, furthermore, we must discern and respond to the ethical summons issued by the Other that go beyond any codified obligation. Rather than hovering above the fray, a viable metaphysics must enter into the chaos of everyday life while informing an ethic wherein one is summoned to risk one's neck and put oneself on the line. Instead of offering abstract speculation about the neighbor, metaphysics must terminate in service to the widow, the orphan, and the alien.

Third commandment: If we have any desire to claim knowledge of the Absolute, we must foreswear absolute knowledge. We cannot pretend to have privileged access to, or an infallible knowledge of, Truth. Knowledge of God arises indirectly, amidst the flux, as we are moved by metaphors and "thrown above" by hyperboles (*hyper* + *ballein*) toward an encounter with God. The God of metaphysics cannot be one we craft as an idol. A God worthy of the name is not a god conjured from our resources. A praiseworthy God arrives unbidden, unexpectedly, at God's initiative, and catches us off guard. We possess no skill, no *technē*, to wring a confession out of the Holy One. Within the flux, we are condemned to fragmented knowledge and must be wary of settling on any idol, or graven image, or "Truth" that claims to settle matters once and for all.

Richard Kearney

At first blush, Richard Kearney might appear more comfortable being grouped among those who knock metaphysics. He writes, for instance,

"For too long theology and metaphysics have identified the divine with the most all-powerful of Beings. Sovereign, Self-sufficient substances. Transcendental Forms. First and Final Causes. Immutable essences."[47] With Paul Ricoeur, furthermore, he observes that "without the encounter of Greek metaphysics with biblical religious thought, philosophers 'would have never reached the idea that Being is the proper name of God and that this name designates God's very essence.' . . . this conjunction of God and Being was to survive for many centuries—from Bonaventure and Aquinas to Gilson and the neo-Scholastics. Thus did the God of Exodus secure ontological tenure in the God of metaphysics."[48]

Like Heidegger, Kearney regards God's co-option into metaphysics as ontotheology's key transgression because of its "tendency to reify God by reducing Him to a being (*Seinde*)—albeit the highest, first, and most indeterminate of all beings."[49]

When Nietzsche and Freud trumpet God's death, Kearney once again agrees with Ricoeur: the death of god they celebrate is the false god of ontotheology, the god "who deserves to die."[50] After the atrocities of the *Shoah* "so dies the omnipotent God of ontotheology understood as Emperor of the World. So also dies the omniscient God of 'self-sufficient knowledge' that places the 'powerful over the good and law over love and humility that are superior to law.' And along with the omnipotent and omniscient God goes the omnipresent God who condones evil as well as good. So dies, in short, the Omni-God of theodicy invoked to justify the worst atrocities as part of some Ultimate Design."[51]

One imagines Kearney presiding at the wake of the "Omni-God," reciting over the casket Etty Hillesum's prayer: "You, God, cannot be God unless we create a dwelling place for you in our hearts."[52] We must abandon the God of "power and might" and risk an encounter with the *kenotic* God of the Incarnation, the one who divests the divine being of omnipotence. The God who comes *after* the death of the God of metaphysics is not the "Highest Being" but, rather, one encountered as pure possibility, pure *posse* rather than *esse*, as a "promise, a call, a desire to love and be loved that can not *be* at all unless we allow God to be God."[53]

Amidst the rubble of a collapsed "Grand Metaphysical Systems that construed God in terms of formal universals and abstract essences,"[54] Kearney does not leave us destitute and godless. In fact, amidst the debris he charts a return to God, or perhaps God's return to us, by what he calls "anatheism." Anatheism, Kearney believes, is capable of opening a space "where we are free to choose between faith or nonfaith. As such, anatheism is about the *option* of retrieved belief. It operates *before* as well as *after* the division between theism and atheism, and it makes both possible. Anatheism, in short, is an invitation to revisit what might be termed a primary scene of religion: the encounter with a radical Stranger who we choose, or don't choose, to call God."[55]

Kearney's anatheism does not rest on metaphysical certainties or syllogisms; it makes, instead, a wager or induces an "existential drama" calling us to discernment and decision.[56] We may return to God; we may not. Anatheism is less a command than a coax to openness "to someone or something that was lost and forgotten by Western metaphysics."[57] We cannot dance before or sing praises to the Omni-God, nor can the God of metaphysics still our restless hearts. Perhaps, though, the opening of anatheism can lead us to the God who comes after the God of metaphysics, enabling us to hear the call of the God who may be, a God who will and wants to be God for us . . . *if* we allow it. The key word, of course, is *if*: *if* we make ourselves open and vulnerable for God to appear not in acts of power but in the arrival, oft unbidden, of the Stranger.

In place of the "Grand System," Kearney privileges what he calls "micro-eschatologies," or events manifesting and disclosing God in the everyday. For Kearney, the *eschaton* is not a cataclysmic event; it is a "sundering," a breaking open and revealing the divine in the everyday, a "sacramental vision" attuned to immanent transcendence.[58] Through the concept of micro-eschatology, Kearney exhorts us to train our eyes not to a far-off horizon but to the quotidian where we encounter the divine in the daily and discern the woo of the Holy One in "the least ones calling for a cup of cold water, asking to be fed, clothed, cared for, heard, loved."[59] He calls this a micro-eschatological "fourth reduction" returning us to the everyday and thrusting us into "face-to-face encounters of our ordinary universe" where the divine is disclosed in the face of the stranger, where we intuit the presence of the divine amidst St. Teresa's pots and pans.

In his critique of metaphysics, Kearney aligns with Heidegger; in his call for us to remain in the day-to-day, he stands with Caputo. On his own, he remains without peer as an expositor of texts. He does not merely write about texts but thinks and philosophizes through them.

His hermeneutical phenomenology, moreover, extends beyond the text toward a hermeneutic of lived existence. This Ricoeur-inspired movement from text to life allows him to offer "a number of more personal reflections on the enigma of transfiguration, as it relates to the specifically paschal testimonies of the resurrected Christ."[60] Kearney writes:

> The post-paschal stories of the transfiguring *persona* remind us that the Kingdom is given to hapless fishermen and spurned women, to those lost and wandering on the road from Jerusalem to nowhere, to the wounded and weak and hungry, to those who lack and do not despair of their lack, to little people "poor in spirit." The narratives of the transfigured-resurrected Christ testify that after the long night of fasting and waiting and darkness and need—afloat on a wilderness of sea—breakfast is always ready. The transfiguring *persona* signals the ultimate solidarity, indeed indissociability, of spirit and flesh.[61]

If God is to be credible after the Shoah, this God will be no "Omni-God." It will be, instead, the Kingdom's God who communicates not through deeds of power but subtly, "in stories and act of love and justice, the giving to the least of creatures, the caring for orphans, widows, and strangers; stories and acts which bear testimony—as transfiguring gestures do—to that God of little things."[62] The micro-eschatological reduction awakens us to the immanent transcendence of the little things and gives us to behold the world with eyes open and alert to the everyday epiphanies of the divine.

From Kearney we craft a fourth commandment: *Thou shalt be attuned and attentive to everyday disclosures.* A compliant metaphysics will not impose categories or preset how and where the divine will make itself manifest. Instead, we must choose to interpret the day-to-day with an eye attentive to the "small things left behind, unheard and unseen, discarded and neglected."[63] It calls for a hermeneutical metaphysics that does not pine for a different world, but one that makes it possible for us construe and comport ourselves in the world differently, newly conscious of the "epiphanies of the quotidian" revealing the divine not in power and might but in "mustard seeds, grains of yeast, tiny pearls, cups of water."[64] Kearney's counsel to any would-be metaphysics would insist that it remain open to discovering the holy in the humdrum and the mystical in the mundane.

Merold Westphal

I treat Merold Westphal last not only because he is the most hospitable of our thinkers to a theological engagement with metaphysics, but also, and blessedly, because he sets out his own criteria. But before I enumerate these and try to formulate his commandment, let me position him vis-à-vis the other thinkers.

Like Heidegger, Caputo, and Kearney, Westphal insists on the need to overcome ontotheology. And, like Kearney and Caputo, he is committed to a form of hermeneutic phenomenology. But compare the following with Caputo's take on "the Truth": "The truth is that there is Truth, but in our finitude and fallenness we do not have access to it. We'll have to make do with the truths available to us; but that does not mean either that we should deny the reality of Truth or that we should abandon the distinction between truth and falsity. Moreover, the most we should claim for this claim itself is that it is true, that it is the best way for us humans to think about the matter."[65] He recalls Kearney's refusal of the metaphysical traits ascribed to the "Omni-God": "In order to have a biblical, personal, eschatological, and ethical God, the goal Kearney and I share, it is necessary to overcome ontotheology. This does not require that we abandon abstract and impersonal metaphysical categories in our God talk, but only that we put them in their proper, subordinate place."[66]

We must overcome ontotheology, but this overcoming need not require abandoning metaphysics. We need, instead, a chastened metaphysics that recognizes the limits of human reason and puts metaphysics at the service of faith.

In a recent article, Westphal engages Kant, Heidegger, and Jean-Luc Marion in an effort to understand why "metaphysics is seen as abusing the life of faith" because, within the confines of the metaphysical system, it leaves no room for faith.[67] In his treatment of Kant, for instance, he detects an apparent paradox: "We seem to be overcoming metaphysics in order to make room for metaphysics. But there is no contradiction here. The metaphysics to be overcome is not the same as the metaphysics for which room is made. The one is an enemy of faith, the other is an essential component thereof."[68] On Westphal's reading, Kant resists the encroachment of any dogmatic metaphysics that either asserts human reason as the "highest tribunal by which all questions of right (*quid juris*) regarding our God talk are to be settled" or that reshapes God to "fit the Procrustean bed by which it defines human rationality."[69] Nevertheless, neither this critique nor those of Heidegger or Marion deal the death stroke to metaphysics. Quite to the contrary, Westphal reads these critiques as having the potential to capacitate a metaphysics that can contribute to and serve the life of faith.

The capacitating power of his critique becomes evident in the essay's conclusion. Westphal reminds his reader that up until this point he has been "focused on overcoming metaphysics, on its danger to the life of faith, its role as abuser of biblical faith."[70] And by "overcoming metaphysics" he means the metaphysics that would fall prey to the charge of ontotheology. So far, nothing new. Then he writes, "But I have said only three things, and ever so briefly, about the use of metaphysics for the life of faith: first, that faith and the theology that accompanies it presuppose and include metaphysical beliefs; second, that this metaphysics can be and must be different from the metaphysics that needs to be overcome . . . third, that this metaphysics will need to be a humble metaphysics, acknowledging that it rests on faith and not pretending to be the Voice of Pure Reason."[71]

In other words: some practice of metaphysics is inescapable; ontotheology will not fit the bill; and the metaphysics needed to serve faith must emerge from faith. Ultimately, the metaphysics he envisions as best capable of serving faith will be a "pragmatic metaphysics," one rooted within the practice of faith and arising from faith to nourish "private prayer, character formation, public worship, and service to others." No disengaged or abstract speculation, Westphal envisions it as a living and dynamic practice "embedded in a spirituality that is simultaneously an inward journey, and upward journey, and an outward journey. It is not a preamble to faith but a reflection that arises out of faith and seeks to serve the life of faith."[72] Metaphysics, as Westphal envisions it, is not idle speculation but a living summons to ongoing inquiry. It is a moment within, and always at the service of, *fides quaerens intellectum* (faith seeking understanding).

From Westphal we draw our fifth commandment: *Be still and know: Metaphysics is a vocation.* A theologically viable metaphysics will recognize that metaphysics finds its origin as a response to something other to and in excess of human rationality. Rather than a neutral practice of abstract reflection, metaphysics arises because of a presentiment that its searching is a consequence of having first been sought and called by a presence anterior to it. The overcoming of metaphysics as ontotheology may, should we allow Westphal to play the role of Moses, deliver us from the land of idolatrous captivity and free us to take faltering steps out into the promised land led by the voice of the One who bids us to follow. Thus, a theologically serviceable metaphysics, in obeying commandment, will be alert and responsive to God's call.

Capacitating Metaphysics

In an effort to emulate Taylor's ad hominem strategy of argument, I have tried to engage Heidegger, Caputo, Kearney, and Westphal as representing a continuum of boosters and knockers. Each "no" raised in a justified refusal of earlier practices of metaphysics, I am claiming, need not be read as an embargo on all future metaphysics. On the contrary, each offers a corrective negation, a "no" affirming an absence, indicating that something has been recessed and is in need of being surfaced. Metaphysics, in effect, can be capacitated by learning from previous missteps. Allow me, then, to propose Desmond's philosophy as a viable metaphysics in compliance with our five commandments:

1. *Thou shalt not index the divine to human reason* (Heidegger)
2. *Thou shalt not be faithless to the flux* (Caputo)
3. *Thou shalt not produce counterfeit gods* (Caputo)
4. *Thou shalt be attuned and attentive to everyday disclosures* (Kearney)
5. *Be still and know: Metaphysics is a vocation* (Westphal)

Throughout the forthcoming exposition of Desmond's philosophy, I advert attention to the ways in which metaxology proves faithful to these commandments. There may be practices of metaphysics that fall afoul of these warrants, but metaxology will prove not to be one of them.

By no means is it my intention to promote Desmond as the savior of metaphysics. Metaphysics might not need as much "saving" as Manoussakis's comment might lead one to believe. Dominique Janicaud wryly observes the "theme of onto-theology has so intimately penetrated reflection on the history of metaphysics that it seems quite legitimate to turn this magic wand back on contemporary writings whose 'post-metaphysical' character is often more proclaimed than proved."[73] A few pages later, he continues, "Husserl shows quite clearly that a metaphysical phenomenology is possible; ought we to add, more categorically perhaps, that phenomenology, radically implemented and methodically conducted, can only be metaphysical (in the sense of *metaphysica generalis*)?"[74] Even some hard-liners against any attempts at metaphysics have softened. Jean-Luc Marion, in the new edition of *God without Being*, changes his position in regard to Aquinas, writing, "I am ready to maintain today the apparent paradox that Thomas Aquinas *did not* identify the question of God, nor that of his names, with Being, or at least with Being as metaphysics understands within its 'concept of Being.'"[75] Marion's former student Emanuel Falque asks whether "this putative metaphysics understood as ontotheology—namely the act of leading being *qua* being [*ontos*] back to God as the super Being [*theos*]—is not another one of those paradises that is illusory and impossible to find."[76] So, if the search for a metaphysics-as-ontotheology turns out to be a snipe hunt, the exercise of trying to understand how previous metaphysics overstepped their bounds has generated guidelines for our inquiry. Our time with Heidegger, Caputo, Kearney, and Westphal has not been in vain.

If Desmond is not *the* messiah of metaphysics, he has nevertheless a pivotal role to play in overcoming the "overcoming of metaphysics." He demonstrates, I believe, that metaphysics has not died out but, if it is to have a future, must be tried out, and, if my reading of his philosophy bears out, lived out. And so with philosophical passports in hand, let us venture into the *metaxu*. Let us accompany him on a philosophical journey and be tutored as we travel. At our journey's end, I am confident we will have been informed by his efforts to think in a metaphysical key. But it is my hope that our time together will show how his philosophy, undertaken as a practice, can transform the way we perceive the world. Without further ado, and with philosophical passports in hand, let us venture into the *metaxu*.

SPEAKING METAXOLOGICALLY: WORDING THE *METAXU*

I subtitle this admittedly lengthy section "Wording the *Metaxu*" because it introduces the categories and vocabulary Desmond uses throughout his philosophy. There is truth in Catherine Pickstock's claim that "Desmond is astonishingly direct and astonishingly clear,"[77] but Simpson's observation is equally apt: "Desmond's work can be complex, dense, meditative, and full of neologisms."[78] I begin with the nature and task of Desmond's metaphysics. I then take up key categories: "ethos," the "fourfold way," and his tripartite understanding of transcendence. These furnish our grammar for speaking metaxologically, a language we will develop and enrich throughout our journey.

Metaphysics: Its Nature and Task

Desmond's *Being and Between* opens with the primordial metaphysical question: What is being? What does it mean to be?[79] This is not the question of what it means to be this or that but what it means to be at all. A simple-seeming question becomes, upon reflection, maddeningly complex; for, as Aristotle observed, "there are many senses in which a thing may be said to 'be' (*to on legetai pollachōs*)."[80] Aristotle and Aquinas, for instance, recognized three ways being can be "said": the *univocal*, the *equivocal*, and the *analogical*. Each understood, moreover, the inability of any one way to provide an exhaustive account of being. Indeed, it is part of the metaphysician's vocation to accept that metaphysics "*does* often put a strain on language, seeming to make it other to so-called 'ordinary' usage."[81] Even those who claim to be "postmetaphysical" or who believe metaphysics to have been overcome cannot evade raising the question of being because "in all our thinking, and living, certain fundamental senses of being are already at work, and continue to be at work."[82] Ironically, any effort to dismiss metaphysics necessitates its invocation. Some engagement in metaphysical reflection is unavoidable.

If Desmond is correct, if some type of metaphysics is necessary, then which one? If a theologian wants to make friends with a metaphysician, to whom should she turn? There is a range of options, from Aristotle to

Aquinas to Hegel to Badiou. Some fall afoul of our five commandments: Aristotle and Hegel were, for Heidegger, culprits of ontotheology. Materialists such as Badiou manifest little interest in the God question and assume atheism as axiomatic. In my estimation, Desmond is a theologian-friendly metaphysician who harbors no aspiration to construct a grand "system" in which to schematize or explain the whole of being. His goal, Thomas Kelly observes, is "to revitalize the transcendent and to show its ineluctability for the ontological constitution of the human and any understanding of the human which can lay claim to adequacy."[83] Desmond wants to demonstrate that we cannot adequately understand what it means to be human without considering our openness to and intimacy with the Divine.

In a gesture sure to allay some of metaphysics' knockers, Desmond offers no totalizing system but "a form of reflective thinking under fidelity to the truth of what is thus at play."[84] The final phrase is key: *at play* indicates how he regards his philosophy as arising in the midst of, and as a response to, finding oneself "in the midst of beings."[85] Instead of offering an abstract answer to the question of being, Desmond's metaphysics is better thought of as a method of reflection leading us along the road as we plumb the question of being. By remaining faithful to what is at play, his philosophy originates in, and stays faithful to, everyday flux. This becomes clear if, recalling the dual meaning of *meta* ("in the midst" and "beyond"), we follow his suggestion that "this double sense of 'meta' can be taken to correspond to the difference of *ontology* and *metaphysics*. Ontology (as a *logos* of *to on*) can be taken as an exploration of given being as immanent; metaphysics can be seen as opening a self-surpassing movement of thought that points us to the porous boundary between immanence and what cannot be determined entirely in immanent terms."[86]

The question of being that arises from dwelling amidst beings (ontology) can spur us into an attentiveness to what is in excess of and beyond finite being (metaphysics). Rather than a denial of the quotidian, metaphysics begins amidst the flux and enjoins reflection on the fact that "all beings, events, processes are, or happen to be. That they are *at all* is something that exceeds what they are."[87] Renewed attention to the beings encountered in ordinary life engenders an appreciation for how extraordinary being is.

We need a renewal of attentiveness because—and here Desmond and Taylor align—we have lost our sense of wonder at the sheer existence of being. One of the symptoms of the eclipse of God has been the modern imagination's "epistemic irritability with the equivocity of being,"[88] which has fueled its rage for imposing order: "One thinks of the modern mathematization of nature and the hope of empowering technological interventions. One thinks of how in the scientific objectification of nature, externality is stripped of all its qualitative textures, these being consigned to mere secondary qualities. . . . There is an evaporation of the good as defining the teleology of being. The good of the whole is no longer there, and in its place we find ontologically devalued thereness."[89]

Like Taylor, Desmond detects a shift away from appeals to God and an increasing reliance on the power of human reason. He, too, notes how the nature of metaphysical reflection has been transformed, if not degraded, throughout modernity. What began as a festive mindfulness of an "enchanted" world, porous to intermediation with the divine, was strangled as the passages between the immanent and the transcendent realms became clogged. Desmond, expanding one of Taylor's insights, notes how "the movement to this Western buffered self goes together with the disenchantment of the world and the construction of the immanent frame. This construction leads by circuitous ways to *default atheism*, as I would put it."[90]

Desmond does not respond to this clogging or buffering, as Taylor does, by offering a counternarrative. He calls, instead, for a "return to the sources of metaphysical thinking."[91] He hearkens us to heed and take to heart Socrates's claim, namely, that "this is an experience which is characteristic of a philosopher, this wondering (*thaumazein*): this is where philosophy begins and nowhere else."[92] Metaphysical thinking begins in primal astonishment: "Astonishment itself is primal. It is elemental and irreducible. Plato speaks of *thaumazein* as the *pathos* of the philosopher. This is sometimes translated as wonder and this is not inappropriate. Astonishment, however, captures the sense of being rocked back on one's heels, as it were, by the otherness of being in its givenness. Plato says *pathos*: there is a pathology in metaphysics. There is a suffering, an undergoing; there is a patience of being; there is a receiving that is not the production of the metaphysician or mind."[93]

Herein we find a synopsis of what Desmond takes to be the nature and task of metaphysics. Its nature: metaphysics originates as a response to suffering a "certain shock or bite of otherness."[94] It reflects *being opened*, both *being* as opened toward us and our being *opened* as a result of it addressing us. Its task: to keep alive this astonishment and to remain faithful to the vocation to renew the "opening to transcendence that comes first to us."[95]

Thus far, Desmond avoids transgressing our commandments. Whatever the cause of astonishment, he recognizes (1) that metaphysics is a vocation responding to the summons of a transcendent source, (2) that this vocation arises from the flux of daily life and must remain faithful to life's flux, and (3) that its attentiveness to disclosures "amidst" beings must guide its gaze "beyond" being. Hardly a disengaged "taking a look," Desmond envisions metaphysics as a passionate endeavor, an undertaking and an undergoing. Instead of idle speculation, we shall see his metaphysics as a mode of existence aimed at returning its practitioners to the primordial sources that elicit, and that promise to refresh, our sense of astonishment that being *is* at all.

In place of a totalizing system of concepts, Desmond invites us to consider anew how our comportment amidst beings (*meta*) can be directed toward and alerted to what is beyond and in excess of finite beings (*meta*). In place of "the system" he articulates a systematic approach keen on probing the interconnections and intermediations between beings and discovering how our inquiry points us, ultimately, beyond finite being toward the infinite source of all being. This is not an ontotheological effort to inscribe the deity within a conceptual system. Nor is it an exercise of an "instrumental mind," which, as a hallmark of modernity,

> takes for granted, in a potentially mindless way, the beings that are given, and goes to work with its categories on what is there, devoid of metaphysical astonishment before the *that* of its being there at all. It bustles with activity, but [this activity] may crowd out an essential otherness. To restore mindfulness of this, one must stop thinking in that mode, stop thinking that instrumental thought exhausts the energy of thinking. Silence, patience, a different ontological vigilance is needed. Solitude may prepare an opening for different thought, for a celebrating mindfulness of being.[96]

. Desmond's philosophy encourages and seeks to cultivate an "onto-logical vigilance" sensitive to what "instrumental mind" brackets out. Metaphysics, as a practice, puts us in touch with energies otherwise re-cessed and ignored in modernity. If modernity takes being *for* granted, this contemplative receptivity perceives being *as* granted and, attuned to its gratuity, invites us to dwell anew within what he calls the *metaxu*, or ethos of being.

The Ethos of Being: The *Metaxu*

Desmond's metaphysics arises "in the midst" of beings and responds to finding oneself astonished by being's givenness. Astonishment refreshes our sense of what it means to be: beings are not "just there" but a part of a dynamic system of signs pointing beyond themselves toward an ulti-mate origin. Refusing to separate ontology from metaphysics leads him to plead for "a practice of philosophical thinking that does not float above the ethos of being in abstraction, but comes to itself in the midst of things. There the astonishing being given of being(s) opens us for thought, and cries out against any form of Laputan abstraction. We start in the midst of things, and we are open to things. We are open because we are already opened. Before we come to ourselves as more reflectively thoughtful, we already are in a porosity of being, and are ourselves as this porosity of being become mindful of itself."[97]

Unlike the residents of Swift's Laputa, the floating island whose residents become lost in abstractions and must be struck with a "bladder" to remind them to move, Desmond's metaphysician remains engaged with the happening of being; metaphysics enjoins a practice of dwelling amidst beings mindful of a creative source in excess of finite being.

Having considered the what of metaphysics, we need to consider its whence. Central to Desmond's vision: metaphysics originates in "the between" or, as found in Plato's *Symposium*, the *metaxu*. He explains his neologism: "'*Metaxu*' is the Greek word for 'between,' while '*logos*' can mean an accounting, or reasoning, or wording. A metaxological phi-losophy is concerned with a *logos* of the *metaxu*, or a wording of the be-tween. Such a philosophy is concerned with life itself as a between space, a *metaxu*, and with the fact that this between is an articulated middle or intermedium."[98]

Our lives unfold within and upon the *metaxu*, between birth and death, being and nothingness, the finite and the infinite. Metaxology offers an account of the *metaxu* as the embracing "ontological context or overdetermined matrix of value in which our human ethos and ethics come to be articulated. This is prior to, and in excess of, every specific ethical determination that we define. For we reconfigure the elemental ethos, and so stay true or betray or disfigure its promise. What is at play in it cannot be stated univocally or made fully evident at the outset, since it is through the reconfigured *ethe* that we gain some sense of its potencies."[99]

Here Desmond makes a distinction between the "reconfigured" and "primal" ethos of being. In every age, humans dwell and negotiate their lives within the *metaxu*. We need, Desmond believes, to step back and look critically at our ethos and discern how our era reflects, or distorts, the potency of the primal ethos. Do we live in concert with creation or at cross-purposes with it? This is an archaeological initiative, one that peers beneath the practices and values that define our reconfigured ethos in order to explore "the enabling sources and powers that give being to be as it is, and give it to be as good."[100] Have we remained true to the goodness of creation or have we betrayed it in a quest for riches or power? Do our communities reflect our interdependence or are we increasingly closed off from one another?

This may become clearer if we connect Desmond's *metaxu* or ethos with Taylor's "social imaginary." The social imaginary, Taylor writes, is broader and deeper "than the intellectual schemes people may entertain when they think about social reality in a disengaged mode. I am thinking, rather, of the ways people imagine their social existence, how they fit together with others, how things go on between them and their fellows, the expectations that are normally met, and the deeper normative notions and images that underlie these expectations."[101]

Both Taylor and Desmond emphasize the social imaginary and *metaxu* as anterior; they are better thought of as backgrounds than foregrounds, the backdrop and setting of the stage on which our lives are acted out. Rather than determinate "things," it is better to think of each as a matrix or encompassing context providing us with the know-how by which we negotiate shared space. Both reflect the "common understanding which makes possible common practices and a widely shared sense of legitimacy"[102] expressed in cultural mores, customs, institutions, and expectations. But because they operate in the background, we are seldom aware of them—only when a breakdown or an interference with the normal flow of events takes place do we become thematically aware of the assumptions informing our practices.

We should resist, however, conflating the social imaginary with the *metaxu*. To employ a distinction Desmond draws, the social imaginary is better situated within a narrower realm of ontology, whereas the *metaxu* offers a more capacious metaphysical view. For Desmond, ontology and metaphysics are distinct yet inseparable: "Ontology deals with being as immanent, and as such it tends to culminate in something like Hegel's system of self-determining thought, or perhaps the existential recoil back to human immanence in terms of fundamental ontology, such as that of Heidegger. Metaphysics, by contrast, is more metaxological in the sense of opening mindfulness to transcendence by means of an exploration of the signs of irreducible otherness, even in immanence."[103]

Taylor's social imaginary describes the immanent realm in which we live, and move, and have our being. It furnishes and describes the pre-theoretical way we function and negotiate our lives together. It describes this background as the "largely unstructured and inarticulate understanding of our whole situation, within which particular features of our world show up for us in the sense they have."[104] These often unstated and presumed assumptions inform, shape, and give coherence to our practices: things make sense against this horizon. Yet the accent is primarily ontological in describing how "ordinary people 'imagine' their social surroundings"[105] and live in the midst of other beings.

It may be helpful here to recall Janz's critique of Taylor. Janz accuses Taylor of an oversight because "the term 'transcendence' is not, as Taylor uses it, an independent or 'ontological' *source* of anything; it is rather solely the *product* of logical thinking."[106] Taylor refers repeatedly to our potential for transcendence and offers examples of those who have come into contact with God, yet he never offers a substantive account for God's existence. The lacuna: Taylor may tell us a great deal about how our age came to pass, he may tell us much about how it feels to live within a world where divine light appears to have been eclipsed, but he never provides a substantive account for God's existence. In Desmondian terms, Taylor offers an ontological account dealing with being as immanent and describes our being *amidst* beings. Limited to this first sense of *meta*, Taylor's map requires a metaphysical supplement to convince the seeker—even if via indirections—to venture *beyond* the immanent order because the fullness of life and source of flourishing comes from a transcendent source.

Let me suggest how Desmond's *metaxu* provides the metaphysical supplement required to help flesh out Taylor's map. Taylor's genealogy accounts for how we came to live and negotiate our lives within the "immanent frame" in a way either open or closed to the question of God. It is a suggestive ontological and phenomenological portrait of how the "social imaginary" was formed, what was gained and lost through its formation, and it performs to the extent it induces us to experience the "cross-pressures" pulling us simultaneously toward belief and unbelief. As we search for what will ensure our flourishing, we ask: Must we make some sort of appeal to God? On our own, do we have sufficient resources to bring about flourishing or must it come from a source beyond ourselves? Taylor, for his part, thinks we need to make some appeal to a theological view. The constraint placed on Taylor's map, however, is that it paints a vibrant ontological portrait of our age but fails to take up the metaphysical questions besetting seekers. He refers to experiences of prayer and fullness, adduces instances of others' attainment of human flourishing, but offers no substantive account for the source of this fullness. Taylor assumes what needs to be argued, but offers no pathway leading toward God.

Desmond's metaphysical enterprise can complement and complete Taylor's project. This is because the *metaxu* encompasses an ontological concern for being amidst beings (first *meta*) and a metaphysical appreciation for how beings point to what is beyond finite being (second *meta*). But we only arrive at the second *meta* by considering and contemplating the first. As a form of reflection, metaxology inculcates an openness "to transcendence by means of an exploration of the signs of irreducible otherness, even in immanence."[107] This complements Taylor by making possible a new way of comporting oneself within our age. If Taylor's ontological approach takes being for granted, Desmond's approach corrects it by restoring a sense of being as gratuitously granted by a creative origin. Metaxology tutors us to read Taylor's map anew, guiding our gaze from the ontological realm of being toward the meta-physical source of all that is. To read Taylor's map with metaxologically opened eyes is to discover the map's depths disclosed and to find that there is more to it than meets the untrained eye.

Such a disclosure is necessary to respond to Janz's critique and to negotiate the terrain beneath the eclipse. As we referenced, Desmond shares a common cause with Taylor in desiring to resist the encroachment of "instrumental mind." The consequence of instrumental mindfulness is the "devaluing objectification of being" and "subjectification of value."[108] Desmond describes the reductive tendency: "Being is objectified in that it is neutralized or devalued or evacuated—emptied of any value or worth or goodness in itself—and made into a 'merely empirical' mechanism. The subjectification of value comes about as there is a 'revaluation' of value in terms of human self-determination that comes to see the supreme value as freedom understood in terms of human autonomy—ultimately flowering to reveal its core in the will to power."[109]

The dialectic between "objectification of being" and "subjectification of value" is, Simpson notes, reciprocal. Its movement generates a belief that "humans cannot be truly autonomous if there is any value or good other than that which they create."[110] This, for Desmond, results in the antinomy between autonomy and transcendence. "The antimony," he writes, "absolutizes autonomy, and you relativize the good as other, or more than our self-determination; absolutize the good as other and you must relativize autonomy."[111] One naturally thinks of Kant, but Nietzsche is no less beholden to an antinomy between an autonomous self-determination that rejects any semblance of heteronomic interference.[112]

The modern reconfiguration of the ethos, pitting God against the human in a zero-sum contest, does not tell the whole story. In fact, one important contribution of deconstruction has been to challenge modernity's "notion of a fixed univocal unity."[113] Deconstruction destabilizes the sediment of modernity and thereby exposes our ethos as but one possible figuration; we have reconfigured the ethos in *this* way, but there could well have been, or there may yet be, others. Instead of taking the modern ethos for granted or as inevitable, deconstruction gives us to see how it is an achievement, how the present reconfiguration is one of many possible alternatives. Yet Desmond does not rush in, blueprints in hand, to rebuild after the deconstructionist's hammer has been swung. We find him, rather, exploring the primordial ground deconstruction has brought to light. He invites us to join him in marveling at the protean nature of the primal ethos, how it has been and can be shaped and reshaped. Before trying to build on the newly uncovered ground, Desmond surveys the territory and asks how we might make good on the promise and potency of the elemental ethos. We are not condemned, he would have us believe, to repeat the mistakes of the past. We can build in fidelity to the promise and goodness of being.

Metaxological metaphysics, far from running away from daily life, demands fidelity to the *metaxu*. It bids us to become aware once more of the primal ethos disclosed beneath the destabilized sediment of each era and to encounter within the *metaxu* what he calls the "intimate strangeness of being." Strangeness: being has "an otherness, indeed marvel, of which we are not the conceptual masters." Intimate: "this very strangeness allows no stance of thinking 'outside' being—we are participants in what we think about."[114] A metaxologically attuned mind perceives in every era the various fissures and "cracks" through which the intimate strangeness of being can address us. Our duty is to respond to this call, not by seeking to silence it but by being directed through the crack in every reconfigured ethos toward the elemental *metaxu* where we may drink, and remember once more, the goodness of what it means "to be" at all.

Easier said than done! Desmond describes our era as reconfigured by what he calls "postulatory finitism." Postulatory finitism, he writes, "first supposes, then later presupposes, that the finite and nothing but the finite constitutes the ultimate horizon for human thinking, one greater than which none can be thought."[115] Or, stated otherwise, it lays down the "rules" for what philosophy can talk about. It postulates, and presumes as a given, that we can neither raise nor answer questions of the infinite. The question of God, then, has no place on the philosophical agenda. Desmond recalls "a time when to mention God or religion in the company of advanced intellectuals was like mentioning sex in a prudish Victorian drawing room. An icy silence would descend, and the silence communicated more than overt argument possibly could: *we* do not now talk of these things."[116] Among an increasing segment of the West's population, the question of God has ceased to be a question. Ours is a time, as Desmond mentioned, of default atheism.

By daring to speak of a metaphysics open to self-transcendence and hospitable to the religious question of God, Desmond challenges this postulatory finitism. Taylor might regard his project as disrupting the "secularist spin" that buffers us from experiencing the push and pull of the Jamesian open space. Desmond wants to reignite a sense of astonishment at the givenness of being and, in so doing, reopen the question of God. Nietzsche's madman spoke too soon: God is not dead, but we need to be provoked into raising the God question once more. Desmond can, I believe, lead those willing to accompany him on a purgative itinerary capable of reopening the question of God, and lead us toward an encounter with the Creator on whose account, Gerard Manley Hopkins writes, "nature is never spent" and because of whom there continues to abide within the *metaxu* "the dearest freshness deep down things."[117]

The Fourfold Sense of Being

I pivot now to Desmond's fourfold—metaxology's *how*—by linking the *metaxu* with metaphysics. Our lives, he writes, unfold upon the *metaxu* "between diverse extremes: birth and death, nothing and infinity, abysses of abjectness and superlatives of heights, interiorities of secret intensity and exteriorities of vast extension. Human being is a between-being, but more often than not these extremes are recessed in the domestication of everyday life."[118] By no means is metaxology limited to reflecting on human being, for it seeks to discern "in the very ontological robustness of immanent otherness an original communication of an even more radical otherness, hyperbolic to the terms of immanence alone."[119] A searching metaphysics, metaxology ranges across the ethos attentive to disclosures of a presence that transcends and exceeds the boundaries of immanence. It remains open to such irruptions because it is mindful that "what is hyperbolic *in* immanence points to what is hyperbolic *to* immanence."[120] We cannot abandon the flux because we come to self-presence within it. Our question is not whether to dwell in the ethos, but how: "If there is a return to the recalcitrances of given immanence, in their otherness to self-defining thought, there is also a searching of the 'more' of the given world, as charged with signs of what exceeds immanence alone. Reading the signs of this 'more' as communicated in the saturated equivocity of the given world is intimate to the vocation of metaxological metaphysics."[121]

To interpret these signs, we turn to the "fourfold sense of being" to orient us to a practice of metaphysics enabling us to recognize the *metaxu* as a milieu allowing communication with other beings and as porous to the creative and sustaining source of all being.

Desmond's "fourfold" takes to heart Aristotle's observation that "being is said in many ways." The fourfold provides systematic categories for thinking and speaking about being without any pretense to being "the system" in which being is schematized or dominated. As both systematic and hermeneutic, it "offers itself as an unfolding interpretation of the many sides of the plenitude of the happening of being, as manifest to mindfulness in the between."[122] This is a fraught undertaking because remaining "absolutely true to the plenitude of this happening is all but impossible for us, and indeed failure of some sort is inevitable. But this impossible truthfulness is asked of us, even if inevitable failure brings us back to the truth of our finitude. This failure may itself be a success of sorts, in renewing metaphysical astonishment before the enigma of being that was, and is, and always will be too much for us, in excess of our groping efforts."[123]

The inevitable failure of metaphysics to be "absolutely true" chastens the metaxological imagination. As we learned from Caputo, we cannot ever claim to have attained the "Truth," full stop. We will always come up short as we stutter and stammer to speak what exceeds speech. Like Levinas for whom the Saying always exceeds the Said, we might say that within the metaphysician's vocation the act of Responding always exceeds any Response.

The fourfold denominates four senses of being: univocal, equivocal, dialectical, and metaxological. If being can be said in many ways, we need to draw upon each of these ways in order to speak adequately, if never exhaustively, of being's plurivocity. This is essential if we wish to articulate a coherent metaphysics given that "our understanding of what it means to be comes to definition in a complex interplay between indetermination and determination, transcendence and immanence, otherness and sameness, difference and identity. To be true to the *metaxu* we need a way to speak faithfully of determinacy (univocity) and indeterminacy (equivocity), the comingling of immanence and transcendence, and of the interplay between otherness and sameness (ongoing metaxological intermediation rather than a resolved dialectic). The fourfold provides a set of imbricating lenses offering a finessed way to think about and respond to being. Rather than seeking to dissolve metaphysical per-plexities, the fourfold (re)attunes us to the plurivocity of being and bids us to remain open to the sources of wonder and astonishment that inau-gurate and perpetuate the vocation of philosophical inquiry.

Univocity and Its Limits

We begin with the univocal sense of being, which Desmond takes to be "motivated by a desire to reduce the manifoldness of given being to one essential meaning."[124] Univocity stresses "sameness, or unity, indeed sometimes immediate sameness, of mind and being."[125] No doubt, uni-vocity speaks to common sense and we are reminded of Bishop Butler's quip, "A thing is itself and not any other."[126] Univocity's rallying cry: *to be is to be intelligible, and to be intelligible is to be determinate.*[127]

We daily talk of discrete things—*this* jar, *that* car. Certain fields of inquiry, such as math, science, and engineering, require univocal preci-sion: the 1999 Mars Climate Orbiter failed because English units were not converted to the metric system; in 1968, Mariner I's failure was due to a misplaced hyphen.[128] Without gainsaying the need for determinacy, Desmond observes how "recurrently throughout modernity, certain sci-entific orientations to nature have tended toward the reductive."[129] We require univocity to identify and distinguish beings, but we know there remains an excess, an irresolvable remainder. Being is more ambiguous than univocal, or scientistically reductive, approaches would have us believe.

Yet it takes but a cursory look at philosophy's history to reveal no shortage of thinkers who take univocity as the canon of human knowl-edge. In its ontological and logical forms, one thinks of Parmenides, Py-thagoras, Aristotle, Duns Scotus, and Spinoza. For univocity in the form of a "calculative *mathesis*"[130] one turns to Descartes, the early Wittgen-stein, and Badiou. Additionally, the siren's song of univocity continues to be heard in our own day. When Thomas Nagel published *Mind and Cosmos* as a challenge to "reductive materialism," the outcry was aston-ishing. Steven Pinker denounced the book as "the shoddy reasoning of a once-great thinker," and Daniel Dennett described Nagel as part of a "retrograde gang" whose work is "cute and it's clever and it's not worth a damn."[131] Nagel's heresy? The audacity to claim "the great advances in the physical and biological sciences were made possible by excluding the mind from the physical world. This has permitted a quantitative understanding of that world, expressed in timeless, mathematically formulated physical laws. But at some point it will be necessary to make a new start on a more comprehensive understanding that includes the mind."[132]

Without denying the power of math and sciences, Nagel recognized their inability to wholly and definitively explain all phenomena. A more comprehensive approach is needed to accommodate what more reductive accounts leave out. This critique of reductive materialism comes, no less, from a philosopher who not only lacks a *sensus divinitatis* but also strongly opposes any invocation of any sort of transcendent being.[133]

Neither Nagel nor Desmond rejects univocity; univocal or determinate speech is necessary for intelligibility. They deny, though, that univocal determinacy exhausts the range of intelligible speech. In fact, Desmond argues, "the will to absolute univocity is self-subverting, and cannot evade its own opposite, equivocity. This very insistence on univocity itself proves to be equivocal, for no univocal meaning can be given to the univocal insistence."[134] Reductive materialism abstracts from the plurivocal flux and fails to account for the emergence of the mind. This leads him to observe that "simply as self-transcending, mind is an anomaly to the universal mechanism; it is excess, a surplus, ultimately indeed a surd. In a word, scientific univocity reduces being to something that cannot account for scientific mind itself."[135]

In Plato's philosophy, Desmond finds an intimation of a way to preserve the determinacy of univocity without the pretense of rendering all being determinate. He recalls that above the gates to Plato's Academy a sign is said to have read: "Let none who has not studied geometry enter here!" For Plato, the rigors of geometry were propaedeutic for the study of philosophy. Desmond contrasts Plato with Aristotle, for whom *thaumazein* (to wonder) terminates in "a determinate *logos* of a determinate somewhat, a *tode ti*. But this end is a death of wonder, not its refreshening at a level of mindfulness marked by deeper or higher metaphysical sophistication. Not surprisingly, Aristotle invokes geometry to illustrate the teleological thrust of the desire to know (*Metaphysics* 983a13ff). What is geometry but a figure for determinate knowing in which all the ambiguity of perplexity is overcome or dissolved in the solution."[136]

Geometry was regarded essential to philosophical inquiry because it trained the would-be philosopher in the rigors of logical inquiry. Philosophy, for Plato, requires "midwives" possessing, like Socrates, the know-how and finesse to help others "discover within themselves a multitude of beautiful things, which they bring forth into the light. But it is I, with God's help, who deliver them of this offspring."[137] For Aristotle, by contrast, geometric precision becomes the ideal and *telos* of inquiry. If Plato sought to preserve and refresh wonder, then Aristotle sought the obverse. "For all men begin, as we said, by wondering that the matter is so. . . . But we must end in the contrary and, according to the proverb, the better state, as is the case in these instances when men learn the cause."[138] Nor is the desire for precision exclusive to Aristotle: one may think of Descartes, Spinoza's *ordo geometricus*, Kant, and Husserl.[139] Desmond, moreover, detects a direct line leading from "Aristotle to logical positivism with respect to this ideal of determinate intelligibility."[140]

The rage for order leading to the privileging of geometric precision as the standard for knowledge is not limited to philosophy or its history: there is no shortage of reductive approaches—Taylor's bête noire is behaviorism—requiring being to fit within a determinate system of categories. Such efforts manifest the ongoing relevance of what Pascal considered the *l'esprit de géometrie*: the "geometric mind" fixates on "objective truths such as we pursue in the hard sciences and mathematics."[141] Desmond playfully describes the geometrically minded systematizers as those "who (mis)behave like the ugly sisters of Cinderella: the glass slipper will fit the foot, must fit the foot, never mind the blood on the carpet!"[142] The ambiguities of human reality cannot all be fitted into a single system; we require, rather, Pascal's *l'esprit de finesse*. A spirit of finesse resists temptations to dominate being, preferring instead a subtler and more discerning approach. It recognizes and appreciates being's inherent equivocity and, rather than squelching it, remains mindful of being's ambiguity. The finessed mind does not revile geometry or univocity but relativizes this mode of thought and preserves the dynamism of the whole.

Equivocity and the Restlessness Search for Wholeness

Desmond's equivocal sense of being refers "to a plurality that resists reduction to one univocal meaning and one alone."[143] Whereas univocity

accents unity, sameness, and clarity, equivocity stresses manyness, difference, and ambiguity. One is reminded how the word "dog" can refer both
to a pet or to a star with "no community of meaning between the earthly
and heavenly dog."[144] Taken equivocally, "dog" has two distinct meanings. There is a limit, though, to the fluidity of equivocal speech. Just as
pure univocity "is a limit, so it is difficult to find absolutely pure instances
of equivocity, which would imply a difference without even the hint of a
possible mediation. Absolutely unmediated difference seems to be absolutely unintelligible; for even to state the putative absolute difference is
in some way already to transcend it."[145] Any attempt at absolute equivocity proves self-subverting because equivocity is limited by an unavoidable recourse to determinacy: to talk with another, one must say
something about something. For equivocal speech to be communicative,
it must speak using determinate words about some determinate something. Thus, despite its recognition of fragmentation and flux, equivocity
cannot evade speaking of integral beings, even if only to call their integrity into question.

Within our daily lives, we find ourselves situated between the theoretical limits of absolute univocity and absolute equivocity, inflexible
determinacy and unremitting flux. Aristotle took a dim view of equivocity because of his commitment "to the law of identity and the law of
excluded middle. A being is itself and not another thing. It is logically
impossible to suppose that the same thing is and is not, as some think
Heraclitus said. To be is to be determinate, a *tode ti*. If this is the case, our
quest for intelligibility will always be marked by a certain predilection
for univocity."[146]

Elsewhere, in book 3 of *Rhetoric*, we find one of Aristotle's more
ironic statements: "It is a general rule that a written composition should
be easy to read and therefore easy to deliver."[147] Aristotle's target is not
surprising: Heraclitus. He continues: "To punctuate Heraclitus is no
easy task, because we often cannot tell whether a particular word belongs
to what precedes or what follows it. Thus, at the outset of his treatise he
says, 'Though this truth is always men understand it not,' where it is not
clear to which of the two clauses the world 'always' belongs."[148]

For a thinker such as Aristotle, for whom geometric precision serves
as the ideal canon for human reasoning, any trace of Heraclitean flux
must be brought to heel and explained. And, as we have seen, he is not
alone in desiring to exorcise ambiguity. Descartes, in the *Discourse on*

Method, articulates as his first rule that the investigator ought "never to accept anything as true that I did not plainly know to be such; that is to say, carefully to avoid hasty judgment and prejudice; and to include nothing more in my judgments than what presented itself to my mind so clearly and so distinctly that I had no occasion to call it into doubt."[149]

Let there be no doubt: this *l'esprit de géometrie* abides long after Descartes's death. Just recall the tension between "Continental" and "analytic" philosophers. It is true, as Terry Pinkard observes, that dismissing the Continentals as "a bunch of wooly minded gasbags"[150] no longer carries the punch it once did. Cool comfort, indeed. Now that most Anglo-American philosophy departments are analytic in orientation, the token "wooly" thinker may be tolerated, but toleration is hardly the same as celebration or appreciation.

It is not Desmond's desire to disentangle "wooly" thought or spin it into a univocal yarn. His commitment to preserving a healthy sense of equivocity and his sensitivity to the plurality of voices at play, in fact, leads him to embrace "wooliness" as inescapable. In this, he makes common cause with a number of postmodern thinkers. Desmond can, I believe, take on board Caputo's description of deconstruction as "organized around the idea that things contain a kind of uncontainable truth, that they contain what they cannot contain. Nobody has to come along and 'deconstruct' things. Things are auto-deconstructed by the tendencies of their own inner truth. In a deconstruction, the 'other' is the one who tells the truth on the 'same'; the other is the truth of the same, the truth that has been repressed and suppressed, omitted and marginalized, or sometimes just plain murdered."[151]

Desmond, too, recognizes in being an inextirpable ambiguity. Hence the contribution of deconstruction in unsettling univocal complacency. The "inner truth" of being, perceived by Iris Murdoch's contemplative gaze, refuses to be constrained, and it struggles to communicate itself by calling out to us, demanding we open ourselves to its reality and welcome what has been concealed beneath the too neat and too tidy accounts rendered by univocal reduction.

This appreciation of equivocity's truth does not rely solely on philosophers. Long before Derrida, Caputo, Foucault, and Judith Butler, Shakespeare penned *Macbeth* as *the* play about equivocity: "Radical equivocity attaches to time, to daring, to trust, to power, to the elementals, to the nefarious powers, to sleep, to life itself and to death. 'Fair is foul and foul is fair.'"[152] It is the story of double appearances: a loyal vassal and his hospitable wife exposed through their act of traitorous regicide.[153] Note the flux following Duncan's death:

Old Man   'Tis unnatural,
Even like the deed that's done. On Tuesday last,
A falcon, tow'ring in her pride of place,
Was by a mousing owl hawked at and killed.

Ross
And Duncan's horses (a thing most strange and certain),
Beauteous and swift, the minions of their race,
Turned wild in nature, broke their stalls, flung out,
Contending 'gainst obedience, as they would make
War with mankind.[154]

Throughout *Macbeth*, Shakespeare deconstructs the stable categories of good and evil, light and darkness, pure and impure. Hands are washed free of blood yet remain bloody; courage screwed to the sticking place is cowardice. Perhaps there is no better instance of the suppressed "truth of the other" than the ghost of murdered Banquo, who bursts death's constraint to give silent testimony to his concealed, nay murdered, truth.

Mindful attention to equivocity requires an ongoing hermeneutic of the interplay of text and action. Actions, like words, can bear of multiple meanings. Take *Casablanca*'s famous song:

You must remember this
A kiss is just a kiss, a sigh is just a sigh.
The fundamental things apply
As time goes by.

A lovely sentiment, but true? Univocal reasoning wishes it so: everything is what it is, and no other. Equivocal reasoning notes a difference: the kiss of "Let him kiss me with the kisses of his mouth!" (Song of Solomon 1:2) is not the same as "Judas, is it with a kiss that you are betraying the Son of Man?" (Luke 14:48). A kiss can be a kiss, a physical gesture, but it cannot be reduced only to a gesture; there is more to it than univocity can convey.

It is here we see metaxology's ability to negotiate the space between univocity and equivocity by preserving the truth of each and refusing to slide into univocal dogmatism or equivocal skepticism. Metaxology neither insists on a single univocal *regula* nor does it valorize equivocal flux in its indeterminacy. What recommends Desmond's approach is its ability to mediate between those "who are obsessed with inflexible determinacy and those who turn away from any kind of determinacy with disgust."[155]

This becomes clearer if we consider how the dynamism of our desire bespeaks a restless longing for wholeness. Desmond, showing his Platonic slip, recalls the *Symposium*'s[156] discussion of desire, where Socrates claims that "anyone who has a desire desires what is not at hand and not present, what he does not have, and what he is not, and that of which he is in need; for such are the objects of desire and love." Desire is not self-enclosed and has not the resources to sate its lack. Desire is intentional, it is *for* something and, he writes, "reaches beyond itself. For this reason, lack is not solely negative: it attests to the stirring of an impetuous power through which desire begins to be more than itself. Negatively understood, it is a witness to unfulfillment; positively understood, it may make desire aware of itself and so awaken it to what is more than itself."[157] Desire impels us to reach outside of ourselves in a quest for wholeness. We do not merely have desire; desire, rather, is constitutive of creaturehood. It is "a form of life which, while originating in lack, wars with lack, seeking thereby to keep despair at bay."[158] But this lack does not betray desire as indigent or impoverished. Though the end is absent—otherwise we would not desire it—it is not wholly absent because desire intimates the presence of something missing and clamors to attain it. Desire's lack drives its quest for fulfillment.

For Desmond, desire's *telos* (end) is present at its origin, disquieting desire by reminding it of its lack and as yet unachieved wholeness. Yet it is nothing less than the presence of the *telos* that impels us to begin the adventure of negotiating our identity in a process Desmond calls "selving."[159] Like the *metaxu*, the self is also a dynamic process. What Desmond calls "selving" expresses the ongoing process of the self's becoming as it intermediates with the world around us. This "selving" is fueled by disquieted desire and propels us on a passionate itinerary, which, recalling Plato, is driven by eros as "the name for our pursuit of wholeness, for our desire to be complete."[160] We are, from the beginning, drawn by our *telos* toward our *telos*. Augustine and Aquinas, were they consulted, would recognize this impulse:

> You stir man to take pleasure in praising you, because you have made us for yourself, and our heart is restless until it rests in you.[161]

> Because the will is a power of the rational soul, which is caused by God alone, by creation. . . . Second, it is evident from the fact that the will is ordained to the universal good. Wherefore nothing else can be the cause of the will, except God Himself, Who is the universal good: while every other good is good by participation, and is some particular good, and a particular cause does not give a universal inclination.[162]

We are agents of desire, unsettled and driven by a longing impelling us outward in search of fulfilment. No matter what we count as possessions, we are always first possessed by a desire admitting no finite satisfaction: ours is a restless quest for wholeness.

This quest for wholeness, though, begins amidst constant flux. We come to ourselves, become aware of ourselves, in a world of constant flux. Beings are born and die, come into being and pass away. We are constantly bombarded by what can appear as an "infinite succession" of beings.[163] Human desire is elicited amidst this flux and is the driving force as we negotiate the inescapability of its vicissitudes. Desmond observes, "Our immediate inclination is to perceive the external world as a dispersed multiplicity of univocal particulars. In time, inevitably, this fixed definiteness is loosened up by our recognition of becoming and its open-endedness. Things in their determinate particularity, carried beyond themselves by the generating power of becoming, pass away and ultimately disappear into the indefinite succession of other particulars."[164] Human desire reaches intentionally toward an integrating source beyond the flux, a *telos* that directs and promises wholeness. In this way, desire negotiates the creative tension between univocity and equivocity, of discovering ourselves surrounded by finite beings as they come into and pass out of existence.

The human subject is, in this way, an incarnate *metaxu* where uni-vocity and equivocity intermediate. Though we desire *this* or *that*, we know no univocal entity will satisfy our longing; we desire, always, more. Metaxology allows us to speak faithfully of both senses of being. Unbri-dled univocity downplays flux in favor of determinacy. Unconstrained equivocity revels in indeterminacy but betrays particularity. Both capture elements of the truth, but neither captures being's truth fully. By resisting the pressure to force an either/or decision about how to speak of the uni-versal impermanence of being, metaxology preserves the truth of each to offer a finessed understanding of the infinite succession of beings en-countered daily and the way our desire for wholeness is elicited by and oriented toward a transcendent end or *telos*.

The Dialectical Sense of Being

The dialectical sense of being draws attention to "a *process of interplay* between same and different, between self and other."[165] Dialectic is "ety-mologically in the same family as 'dialogue': mindful communication between self and other. Dialectic can refer us to a rhythmic process of unfolding, whether of process or events, thoughtful articulations or communications. There are many forms of dialectic. Socratic-Platonic dialectic, for instance, is bound up with dialogical openness to others. Modern dialectic, of which Hegel is perhaps the master exponent, is shaped by the ideal of autonomous thinking in which the self-determination of a process tends to be given primary place."[166]

In this subsection, we consider how the practice of dialectic medi-ates between the self and other in search of a more inclusive unity. Rather than denying ambiguity, dialectic "thinks through" equivocity en route to a whole capable of reconciling differences.[167] The question is this: Does the sense of the "whole" attained by dialectic remain truthful to being?

For Desmond, the practice of dialectic "seeks to recover what the univocal sense offers"[168] without turning away from the complexities and ambiguities of the equivocal. It claims to uncover a unity *beyond* flux, a deeper and more abiding totality comprising a coherent whole. In think-ing *through* the flux and gathering it into a whole, dialectic offers a nu-anced version of univocity's mantra. Yes: *to be is to be intelligible*, but *to be wholly intelligible is to part of an encompassing whole.*

Hegel serves as the exemplar of modern dialectic. We risk, though, misreading him if we forget, as Desmond reminds us, that "Hegel offers no static formalization of thesis, antithesis, synthesis (now recognized by scholars to be attributed to Fichte, more properly speaking)."[169] Taylor reinforces this, noting how dialectic is neither a method nor an approach: "If we want to characterize Hegel's method in his great demonstrations we might just as well speak of it as 'descriptive,' following Kenley Dove. For [Hegel's] aim is simply to follow the movement in his object of study. The task of the philosopher is 'to submerge his freedom in [the content], and let it be moved by its own nature.' If the argument follows a dialectical movement, then this must be in the things themselves, not just in the way we reason about them."[170]

To borrow from Taylor, Desmond reads Hegel as offering a hermeneutical dialectics "which convince us by the overall plausibility of the interpretations they give."[171] Hegel's system has been regarded as the apex of metaphysics and the "the consummation of reason."[172] Desmond rejects this. For Hegel "hides nuances, nuances that, if resurrected for re-thinking, shed a different light on metaphysical thinking, and the possibilities of its contemporary renewal."[173] By inquiring into the truth and limits of dialectic, Desmond exposes the oft-imperceptible cracks in Hegel's philosophy, passages capable of leading us toward a renewal of metaphysical thought.

The goal of Hegel's *Phenomenology of Spirit*, Desmond suggests, is to give an "insight into what knowing is."[174] This requires an investigation into the role of mediation. Mediation, for Hegel, "is nothing but self-identity working itself out through an active self-directed process."[175] The following gives a sense of this process:

> The movement of a being that immediately is, consists partly in becoming an other than itself, and thus becoming its own immanent content; partly in taking back into itself this unfolding [of its content] or this existence of it, i.e. in making *itself* into a moment, and simplifying itself into something determinate. In the former movement, *negativity* is the differentiating and positing of *existence*; in this return into self, it is the becoming of the *determinate simplicity*. It is in this way that the content shows that its determinateness is not received from something else, nor externally attached to it, but

that it determines itself, and ranges itself as a moment having its own place in the whole.[176]

Hegelian mediation is self-mediation: "Through self-mediation he endeavors to complete (captured pictorially in the image of the circle) the incomplete self-knowledge of immediacy."[177] In a line sending shivers down Caputo's spine, the consummation of Spirit's self-mediation leads to totality: *Das Wahre ist das Ganze*, "the true is the whole."[178]

We should register no small degree of awe at the scope of Hegel's self-mediating Spirit. Here we find an approach with much to recommend itself to those who wish to preserve the truth of univocity and equivocity. Hegelian dialectic, first, describes a dynamic and gradually unfolding process that remains true to the flux of change over time. His own example of the bud → blossom → fruit illustrates a finessed understanding of the organic unfolding of this process.[179] Second, dialectic does not shirk from having to take account of the other; indeed, what Hegel calls the process of self-sublation (*aufheben*) describes how the subject becomes determinate by sublating its other in a process that simultaneously cancels and preserves the other. Through sublation, the distinction between "self" and "other" is abolished by preserving the "other" within the self. Thus, Hegel's dialectic holds out the promise of guiding us safely between the Scylla of a dogmatic univocity and the Charybdis of a chaotic equivocity. And, if we take the unfolding of Hegelian dialectic as a description of history's unfolding, we could chart through the ages a record of inexorable progress as *Geist* unfolds itself forward in time as it becomes increasingly determinate and moves toward its ultimate consummation.

Nevertheless, we must exercise caution against the seductions of Hegel's system. For though dialectic does take account of equivocity, it does so in a way that fails to respect the irreducible alterity of the other. As Simpson writes, "The dialectical sense taken on its own tends to absolutize itself and its self-mediation such that thought thinking itself becomes a univocal totality that is deaf to any mediation but its own—a solipsistic circle that closes in on itself."[180] In other words, though dialectic does account for plurality, it is a plurality subsumed into a larger whole. This, Desmond contends, is clearest in Hegel's theology where God "others" himself "in finite creation, not to allow finite creation to be as irreducibly other to Himself, but because without God's own self-othering, God Himself as beginning is all but nothing. The creation is God's self-othering and hence not other, but the ontological mediating detour in God's dialectical self-mediation with Himself."[181]

Desmond refuses to take part in the "coronation of absolute spirit" or consummation of Hegel's "system" when "Hegel places the crown on its head, and the hymn he sings is Aristotle's *Te Deum* to *noesis tes noeseos*. This is Hegel's highest amen to being."[182] It is an "amen" directed not toward the God who transcends the whole but to the God who has become one with the whole. If this is Hegel's god, then it should come as no surprise that Heidegger saw no way to sing or dance before it.

Modern dialectic—in its Hegelian iteration—runs aground because it subsumes alterity into a totalizing whole: "Hegel's speculative unity is marked by, as we might call it, a kind of 'dialectical univocity.'"[183] Hegelian self-mediation results in a closed system unfolding from germ to full maturity according to its own logic. Looked at theologically, although it pays lip service to God, it cannot admit of revelation or irruptive grace, as these would require an intrusion into the system by a God who transcends it. Moreover, this would be a deity alien to orthodox Christianity: Hegel's dialectic unfolds from a state of lack and moves through stages toward ever-greater determinacy. Hegel's God, in effect, must become God over time. Prayerful appeal to the Transcendent is likewise ruled out because, in this system, there exists no transcendent Other. Hegel's God occupies the same plain as humans. We are left, Desmond writes, with God's "counterfeit double," a false god who masquerades as the Transcendent yet remains firmly ensconced within the immanent realm.[184]

In attempting to think through the equivocity of becoming to recuperate a sense of univocity, Hegel's dialectic overreaches and inscribes its god into its conceptual system. It reduces God's alterity to an instance of categorical sameness. Thus, this is not the god to whom we bow, but the one who subtends human centrality and makes reality transparent. Hegel writes:

> The love of truth, faith in the power of mind, is the first condition in philosophy. Man, because he is mind, should and must deem himself worthy of the highest: he cannot think too highly of the greatness and the power of his mind, and with this belief, nothing

will be so difficult and hard that it will not reveal itself [*sich eröffnete*] to him. The essence of the universe at first hidden and concealed [*verborgene und verschlossene*], has no power which can offer resistance to the search for knowledge; it has to lay itself open before the seeker—to set before his eyes and give for his enjoyment, its riches and its depths.[185]

In mediating between self and otherness, Hegelian dialectic places humans center stage. *Geist*, Taylor observes, "lives as spirit only through men. They are the vehicles, and the indispensable vehicles, of his spiritual existence, as consciousness, rationality, will."[186] He continues, noting how for Hegel "*I* as a human being have the vocation of realizing a nature which is given: and even if I am called on to be original, to realize myself in the way uniquely suited to myself, nevertheless the scope for originality is itself given as an integral part of human nature, as are those unique features of me on which my originality builds. Freedom for man thus means the free realization of a vocation which is largely given."[187]

Desmond sees Hegel as "dialectically instrumentalizing" the individual, who becomes "an instrument of the absolute whole: man, so to say, is the means by which God comes to self-determination; man is the medium of God's knowing."[188] Hegel's counterfeit god uses us, in fact *needs* us, in order to actualize its potentiality.

Hegel's practice of dialectic is wanting because, in its commitment to recuperating univocity, it too severely downplays equivocity. It pays lip service to alterity, but fails to preserve it. Hegel, in other words, overemphasizes the "self" in self-determination and reduces the Other to an instance of the Same. In this system, there is a place for everything and everything has its place. This god "fits" and, if you cock your ear aright, you can hear the howls coming from Caputo's office!

This becomes clearer by situating the practice of dialectic within the *metaxu*. Recall the question posed earlier: How do we mediate with an infinite succession of beings? Infinite succession, we saw, describes the external world of becoming. Confronted by an infinite stream of beings who come to be and pass away, how do we make sense of the external world of becoming? Impelled by a desire for wholeness, how do we remain true to being's determinacy and ambiguity? Alone, neither univocity nor equivocity is sufficient: univocity without equivocity is static lifelessness, and equivocity without univocal determinacy would overwhelm us with chaotic flux. Though we desire wholeness, neither one satisfies our restlessness. How, then, are we to respond from within the *metaxu*, the "Desmondian open space" where we feel wooed by both voices and their promise for wholeness?

What keeps us intact and permits us to withstand the univocal and equivocal forces buffeting us is called *intentional infinitude*, or "the power of open dialectical self-mediation displayed in the articulation of human desire."[189] Intentional infinitude refers to our longing for the infinite. Our desire to mediate between unity and multiplicity, René Ryan writes, "seeks unity, rather than dispersal. We want to mediate between ourselves and the world; but more, we want to communicate ourselves to ourselves. Desmond describes this potency as circular, though not in a closed way, and founded in the appreciation that humans seek to know themselves. In this search they strive for open wholeness, as the desired end to their infinite restlessness."[190]

A single clause distinguishes Desmond's intentional infinitude from Hegel's dialectic: "circular, though not in a closed way." Indeed, if we trace its roots to more ancient practices, intentional infinitude attests to the salutary potential of dialectic. In Socratic-Platonic dialogues, interlocutors journey together and engage in open-ended and cooperative argument that seldom terminates in cut-and-dry answers. Perhaps this is the point: instead of giving "the answer" they offer "the invitation" to discern for oneself what it is that we love and, through discernment, grow in articulacy about their loves. As an exercise in ongoing conversation, dialectic preserves practitioners from complacency by reminding them that no single answer, no *thing* of any sort, can still the restless questioning of the mind or sate the hunger of the heart.

Compared with the Socratic-Platonic version, Hegel's totalizing system represents dialectic's modern mutation. Whereas dialectic was an ongoing and unending practice for Socrates, Hegel employs dialectic in a way privileging self-mediation and "takes its sights from the ability of thought to think what is other, and to bring the other into relativity to itself. The conclusion then drawn is that the thought that thinks the other overreaches the other; hence in thinking the other as a thought, it ends up as the thought that thinks itself, but now inclusive of otherness."[191]

By closing the circle and resolving the dialectic in favor of the self, Hegel betrays the *dia* by abrogating the open-endedness of intermediation. Dialectic's rhythmic give-and-take, call-and-response, is arrested and freezes the other into a totalized whole. Its sentiment: "I go toward the other out of my own lack, I tend to the other not primarily to attend to the other, but as perhaps requiting my own lack. I am tempted to possess the other to enable my own achieved self-possession."[192] There is something vampiric about the self, or the Spirit, who brings itself about not by reverencing the other but by using the other instrumentally to effect its emergence.

In the end, although it succeeds in recuperating a sense of univocity from the flux of equivocity, modern dialectic fails to account fully for the ambiguity and universal impermanence of being. Dialectic recognizes alterity, but only in order to instrumentalize the other to achieve its own end. Dialectic betrays eros by settling for what is not infinite. The problem: dialectic enacts a closure upon itself, creating a system in which individuals are sublated into the larger whole. Otherness is preserved, but at the cost of being counted now amidst the Same. The accusation of ontotheology sticks: this is not the God *of* the Whole but God *as* the Whole.

The Metaxological Sense of Being

Metaxology, Desmond writes, "sees philosophy as seeking a logos of the metaxu, an intelligible account of what it means to be between or intermediate."[193] It stresses "the mediated community of mind and being, but not in terms of the self-mediation of the same. It calls attention to a pluralized mediation, beyond closed self-mediation from the side of the same, and hospitable to the mediation of the other, or transcendent, out of its own otherness. It puts the emphasis on an intermediation, not a self-mediation, however dialectically qualified."[194] In emphasizing pluralized mediation, Desmond refuses to freeze—as dialectic is wont to do—the ongoing interplay. In preserving the dynamism, metaxology effects a delicate yet dynamic balance between equivocity and univocity.

Jere O'Neill Surber identifies three ways metaxology surpasses Hegel's dialectic:

1. While univocity and equivocity remain . . . complexly interrelated, the true complexity and nuance of their interrelations cannot be adequately described in terms of some dialectical synthesis or "higher univocity."

2. Although a systematic framework for exploring this complex web of interrelations is indispensable, it cannot constitute the sort of "closed system" that the dialectical stance implies.

3. While a metaxological perspective is not opposed to concepts . . . its concepts must continually maintain their connection with concrete experience, which lends to them a sort of openness and "jaggedness" or "irregularity of contour" suppressed in the dialectical approach.[195]

A metaxological philosophy, in other words, (1) preserves the truthfulness of univocity and equivocity, (2) resists closure upon itself as "the system" while remaining open to the happening of being, and (3) swears off "taking the measure of" or imposing a measure on being. Its "jagged" concepts stay open to what cannot be contained within any finite category. Instead of closing in on itself in a self-contained whole, metaxology's openness permits it to interface with the texture of reality. No grand system, metaxology responds to the complexities of creation and reflects on them systematically. In Surber's characterization of metaxology we find further confirmation that Desmond does not violate any of our five commandments.

Though not antagonistic to *all* practices of dialectic, metaxology employs dialectic in a way that avoids succumbing to Hegel's "dialectical reduction."[196] Whereas Hegelian dialectic privileges a singular self-mediation encompassing the Other within the Same, metaxology remains committed to a form of ongoing double-mediation. To be true to the *metaxu* requires remaining attentive to both self-mediation and to the ongoing inter-mediation of being as other to oneself. "Genuine philosophical thinking," Desmond avers, "must be *both* self-mediating and also open to the intermediation between thought and what is other to thought, precisely as other."[197] In this way, metaxology makes good on the promise of the *dia* in dialectic by resisting efforts to subsume the other into its categories, preferring instead to initiate a dialogue *with* the other. Such a give-and-take, essential to metaxology, renders it a dialogical, rather than a monological, practice. Instead of a soliloquy delivered by one who "struts and frets his hour upon the stage," it initiates dialogue. To be metaxological means that one dwells "with the interplay of sameness and difference, identity and otherness, not by mediating a more inclusive whole but by recurrence to the rich ambiguities of the middle, and with due respect for forms of otherness that are dubiously included in the immanence of a dialectical whole."[198] In its commitment to remaining within the flux of existence, in its mindfulness of voices suppressed by other philosophical practices, metaxology assumes a stance of vigilant discernment. In its openness and responsiveness to the call of the other, or the Holy Other, metaxology might even be regarded as a form of philosophical prayer.

It is this openness, this refusal to regard the whole as "complete" or "closed," that sets Desmond apart from Hegel and Aristotle. Metaxology retains a sense of open-endedness; it proceeds tentatively, not by imposing categories but by engaging in a form of Socratic-Platonic dialogue. "I think of Socratic dialogue as witnessing to an honesty to where we find ourselves," he writes, "an honesty also willing to confess that in the midst of the ordinary something beyond comes to make a call on us. We can receive the call(er), or we can turn away from the invitation."[199] The metaxological both/and does not pit immanence against transcendence but sees the *metaxu* as the porous intermediation of both where one can discern, and respond, to the call of the Other. Upon hearing this, Westphal and Kearney nod in agreement, for Desmond manifests an openness to Kearney's micro-eschatologies, the many and various disclosures of the divine within the immanent realm, and to Westphal's sense of metaphysics as a vocation, a response to having first been called.

Instead of depicting metaxology as a penthouse on top of the univocal, equivocal, and dialectic sense of being, Desmond envisions it as a way of bringing "to truer articulation what is at work in them."[200] His Hegelian slip shows as each sense of being is *aufgehoben* and incorporated into the metaxological. But metaxology neither supplants nor annuls these voices but holds them together to allow each, in its own way, to speak of being. It symphonically weaves together each voice and allows it to speak its truth, yet balances these voices so no one dominates the other; one need not choose between the "one" and the "many" but can preserve both. As a task, then, metaxology leads to a finessed "*practice* of a kind of thinking"[201] mindful of the plurality of voices at play within being.

So, like dialectic, metaxology is a mode of philosophical mindfulness keen to think beyond the binary opposition of univocity and equivocity. When practiced well, dialectic initiates an ongoing cycle of discernment. Metaxology, similarly, unfolds as a ceaseless dialogue—a process of being questioned and questioning—with being. Yet this surfaces a paradox: every time we question, we acknowledge a lack (otherwise we would not ask) and a presentiment of what is missing (we are, after all, asking about something). So, Desmond asks, "How can mind be beyond lack, be somehow already full?"[202] His answer: "If we are in search, how do we recognize what we seek, did we not already have some sense of what we seek? If we did not have this prior sense of what we seek, we could not seek it at all in the first place. Contrariwise, if we do have this prior sense, why do we seek at all, since we already seem to have what we seek, and we cannot really seek what we already have?"[203]

For Desmond, the paradoxical lack points "deeper than lack to a more positive condition of being."[204] Like Plato, Augustine, and Aquinas, Desmond posits the presence of the end (*telos*) as abiding at the origin of our search (*arche*). Desire moves not from total lack to fullness but from the presentiment of plenitude toward actual plenitude.

It may be helpful to recall the *Symposium* where Socrates, speaking in Diotima's voice, recounts Eros's birth to those gathered at Callias's bacchanal. Eros was conceived on the night of Aphrodite's birthday. *Poros*, "resource," became drunk and fell asleep in the garden. *Penia*, "poverty," who had been begging outside the gates, seized the opportunity to "relieve her lack of resources: she would get a child from *Poros*." The offspring of Poros and Penia, Eros bears a likeness to both:

> He is always poor, and he's far from being delicate and beautiful (as ordinary people think he is); instead, he is rough and shriveled and shoeless and homeless, always lying on the dirt without a bed, sleeping at people's doorsteps and in roadsides under the sky, having his mother's nature, always living in Need. But on his father's side he is a schemer after the beautiful and the good; he is brave, impetuous, and intense, an awesome hunter, always weaving snares, resourceful in his pursuit of intelligence, a love of wisdom through all his life, a genius with enchantments, potions, and clever pleadings. (203d)

Eros is a being of the between: between mortality and immortality, poverty and riches, wisdom and ignorance. Indeed, Eros serves as one of the daimons, traversing the space between gods and mortals "conveying prayer and sacrifice from men to gods, while to men they bring commands from the gods and gifts in return for sacrifices" (203a). Eros appears as the "paradoxical mixture of poverty and plenitude,"[205] the child in whom abundance and lack intermingle.

Too often forgotten is the dual parentage of Eros as the offspring of Poros and Penia. Hegel, for one, so stressed the indigence of *Geist* that no heed was paid to Poros; Hegel's counterfeit god moves from lack to fullness, from indeterminacy to determinacy, through a process of self-determination that overcomes what is lacking. A metaxological consideration of desire remains attentive, however, to Eros's dual inheritance: the wealth of Poros and the poverty of Penia. Heir of both, Eros is born into a state of enriched poverty, bearing within itself a promissory note guaranteed by Poros's riches. Though it does not yet possess the fullness of its patrimony, the promise of eventual fulfillment animates Eros's restless seeking. Contrary to the image portrayed in movies, a properly erotic itinerary is not one of promiscuity but of pilgrimage guided by desire's relentless straining toward the promise of infinite fulfillment.

Our desire for fulfillment, animated by the enriched poverty of Eros, implicates us in the *metaxu* and as a *metaxu*. The between describes not only where we find ourselves on the map of being (topology) but also who we are as beings (anthropology). We saw this initially when discussing "intentional finitude" as the way we respond to infinite succession. Faced with the coming to be and passing away of beings, we experience a drive to "mediate between unity and multiplicity in our search for wholeness."[206] We experience ourselves situated between lack and fullness and we intermediate between ourselves and things in search of wholeness. Our enriched poverty resists closure: no, this will not satisfy . . . continue searching. Metaxology does not resolve this tension or sate this desire. Instead, it challenges us to strike out with courage in search of that for which our hearts and minds most desperately long. It implicates us in a quest.

Transcendence: Exterior, Interior, Superior

I now consider the nature of metaxological "transcendence." Transcendence, like being, can be said in many ways. We have, in fact, anticipated this discussion when we discussed infinite succession, intentional infinitude, and actual infinitude. We need to clarify how Desmond's three "transcendences" arise from amidst the between and point beyond the *metaxu*. If metaphysical attentiveness arises amidst beings, then "the question of transcendence has nothing to do with a leap out of being into the void, but with the deepest mindfulness of what is emergent in the middle itself. Again, the double meaning of *meta* is relevant. '*Meta*' is being in the midst; '*meta*' is also a reference to what is beyond, what is transcendent. Metaxological metaphysics must think the doubleness of this tension between being in the midst and being referred by self-transcendence to the transcendence of what is other, what is over and above."[207]

Tutored to perceive the world metaxologically, we recognize how signs encountered in the midst of the *metaxu* point beyond immanence toward a superior transcendence, toward God, on account of whom being *is* and continues to be at all.

Exterior Transcendence (T₁)

Desmond claims: "The happening of the between is a metaxological community of transcendences."[208] Note: the between, or *metaxu*, is not static but energetic and vital. Metaxology reflects upon this happening in a plurivocal manner:

> Univocity puts the stress on something or someone *determinate*, this or that character or thing. Equivocity puts the stress on something more *indeterminate*, something neither this nor that, something ambiguous, especially in the heart of acting human beings. Dialectic puts the stress on a togetherness of oneself and others, on a meditation of our differences in the exchange with each other. Metaxology does not dispose of these three senses but aligns them more truly with what in the between is *more than determinable* and *beyond our self-determination*. It is attentive to many-meaninged inter-play, bringing more to the fore the plurivocity of inter-mediations between oneself and others.[209]

As an intermediating happening, the *metaxu* is also communal. The "happening" does not take place solely within each being; it happens between and amidst them. Thus, when Desmond refers to the "community of transcendences," he indicates how, at its basic and most primordial level of being, each being is in relationship with what is other to it. Norris Clarke makes a similar observation, noting how "the intrinsic structure of all being is irreducibly dyadic: substance-in-relation."[210] To be at all is to be in relationship because being is relational.

The first transcendence is called "exterior transcendence" (T_1). We saw this above when we treated infinite succession which, for Desmond, refers to "the transcendence of beings as other in exteriority."[211] It is easy to take for granted that beings are other to and exist independently of us. Exterior transcendence, Simpson observes, reminds us that "the otherness of the world precedes and exceeds our thinking of it."[212] There are determinate beings other to us and irreducible to any system; being, in its intransigent resistance to schematization, bears witness to something in excess of determinacy. Being as other to us is not *indeterminate* or awaiting our impress to give it form; being as other to us is and remains *overdeterminate* and cannot be fixed or frozen in place. *Esse semper maius*: being is always greater than any concept or system. Being is not *this* or *that* thing but the mysterious source of everything.

A metaxological mindfulness of T_1 remains alert to our immersion within a world of beings. Beings come into being and pass away; flowers bloom and wither, animals are born and die: "There is a constitutive doubleness that, as coming to be and passing away, is inscribed ontologically on their being as becoming."[213] This doubleness affects how we reflect upon what it means to be. In the tree outside my window, a robin builds her next. Ontically, I know *what* she is: a bird. I am aware of her ontological doubleness: last spring, she was not but now in late summer, she is; in three years, she will be no longer. She has being now, but only fleetingly.

Metaxological mindfulness does not despair at the inherent fragility of being. This is because the wash of infinite succession can both "appall us and exalt us. We face our own nothingness, and yet we feel ourselves strangely native to the cosmos. We shrink to nothing before the immensity, and yet we sing our thanks out into the openness. And there are breakthroughs beyond the sense of void infinity, such as made Pascal afraid, into an appreciation of infinitude as plenitude. We breathe the glory of the sublime creation, in its disproportion to our power to master it."[214]

Where the ontic question probes *what* something is in its determinacy, and the ontological question considers *how* something perdures as an identity-in-impermanence, it falls to the metaphysical question to ask after the whole of being: Why being at all?

The question of why being and not nothing erupts as a response to having heard the call of being. We come to be in the midst of being's happening and become attentive to how beings intermediate with one another. This is metaphysics as a response to dwelling amidst and being stirred into mindfulness by being. The external world communicates itself, as Gerard Manley Hopkins expressed poetically in "As Kingfishers Catch Fire":

Each mortal thing does one thing and the same:
Deals out that being indoors each one dwells;
Selves—goes its self; *myself* it speaks and spells,
Crying *What I do is me: for that I came.*[215]

Metaxology responds to the address of exterior transcendence and empowers our response. Each "mortal thing" is expressive; each being "selves" and communicates itself to the world around us. No being must be tortured into speech because from its innermost core all beings proclaim themselves. For those who have ears to hear, the *metaxu* pulsates and sings of this communication. In our modern era, we have grown deaf to this chorus of voices. Philosophical inquiry inspired by Descartes, for instance, would look claim, perhaps even deem, it eccentric. Such a critique would be quite right, for metaxology is eccentric: it is neither centered in nor does it index being to the *cogito* because it is an elicited response in a dialogue initiated from outside the self.

The vector directing every act of self-transcendence finds its origin, accordingly, not in the self but in the advent of transcendence. Again, recall Augustine's response to creation as he seeks the object of his love. No being satisfies his quest, each pointing beyond itself and the created order toward its Creator.[216] Far from a dispassionate search, his odyssey is an eccentric quest in response to the call of exterior transcendence perceived in beauty. Augustine, addressed by the natural world, turned to beings external to himself (T_1). Not even the totality of finite creation could satisfy his restlessness. Yet, in opening himself to exterior transcendence, he hears creation singing of the Creator who made them (Ps. 99:3). Creation's song is, in this way, robustly *meta*-physical because it points beyond immanence toward the transcendent Creator.

Interior Transcendence (T$_2$)

Confronted by the oscillation of exterior beings as they come to be and pass away, we are struck: Why anything at all? Being does not unfold neutrally before us; rather, we are drawn into its interplay. What Desmond calls *intentional infinitude* implicates us in two ways: it launches us into a quest for an ultimate origin and it exposes within ourselves the abyssal depths of desire's longing. The "transcendence" in self-transcendence conveys both the act of reaching out beyond oneself and an awareness of a transcendence abiding within one's depths. Interior transcendence (T$_2$) indicates "the transcendence of *self-being* such as we meet especially in the self-surpassing power of the human being."[217] The capacity for self-transcendence renders us creatures of possibility who, in freedom, take a stand on who we become: "The meaning of possibility can here be defined immanently rather than just determined externally. There is possibility as freedom, perhaps even as the promise of free finite creativity. Human self-transcendence awakens to itself in the astonishing givenness of being, awakens to its own astonishing powers of self-surpassing. Human beings are finite yet exceed finitude in their self-surpassing."[218]

Self-transcendence bears the dual mark of eccentricity and ecstasy. As eccentric, it originates as a response to a call from outside or beyond the self; as ecstatic, it is both outer reaching and other reaching. That is, self-transcendence intentionally reaches toward being as *other* to and outside of the self. Self-transcendence is not *autotelic* but directed by a summons directed from without. We are open *to* acts of self-transcendence, to reaching beyond ourselves, because we are first opened *by* transcendence. Disquieted yet enticed by the call from outside ourselves, beyond ourselves, we reach outward and other-ward.

Self-transcendence is awakened and guided by our becoming aware of what we earlier encountered as the "intimate strangeness of being." This intimate strangeness refers to the "middle condition of our thought of being: being is strange because it has an otherness, indeed marvel, of which we are not the conceptual masters; it is intimate, in that this very strangeness allows no stance of thinking 'outside' being—we are participants in what we think about. Being indeed gives us to be before we think about the meaning of what it is to be. The strangeness of being is as much about us, as we are within it."[219]

Stirred by being's advent and call, one knows oneself as one among other beings yet recognizes that their "strangeness" eludes any conceptual schema. We know beings intimately because we are among them and we are because of them, yet they elude capture by our concepts. Self-transcendence possesses, then, a double movement. The self is awakened *by* the advent of transcendence, the address of a being other to self; the self is awakened *to* transcendence, impelling it outward in a ceaseless quest for wholeness.

Superior Transcendence (T_3)

We turn now to what Desmond calls actual infinitude, superior transcendence, or *transcendence itself* (T_3). This is not to be confused with any ontotheological "highest being in the sense with which God is often identified—namely, the *ens realissimum*."[220] The God of whom he writes is not *a* being because transcendence itself (T_3) is in excess of determinate "beings, as their original ground; it would be in excess of our self-transcendence, as its most ultimate possibilizing source. It would be beyond the ordinary doublet of possibility/reality, as their possibilizing source; it could not be just a possibility, nor indeed a realization of possibility. It would have to be 'real' possibilizing power, more original and other than finite possibility and realization. It would have to be possibilizing beyond determinate possibility, and 'real' beyond all determinate realization."[221]

What is distinctive about "transcendence itself," what we have nominalized as the Transcendent or God, can be expressed in a word: possibilizing.[222] Transcendence itself (T_3) is the possibilizing source of the other two transcendences (T_1, T_2) as their origin, the pure act that, as such, is the source of all finite existence. To the question, Why anything at all? comes the response: because Transcendence itself, the Transcendent, is and makes it to be.

An anecdote: I used to teach high school sophomores, who were generally incredulous about God's existence. Many had absorbed enough

New Atheism to label themselves skeptics if not unbelievers. Nevertheless, I found using a finessed approach to Aquinas's Third Way—the argument from contingency—sprinkled with humor would intrigue them enough to get them to entertain the "God question." The guiding question for that day's class: What is God's job requirement? If we were to embark upon a job search for a new God, could we think of the absolute bare minimum qualification needed to fill the position? Not surprisingly, the nascent skeptics never mentioned being Triune or gracious but limited themselves to traits such as kindness, power, and omniscience. After entertaining all of these and working our way through Aquinas's demonstration, I set out what I considered to be the entry-level requirement: "God's job, most basically, is to make things *to be*." Then, knowing my sophomores would be tickled by a slightly risqué answer, I would continue: "What sort of things? Everything. From aardvarks and angels to zygotes and zebras. God makes the whole damn thing to be!" Then, with some gusto, I'd conclude: "Alas, I cannot make a single glass of wine to be—if I could, I would not be standing here because I wouldn't be standing at all—so, sorry to say, I'm out of the running for the job." There is, I hear, a Facebook page where this quote is enshrined by some alumni.

This, I think, is what a possibilizing God makes possible: the existence of anything at all, the reason there is something rather than nothing.

Desmond's "possibilizing" God bears no relation to the god rejected as ontotheological. Ontotheology's god takes up residence and has a job to do *within* the immanent order. Such a god becomes, as Westphal writes, "a Highest Being who is the key to the meaning of the whole of being."[223] Desmond regards Hegel as an ontotheologian, for his counterfeit "God 'needs' man, and hence is defined as what it is or may be in terms of its relativity to us."[224] Rather than a possibilizing divinity, Hegel's god is one for whom divinity is a possibility: "A God that is not truly what it may be in the beginning, but has to become itself, fully realizes what it might be, or may be, in a process of becoming or self-becoming, in which it is teleologically, or eschatologically, more fully itself or complete at the end of the process. I think this way of thinking runs a grave risk of producing counterfeit doubles of God, even it gives to some the satisfaction of being needed by God."[225]

Hegel's counterfeit god is an "erotic absolute" defined by an "indefinite abstraction or lack; self-exit into otherness; return to self through and from the otherness; now in the end explicit self-constitution, finally determined as fully real."[226] This god unfolds and is driven by the indigent lack of Penia with scant recognition of the enriched poverty inherited from Poros.

Desmond's God is not *a* being but, rather, the Origin, Creator, and Sustainer of being. This is not a God of inner potentiality who has any need to create. God's relationship to the whole is asymmetrical and nonreciprocal: God creates and sustains being, God gives being to be *at all*, but not to achieve any self-serving goal. God does not need humanity to work out God's issues or to become God. The Creator creates not out of poverty but from overabundance; God possibilizes the whole for no "reason" other than the sheer goodness of being itself.

Any recourse to a God not confined to our immanent order cannot fail to tax and strain our language. Indeed, Desmond recurs to several metaphors in an effort to express a sense of the God who evades capture in finite speech. Instead of the "erotic absolute" who *needs* creation, he employs metaphors of the agapeic absolute,[227] absolute original[228] and agapeic origin[229] to draw attention to the "too muchness" and excess of God's creative power. Metaphoric speech is inescapable when speaking of God. For instance:

> The absolute original as depth is a metaphor for the ground of being. Interestingly, the Latin for "high," *altus*, can also mean "deep." . . . As a vertical transcendence, the absolute original is beyond a univocal either/or; it is double, both high and deep. It requires a metaxological both/and. As height, it is transcendent to the world; as depth, it is its immanent ground. . . . To say that the absolute original is the ground is to say that all finite being is shot through with its own dynamic orientation toward absoluteness, toward its own potential wholeness and participation in infinity for which all creation groans.[230]

Note how the metaphor works to portray "transcendence itself" as intimately present to the whole of creation. It spans the heights and depths of created being; indeed, by grounding creation it leaves upon the created order a trace of its creative excess, an enriched poverty, orienting us toward fulfillment. The metaphor asks us to reflect upon what it means to be amidst finite being (*meta*) and gestures at the same time toward what is beyond being (*meta*) and makes being *to be*: the creative and possibilizing source of the whole damn thing.

I conclude by drawing on Kearney's meditation on the Song of Solomon 3:1–4. This not only provides a better sense of Desmond's three transcendences but also shows how they implicate one another. Kearney begins by quoting the Shulamite bride:

> Upon my bed at night I sought him whom my soul loves;
> I sought him, but found him not; I called him, but he gave no answer.
> "I will rise now and go about the city, in the streets and in the squares;
> I will seek him whom my soul loves." I sought him, but found him not.
> The sentinels found me, as they went about in the city.
> "Have you seen him whom my soul loves?"
> Scarcely had I passed them, when I found him whom my soul loves.

For Kearney, "the anxious, expectant seeking of the love-struck bride is reversed into a *being-found*, that is, a *being desired*."[231] A nocturnal yearning stirs the bride and impels her from the bedchamber. This is not a feckless search, a random casting about, but a deliberate quest for her beloved. She knows the one for whom she seeks, the one who awakened within her the stirring of a desire that takes her out into the city streets (T_2). She canvasses the city in search of traces of her beloved (T_1). But, "it is only *after* the bride has passed the sentinels who found *her* that she finds *Him* whom her soul loves."[232] It is because God first calls to us, calls us into being, calls us into relationship, that we can call out and search for God. The longing of the heart is an enriched poverty endowed by its Creator, desire's origin and end, its *arche* and *telos*.

The range of transcendences (T_1 to T_3) comprise the metaxological community of being. As should be clear from his inclusion of self-transcendence, we are each of us included within the community of transcendence where each being intermediates with what is other to itself. The world around us is not a neutral tableau populated by monads; creation has been called into being and is sustained by actual transcendence, the transcendent Creator (T_3). The beauty of creation addresses us as we are struck, or pierced, by a face, a vista, a song. Metaxology does not lead us into the community of transcendence; it arises as a response to awakening within the *metaxu* and finding ourselves bidden to speak, or sing, of the God who is glimpsed in us yet remains always beyond us.

MINDING THE BETWEEN: THE FURROWING BROW OF IMMANENCE

I round out this initial survey of Desmond's metaphysics by thinking through the modes of "minding" the between. For Desmond, mindfulness of being unfolds and evolves in three stages: astonishment, perplexity, and curiosity. There is, he holds, "something excessive and overdetermined about the astonishing beginning; then there is a troubled indeterminacy and sense of lack, in the perplexity of mind that is subsequently precipitated; finally, there is a drive to definitive and determination in curiosity that seeks to overcome any survival of troubled indefiniteness and lack, such as we find in perplexity."[233]

He distinguishes these three modes because, in the modern era, we have stressed the determinate drive of curiosity and recessed the other two. In tracing the evolution of our mindfulness of the *metaxu*, he gives us a metaphysical genealogy in many ways complementary to Taylor's. Hence "the furrowing brow of immanence" purports to describe the historical process moving from an initial "wide-eyed astonishment" to a narrowing "squint-eyed perplexity" to, finally, the "furrowed brow of curiosity" that insists on total determinacy.

On the ontological level, Desmond's description of our age's preference for *l'esprit de géometrie* over *l'esprit de finesse* complements Taylor's moral corral. But, in his metaphysical account, he opens up a new vista for us to explore: for though the modes of mindfulness may forget their origin in astonishment, they can never un-inherit their ancestry. The curious mind may bristle at, or think itself allergic to, overdeterminacy, but astonishment abides in its DNA. By reactivating even long-dormant seeds of astonishment, metaxology promises to renew the way we abide in the *metaxu* by refreshing us at the wellspring of primary wonder.

Wide-Eyed Astonishment: Porosity of Being and *passio essendi*

"The beginning of mindfulness," Desmond writes, "is in an original wonder before the givenness of being. Such wonder is often recognized but its significance is not always plumbed."[234] This insight has roots in Aristotle, Plato, and Thales of Miletus. Thales, Plato writes in the *Theaetetus*, was so enraptured by the stars that he fell into a well.[235] In keeping with these figures, Desmond considers that "the advent of metaphysical thinking is in a primal astonishment." Indeed, this astonishment is primal, elemental, and irreducible: "Plato speaks of *thaumazein* as the *pathos* of the philosopher. This is sometimes translated as *wonder* and this is not inappropriate. Astonishment, however, captures the sense of being rocked back on one's heels as it were, by the otherness of being in its givenness. Plato says *pathos*: there is a pathology in metaphysics. There is a suffering, an undergoing; there is a patience of being; there is a receiving that is not the production of the metaphysician or mind."[236]

We are, for Desmond, *rocked back*, we *suffer*, and we *undergo* the address of what is other to ourselves. In astonishment, the "bite of otherness"[237] inflicts a wound and opens us to what is other than ourselves. In a sense, we are open to the world because we have been opened by the givenness of being; we are subjects because we have been subjected to the address of what transcends us. In astonishment, the overdeterminacy of being breaks upon us as a "rupture and renewal, at once a refreshed distancing and a drawing close of mind and being."[238] Unlike Frodo, who bore a sliver of the Morgul-knife within his shoulder, this wound does not hamper or undermine our journey; to the contrary, the rupture stirs us to ask, What gave, or gives, us to be?

Let us consider the following description of astonishment as the wellspring of metaphysical reflection. Astonishment "is a precipitation of mindfulness before something admirable, or loveable, or marvelous, communicated from an otherness that has the priority in speaking to the porosity of our being. It comes to us, comes over us, and we open up in response. We do not first go toward something, but find ourselves going out of ourselves because something has made its way, often in startling communication, in the very depths or roots of our being, beyond our self-determination."[239]

Because metaxological mindfulness remains true to its origin in astonishment, punches thrown by metaphysics' critics lose their forcefulness. Instead of arising from a dominative attempt to grasp and control, metaxology responds to the address of what is other to and in excess of ourselves. To Caputo's relief, it makes no claim to possess "the Truth." Instead, it remains alert in the everyday to those moments when what is "admirable, or loveable, or marvelous" discloses itself to us. Metaxology discerns the call heard as we stand amidst beings (*meta*), a call that directs us beyond beings (*meta*) to being's source. Opened by astonishment, we are creatures of ecstatic desire reaching outward and other-ward from the abyssal depths of our enriched poverty as our desires strain forward toward the promise of ultimate fulfillment.

There is something childlike about astonishment. A girl grasps her father's hand and says in awe, "Look, the moon!" A boy devours fairy tales and play-acts them for his family. Children live easily with astonishment, unafraid to show their wonder or to ask the questions adults find trivial. Indeed, childhood astonishment may augur the future: she may become a physicist, he an actor. Although we grow out of childhood, we need not lose a capacity for awe. Desmond observes, "The child is not only the father to the man, but the man is the shield of time that shelters, or denies, the idiotic child he was born as."[240] How many of us began careers only to lose our zest because, rather than nurturing awe, we banish our inner child to the cellar?

My point: this description of astonishment not only *informs* by describing it, but in leading us to its origin it *invites* us to recollect experiences of being "rocked back" or "struck." This invitation requires a level of finesse, a certain patience, and a willingness to consider "the nuances of singular occasions."[241] But by ruminating on the "nuances of the singular," metaxology brings to light otherwise concealed depths. This ruminative tactic can be used to probe two concepts central to Desmond's work: the "porosity of being" and the *passio essendi*. We may find the following example taken from Hans Urs von Balthasar helpful.

Balthasar describes how "the little child awakens to self-consciousness in his being-called by the love of his mother."[242] Translated into metaxological terms: the advent of the mother is irruptive and invitatory; her loving smile and tender caress address the child, enabling and inviting the child's response. Balthasar continues:

Since, however, the child in this process replies and responds to a directive that cannot in any way have come from within its own self—it would never occur to the child that it itself had produced the mother's smile—the entire paradise of reality that unfolds around the "I" stands there as an incomprehensible miracle: it is not thanks to the gracious favor of the "I" that space and the world exist, but thanks to the gracious favor of the "Thou." And if the "I" is permitted to walk upon the ground of reality and to cross the distance to reach the other, this is due to an original favor bestowed on him, something for which, a priori, the "I" will never find the sufficient reason in himself.[243]

Desmond and Balthasar recognize that the "self" is inescapably in relation to an other who transcends it. As the caress of the mother awakens the child's "I," likewise does the call of transcendence engender every act of self-assertion and self-transcendence. The summons of the other, the inbreaking of the other's address, capacitates the "I" by astonishing the "I" into movement. What, then, does metaxology add to Balthasar's account?

To start, metaxology foregrounds the means by which intermediation is possible. Desmond call this the porosity of being. This porosity is the "between space where there is no fixation of the difference of minding and things, where our mindfulness wakes to itself by being woken up by the communication of being in its emphatic otherness."[244] We must resist reifying this thinking of discrete beings as having fixed "pores" or "openings" that permit transit and mediation. Porosity is not something a being "has" because it is no *thing* at all. Still, if porosity "is not determinate objectivity neither is it indeterminate or self-determining subjectivity. There is fluidity and passing—a liquid matrix. The porosity is prior to univocal objectivity and it is prior to intentionality. In and through it we are given to be in a patience of being more primal than any cognitive or pragmatic endeavor to be."[245] Irish musicians in a *seisiún* experience this porosity as making the music possible. For they intermediate with one another, each shaping and being shaped as the tunes are played. The space between fiddle, harp, and flute neither fixes nor dissolves the musical voices but allows them to pass into one another. For Desmond, the porosity that enables a musical tradition to spring to life and be handed down to future generations is a characteristic of all finite being: all beings are porous to one another and to their enabling source. This porosity, Desmond admits, appears paradoxical: "Strange wording: filled with openness. For such a porosity looks like nothing determinate and hence seems almost nothing, even entirely empty. We cannot avoid what looks like the paradoxical conjunction of fullness and emptiness: being filled with openness and yet being empty. This is what makes possible all our determinate relations to determinate beings and process, whether these relations be knowing ones or unknowing."[246]

As a ceaseless happening, porosity is an energetic "passing in passage," an ongoing and fluid to-and-fro of intermediation between beings. This porosity, the constitutive openness of all beings to one another and to being's creative source, is a feature of the *metaxu* where all things live and move and have their being. This porosity—playing on Poros—is creation's endowing endowment: it is given to be through God's creative act and its openness renders creation a happening. Attuned to this porosity, we behold creation not as an inert "block" but a vibrant field of intermediation. Indeed, the entire community of transcendence (T_1 to T_3) does not stand upon the *metaxu* as though fixed like furniture on a theater stage. For the *metaxu* shimmers and pulses with a ceaseless "passing in passage" that binds all of creation together. The "porosity of being" means there is indeed a crack in everything . . . and everyone. We are ourselves "the porosity of being become mindful."[247]

Every "social imaginary" or reconfigured ethos, is relative to the primal ethos: each era shapes and forms it, but no reconfiguration ever exhausts it. Each ethos may be more, or less, faithful to the "promise of the original givenness," but no single ethos expresses fully its endowment; more will always remain.

Modern philosophy, if not modernity itself, has suffered something of a metaphysical amnesia leading us to forget being's porosity. A recuperation of our sense of porosity would have theological consequences: "Perhaps it is the case today that many people have difficulty praying because we have a diminished feel for this more original porosity of being. Of course, if it is true as Professor Taylor says that we have become buffered ourselves, this should not be at all surprising. In the process of buffering ourselves we have not more truly realized our promise, in fact, to the contrary, we have reconfigured ourselves in forgetfulness, if not in mutilation, of the communication of original porosity."[248]

For Desmond, the distinction is not that we were porous and are now buffered. This latter description would be untrue and betray our constitutive porosity: we may be clogged or reconfigured against porosity, but porosity cannot be annihilated or overcome. It needs to be purged and awakened through a renewed sense of astonishment.

To Balthasar's account, metaxology adds an expanded and enriched horizon in which the address of being can be issued and answered. For there is something instinctively right about Balthasar's observation: ideally it is the mother (or father) whose love awakens the child to itself. As Kearney urges, we need always be on the lookout for micro-eschatologies, epiphanies of the everyday. By recollecting experiences of astonishment, by meditating on the overdeterminate happening of being, we can become alert to how the "nuances of the singular" communicate something in excess of singularity. We can be stirred by the intimation of transcendence within us, passing in passage through us, weaving us into the *metaxu*. We cannot find wholeness apart from the *metaxu* but only as a part of it.

In addition, there is at the heart of Desmond's treatment of being's porosity what he calls the *passio essendi*. The *passio* conveys the sense that before we grasp at being (*conatus essendi*) we have first to be given to be. We are not self-creating but, instead, the recipients of being; my being is mine, but I did not give myself being. For Desmond, the *passio essendi*

> refers to a certain ontological patience signaled by the fact that we are first recipients of being, of being received in being, before we flower as being active. There is an ontological receiving before there is an existential acting. As something ontological, this receiving is constitutive of our being but it is not self-constituted. To call it *passio* is not to imply a mere dead thereness devoid of its own energetic life. Its own life is not first owned by it; it is given to be its own on the basis of a giving that is not its own.[249]

By no means does the *passio* indicate feeble receptivity, like a deflated balloon awaiting a strong breath. It describes, instead, the givenness of created being: because no being is *causa sui*, all beings have first to be given to be. Aardvark or angel, human or hyena, every finite being must first "come to be" before it can take a stand on itself in freedom.

Before I can "become" something I must first "come to be" through the act of creation.

Students of philosophy are more familiar with the *passio's* younger twin, the *conatus essendi*, who figures prominently in Spinoza's thought. The *conatus* communicates a sense of grasping at being and self-assertion. Its exemplars include Thrasymachus, Machiavelli, Hobbes, Spinoza, Hegel's self-determining *Geist*, Kant's autonomous subject, and Nietzsche's *Übermensch*. Over the course of modernity, "the intimacy of being, articulated as *passio essendi* and *conatus essendi*, mutates into the twins of subordination and dominion, submission and overcoming. The first is the *passio* made abject, the second the *conatus* made superject."[250] The *passio's* recession and porosity's clogging left the *conatus* to seize center stage.

Now, Desmond wants neither to deny nor to downplay the importance the *conatus*. He seeks only to relativize the *conatus* by underscoring the *passio* as prior to and as having priority: "This passion of being is more primal because life opens us before we open to life. We are given to be as living before we give ourselves to be as determined, or self-determining, in accord with the particular form of life we are. The patience of life—in this sense of its being received from sources beyond self-affirmation—is often hidden from sight when the *conatus essendi* is wrongly claimed to be the essence of life itself.[251] In our very selves, we incarnate both "patience of being" and the "endeavor to be." Where the *conatus* overemphasizes competitive striving, the *passio* corrects for this and insists that before being can be grasped, it must be given. Not just my being, or human being, but the whole of being. All that is, is, not as a self-wrought achievement but as the result of a gift.

Metaxology is rooted in the experience of astonishment enkindled by recognizing being's gratuity. Astonishment is a wide-eyed response: eyes expand in order to take in the happening, but there is too much to apprehend all at once. Considered metaxologically, however, astonishment reveals more than the bite of otherness catching us off guard. Astonished eyes perceive dimensions of the *metaxu* we otherwise take for granted. The givenness of being points toward a giver, toward a *passio essendi* that we undergo in common with all of creation. This ongoing creativity, furthermore, bespeaks a constitutive openness between all beings, a porosity that makes the *metaxu* a communion of being. We contemplate within the *metaxu* and our minds are thrust beyond it: I am, but I need not be. Try as we might, being exceeds our grasp and remains always overdeterminate.

Desmond refers to this astonishment as "agapeic" because "it arises from a surplus or excess out of which an affirmative movement of mind as self-transcending emerges."[252] And, elicited and oriented by this agapeic advent, self-transcendence is never for the "purposes of a return to the self. I do not go out from myself toward the other to appropriate the other and through the other to return to myself. I go toward the other because the other is for itself and always irreducible to what it is for me."[253] Agapeic astonishment possesses a festive prodigality that communicates surplus and invites our participation within it. Enlivened by astonishment, we become possessors of what Desmond calls agapeic mind, "a mode of thought thinking what is other to thought, in which there is a release of thinking from itself toward the other as other."[254] This is not thought trying to constrain the Other into one's categories, or through indexing the Other to the canon of human reason. This is a thought provoked by the advent of the Other who invites one to participate in its overfullness. As we consider the furrowing of immanence's brow, what we find is a lessening of this festive sense of being's exuberance and excess.

Perplexity's Squint

As we have seen, a metaxological understanding of astonishment points to two openings. There is, first, an "inarticulate coming towards us of the intimacy of being."[255] Metaxology does not duplicate the rupture of being's advent. Instead, metaxology disrupts our ordinary patterns of thought and behavior by recalling us to the prior *passio essendi* and the fundamental porosity of being. We are not, to use an Irish music image, solo instrumentalists but always already participants in the *seisiún* of being where its rhythm animates and binds together all things. Second, having been opened, every act of self-transcendence records an individual's effort to exercise freedom in search of greater determinacy. The givingness of the *passio essendi* empowers the *conatus essendi*'s adventuring. Metaxology invites us to dwell ruminatively on both aspects of our existence, holding in creative tension the "coming to be" of the *passio* and the self-directive "becoming" of the *conatus*.

For Desmond, human perplexity arises subsequent to astonishment and denotes a mode of mindfulness increasingly governed by conative striving and self-assertion. Perplexity arises subsequent to astonishment. As Simpson notes, "The intimate strangeness of being gives rise not only to astonishment but also to perplexity. In perplexity, one's attention is drawn to the strangeness of being, while the intimacy of being becomes recessed, ambiguous, ambivalent."[256] Whereas astonishment luxuriates in being's overdeterminacy, perplexity finds itself ill at ease. Instead of astonishing overdeterminacy, perplexity sees negative indeterminacy. Thus perplexity, astonishment's prodigal son, renounces the surplus of its father's house and sets out to make sense of the excess the father too easily takes for granted. Perplexity puts the stick to the *conatus* and tries to make its own way on its own terms.

In perplexity, the eyes narrow to size up what had bowled one over. Squinting eyes enframe and take the measure of what is other to the self. Whereas the astonished mind is bowled over and rapturously caught up in being's excess, the perplexed mind intuits a lack it feels compelled to fill. Being's overdeterminacy troubles it, so perplexity seeks determinacy. Thus does the exuberant "It is!" of astonishment give way to "What is?" and impel perplexity forward in an act of inquiry. What was undergone and received in the event of astonishment elicits a countermovement, one aimed at making sense or getting to the bottom of what took place.

Perplexity is "erotic" insofar as it arises out a sense of indigence. Erotic perplexity is driven by a desire forgetful of the endowed poverty inherited from Poros. Desiring to overcome its felt lack, erotic perplexity's seeking "is qualified by the aim of alleviating perplexity's own troubled mindfulness. In this regard, it is tempted to turn the self-transcend into a search that finally is for the sake of returning the self to its own epistemic peace or satisfaction with itself. Then I go toward the other out of my own lack, I tend to the other not primarily to attend to the other, but as perhaps requiting my own lack. I am tempted to possess the other to enable my own achieved self-possession."[257]

Erotic perplexity tends to regard what is other to self in terms of instrumentality. Whereas agapeic astonishment's self-transcendence moves in affirmation of otherness, erotic perplexity's self-transcendence tries to utilize otherness to sate its own need.

Perplexity, though, need not and should not sever its ties to astonishment. Let us consider how, in the first chapter of Michael Buckley's

Denying and Disclosing God, he examines the increasingly fraught relationship between science and faith. Galileo accepted, as many today do not, Augustine's insight in *De Genesi ad litteram*: "The language of scripture is adapted to the preconceptions and understanding of the culture in which it was written. Its grammar does not bear upon the issues of astronomical inquiry."[258] Faith and science, as Augustine knew well, could not be rivals because they shared a common origin. Thus, what arose in response to the Holy One's call (faith) could not forbid the exercise of human rationality as it investigated the natural world (science). So long as God was regarded as the single author of both the book of nature and the book of scripture there was no reason for conflict between the two. Only when human reason began to insist that both books be read with one grammar, rather than interpreted in a way appropriate to each, do we find a conflict growing between the science and religion.

We can read the lives of Galileo (1564–1642), Kepler (1571–1630), and Newton (1642–1727), as recording the "perplexed squinting" of human reason that, eventually, erects an impermeable barrier between science and faith. Buckley describes the consequences of this shift as yielding

> three distinct settlements negotiated between the new knowledge and the ancient faith: in Galileo, they are separate enterprises, neither contradicting the other and neither having a place within the other. Where certainty is found, the one will correct the other as is the case with any knowledge. In Kepler, they are finally a single enterprise, a deduction of what is likely and appropriate within the universe from the triune nature of God and the suggestion or the confirmation of that deduction from observation and mathematic. In Newton's universal mechanics, science gives to religion crucially important evidence, its methodology, and its foundation in fundamental religion.[259]

Each in his own way, these were thinkers variously hospitable to God. For Galileo, "religion and science differ in subject matter, purposes, appropriate methods, or procedures, and language. If these differences are maintained, each can contribute to the general advance of human beings toward real knowledge."[260] Kepler, by contrast, took the doctrine of the Trinity as an a priori and sought to unify astronomy and theology. This alignment means scripture *and* geometry are equally theological languages: "The study of geometry, then, and all of those things whose truth is geometrical, is finally the study of God."[261] Newton turns Kepler on his head. Instead of arguing from an a priori belief in the Triune God, Newton frames "a science that was universal in its compass and which argued to the divine reality from the nature of the world."[262] For Newton the basis of creation was not the creative God of whom creation sings but, rather, a universal mechanics giving "a foundation to both mathematics and religious belief."[263]

Tracing an arc from Augustine to Galileo to Newton can give readers a feel for how astonishment ceded to perplexity. In Augustine, there is a sense of porosity between humanity, creation, and the Creator. We saw this both in the *Confessions* and in *De Genesi ad litteram*. By the time of Galileo, however, the balance between the *passio* and the *conatus* has begun to tilt. Instead of fluid intermediation between religion and science, Galileo presages Stephen J. Gould's NOMA (Non-Overlapping Magisteria) that sees science and faith as wholly distinct. Live and let live, as it were. Within a generation, though, we encounter in Newton a thinker of great perplexity. In order to make his mechanics work, he is compelled to fit God into the universe. God is dragooned into the cosmos because, as Buckley writes, the cosmos is "a unity composed of the sun, planets, and comets whose masses and motions are proportioned so carefully that they 'could only proceed from the counsel and dominion of an intelligent and powerful Being.' Mechanics, if it is to be faithful to its reduction of movement back to force, must go beyond mechanical causes."[264] Newton strips the cosmos of metaphysical excess or overdeterminacy, and the etiolated deity invoked is less the God of the scriptures than a *deus ex machina* required to push the start button on the universal mechanism. There is little place in this increasingly determinate system for occurrence of irruptive theophany. Newton's God is neither disclosed nor named through the burning bush, or at Jesus's baptism, or on Easter Sunday. Instead, Newton's god is named "from the mechanics that has furnished the warrant for his existence and attributes."[265]

Newton is not alone in being driven by perplexity's rage for order. Descartes, Hegel, and the early Wittgenstein are all erotic perplexity's epigone inasmuch as each seeks to resolve indeterminacy. As Desmond might frame it, in eras dominated by erotic perplexity, the chiaroscuro of exterior transcendence (T_1) is deemed as a sign of troubling equivocity in need of determination. Hence the squint of perplexity: one squints in order to narrow the range of vision and to bring the object of inquiry into greater relief. In the modern era, wide-eyed astonishment cedes to the perplexed gaze. A mindfulness born in wonder, *It is!*, grew disquieted by its ignorance, by what it did not know, and tried to establish more and more concretely just *what* it is.

As a mode of metaphysical consciousness, perplexity is itself a *metaxu*, between astonishment and curiosity. There is no one-speed perplexity because it admits of a range. It can be wooed by *l'esprit de finesse* and remain in close contact with its roots, preserving a balance between the *conatus* and the *passio*. It can be seduced by *l'esprit de géometrie* to wander from its origin as it strives to get the measure of what it beholds. Newton, to my mind, seems the incarnation of perplexity: harnessing the power of the *conatus*, he works out a mechanics of the cosmos at least prima facie hospitable to the divine. Heidegger's critique of ontotheology's god lands: this is hardly a god before whom one sings, or dances, or offers prayers. Could it be otherwise? Only thinly connected to its origin in astonishment, Newton's "God was not encountered as a presence; God was inferred as a conclusion from what one did encounter."[266]

Curiosity's Furrowed Brow

Desmond's third form of mindfulness is curiosity. When perplexity strays too far from astonishment, it mutates and becomes increasingly hostile toward being. For the curious mind the overdeterminacy of astonishment "can be too easily forgotten, just as also the troubled indeterminacy of perplexity can be dulled. If to be is to be determinate, here to be is nothing if it is not determinate. Being is nothing but determinacy and to be exhausted in the totality of all determinations. The danger: hostility to ontological astonishment is twinned with the annihilation of the wonder of being itself."[267]

Curiosity abhors vagueness and imprecision; for the curious mind "being is a mere strangeness to be domesticated; beings are mere strangers over against us to be fixed and conquered—strangers to be made, by us, no longer strange."[268] The play of equivocity cannot be countenanced and must be brought to heel: to be is to be determinate, and all will be determined. If astonishment was rocked by overdeterminacy, and perplexity sought to get the measure of a seemingly indeterminate happening, the curiosity seeks to give the measure and solve the "problem" of being.

Desmond regards curiosity as astonishment's "ungrateful child." It is modernity's *enfant terrible* at whose impatient insistence the *ethos* has been reconfigured

> out of distrust of equivocity, expressed in the univocalizing mentality of dualistic opposition that produces a devaluing objectification of being on one side and a subjectification of value on the other side. Both sides deprive value of ontological ground, and this devaluation, in turn, forces the subject to step into the emptiness where it manifests itself in a reactive activism, itself expressing a will to power that will to ground itself, or that claims to be self-generating, or indeed that in final exasperation dismisses all grounding and proudly stands there as groundless will to power that will brook no resistance from any other, that will make no apology for itself, but simply will insist that its way will be the way and the truth, and that it will get its way.[269]

Petulant curiosity turns on astonishment (*It is!*) and perplexity (*What is?*) to state with sober, studied indifference *What is it?* as it trains its gaze at the "determinate being there of beings."[270] Wide-eyed astonishment gives way to the cold calculation of being's accountant.

If Newton serves as an exemplar of a hypertrophied perplexity, Denis Diderot (1713–84) and Baron d'Holbach (1723–89) are exemplars of how the narrow eyes of perplexity becomes the furrowed brow of curiosity. At their hands, Newton's universal mechanics undergoes a drastic modification. From Newton, Buckley writes,

> Diderot and d'Holbach accepted the universality of mechanics, that the mechanical method could deal with all of reality from mathematics to theology; what they rejected of Newton was his claim that the mechanical study of natural phenomena necessarily leads to a non-mechanical principle, to a transcendence source above nature, i.e., to God. From Descartes, Diderot and d'Holbach refused his

metaphysics or first philosophy as nonsense—as Newton had before them; but from Descartes, they accepted the autonomy of mechanics, i.e., that all physical reality was mechanical and must be explained through mechanical principles.[271]

For Diderot and d'Holbach, there is no need to invoke the divine in order to make sense of the universe or its operations. The universe is a self-contained whole, closed in upon itself. By enacting a synthesis between "universal mechanics (à la Newton) with only mechanical principles (à la Descartes)" and revolutionizing "natural philosophy by making matter no longer inert, but dynamic," Newton's *deus ex machina* becomes a *deus otiosus*, "not so much denied as unattended to, detached and uninvolved, not influential in the world and of human beings, and finally yielding to oblivion."[272]

One of the key factors contributing to the rise of modern atheism was the inaction of theologians who bracketed appeals to religious experience. Enamored of the explanatory power of science, they appealed less and less to the specifically theological sources that gave life to faith. No appeals to prayer, liturgy, mystical experience, the saints, the scriptures. As Buckley observes, "To bracket the specifically religious in order to defend the God of religion was to assert implicitly the cognitive emptiness of the very reality one was attempting to support."[273] Theologians hitched themselves to the system of universal mechanics, convinced this would provide the sure and steady foundation to ensure the stability of their system. Yet thinkers such as Diderot and d'Holbach saw what Wittgenstein expressed: "A wheel that can be turned though nothing else moves with it, is not part of the mechanism."[274] Curiosity, with its brow furrowed, brushes off appeals to God as "wooly" and unnecessary: if it cannot be measured, it cannot matter. If it cannot be counted, it cannot count. No wonder the metaphysical question Why anything at all? is written off as absurd.

By no means does Desmond reject the importance of curiosity. Like univocity, curiosity's interest in determinacy can speak truly of being. But, as we have seen, we need more than univocity. Like univocity, when curiosity thinks itself sufficient, it betrays the truth of being. Desmond retains the healthy impulse and precision of curiosity, but resists scientistic reductionism. This is because "scientism the outlook takes hold that the univocalizing approach is the one and only approach. This is a contradiction of the plurivocity promised in the other modalities of wonder. Determinate curiosity has its place within the embrace of the more original sense of wonder, and while it occludes it, it cannot itself even function, much less prosper, if it does not dip back again and again into the primal modality of the originating astonishment."[275]

Recalling Taylor, the "buffered" and curious self are homologues. Both have lost a taste for the Transcendent, both affect a pose of aloof or unattached inquiry and self-directed autonomy. They exhibit what Desmond calls an "allergy to transcendence" (T_3) because their understanding of "self-transcendence has been yoked to a model of autonomous self-determination: the self is the law of itself."[276]

Curious and buffered selves need to be led back to the wellspring of astonishment. We may have reconfigured ourselves to be buffered, but "buffering" cannot be, per Desmond's anthropology, an irreversible fait accompli. Not only are we constitutively porous, we are porosity made aware of itself. This porosity permits an intermediation between stages of mindfulness. The *metaxu* admits of other reconfigurations, and we may contribute to future reconfigurations by our efforts to reawaken our age to a sense of astonishment. Human attentiveness is not fated or condemned to sojourn in the *metaxu* bereft of wonder. The furrowed brow of curiosity, too, may be struck by something in excess of determinacy—despite its best efforts—and find itself renewed. Considered ontologically, the map of our age accounts for how curiosity became the dominant mode of mindfulness. Read in a metaxological light, however, one can perceive itineraries conveying us along return routes leading us to a rekindling of astonishment. This is because we move "from ontological astonishment before being toward ontic regard concerning beings, their properties, patterns of developments, determinate formations, and so on. It is essential to the becoming of our mindfulness that we move into curiosity. The overdeterminate is saturated with determinations, not an indefiniteness empty of determinacy. The question 'What is it?' turns toward the given intricacy of this, that, and the other thing, and there can be something even reverent in this turning, for it too shares in our porosity to the astonishing givenness."[277]

Ungrateful curiosity may furrow its brow and lock itself away to obsess on "this, that, and the other thing" but even at its most antisocial, it cannot rid itself of its origin in wonder and awe. Just as the prodigal son in Jesus's parable (Luke 15:11–32) could not, despite his best efforts, un-son himself and sever his relationship with his excessively prodigal father, as a mode of mindfulness curiosity cannot dissolve the deep ties that link it back on its source. Curiosity may train its tunnel-like gaze to focus on what is determinate, it may turn a deaf ear to the clamor of agapeic astonishment, but it cannot deny its heritage. Though it may take time for it to come to its senses as it wanders the *metaxu*, it is not impossible that it could turn about and make its way back to its home where it can join the festivities and proclaim anew, *It is*!

Desmond's metaphysics offers an approach to reflection remarkable in its scope and its ability to offer a finessed account of what it means to live in the *metaxu*. Rather than telling us about it, he tries to develop our ear for the plurivocity of being and train our eyes to recognize the crack in everything. He shows, too, how our mindfulness of being undergoes shifts depending on our proximity to astonishment. This spectrum of attentiveness becomes the speculum in which we are given to recognize ourselves. The renewal of wonder we need, however, is not a once-and-for-all occasion but an ongoing commitment:

> So long as life continues, one has to say yes to wonder. This is not a matter of reviving our capacity for wonder. In a way, we do not have a capacity for wonder; rather we are capacitated by wonder— and capacitated through it to wise mindfulness. Since this capacitation is not determined through ourselves alone, we alone cannot revive it. Wondering is not a power over which we exercise self-determination; it witnesses to a given porosity of being that endows us with the promise of mindfulness. If there is to be a revival of the capacity, it is in coming home again to this porosity—and its capacitating of our powers.[278]

We may not be able to induce astonishment within ourselves, but I believe we can undertake exercises to render us open and hospitable to such experiences. We began this process when we explored the grammar and the nature of metaxological metaphysics. Metaxology's paradox: we are capacitated by knowing our incapacitation. This is a lesson learned in various ways: metaphysics is capacitated by an external call, by the advent of the Transcendent; our grasping at being (*conatus*) is capacitated by our first being given to be (*passio*); our incapacity to reduce being's flux capacitates us to perceive the irreducible porosity of being and to perceive the "crack in everything." Our incapacity to sate our restlessness capacitates us to embark on the adventure of selving as we journey forward toward the promise of wholeness for which we most desperately long. Recognizing our incapacity to control God capacitates us to develop a form of patient mindfulness, attuned to the goodness and gratuity of creation, as we await in hope for any signs or hints of the advent of the One who sings us into and sustains creation in being.

DISCOVERING THE "CRACK" IN EVERYTHING

In *Philosophy and Its Others*, Desmond describes "the naming act of philosophical mindfulness as thought singing its other; for in singing we meet an outpouring of articulation of enigmatic affirmative power, even when the song airs the grief of suffering being."[279] In keeping with this theme of *singing*, I conclude this chapter with three tasks.

First task: allow me to offer another word about the relationship between Taylor and Desmond. At the end of chapter 1, I expressed my belief that Desmond preserves and advances Taylor's project. In this chapter, I have suggested a way of reading Desmond's understanding of the *metaxu* as a metaphysical supplement to Taylor's ontological "social imaginary." A metaphysical supplement, attentive not only to *how* beings are but *why* they are, may help to allay Janz's concern over Taylor's reticence about offering a demonstrative proof for God. Desmond, we shall see soon enough, offers a series of indirect "ways to God." In this way, we might think of Desmond as Taylor's consigliere, who assures Janz, "Yes, yes, there is a *there* there. His map is trustworthy." Capiche?

In addition to providing indirect ways to God, Desmond's philosophy tutors us in what Taylor calls a "subtler language."[280] This is needful because our modern language

1. Has lost, and needs to have restored to it, its constitutive power.
2. The loss of this power means we deal instrumentally with the realities which surround us; their deeper meaning, the background in

which they exist, the higher reality which finds expression in them, remain ignored.

3. Our language has lost power to Name things in their embedding in this deeper/higher reality.

4. This incapacity of language is a crucial facet of an incapacity of being, that our lives are reduced, flattened.[281]

In its attentiveness to the plurivocity of being, metaxology attunes us to being's otherwise obscured depths. The language of metaxology works to *inform* and *form* the reader. Cyril O'Regan identifies it as moving beyond the level of flattened discourse when he describes it as doubly poetic "in the discursive sense that philosophy is a raid on the inarticulate that enlists in its articulation any and all available forms of discourse (e.g. symbol, myth, comedy, tragedy), and second in that the making (also unmaking) of selves and community has dramatic pattern with both comic and tragic elements."[282] Desmond's texts, he notes elsewhere, "perform nothing less than a fundamental reopening of a philosophical discourse, which, from its first appearance in the Occidental tradition, intends the origin as the really real."[283] Desmond sings us a philosophical lullaby, not to put us to sleep but to still the curious mind and lead it, gently, back to the sources of astonishment. We are sung into metaphysical contemplation.

A temptation, known well to Gerard Manley Hopkins, besets the curious mind. When faced with the mystery of God, it tries to get the measure of the Holy One and put it to use. So, rather than letting God be God, rather than acquiescing before the advent of God's Mystery, we nip and tuck the Transcendent and try to fit it into our immanent categories. Hopkins saw this:

We guess; we clothe Thee, unseen King,
With attributes we deem are meet;
Each in his own imagining
Sets up a shadow in thy seat.[284]

Desmond offers us a metaphysically rich yet ever-humble form of speech cognizant of its own limitations. Metaxology is wounded speech, bearing within it a graced rupture left by the advent of the Transcendent.

But we are capacitated by this wound not only to speak a subtle language but also, and more importantly, to watch vigilantly for any sign or disclosure of God's advent. In adjuring us to a patient watchfulness, metaxology becomes for us a way of living something akin to a philosophical prayer arising in response to natural religious wonder.

Second task: I return to Emerson, for whom the presence of "a crack in everything God has made"[285] points to an intrinsic vulnerability of all finite beings. His quote invokes two flawed heroes—Achilles and Siegfried—but the truth of his observation holds universally. Hero or villain, saint or scoundrel, every being bears a crack. Yet the crack, metaxologically rendered, is no occasion for sorrow. We bear upon us, within us, a wound resistant to closure. In the *metaxu*, we see this crack as an opened opening, a rupture of the self *by* the Transcendent that opens us *to* the Transcendent. We bear this wound as a mark of our eccentricity, as it comes from outside ourselves, and this wound renders us beings of ecstasy capable of reaching beyond ourselves to the one who awakened us. In the *metaxu*, the crack is at once a sign of fragility and gratuity. We turn inward, to our abyssal depths where, in the intentional solitude of prayer, we encounter an abiding otherness "marking one's intimacy to self. There is also the communication of the incognito God in the deepest ontological porosity of one's soul, so deep that it seems like nothing, since too the porosity is itself no thing—the open between space in which communication of the power to be is given and different selvings take determinate form. One is never alone, even when one is alone."[286]

On account of the crack in everything, ourselves included, we can awaken to the intimate universal: an interior presence weaving us into community with the whole of being.

Third task: philosophy as *singing* its other. There is an expression regularly heard through the pubs of Desmond's native Ireland: How's the crack? (*craic* in Irish/Gaelic). In a pub, the "crack" is not a thing, but it is also not nothing. The crack is the milieu, the happening, the intermediation of beings, the "passing in passage" between the bar and the musicians playing in the corner and the laughter and stories shared at tables. A night of good crack: family from overseas are in town and the whole family turns out for a few pints. A fiddle player taps her bow and the *seisiún* lifts off with a set of fiery reels. An elderly couple, whose dancing days should be long behind them, forget themselves and dance a two-hand. A poem recited, a song sung, an air played: the gathering goes quiet. A joke brings peals of laughter. A marriage proposal. A kiss. Love. No one element makes the night, no one instrument accounts for all the music, but in the "passing in passage" they interweave and contribute to the happening of the night. Good crack.

Good crack must not be taken *for* granted but *as* granted, an unexpected and welcome happening, never duplicable and always unique. It cannot be planned and must emerge of its own accord, unfolding organically and drawing participants into itself. It is not the achievement of the *conatus* as an endeavor, but the *co-natus* as a "being born with" each other in the moment. This rebirth itself is a shared undergoing, a suffering of something that exceeds the group and galvanizes the evening, leaving all in attendance wanting more. One becomes attuned to the crack and develops a knack for "sniffing it out."

Desmond offers us a metaphysics of the crack. As a happening, we only come to recognize the crack when we are in the middle of it. By the time we are asked, "How's the crack," it already englobes us. To respond, "Ah, it's good crack," says almost nothing, but how to say more? Any responder will stammer because no word can say it all. To describe the crack risks betraying it. Sometimes we must find other ways of speaking—art or poetry or song—to convey the too-muchness. Desmond gives us the subtler language needed to speak faithfully of the *metaxu*. Rather than imposing an interpretation or trying to capture the between, he leads us into it with a renewed mindfulness of its richness. Desmond gives us a way of wording the between, of standing within the *metaxu* in a way open to undergoing it. Though Wordsworth's entire poem sings of this, let me quote the last two stanzas of "The Tables Turned":

Sweet is the lore which Nature brings;
Our meddling intellect
Mis-shapes the beauteous forms of things:
We murder to dissect.

Enough of Science and of Art;
Close up those barren leaves;
Come forth, and bring with you a heart
That watches and receives.[287]

We, too, must arise and "quit" our books and venture, adventure, into the *metaxu*. We must stay the knife of murderous concepts and wait in watchful receptivity. Like the happening of a *seisiún*, we cannot close ourselves off to what unfolds around us. We are bid to take our place, to enter the performance, and undergo what it means to be in the between.

To further this claim, I turn in chapter 3 to consider "The Poetics of the Between" and offer an account for how Desmond's philosophy works as a form of "spiritual exercise." As we walk more intensively with Desmond, we invite French philosopher Pierre Hadot to join us as we consider how metaxology, taken as making possible a philosophical way of life, has precedent in the history of Western thought.

THREE

The Poetics of the Between

Metaxological Metaphysics as Spiritual Exercise

> What is needed is a conversion to an attitude in which existing is
> more than taking, acting more than making, meaning more than
> function—an attitude in which there is enough leisure for wonder
> and enough detachment for transcendence. What is needed most
> of all is an attitude in which transcendence *can be recognized again.*
> —Louis Dupré, *Transcendent Selfhood*

In its infinitive form, "to exercise" can be taken in two ways. In some
contexts, it means "to vex" or "to exasperate"; or it can mean "to engage"
or "to practice." In chapters 1 and 2, we explored why Charles Taylor and
William Desmond regard the question of transcendence as "exercising"
in the first sense. Taylor's immanent frame and Desmond's reconfigured
ethos both describe what many today experience as an "eclipse of the
transcendent." In chapter 1, I considered how *A Secular Age* offered a per-
suasive historical narrative of this eclipse. Taylor's map, I argued, works
to implicate the reader: Taylor does not simply tell us *a* story but tells us
our story. By weaving us into the map, his text performs by inducing a
sense of the cross-pressures experienced by those dwelling within the

immanent frame. I concluded by surfacing Paul Janz's critique of Taylor and suggested we take a trip to Ireland where, with Desmond's assistance, we might discover a way to fill in Taylor's map.

In chapter 2, I introduced Desmond's systematic metaphysics as a resource for reflecting on what it means to be "in the between." Metaxological philosophy, like Taylor's map, also implicates its reader and works to reorient the way one perceives the ongoing happening of the *metaxu*. We probed Desmond's "systematic" philosophy "in the sense of a disciplined understanding of enabling connections; connections stabilized but not frozen by sameness; connections defined and developed by dynamic difference; connections not enclosed in one immanent whole; and all in all, connections enabling complex interplays between sameness and difference, interplays exceeding the closure of every whole on itself."[1]

Yet metaxology is not the architectonic "system" rejected by many of metaphysics' critics, for it neither dragoons God into its service (ontotheology) nor claims an exclusive possession of "the Truth." It remains true to its humble origins, arising as a response to having been provoked by astonishment. Desmond's is a finessed metaphysics, attentive to being's plurivocity and committed to keeping the voices in play within an open and porous whole. Along the way, I gestured to ways in which metaxology complements and fortifies Taylor's map.

This chapter argues for reading metaxology as a form of "spiritual exercise" and does so by considering the poetic dimension of Desmond's thought. Like "exercise," I take the word "poetic" to possess a double meaning. In a first sense, it distinguishes poetics from systematics: "Poetics deals with creative overdetermination; systematics with created determinations and self-determinations. Poetics reveals the more original coming to be, or showing; systematics articulates forms of interconnection that issue from the more original forming. Poetics concerns the forming power(s), prior to and in excess of determinate form, for it is intimate with the overdetermination of the original source(s)."[2]

Echoes of *passio essendi*, for being must be given to be before it can be reflected upon. Systematics reflects upon what Desmond calls "becoming" wherein "one becomes a determinate something, out of a prior condition of determinate being and towards a further more realized or differently realized determination of one's being."[3] Desmond's poetics does more than point or designate; it is revelatory and performs by permitting us to peer beneath the surface of "becoming" to consider the dynamic process of "coming to be." As he observes, "Becoming itself suggests something more primordial about coming to be. Creation is connected with this more primordial coming to be—a coming to be that makes finite becoming itself possible but that is not itself a finite becoming."[4] Singing within the reconfigured *metaxu* or the immanent frame, Peggy Lee croons, "Is that all there is?," and Desmond responds with a lilting *no*. No: every finite being points back to and serves as a sign of a more originative power giving being to be *at all*. Metaxology's poetics sensitizes and attunes us to the primordial rhythm of the original source of being as it pulses within the *metaxu*.

There is also a second sense of poetics as performative. Poetic language, for Desmond, is neither epiphenomenal nor merely a rhetorical "embellishment that otherwise puts drapery over the sturdy drab furniture of thinking. It has more to do with *enactment*: the words are not just a matter of 'talk about' a something, but are uttered or written somehow to bring to pass a happening, to enact it mindfully. Performance is a (per) forming, a coming to be of significant form, through (*per*) a passing from silence to speaking. The saying is as important as the said; and sometimes the saying says more than the said."[5]

"Poetic" in this case expresses how a text's language enacts a performance, how it implicates the reader in a transformative process, or *poiesis*. Although not bereft of insightful philosophical propositions, the poetic nature of Desmond's prose can shift and transform readers' dispositions. At times, his texts roil and vibrate as metaphor, allusion, symbol, and hyperbole collide. This is hardly a result of careless writing: metaxological poetics enacts a discursive performance aimed at arousing a sense of the *metaxu*'s dynamism and rhythm. Desmond's texts, I contend, cannot simply be "gone over" and mined for analytic arguments or syllogism. To be appreciated, they must instead be "undergone" as a form of spiritual exercise. So considered, metaxology becomes both a way of thinking and a way of being, a mode of perception and a mode of life. In terms of our chapter 2, I believe metaxology tutors us to detect the "crack in everything" and discern how the "crack" functions as a trace of the divine, pointing beyond the immanent order toward the origin of being itself. Metaxology invites us to put our ear to the "crack" and be carried by the music within.

Approaching metaxology as a spiritual exercise can cultivate an attitude in which, as Dupré notes in our epigraph, transcendence can be recognized again. I begin with Pierre Hadot, for whom philosophy is "a concrete act, which change[s] our perception of the world, and our life: not the construction of a system. It is a life, not a discourse."[6] By exploring Hadot's understanding of spiritual exercises, we gain insight into (1) how they cultivate philosophy as a way of life and (2) how metaxology might be interpreted similarly. I then test my wager by interpreting Desmond's "return to zero" as an exercise in "learning how to die." By pushing nihilism to its limits, this exercise induces not despondency but "a different nihilism: a nihilating of despair in despair."[7] He guides us into the night of nihilism in order to be reborn into a state of what he calls "posthumous mindfulness." Next I consider how posthumous mindfulness attunes us to the poetics of the between, what Desmond calls the "hyperboles of being," as pointing beyond the immanent order (T_1 and T_2) toward actual transcendence or God (T_3). Finally, these hyperboles lead me to propose how metaxology opens to us four "itineraries to the sacred," fitting for those who desire to return to God, in our secular age.

PIERRE HADOT: PHILOSOPHY AS A WAY OF LIFE

Mention of "spiritual exercise," at least in the company of those familiar with Christian spirituality, will likely evoke Ignatius of Loyola's *Spiritual Exercises*. By the idea of "spiritual exercises," Ignatius meant to indicate every method "of examination of conscience, meditation, contemplation, vocal or mental prayer, and other spiritual activities, such as will be mentioned later. For just as taking a walk, traveling on foot, and running are physical exercises, so is the name of spiritual exercises given to any means of preparing and disposing our soul to rid itself of all its disordered affections and then, after their removal, of seeking and finding God's will in the ordering of our life for the salvation of our soul."[8]

The *Spiritual Exercises* unfolds over the course of four "weeks" as the retreatant undertakes a process of coming to know and accept God's will for one's life. The goal of the thirty-day retreat is not to arrive, like a tourist, at a preset destination. Instead, the *Exercises* are a type of spiritual journey or pilgrimage that invites the retreatant to meditate upon and embrace more fully the truths of Christian life. Over the course of these "weeks," one considers the warp and woof of salvation history: the goodness of creation, the consequences of sin and the grace of forgiveness, the life and work of Jesus Christ and his call to discipleship, the mystery of suffering and death, and the triumph of the Resurrection. No bystander, the retreatant is actively engaged in discerning how one is being called by God to live out, now, Jesus Christ's mission. Thus, in place of acquiring more information about Jesus, or about Christianity, the retreatant prayerfully draws near to Jesus in order to "love him more intensely and follow him more closely."[9] Ignatius's *Exercises* are not meant studied but received, prayed through, and lived out in the world by answering one's call to discipleship.[10]

Though regarded as an innovation in Christian spirituality, the *Spiritual Exercises* are not without precedent. Paul Rabbow's *Seelenführung* convincingly demonstrates how Stoic and Epicurean philosophies both contained "*spiritual* exercises of the same kind as we find in Ignatius of Loyola."[11] Extending Rabbow's insight, Hadot observes how the Stoics "declared that philosophy, for them, was an 'exercise.' In their view, philosophy did not consist in teaching an abstract theory—much less in the exegesis of texts—but rather in the art of living. It is a concrete attitude and determinate lifestyle, which engages the whole of existence. The philosophical act is not situated merely on the cognitive level, but on that of the self and of being. It is a progress which causes us to *be* more fully, and makes us better."[12]

Unlike today, where philosophy is typically approached as an abstract or theoretical discipline, ancient philosophy was approached as a *praxis* that engaged the person's mind and body. This insight is a signal contribution of Hadot's scholarship, for he advocates a view of philosophy not just as a disengaged way of thinking but as a fully engaged way of being in the world. Ancient philosophy, he claims, was "above all, a way of life."[13]

Hadot defines spiritual exercises as "voluntary, personal practices intended to bring about a transformation of the individual, a transformation of the self."[14] As Maria Antonaccio observes, "This idea of self-training is at the heart of Hadot's thesis that ancient philosophy was not primarily an abstract mode of discourse, but rather a form of *askesis*, a practice of shaping oneself to an ideal of wisdom."[15] Marcus Aurelius's *Meditations* are not, then, abstract musings on human life but a training manual or guide to daily life. More than 1,800 years after his death, readers who struggle to rise from bed in the morning might follow the following counsel: "When you have trouble getting up in the morning, let this thought be in your mind: I'm waking up in order to do a man's work."[16] So, why read the *Meditations* today? For Hadot, it is because in them we "catch a person in the process of doing what we are all trying to do: to give a meaning to our life, to strive to live in a state of perfect awareness and to give each life's instant its full value."[17] These meditations do not tell one what to think, but they shape how one perceives and lives.

To provide a sense of how philosophy can become a way of life, Hadot distinguishes "between *discourse about* philosophy and *philosophy itself*."[18] *Philosophical discourse* was divided into three parts: logic, ethics, and physics. When "it comes to teaching philosophy, it is necessary to set forth a theory of logic, a theory of physics, and a theory of ethics. The exigencies of discourse, both logical and pedagogical, require that these distinctions be made. But philosophy itself—that is, the philosophical way of life—is no longer a theory divided into parts, but a unitary act, which consists in *living* logic, physics, and ethics."[19]

Stoic philosophy, for example, required putting theory into practice. Epictetus: "A carpenter does not come up to you and say, 'Listen to me discourse about the art of carpentry,' but he makes a contract for a house and builds it . . . do the same thing yourself."[20] Philosophical discourse and philosophical life are incommensurable yet inseparable; presaging Kant, the ancients understood: philosophical discourse without practice is empty, philosophical practice without theory is blind.[21] More colloquially: if you want to talk the talk, you must walk the walk.

How does one move from discourse about philosophy to its practice? How does one learn to live the philosophical life? Unfortunately, "although many texts allude to them, there is no systematic treatise which exhaustively codifies the theory and technique of philosophical exercises (*askesis*)."[22] Still, we have clues. Musonius Rufus, in his *On Exercises*, "affirms that people who undertake to philosophize need to exercise."[23] This provides us with a clue that the notion "of philosophical exercises has its roots in the ideal of athleticism and in the habitual practice of physical culture typical of gymnasia. Just as the athlete gave new strength and form to his body by means of repeated bodily exercises, so the philosopher developed his strength of soul by means of philosophical exercises, and transformed himself."[24] We find, moreover, in Philo of Alexandria two lists of spiritual exercises: "One of these lists enumerates the following elements: research (*zetesis*), thorough investigation (*skepsis*), reading (*anagnosis*), listening (*akroasis*), attention (*prosoche*), self-mastery (*enkrateia*), and indifference to indifferent things. The other names successively: reading, meditations (*meletai*), therapies of the passions, remembrance of good things, self-mastery (*enkrateia*), and the accomplishment of duties."[25]

The range of activities indicates just how "these exercises in fact correspond to a transformation of our vision of the world, and a transformation of our personality."[26] One does not undertake spiritual exercise only to *think* differently; one does so to be-in-the-world in a transformed manner. The goal is to be transformed, not just informed.

A full treatment of ancient spiritual exercises is beyond my scope and exceeds my competence. My hope is to engage Hadot's work to show how philosophy in general, and Desmond's in particular, might be read as a spiritual exercise. I examine philosophy as an exercise in (1) learning to live, (2) learning to die, and (3) learning to read. In each, I try to clarify how philosophy can be undertaken as a way of life and how this approach allows us to read metaxology as a spiritual exercise capable of transforming the way we live in and perceive the world around us.

Learning to Live

For Hadot, "the passage from discourse to life is a tightrope walk that is hard to make up one's mind to try."[27] This seems an odd claim, especially if the goal of ancient philosophy was to transform one's life by raising "the individual from an inauthentic condition of life, darkened by unconsciousness and harassed by worry, to an authentic state of life, in which he attains self-consciousness, an exact vision of the world, inner peace, and freedom."[28] Who would not want to live authentically? As we shall see, putting philosophy into practice requires more than reading about philosophy. It requires self-investment and risk as one undertakes a sustained effort to recognize and retrain one's passions. The tightrope image is apt, for like the Jamesian open space, it depicts philosophy's practitioner as prone to pushes, pulls, and wobbles; no self-assured sage, the real philosopher is forever exposed and vulnerable. One ventures out on the tightrope, steps away from settled certainties, and discovers oneself hovering above an abyss. Bereft of harness or handrail, the philosopher must decide whether to forge onward into the unknown and uncertain or retreat to the known. If we took this risk more seriously, we might well append to Philosophy 101 courses a warning: Beware! Practice at your own risk!

The obstacle to attaining the balance necessary to cross the abyss, let alone taking the first step out upon the tightrope, can be summed up in a single word: *passions*. For the ancients, the "principal cause of suffering, disorder, and unconsciousness were the passions: that is, unregulated desires and exaggerated fears."[29] Each philosophical school regarded philosophy as "therapeutic of the passions" capable of transforming an "individual's mode of seeing and being."[30] Stoics believed "all mankind's woes derive from the fact that he seeks to acquire or keep possessions that he may either lose or fail to obtain, and from the fact that he tries to avoid misfortunes which are often inevitable."[31] Epictetus's *Enchiridion* begins with an observation: "Of things some are in our power, and others are not. In our power are opinion, movement toward a thing, desire, aversion (turning from a thing); and in a word, whatever are our own acts: not in our power are the body, property, reputation, offices (magisterial power), and in a word, whatever are not our own acts."[32] We should focus only on things within our control, for these are "by nature free, unrestrained, unhindered." Things outside our control should be regarded as "weak, slavish, restrained, belonging to others." As a therapeutic *praxis*, Stoicism trained practitioners to discern the difference between what can and cannot be controlled and to find a sense of equanimity as one stood between them. One could take Epictetus's words as a sort of mantra: "Work, therefore, to be able to say to every harsh appearance, 'You are but an appearance, and not absolutely the thing you appear to be.' And then examine it by those rules which you have, and first, and chiefly, by this: whether it concerns the things which are in our own control, or those which are not; and, if it concerns anything not in our control, be prepared to say that it is nothing to you."[33]

Such a transformation of vision does not occur instantaneously nor can it be achieved simply by reading about discernment. It requires concerted effort to recognize disordered passions and to bring these passions into balance. This cannot be done, however, from the safety of an armchair. It requires self-discipline and risk: one must venture out onto the tightrope at some point to test oneself and develop one's balance.

One way to develop the balance integral to the philosophical life is through the practice of attention (*prosoche*). Hadot describes this as "a continuous vigilance and presence of mind, self-consciousness which never sleeps, and a constant tension of the spirit."[34] Attention is cultivated through and enacted as an active stance before the real in which "the philosopher is fully aware of what he does at each instant, and he *wills* his actions fully."[35] Hardly an abstract or purely cognitive act, this attentiveness is an embodied disposition or a way of living in the world. Ongoing practice fosters attentiveness as a *habitus*, a settled disposition; *prosoche* allows its practitioner to concentrate fully on the present moment by bracketing out extraneous and nonessential impingements.[36] Attention makes possible a releasement, a letting-things-be, even in the midst of chaos; instead of trying to control everything exterior to the self, one allows what is other to be other. Arduous work, but not without reward. The fruit of developed attention, as Iris Murdoch observed centuries later, offers "a progressive revelation of something which exists independently of me. Attention is rewarded by a knowledge of reality."[37]

As a practice of metaphysical thinking, metaxology insists on remaining attentive to the ceaseless intermediation between individual beings and between finite being and the transcendent source of being. Metaxological mindfulness does not float above the *metaxu* but, because it knows itself to have been awakened within the *metaxu*, insists on remaining faithful to the ethos. In the *metaxu*, each created entity is an intermediary; the crack of finitude is an opening to the infinite. One needs, though, to develop practices of attention to recognize such signs. Simone Weil, for instance, describes this sort of attention as consisting

of suspending our thought, leaving it detached, empty, and ready to be penetrated by the object; it means holding in our minds, within reach of this thought, but on a lower level and not in contact with it, the diverse knowledge we have acquired which we are forced to make use of. Our thought should be in relation to all particular and already formulated thoughts, as a man on a mountain who, as he looks forward, sees also below him, without actually looking at them, a great many forests and plains. Above all our thought should be empty, waiting, not seeking anything, but ready to receive in its naked truth the object that is to penetrate it.[38]

Attention is a practice through which self-presence grows more receptive to what is other to the self and welcoming to this alterity as it presents itself on its own terms. It requires not an assertion of self, an act of *conatus essendi*, but surrender to the *passio essendi*. To give a popular example of such a surrender, think of Luke Skywalker in the climactic scene of the original *Star Wars*. Amidst heavy enemy fire, he prepares to fire his proton torpedo into the Death Star's structural flaw. As he closes in, he hears the voice of Obi-Wan Kenobi: "Use the Force, Luke. Let Go. Luke, trust me." To the consternation of those in the command post, he turns off his targeting software. He focuses, surrenders himself, fires, and saves the day. Attention did not remove him from the flux but let him be fully present within it. In a far less dramatic way, Desmond observes that "human living is not abstract theory but also practical and ethical. Our being in the midst extends to a mindful way of life and a life of mindfulness. There is something before the contrast of theory and practice, or the subordination of one to the other. Original mindfulness is not so much an act as a passion. It is a patience before it is an endeavor, a receiving before it is an activity."[39]

Metaxology tutors one to live within the vicissitudes of the *metaxu*, mindful that before we take a stand on or grasp at being (*conatus*), we have first to be given to be (*passio*). Metaxology possibilizes a meditative way of dwelling within the *metaxu*, attentive to "certain elemental experiences or happenings, or exposures that keep the soul alive to the enigma of the divine."[40] This is a form of watchfulness keen to discern within the *metaxu* how the "crack" in everything can be interpreted an opening for a potential encounter with the holy.

In the writings of the Stoics, we find techniques for cultivating *prosoche*. One of these, the premeditation on evils (*praemeditatio malorum*) asks us to " represent to ourselves poverty, suffering, and death. We must confront life's difficulties face to face, remembering that they are not evils, since they do not depend on us."[41] William Irvine calls this technique "negative visualization" aimed at rousing us into an appreciation of what we have.[42] He cites Epictetus's advice to parents: when you kiss your child good night, "silently reflect on the possibility that she will die tomorrow."[43] In the next section, we shall consider how Desmond offers a variant of this meditation—the "return to zero"—as a meditative practice necessary to reawaken the sense of astonishment that is the wellspring and vital force of metaphysical reflection.

Another method Hadot describes—the "method of physical definition"—was practiced by Marcus Aurelius. As a teacher, I have found this practice enormously helpful with students who become anxious when facing large or complicated assignments. Instead of seeing it as a monolithic task, you break the project down into its constitutive elements. So broken-down or decomposed, the project is less intimidating. For Hadot, this method permits one to behold a reality "in its nudity, by separating it from the value-judgments which people feel obliged to add to it, whether by habit, under the influence of social prejudice, or out of passion."[44] Sex, when decomposed, becomes the "rubbing together of abdomens, accompanied by the spasmodic ejaculation of a sticky liquid."[45] Music, whether Mozart or Madonna, fares no better:

> A seductive melody . . . you can despise it if you divide it into each of its sounds, and if you ask yourself if you are lesser than each one of them taken separately; if you are, you would be filled with shame. The same thing will happen if you repeat this procedure in the case of the dance, by decomposing it into each movement or each figure. . . . In general, then, and with the exception of virtue and its effects, remember to head as quickly as you can for the parts of a process, in order, by dividing them, to get to the point where you have contempt for them. *Transpose this method, moreover, to life in its entirety.*[46]

Neither music nor dance should induce a person to get "carried away," so by breaking each into its elements, one can gain only on a perspective on it but also, by seeing it as nothing more than an assembly of notes or physical gestures, one gains control over it. This is an exercise in dividing and conquering: even the most daunting tasks can be decomposed into smaller, more manageable, parts. As a way of life, this is a stance of ongoing vigilance within each moment enabling one to resist being overwhelmed even by unexpected occurrences.

Metaxology employs its own method of decomposition. It, too, discerns the voices at play within the happening of the *metaxu*. Space is made for the symphonic interplay between univocity, equivocity, and dialectic. One "decomposes" the senses of being into its parts, not to vitiate the *metaxu* but to discern within each voice its contribution to the happening of the whole. Unlike Marcus Aurelius, for whom decomposition sought to attain to mastery, metaxological decomposition seeks only to expose the "crack" in everything and awaken within the practitioner a sense of the mystery abiding at the heart of being. No single voice can ever exhaust its richness, for the compulsion of every Saying bursts the bounds of every Said. The rhythm of the *metaxu* requires multiple voices to be harmonized and balanced in creative tension. There is a humility attendant to discovering the rhythm pulsing at the heart of being as we are forced to acknowledge that we have not composed this music. Rather than fleeing or freezing the flux, we commend ourselves to creation's song as we are rhythmically drawn ever deeper into being's inexhaustible and mysterious depths.

Learning to Die

The practice of spiritual exercise, whether cultivated through sustained *prosoche* or through dialogue, serves to affirm one's existence. Ascetic practices enjoined by ancient philosophers sought not to absent us from the quotidian flux but to immerse us within it, albeit with a reformed mode of attention. We practice *praemeditatio malorum* to inure ourselves against the inevitable sting of grief; we undertake Marcus Aurelius's "method of physical definition" to see even the most complicated events in their elemental or atomic form. If spiritual exercise allows one to assume a more equanimous stance toward a chaotic reality, it is because it offers a practitioner a different perspective on reality. Any effort to undertake a spiritual exercise, like any attempt to reflect metaxologically, begins as a part of, and not apart from, the world. Even though we cannot take flight into the empyrean and enjoy an unobstructed view of the whole, there are ways to reform and renew the way we occupy the *metaxu*.

No practice better captures the way spiritual exercise affects our perception of the whole than what Hadot calls "learning how to die." Socrates enjoined this in the *Phaedo*: "I think that a man who has truly spent his life in philosophy is probably right to be of good cheer in the face of death and to be very hopeful that after death he will attain the greatest blessings yonder . . . the one aim of those who practice philosophy in the proper manner is to practice for dying and death."[47] Of course, Socrates did not harbor a secret death wish. He recognized, though, that the practice of death surfaces and sifts through our passions; the practice of death is not pathological but purgative:

> Does purification not turn out to be . . . to separate the soul as far as possible from the body and accustom it to gather itself and collect itself out of every part of the body and to dwell by itself as far as it can both now and in the future, freed, as it were, from the bonds of the body . . . any man whom you see resenting death was not a lover of wisdom but a lover of the body, and also a lover of wealth or of honors, either or both.[48]

No morbid fixation, this is an exercise intending "to liberate ourselves from a partial, passionate point of view—linked to the senses and the body—so as to rise to the universal, normative viewpoint of thought, submitting ourselves to the demand of the Logos and the norm of the Good. Training for death is training to die *to one's individuality and passions*, in order to look at things from the perspective of universality and objectivity."[49]

As an exercise, meditating on death is not limited to Plato. The Epicureans, Seneca, Marcus Aurelius, Montaigne, and Heidegger all wrote of it.[50] Since I treat Desmond's version of this meditation in our next section, let me focus here on its effect. Why, one might wonder, would anyone follow Marcus Aurelius's suggestion to keep death before our eyes? "Each of life's actions must be performed as if it were the last."[51] Why, in the West where church attendance continues to decline, is Ash Wednesday one of the more popular services? Why such a popular embrace of a *memento mori* traced in ash that "you are dust and to dust you shall return" (Gen. 3:19)? Even Charon, the ferryman who bears souls across the River Styx, gets in on the act. Even as pop culture croons of remaining forever young, his ghastly admonition resonates: "Vain crea-tures, why have you set your hearts on these things? Cease toiling, for your lives will not endure forever. Nothing that is in honor here is eter-nal, nor can a man take anything with him when he dies; nay, it is inevi-table that he depart naked, and that his house and his land and his money go first to one and then to another, changing their owners."[52]

Is facing mortality therapeutic? To many, I suspect, meditating on death would appear more as a sordid pathology than salutary exercise. Should we not simply embrace life, live each day as it comes, and content ourselves that we know neither the day nor the hour when death will claim us? Why should meditating on death be suggested as a spiritual exercise?

We meditate on death because "training for death is a spiritual ex-ercise which consists in changing one's point of view. We are to change from a vision of things dominated by individual passions to a represen-tation of the world governed by the universality and objectivity of thought."[53] This conversion involves both an inward contraction as one examines oneself and recognizes one's finitude and an outward expan-sion as the soul soars toward the infinite. Delivered from bodily preoc-cupations, the soul takes wing to range across the expanse of the cosmos. By practicing death, one becomes "aware of his being within the All, as a minuscule point of brief duration, but capable of dilating into the im-mense field of infinite space and seizing the whole of reality in a single intuition."[54] We see things from the other side of death; with Charon we look upon the shores of mortal concern and behold how the things we pursue in life—riches, honors, property, power—come to naught. Imag-ining how we would behold the world from the side of death "confers seriousness, infinite value, and splendor to every present instant of life."[55] Passing beneath death's pall renews our sense of the fragility of our finite existence and the sheer caducity of being. Far from nihilistic, vision purged by passing through death comes to behold the oft-missed splen-dor of nature, now seeing how "all things are mutually intertwined, and the bond is holy; and there is hardly anything unconnected with any other thing. For things have been coordinated, and they combine to form one universal order. For there is one universe made up of things, and one God who pervades all things, and one substance, one law, one common reason . . . and one truth."[56]

The practice of death invites us to examine the present moment and "to rediscover a raw, naïve vision of reality" as we behold "the splendor of the world, which habitually escapes us."[57] To view life from the side of death recalls to consciousness that what is past cannot be undone and what is future cannot be controlled: one can act only in the present moment.

Training for death raises us "from individual, passionate subjectivity to the universal perspective" and is ingredient in the philosopher's "greatness of soul" as one purged of illusion and capable of beholding reality as it is.[58] It is seemingly paradoxical: we learn to live well by learning how to die. Yet, like Plato, Pascal saw the importance of this: "We run heedlessly into the abyss after putting something in front of us to stop us seeing it."[59] Meditating on death strips away the various "somethings" we use to conceal the presence of the abyss. We are thereby delivered from the workaday humdrum, the banal rhythm of the quotidian, to a renewed sense of life's gratuity and fragility.

Learning to Read

At the core of any undertaking of spiritual exercise, and consequently at the core of the philosophical life, rests a desire for transformation. One exercises the spirit with a desire to grow in self-knowledge, to gain control over one's passions, and to lead a more authentic and integrated life. The diastole of *prosoche* contracts the soul inward as it cultivates vigilance and a discerning eye on life's essentials; the systole of *metastrophe* expands the soul toward a cosmic view of nature and a sense of being interwoven within the Whole. The goal of these exercises is a self-formation, of coming to realize and actualize one's potential. Rather than conformity to a social standard, one undertakes these practices to achieve authenticity. The process of uncovering the authentic self admits of multiple metaphors: spiritual gymnastics, Plotinus's image of sculpting, or Plato's allusion to Glaucos, the sea god whose true figure remains hidden until shorn of its barnacles. Each metaphor expresses how spiritual exercises liberate the practitioner by uncovering and recovering the true self.

The philosophical life cannot, for this reason, seek to avoid personal upheaval and reorientation as one embarks on this recovery of the true self. No exercise promises immediate results, and the philosopher will often find herself in an ambiguous place, unsure of whether she is closer to the end or the beginning, nearer to captivity or to freedom. Although this intermediate state often requires periods of solitude for introspection and self-examination, it is not a solitary endeavor. Ilsetraut Hadot describes how, with the rise of philosophical schools in Athens, the philosopher became a "spiritual guide" (*kathegemon*) or "the one who leads, who shows the way."[60] One stands in relation to one's teacher or master, who instructs the student in this way of life. She continues: "In the fourth century BC, all philosophical schools had regarded the written word, the book, only as a temporary measure in place of personal instruction. For Plato the only valid form of philosophical instruction was a dialogue, which consists of questions and answers—dialectic. This form of instruction actually presupposes the active participation of the student, because the dialectical dialogue can only proceed when the respondent gives critical approval at every stage of the dialogue—that is, when questioner and respondent, teacher and student, reach agreement at every stage of thought."[61]

Dialogue between student and teacher, or the inner dialogue required for an ongoing examination of conscience, is unending. The point of philosophical dialogue is not to arrive at a solution, but rather it is to journey along the road together in search of the truth.

Both Hadots suggest the need to approach philosophical texts as dialogue partners. Pierre: "I always prefer to study a philosopher by analyzing his or her works rather than trying to uncover a system by extracting theoretical propositions from these works, separated from their contexts. The works are alive; they are an act, a movement that carries along the author and the reader."[62] A text must be approached as an interlocutor: one must be implicated in its unfolding dialogue, and allow oneself to be questioned and, in turn, be willing to question the text. What Sandra Schneiders says of scripture seems applicable here, for approaching a philosophical text as a dialogue partner means "taking a chance on hearing one's name called at close range."[63]

The challenge we face today, Pierre Hadot contends, is that we have forgotten how to read. We have forgotten how works of philosophy and theology emerge from within life of an author and the author's community. Scripture scholars, of course, know well the importance of the *Sitz im Leben* for exegesis. Yet how many courses present Plato or Augustine, Aquinas, Hume, or Nietzsche without putting them into context? How often do theologians succumb to a form of "theologology" or "talking about talking about God" without actually undertaking philosophical reflection or, dare one say, encouraging prayer?[64] To be sure, it is no mean feat to identify an argument, evaluate its merits, and assess its overall coherence. But Hadot rightly resists reducing philosophy to merely analyzing a text's argument. Philosophy, like theology, should be approached as an exercise teaching us how to read again by training us "how to pause, liberate ourselves from our worries, return into ourselves, and leave aside our search for subtlety and originality, in order to meditate calmly, ruminate, and let the texts speak to us. This, too, is a spiritual exercise, and one of the most difficult."[65]

Commendably, Desmond recognizes how a text's poetic dimension can inform and form a reader. Reflecting on his own work, he writes: "One can find some extremes of abstract dialectic—I can do that—leaving some readers exasperated or gasping for more familiar concreteness—and then, by contrast, the eruption of another language—poetic—seemingly entirely other, imagistically concrete, too concrete for some abstract thinkers. Some of my readers are discomfited by this doubleness. Others, I am happy to report, approve of it in some way. Perhaps the mixture of being discomfited and being moved has something right about it."[66]

Metaxology weaves the abstract and the concrete to refresh our mindfulness of the dynamism of the *metaxu*. Instead of "the system," Desmond provides his reader with an invitation into a meditative consideration of what it means to be. The poetics of the text, intermingling the abstract and the concrete, induce a sense of dis-ease and disorientation. This interplay throws us off step and exposes those places where our pattern of thought has fallen into a rut and how we have grown inured to the plurivocity of being. Metaxology's poetics force us to slow down and to discern the voices at play within the text and, over time, in the *metaxu* itself. Think of it like wine tasting notes: it is one thing to read about the wines but a wholly different, and more engaging, matter to taste for oneself and detect the various flavors present within each vintage. Metaxology develops our metaphysical palate.

In this vein of spiritual exercise, we should see Desmond as teaching us how to read within the space between philosophy and religion. Of his own upbringing he writes: "If the influences shaping me as a young person were those of a strong Irish Catholicism, this was one in which something like a pagan appreciation for the earth was not absent, and no absolute incompatibility between these two was felt. This reflects a feel for nonhuman nature as a creation in which traces of the enigmatic God are not absent."[67] Desmond, you might say, trains us to discern these traces, to stand between philosophy and theology and discover that they are separated not by an insuperable wall but by a porous threshold. Each possesses its own integrity, but this is an integrity-in-relation because both attempt to respond to the intimate strangeness of being. For the philosopher, the intimate strangeness is disclosed in moments of natural wonder; for the theologian, it is disclosed in divine revelation. Instead of relegating each to its own silo or pitting one against the other, Desmond leads us to the threshold between them and invites us to consider, paradoxically, how the poverty of philosophy and religion actually betokens their richness.[68] To occupy the space between philosophy and religion necessitates reflecting on being-as-given and, mindful of the "crack," reflecting on the giver-of-being. Learning to read Desmond's philosophy as a "poetics of the between" does not lead to conceptual mastery over the *metaxu* but enhances one's ability to recognize the mystery at the heart of being that flows into and animates philosophical and theological inquiry.

We turn now to immerse ourselves in the "poetics" of metaxology by exploring how it "works" to renew our mindfulness of the between. Although these exercises are analogous to the *psychagogy* of Platonic or Stoic practices, they possess a pronounced theological character, rendering them *mystagogic* exercises. As I argued previously, metaxological metaphysics originates in being awakened by the advent of transcendence; it is, first and foremost, a response to the poetics of the *metaxu*. In this it is akin to the way "a bicycle's movement provided for its lights. In the night one needs a light that illuminates and allows one to guide oneself (this is theoretical reflection), but in order to have light, the generator has to turn by the movement of the wheel. The movement of the wheel is the choice of life. Then one could move forward, but one had to begin by moving for a very short time in the dark."[69]

Our first exercises explores how metaxology teaches us "how to die." We begin by peddling in the dark, beneath the "eclipse of the transcendent" in the hope that by turning our metaphysical wheels we might produce light enough to navigate the darkness.

METAPHYSICS AS *ASKESIS*: "RETURN TO ZERO" AND POSTHUMOUS MIND

It is time to test my wager that Desmond's metaphysics can be undergone as a form of spiritual exercise. Metaxology, to borrow from Charles Taylor, can be "tested in practice."[70] To test a theory in practice means "not to see how well the theory describes the practices as a range of independent entities; but rather to judge how practices fare when informed by the theory."[71] Approaching metaxology as a "way of life" requires reading the text with a willingness to be informed about a style of metaphysics and to be formed or transformed by undergoing it.

Given my interest in Desmond's contribution to theology, I focus primarily on *God and the Between*, which concludes a metaphysical trilogy published between 1995 and 2008 and manifests a rich maturing of his thought.[72] There is a pragmatism behind this choice: few readers will work through the whole of the thinker's oeuvre. Given my interest in encouraging theologians to "take up and read" Desmond, this is an ideal text because it can be read as a performance of philosophical theology. *God and the Between* unfolds in four parts. Part I, "Godlessness," gives a tour of modernity's "godless" ethos. He asks readers to consider whether we are bereft of the divine or, perhaps, we have been bewitched into thinking true the madman's cry: God is dead. In part II, "Ways to God," Desmond equips us to sojourn in the desert of atheism by identifying a series of metaxological "indirections" capable of renewing our sense of God. In part III, "Gods," he explores various concepts of God and identifies what is true, and what is incomplete, in each. In part IV, "God," he embarks on a project of philosophical poetics. Through a series of metaphysical cantos, he invites us to rethink the traditional attributes of God. Each canto expresses, in poetic form, the germ of what he explicates in prose. This is a radically innovative approach without, it seems, parallel in contemporary Continental philosophy: we are guided and drawn into a series of poetic passages—a poetic porosity—to encounter the divine anew.

Finally, I believe Desmond offers our age something akin to what Jean LeClercq describes as *philosophia*, or a practice designating "not a theory or a way of knowing, but a lived wisdom, a way of living according to reason."[73] What LeClercq observes of Rupert of Deutz applies equally to Desmond: Rupert writes "with such a deeply religious feeling and such a rich poetic orchestration that he awakens in his reader new conceptions of mysteries."[74] And I should hasten to add that my proposals here are exploratory and experimental: Desmond does not cast his thought within the mold of "spiritual exercise." Yet I recall one of the epigraphs to *The Intimate Universal* where he cites Matthew 13:51–52:

> "Have you understood all this?" The disciples said, "Yes." And Jesus said to them, "Well, then, every scribe who becomes a disciple of the kingdom of heaven is like a householder who brings out from his storeroom things both old and new."

I want to venture into metaxology's storeroom and bring to light "things both old and new" and offer them to the inquisitive reader. Instead of "showing and telling," I invite readers to "taste and see," to experience for themselves the promise and potential of metaxology as an ascetic practice.

As a Jesuit priest, my spiritual roots—my Ignatian slip!—will be apparent.[75] A son of Ignatius, I begin by giving a metaxological "composition of place." Next, I follow Desmond's invitation to undergo the throes of nihilism in a meditation he entitles the "Return to Zero." Finally, I examine the "fruit" or "grace" of this exercise by considering what Desmond calls "posthumous mind." If this succeeds in suggesting how this exercise might inculcate a renewed mode of metaphysical consciousness, in the next section I can consider what posthumous mind permits us to perceive.

Composition of Place: The Reconfigured *Metaxu*

As we mentioned, there survives no extant treatise codifying the practice of ancient spiritual exercise. Yet, given the rootedness of Ignatius's

Spiritual Exercises in ancient soil, it seems warranted to use his text as a template for reading metaxology as a part of this tradition. For although the content of the exercises varies over the course of the retreat, the approach one takes to each meditation remains basically the same. Before entering into each prayer period, Ignatius counsels the exercitant to offer a preparatory prayer: "Ask God our Lord for the grace that all my intentions, actions, and operations may be ordered purely to the service and praise of his Divine Majesty."[76] What Hadot observed of ancient practices remains true even within contemporary approaches to Ignatian spirituality: one undertakes the exercises with a desire for transformation. After this prayer stating one's desire, Ignatius turns to a "first prelude" called the "composition of place." Michael Ivens comments, "In imaginatively composing a place or situation corresponding to the subject of prayer, one 'composes oneself,' in the sense of 'getting oneself together,' or becoming recollected."[77] One recollects, deliberately and thematically, where one is now and how one stands before God. One steps back from the quotidian to gain perspective on one's life. Composition of place is not a flight from the real, but an intensification of attention to it, allowing the present moment to manifest itself fully. This is an Ignatian iteration of *prosoche* whereby one opens oneself to being addressed by the real. For Ignatius, all creation—from our innermost desires to nature's beauty—can be a locus of encounter with God.

A metaxological "composition of place" begins in "the between" and reflects on how our age has reconfigured the primal ethos. For Desmond, our age has been configured according to the drive of the curious mind: "The momentum of modernity dominantly conceives our development as away from astonishment and perplexity towards as definite a determinate cognition as possible."[78] This momentum can be variously described. One might see it as a "coming of age story" in which scientific materialism "is seen as the stance of maturity, of course, of manliness, over against childish fears and sentimentality."[79] For New Atheists, such as Sam Harris, Richard Dawkins, and Daniel Dennett, any vestige of mystery needs to be exorcised. Our era, it seems, has been entranced by a Cartesian dream of *mathesis universalis* that inspires "an unprecedented will to univocalize being."[80] Thus we try to fit the whole of being into the Procrustean bed of univocity. Anything that cannot be counted by univocal categories—Plato's Good, revelation's God, or a sense of final causality—

is written off as wooly. Loss of final causality, especially, exacted a toll because, as Michael Buckley writes, "the self-enclosed physics of Descartes was established as autonomous, however much it might find its roots in first philosophy. Once launched, it was on its own with matter in movement inevitably finding its predetermined contours. With the Universal Mathematics, Descartes removed any final causes, any notae or *vestigial* of god, from the world."[81] A point of contrast: Augustine heard creation sing of its Creator, whereas the Cartesian universe is mute. Descartes's universe invokes an ontotheological god as a divine linchpin to hold the system in place. Heidegger rightly rolls his eyes. Before this god, there can be no singing and dancing.

Our composition of place, stated metaxologically, must acknowledge that today we live in an era wherein "our *conatus essendi* seems rather spurred into an activism, a self-activation that can lead even to an extreme of hyper-activism. Then the *passio essendi* is forced into recess as the *conatus essendi*, expressing itself without hindrance, goes into overdrive."[82] A hypertrophied *conatus* coupled with the devaluation of being leaves us in a state of ontological nihilism. Modern thought has, Desmond notes, grown accustomed to the standard "distinction of fact and value. We think of being as there, just there, a fact or set of facts. We think of values as human constructions that are imposed or projected on the otherwise valueless being. By itself, being is worthless. The degrading of being's value is itself the product of the mind of mathematical and scientistic univocity; it lacks the sense of metaphysical integrity that the univocal can sometimes reveal. This scientistic univocity produces ontological nihilism."[83]

Given this image of the human agent as sole author and determiner of being's value, it is little wonder we see the development of an antinomy between autonomy and transcendence. As Ludwig Feuerbach puts it: "To enrich God, man must become poor; that God may be all, man must be nothing."[84] So also Zarathustra:

Before God! But now this God has died! You Higher Men, this God was your greatest danger.
Only since he has lain in the grave have you again been resurrected.
Only now does the great noontide come, only now does the Higher Man become—lord and master.

Have you understood this saying, O my brothers? Are you terrified:
do your hearts fail?
Does the abyss here yawn for you? Does the hound of Hell here
yelp at you?
Very Well! Come on, you Higher Men! Only now does the mountain of mankind's future labour. God has died: now *we* desire—that
the Superman shall live.[85]

The self-assertion of autonomy has no tolerance for talk of God.
Zarathustra: *If* there were gods, how could I endure not to be a god?
Therefore there are no gods.[86]

Louis Dupré captures well the consequence of modernity's ethos:
"In the present situation, the very reality of the transcendent is at stake,
more than its specific conceptualization. The very possibility of a relation
to the transcendent in the modern world has come under fire."[87] In *God
and the Between*, Desmond offers a metaxological spin on this insight:
"Third transcendence (T_3) has been made problematic in modernity,
both by a univocalizing objectification of first transcendence (T_1), and by
developments of second transcendence (T_2), especially when this last defines itself in terms of its own autonomy. Then a logic of *self-determination*
stands guard over all our thinking, and the thinking of what is other to
our self-determination."[88] For Desmond, in an age moved by a drive to
univocal determination, actual transcendence can neither be measured
nor managed, and so cannot count. Any self-transcendence (T_2) fixated
on preserving autonomy cannot but deem actual transcendence (T_3) as a
threat. In this configuration of our ethos, we are drawn to Zarathustra,
for if we cannot be gods, then the gods must be rejected. Given this
hostile antinomy, the "eclipse of the transcendent" is a triumph of the
human.

Desmond refuses to retreat from this eclipse whose shadow engulfs
our ethos. In fact, Desmond insists we stand firm beneath its hoary light
and think through the consequences of our growing sense of godlessness.
He wants us to compose ourselves within a milieu bereft of God, an
ethos that possesses no value other than what we endow it with. He invites us, in short, to ruminate on the implications of a thoroughgoing nihilism. "Valueless being leads to nihilism," he writes, and "it does not
matter whether by a scientific, political, or aesthetic route."[89] Indeed, it is

hard not to see the signs of such nihilism surrounding us: ecological crises, surging nationalism, global poverty and inequality. As Pope Francis observes in *Evangelii gaudium*: "Today we also have to say 'thou shalt not' to an economy of exclusion and inequality. Such an economy kills. How can it be that it is not a news item when an elderly homeless person dies of exposure, but it is news when the stock market loses two points?"[90] Nietzsche extolled the will to power as a substitute for God's death: "*This world is the will to power—and nothing besides! And you yourselves are also this will to power—and nothing besides!*"[91] Yet, if we have truly succeeded in "wiping away the entire horizon" and "drinking up the sea,"[92] these words seem cool comfort. For Desmond, "if all being is valueless, we too are valueless finally, in the valueless whole, and all our brave, heroic valuing is swallowed by the valueless whole."[93] Severed from a creative origin, is not every instance of self-assertive striving little more than a "tale, told by an idiot, full of sound and fury, signifying nothing"?[94] Beneath the eclipse, we must stand within the "Desmondian open space," where we feel the buffets and pull of the wind and the tension of the crushing silence of the *nihil*.

Our task now is to discern the nature of this *nihil*: Is the silent darkness a devastating negation, a sign of God's utter absence or nonexistence? Or perhaps what appears as the engulfing darkness of the eclipse is but a prelude requiring us, as its first act, to feel the force of Aristotle's observation: "For as the eyes of bats are to the blaze of day, so is the reason in our soul to the things which are by nature most evident of all."[95] We are not undertaking this exercise to perceive another world but to see if we might come to behold our world otherwise. In in the depths of its darkness, we must strain to discern within the *nihil* some sign, some intimation, of the divine light that portends the eclipse's reversal.

Exercising Nihilism? The "Return to Zero"

Desmond's "return to zero" is a meditation on the implications of the loss of the divine. It is meant to *exercise* and to provoke those undertaking it. He writes: "Suppose though there is *some* truth to nihilism. Suppose the origin is worthless, the world void of inherent value, our energy of being either reactive to or transformative of this worthlessness. What then? No transformation we can effect will change the basic truth of being: It all comes to nothing. But this outcome also includes *us*, and all our grand projects come to nothing. Our reconfiguration of the primal ethos comes to lack any ultimate point."[96]

Existence is worthless. Nothing we do can change this: the absence of value goes all the way down and includes ourselves. The weight of nothingness presses upon us and penetrates the marrow of our being. In this meditation, we are meant to experience "such coming to nothing in our knowing, our doing, our feeling for life."[97] Desmond wants us not only to *think about* but to *feel* how the crush of the *nihil* recasts our lives. We are implicated in the following:

1. *Knowing*: the more we rationalize life the more life seems to lack reason. Englobed by the *nihil* of nihilism, the *ohne warum* (without why) of the rose is hardly a mystical insight, the threshold of reason. Without a determinate *why* reason comes to see itself a surd.
2. *Doing*: Nietzsche's "will to power" may encourage us to leave our mark upon being, but what fuels this courage?
3. *Feeling*: "the élan of life is drained when we lose the aesthetic feel of the agape of being." We move from cheap thrill to cheap thrill—think of the popularity of horror films—but, in the end, it all comes to nothing.[98]

We are indeed clever animals, capable of any number of ruses to anesthetize ourselves against the *nihil*. So, embrace the implications of nihilism and experience the consequences of sheer finitude. Desmond extends a dark mirror and asks, "Can you see yourself? Can you feel in your blood the icy despair of this nothingness?"

In effect, Desmond invites us to stroll along the shore of Matthew Arnold's Dover Beach where we stand at the shore and behold how

The Sea of Faith
Was once, too, at the full, and round earth's shore
Lay like the folds of a bright girdle furled.
But now I only hear
Its melancholy, long, withdrawing roar,
Retreat, to the breath

Of the night-wind, down the vast edges drear
And naked shingles of the world.[99]

Desmond would have us stand resolutely upon this "darkling plain."
He bids us to discern within the "melancholy, long, withdrawing roar"
not the end of belief but a silent prelude to a renewed porosity to God.
Passed the gall of *nihilism*, we drink it to the lees.

As an exercise, the "return" asks us to undergo the shattering of nihilism. We must feel for ourselves the full weight of nothingness: "We
do come to nothing. We are as nothing: a double ambiguous conjunction
of being and nothing. We are but as nothing, and experience our nothingness as the frailty of our finitude, as the perplexity of being that resists being dispelled, as the mystery of being that remains despite our
best conceptual maneuvers. The truth brings us to despair of truth, and
of ourselves, and of the good. Nihilism, the truth of nihilism brings us to
despair of God."[100]

This is not the ersatz nihilism of teenage angst. Nor is Desmond
dispassionately informing us about nihilism. This is an *askesis*, a practice
undertaken in order to feel fully the force of the *nihil*. In this exercise,
none is spared the blow of Nietzsche's *Götzen-Dämmerung* as its blows
shatter our idols and bring to nothing even the greatest monuments to
our *conatus essendi*. This exercise leads us into the desert—Shelley's "an-
tique land" or Dupré's desert of modern atheism—where we cannot
evade a sense of tragic irony:

Look on my Works, ye Mighty, and despair!
Nothing beside remains. Round the decay
Of that colossal Wreck, boundless and bare
The lone and level sands stretch far away.[101]

The "return" forces us to face a bleak reality: everything comes to
nothing. The inherent instability and equivocity of being—the "crack in
everything"—inflicts on all finite beings a wound of constitutive nothingness. Ozymandias's epitaph strikes the heart, but not for the reason
he envisioned. What had once been an awesome sight intended to evoke
despair in his enemies remains a source of the deepest despair: the

ravages of time reduced his monument to rubble and will do likewise to our endeavors. Despair indeed. All being is as nothing and will return to the nothing. Finite reality bears the trace of this nothingness. Freighted with this knowledge, we behold our achievements and utter a despondent repetition of Aquinas's assessment of the whole of his work: *mihi videtur ut palea*—"to me it seems like straw."

This evocation of "despair" has theological resonance. The setting of the First Week of Ignatius's *Spiritual Exercises* weaves the retreatant into a dialectic of sin and grace, brokenness and wholeness. One despairs of sin, not to elicit or compel God's mercy, but as a response to realizing the depths of God's love. Despair as a dark grace: we despair of sin as we recognize how feeble our "no" is when placed against the infinite horizon of God's "yes." Our despair becomes a purgative prelude to a revitalizing encounter with God. The paradox of despair's grace echoes in Karl Rahner's Lenten reflection delivered in 1945. Both the nihilist and the fervent believer can find common ground when Rahner writes that the measure of "the true greatness of man is to despair. Only such a despaired one, who has finished and figured out everything and has noticed that behind everything there is nothing, is the actual, the true man, who has elevated himself above the everyday bourgeois, who bravely and honestly professes the only greatness of man that there is: the honest realization of man's nothingness; the greatness of man is the knowledge of his misery."[102]

The nihilist accepts nothingness as a sign of courage and maturity, a mark of having cast off the immaturity of faith. The believer, too, commends herself to the nothing. She knows that true despair dispels illusions, shows the caducity of our idols, and exposes the emptiness of the human heart and its longing for ultimate fulfilment. Yet the believer stands resolute and does not shy away. Thus, Rahner continues in imagery familiar to an audience who had lived through bombing raids, to exhort his listeners to abide within their "rubbled-over hearts" because

> when you stand firm and don't flee despair, nor in despairing of your former gods—the vital or the intellectual, the beautiful and the respectable, oh, yes, that they are—which you called God, if you don't despair in the true God, if you stand firm—oh, that is already a miracle of grace which shall be bestowed on you—then you sud-

denly will become aware that in truth you are not at all rubbled-over, that your jail is closed only to empty finiteness, that its deadly emptiness is only the false appearance of God, that his silence, the eerie stillness, is filled by the Word without words, by him who is above all names, by him who is everything in everything. And his silence tells you he is there.[103]

Like Rahner, Desmond unflinchingly confronts the winnowing darkness and learns that "whatever can be taken from you is never God."[104] The crisis of despair ("crisis" from the Greek *krinein*, "to decide") rouses us from somnolence and demands we take a stance: "In a paradoxical way, the night of *nihilism* may come to the aid of metaphysical mindfulness. For this night makes *the light itself* perplexing. It makes us wonder if we really know anything important at all, even as we progressively come to know everything determinate."[105] Thus false gods disintegrate beneath the weight of despair, the breakdown of the idols need not break us. Amidst the dust and rubble, this breakdown makes possible God's breakthrough into the darkness. Coming to nothing enacts a purgative route to unclog and reopen being's porosity to what is beyond being. This is an exercise meant to actualize the double potency of *meta*physics: a mindfulness aroused amidst beings that is directed to what is beyond being.

Plato saw philosophy as a training for death, a catalyst for a conversion of the soul. Marcus Aurelius, too, exhorted himself to a mindfulness of death in order to remain attentive to the present moment: "Each of life's actions must be performed as if it were the last."[106] With them, Desmond hears the grating whisper: *memento mori*. Yet Desmond does not want merely to be mindful *of* death but to become possessed of a mindfulness that has passed through and been purified *by* death. Thus, he writes, "the return to zero may be the nihilism of despair, but it need not only be that. It may be a different nihilism: a nihilating of despair in despair."[107] The poetic force of Desmond's prose is apparent in the following:

One wanders a desert that bleaches with burning light, or one is exiled to a Siberia of soul that freezes, or one is fleshed together with perishing, as with one's Siamese twin; one has become as nothing, and one is kissed, before one knows it, by the angel of death. What is the kiss? It is a Golgotha of our human hubris. The kiss opens our sightless eyes. One sees the same things but sees the sameness as other. The wings of the angel beat quietly but in the unbearable terror of her approach being suddenly shows the beauty of thereness as absolute gift. Being is given, and it is given for nothing—nothing beyond the goodness of its being, and of its being given. The terror liquefies the world that one has fixed. The world configured as worthless also seems to dissolve. Something else is offered: a taste of the elemental goodness of the "to be"—abundance without a why, beyond the sweetness of its being at all. Here commences the reversal of nihilism, and a redoubled search for God, for we seem to be given again, redoubled in being.[108]

Recalling the double sense of "poetic," consider first the rhetorical power of the text. This is not an indifferent description but a passionate appeal; from arid desert to frigid tundra to the shadow of death, Desmond wants to involve the whole reader into undergoing this meditation. Carnality and sensuality abound as we are kissed, taste, and see with purged eyes. In a single passage, a phantasmagoria of images and metaphors; the text is saturated with a too-muchness verging on the overwhelming and the hyperbolic.

Desmond seeks, literally and literarily, to "throw us over" (*hyper* + *ballein*) into the happening of which he speaks. Again, rather than telling about this happening, the text implicates the reader in the unfolding of the angel's wings and allows us to undergo the "kiss of death." We are drawn rhetorically into an elemental happening, invited into a purgative unmaking that both threatens and promises some form of remaking. The rhetorical saturation the passage performs by throwing the reader into this *poiesis*, which renews our perception of reality. This is not a proof or a dispassionate argument. It is a passionate wrangling ("passion" from the Latin *patior, pati, passus sum* = to suffer) aimed not at changing minds but at transforming perception. The text is an arena of encounter where, like Jacob at the Jabbok ford, we wrestle with a shadowy figure who seems intent on our demise. We strain against our opponent and at daybreak find ourselves victorious. Successful passage through the "return," however, carries a cost. Jacob limped away from his nocturnal battle with a dislocated hip. Similarly, we suffer an existential dislocation:

the "return" allows us to behold the world with eyes purged by death's kiss. If we sojourn in the desert, we do so as Israel's heirs, as those who struggle with God.

This is a fraught proposition. The "return" is a painful process. We undertake it and risk the shattering of our idols, the dissolution of our illusions, and all of this may lead to the utter despair of godlessness. Yet, amidst the dust and rubble, one may catch sight of the outline of the Angel of Death. Amidst the wreckage and debris of the conatus essendi there is an inbreaking of light and we behold with astonishment the gratuity and nonnecessity of creation: all that is, is, though it need not be. No longer neutral or valueless, we behold being in its elemental goodness. For Bede Griffiths, as Taylor recounts, this is the moment of conversion when the buffered layers are transpierced and the world is viewed, or better re-viewed, with renewed eyes. Even the sky, for Griffiths, was experienced as too awful to behold because "it seemed as though it was but a veil before the face of God."[109] To use a more traditional metaphor, the "return" is a via purgativa through which "we find ourselves in the reversion to what we are without God, which is nothing."[110] Without God we are nothing, yet we are not nothing: we are. We have being, not as something earned or owed, but as a gift.

As an ascetic practice, the "return" functions as a purgative exercise intended to "unclog" our primal porosity and reawaken us to the passio essendi. In a way, it is an archaeological undertaking that leads us downward into the depths of being itself, depths paved over by modernity. This exercise intends to transform our disposition toward creation into one of "deep openness to the ontological enigma of the 'that it is' of beings."[111] The anarchic shattering of the nihil uncovers the archē of existence itself and awakens us to its overdeterminacy. "This is," Desmond writes, "the elemental wonder of metaphysical astonishment: astonishment at the sheer being there of the world, its givenness as given into being, not the 'what' of beings, but 'the that of being at all.'"[112] The kiss of death opens our eyes to the goodness of the elemental ethos whose vibrancy has been covered over or anodized by modernity. Our return to our origin releases us for "a new interface with creation,"[113] mindful of creation's goodness and attentive to the Creator's call. The poetics of the text permit a return to the origin so that we may come to perceive, in the metaxu, the God who is creation's origin and end, its alpha and omega.

Posthumous Mind

Willingly undertaken as a spiritual exercise, meditating through the "return to zero" cultivates a "way of mindfulness, beyond the reductive alternatives either of being as reduced to a particular finite teleology (the kind that some attribute, not justly, to premodern views) or of being as reduced to the valueless world of modernity, be it the worthless thereness of the scientistic picture, or the purposeless being beyond good and evil of Nietzschean becoming."[114] Dubbed "posthumous mindfulness," it is a recurrent theme in Desmond's work. In *Philosophy and Its Others*, he describes it as "a thinking from the future when we are dead, about the ontological worth of the present, imagined from beyond death as our past. (The Irish call death *slí na fírinne*: the way of truth)."[115] With roots tapping into ancient practices, posthumous mindfulness describes how passing through death revitalizes what it means to live:

> So imagine this: what would it be like to die, and come back to your home after a hundred years? Would you like to see everything changed, utterly changed? Would you be dazed? Would you be lost? What would you mourn? What are the nameless, intimate things we now love, and which in our posthumous return we would delight to greet again? Or rather, the intimates of being that might greet us, like old, trusted friends? These things have no name in the technicist's vocabulary, no price in the economist's world. Yet they give charge to life and worth of a different sort. What do we love now, that its loss or desecration would grieve us to the roots on our return? If we cannot name any golden thing, anything that now blesses being, anything that we would want to perpetuate into the future, perpetuate even beyond our death and regardless of death, has not life become metaphysically bankrupt?[116]

For one accustomed to analytic argument, this cannot but be bamboozling. To my mind, the way to make sense of passages such as this—other than writing them off as digressions—is to apply Hadot's observation about ancient philosophers: they "did not aim, above all, to provide a systematic theory of reality, but to teach their disciples a method with which to orient themselves, both in thought and life."[117]

As a way of beholding, posthumous mind stands in continuity with yet moves beyond its forebears. Like Plato, Seneca, and Marcus Aurelius, Desmond's meditation is "linked to the contemplation of the Whole and elevation of thought, which rises from individual, passionate subjectivity to the universal perspective. In other words, it attains to the exercise of pure thought."[118] Still, this "pure thought" does not involve any disengaged, disinterested, or neutral stance toward reality. The posthumous-minded person is not a voyeur peering into the flux or one who stands apart from reality. The opposite is the case: the "return" brings about a rebirth of astonishment at being's givenness. "The kiss of the angel of death awakens posthumous mind to the thought of God," Desmond observes, because "coming to nothing awakens us to finitude as finitude, and thus also to the beyond of finitude in the very gift of finitude."[119]

The reader's eyes glaze: "Enough poetics! Grasp the nettle and give an argument!" Desmond demurs, "there is no absolutely univocal way to God."[120] Any return route must traverse a more indirect pathway. He cites Dostoevsky as an exemplar because, "on the morning of his first death," he undergoes a rebirth of mindfulness:

> He was sentenced to death for political conspiracy. He was halfway into death, on the verge of execution, tilted over the brink of nothing. There was no geometry of death to help. But he was suddenly reprieved, brought back from death, resurrected to life again. The sweetness of the morning air struck him, the song of morning birds, the sky. He was stunned into marveling at the sheer fact of being. This is the resurrection of agapeic astonishment. But it is experienced in a blinding and a groping. Will systematic science ever do justice to what is communicated in this stunning and resurrection?[121]

Unexpectedly drawn back from the abyss, Dostoevsky perceives everything with renewed senses. He sees the world with reborn eyes: he stared into the abyss and his eyes were purged by death. His reprieve gives him, as it were, a "new lease" on life attuned to the very goodness and gratuity of existence. "To be" can no longer be taken *for* granted because, having confronted its fragility, it is beheld in astonishment *as* granted.

Desmond's point is that there are modes of mindfulness beyond Pascal's *esprit de géometrie*, even if these other modes lay fallow or dormant. Indeed, in an increasing secular Western world where the natural order is regarded as "finite and nothing but finite,"[122] one finds it increasingly difficult to imagine, let alone speak, of the inherent goodness of creation. It is as though our minds and tongues have been bewitched with a curse that curtails our patterns of thinking and speaking. Indeed, he asks: "Is it possible that an age could fall under a bewitchment? Could it be that especially since the early nineteenth century many of the major intellectuals of the era live under the bewitchment of godlessness?"[123] What if our age has fallen under a spell and lulled into a sleep of finitude that prevents us from recognizing God?[124] We encountered this spell earlier: postulatory finitism. As a bewitchment, postulatory finitism delimits the agenda of questions our age is permitted ask. It truncates the horizon of our imaginations and ties our tongues to prevent the God question from being raised. Postulatory finitism bewitches us into living *als ob*, "as if," the question of the Ultimate has lost its ultimacy and has ceased to be a live or valid question. Within an ethos dominated by the instrumental mind and mathematical precision, God becomes an irrelevant hypothesis. Still, as Dostoevsky reminds us, there are modes of mindfulness capable of perceiving the elemental goodness of "to be"—even if these modes are wrought through a near-death experience. This leads me to ask: If many in our age have been bewitched into this sleep of finitude, if perhaps we ourselves have felt a sense of drowsiness as our eyelids droop with skepticism, is there no countercharm available? Can this bewitchment be broken?

Alas, there is no technicolor prince(ss) whose kiss can rouse us from our age's slumber. Desmond, though not quite Prince Charming, offers a way of lifting the enchantment. The route he offers is perilous, for it leads along the dark route of nihilism; he asks us to risk the "return" and to push postulatory finitism to its limits. He challenges us to submit to the scourge of the *nihil*, to be flayed by thoughts of coming to nothing, to watch powerlessly as idols erected by the *conatus* crumble. He asks us to sit next to Job, to weather these losses, and to cry into the maelstrom, "I know that my redeemer lives!" (Job 19:25). With Desmond as our guide, we pass through death but do not die; indeed, we are stirred into wakefulness. We sense a seepage, a trickle, as primal porosity unclogs. So we drink from the uncovered well, from a spring ever ancient and ever new, and are regenerated and see the good of "to be." The scene of the breakdown of finitude's idols, after the night of godlessness, occasions a breakthrough. Awakened from the sleep of finitude, we are reborn and released into the world with revitalized senses attuned to perceive the gratuitously given gift that is creation.

MINDFULNESS REBORN: IDIOTIC, AESTHETIC, EROTIC, AGAPEIC

We approach the "return" as a spiritual exercise with a hope of being released from the bewitchment of postulatory finitism. We submit to the Angel of Death's kiss and are plunged into the dark night of the *nihil*. As all our ploys and plans, schemes and schemas crumble, it seems as though all is lost: every stone laid down as testimony to the power of the *conatus* is pulverized and turned to dust. This, though, is hardly the end of the story. For just as the great wave of darkness threatens to suffocate us wholly, the tide turns and rushes out. We are left, gasping for air, and find our eyes and senses to have been purged. We taste and feel and hear and see and smell the elemental goodness of the *to be*, of *our* being, and we behold the *metaxu* anew. Admittedly, we have strayed far from any univocal logical argument—posthumous mind is not the result of a syllogism. It is, rather, the fruit gathered by undertaking, by undergoing, a process that jolts us from somnolence into wakefulness, we traverse a way from life to death to new life. Renewed, one is astonished as the primal ethos shines forth once more.

Posthumous mindfulness resituates the way we abide within the *metaxu* and understand ourselves within the community of transcendence (T_1 to T_3). A rekindled *passio essendi* reminds us that before we take a stand on being, we are given to be. In the fluid intermediation of the porosity of being, we know that *to be* is, mysteriously, to be related to all other beings. The "return" guides us downwards, past the mantle of the reconfigured depths, and commends us to the infernal abyss where our senses are purged and purified. Porosity restored, we grasp how we participate in the *metaxu*'s drama of coming to be and passing away. Yet being's universal impermanence, the mortal wound left by the "crack" in everything, elicits no dirge but a paean to the Creator. Having passed through the way of death, *slí na fírinne*, we behold all things anew. A dark grace, but grace nonetheless.

One must undergo the "return" to grasp, or be grasped by, the power of metaxological metaphysics. Like Taylor's ad hominem argument, this meditation capacitates us to view the *metaxu* from a better vantage point. Just as Taylor does not tell a different history but narrates history differently, so posthumous mind gives us to perceive reality anew. In the next four subsections, I describe how the "return" renders us attentive to the hyperboles of being: idiotic, aesthetic, erotic, and agapeic. We encounter these hyperboles within the immanent order of the *metaxu*, but, as hyperboles, they "throw us over" (*hyperballein*) toward the transcendent dimension. Again, Desmond's hyperbolic language is not merely a form of rhetorical poetics because it performs to direct the reader's attention beyond the between toward God (T_3). In chapter 4, I treat more fully *how* each of these ways offers an "indirection" to God; here, though, I consider *what* posthumous mind gives us to behold within the *metaxu*.

The Idiocy of Being

In modernity's reconfigured ethos, being is taken for granted. To the curious-minded, nature is no more than a neutral substrate to be examined, manipulated, and mastered. Yet, as Desmond describes Dostoevsky's near-death experience, one's perception of the world can be transformed by staring into death's abyss. The world ceases to be "just there" and is seen as though for the first time. There is a disorientation as one is wrenched from the ruts of everyday practice and put on new footing. How many uncounted and unnoticed breaths had Dostoevsky taken before the morning he was to be executed? Pulled back from the brink, he felt his senses purged. Instead of taking his breaths *for* granted, he knows them *as* granted, as gifts. The way of death allowed Dostoevsky, and those who undertake the "return," to reoccupy the present by reawakening them to the singularity, or what Desmond calls the *idiocy*, of being.

By no means is "idiocy" pejorative. Recalling its Greek roots (*idiotes*), Desmond wants "idiocy" to convey a sense of "what is private, intimate, not publicly political."[125] This idiocy "goes to the roots of intimacy of self-being, our pre-objective, indeed pre-subjective, powers of being. Here we come alive again to the porosity of our own being and its *passio essendi*."[126] We find ourselves unclogged, our senses purged, because we are struck by the incommunicable excess of being. The world is beheld as though for the first time and with reignited astonishment. Yet idiocy is not solipsistic, it does not entail any closure upon the self. Idiocy bespeaks a happening, an irruption within the immanent order that opens us to behold the ethos astonished *that anything is at all*. We are propelled outside of ourselves (T_2) in self-transcendence because we find ourselves addressed by and implicated within the happening of exterior being (T_1). The idiocy of being draws our attention to the intimate strangeness of being, a mysterious familiarity so famously captured by Augustine's sense of God as *interior intimo meo* (more intimate to me than I am to myself).[127] What we experience as the idiocy of our being sensitizes us to the idiocy and utter uniqueness of all being. To be at *all*, is to be a being of inestimable ontological value.

Exercising the "return" cultivates an idiotically reborn mindfulness, and this in two ways. First, it occasions a renewed sense of the gratuity of being: *It is!* yet need not be. The fragility of being reminds us that all finite being is marked by a constitutive nothingness: it is, for now, but will eventually cease to be. Posthumous mind, without being blind to this fragility, has a sense of the elemental goodness and gratuity of being. Second, idiotic rebirth affects the way we dwell within the community of beings. Rather than casual onlookers, we are engaged participants in the *metaxu*. Self-transcendence responds to the abiding presence of being's intimate strangeness and bids us to dwell amidst exterior being in a renewed way.

We find in Wittgenstein a similar development in appreciating being's idiocy. Recall how he begins his *Tractatus* with the following propositions:

1.   The world is all that is the case.
1.1.   The world is the totality of facts, not things.
1.11.   The world is determined by the facts, and by their being *all* the facts. [128]

Early in the *Tractatus*, it seems the entirety of world is subsumed into a univocal logic. All that is can be examined as an amalgamation of facts. Yet, at the text's conclusion, there occurs something of a "mystical" upheaval. Wittgenstein's initial attempt to reduce the world to atomistic proposition breaks apart as language cannot exhaust or constrain reality:

6.4321. The facts all contribute only to setting the problem, not to its solution.

6.44. It is not *how* things are in the world that is mystical, but *that* it exists.

6.45. To view the world sub specie aeterni is to view it as a whole—a limited whole. Feeling the world as a limited whole—it is this that is mystical.

6.522. There are, indeed, things that cannot be put into words. They *make themselves manifest.* They are what is mystical.[129]

As he writes in 6.54, his "propositions serve as elucidations" akin to rungs on a ladder allowing us to climb beyond the propositions. Once we have ascended and reached the summit, we kick away the ladder and "see the world aright."[130] He seems to have intuited the "crack" within atomic facts and, rather than mourn the caducity of his system, interpreted these cracks as openings to the inbreaking of divine light.

My point: within the quotidian round, the idiocy of being is easily submerged and forgotten. It is as though we develop cataracts preventing us from seeing the shine of the primal ethos through the chinks and cracks in every era's reconfigured ethos. Denise Levertov puts her finger on this phenomenon of growing deaf or forgetful and being roused once more to mystery:

Days pass when I forget the mystery.
Problems insoluble and problems offering
their own ignored solutions
jostle for my attention, they crowd its antechamber
along with a host of diversions, my courtiers, wearing
Their colored clothes; cap and bells.
         And then
Once more the quiet mystery
Is present to me, the throng's clamor
Recedes: the mystery
that there is anything, anything at all,
let alone cosmos, joy, memory, everything,
rather than void: and that, O Lord,
creator, Hallowed One, You still,
hour by hour sustain it.[131]

The poem begins as a melancholic ode to metaphysical amnesia, to our propensity to forget the mystery of existence amidst the cacophony of life. Problems and distractions clutter the mind; diversions and distractions push now this way, now that way. Primal mystery, wonder's wellspring, becomes clogged and forgotten as each day's demands divert our attention.

Nevertheless, although the courtiers' clamor distracts, they have no power to squelch or exorcise mystery. It abides silently beneath the text's surface, and its advent can rouse us once more from our somnolence, refresh our memory, and renew our porosity. Indeed, the poem itself possesses a textual "crack" separating the first and second stanzas. The poem is porous and recalls its readers to the porosity so often forgotten amidst the din of daily life. Mystery unexpectedly announces itself, and the poet, and the reader, is led into its depths. The result is a renewed sense of being's idiocy and a renewed mindfulness of what is and remains in excess of any system. Our grasping at being (*conatus*) is forced to relax into and recognize the primal *passio*, the originary address of being that remains beyond our control. The woo of mystery calls us to recognize the abiding presence of the intimate universal who abides within our depths and who somehow sustains the whole of creation. With mystery's advent, problems cede to praising as the poem resolves in a doxology born and reborn in primary wonder.

The Aesthetics of Happening

The capaciousness of posthumous mind is reflected both in its ability to be astonished that being is and in its openness to being astonished by the particularity of any given being: that *this* is. For Desmond, in aesthetic rebirth "astonishment becomes ontological appreciation of the incarnate glory of the manifest creation which, showing itself sensuously, exceeds finitization. Native to the material world, our nativity is saturated with rich ambiguity resistant to our intervening domestications. Appreciation of immanence passes a threshold of immanence into mysterious love of transience that exceeds transience."[132]

If this description of this is not entirely clear, perhaps it would help to think of how a father holds his newborn infant. This is not a baby like any other baby, for it is *this* child, *my* child whom I love beyond all telling. The exquisite fragility of each finger and toe, the boundless potential of a life, is swaddled in a blanket and placed gingerly within the father's eager arms. He makes contact, physical contact, not with an anonymous future but with this future, this being, who has a name: *my* daughter, *my* son, *my* beloved.

Aesthetic rebirth reweaves the astonished subject into the community of being. We move from a Cartesian subject-object or disengaged apprehension of the world and find ourselves in congress with reality. This results in a renewed sense of togetherness:

> This togetherness is both "objective" in that *it is there*, out in the world, and "subjective" in that *it is here* in the concrete thereness of our fleshed presence to the world. I call the rebirth aesthetic, because aesthetic invokes both *ta aesthētika* of other-being and *aisthēsis* on our part. There is an immediate dynamic flow back and forth between the aesthetic things and our *aesthēsis*, a fluency richly articulated, though not acknowledged initially in our reflective categories. Our patience of being vibrates in attunement with the saturated glory of creation.[133]

Aesthetic rebirth erupts in ecstatic affirmation: This is beautiful! My precious! My child! There is a surplus incapable of being exhausted by any words. It attunes us to beauty in general and renders us receptive to each being's unique beauty. At no point are we voyeurs peeping in on beauty, at no time do we see without being seen; our flesh, our incarnate being, locates us sensually within the *metaxu*. Caputo and Kearney assent, for we are neither delivered from the flux nor absolved from the call to attend to the needs of those around us: the widow, the orphan, the stranger. The intimate strangeness of being we know idiotically is encountered concretely in and through the face of the other, the stranger, the neighbor.

One literary instance of aesthetic rebirth is found in *The Little Prince*. When the Little Prince meets the fox, he is in a state of sorrow because he has found that the rose on his planet is not unique: in a garden he finds 5,000 roses like his. When he meets the fox, he invites the fox to play with him. Yet the fox demurs and says, "I am not tamed." To tame, the fox observes, "means to establish ties." The bond of friendship, forged over time, transforms the way they behold one another. When they become friends, when they establish ties, then, "To me, you will be unique in all the world. To you, I shall be unique in all the world." In a deceptively simple manner, Antoine de Saint-Exupéry's text guides us into the *poiesis* of friendship. After they become friends, and before the prince leaves to continue his journey, he revisits the rose garden. Once more he stands before the roses but regards them in a new light:

> "You are not at all like my rose," he said. "As yet you are nothing. No one has tamed you, and you have tamed no one. You are like my fox when I first knew him. He was only a fox like a hundred thousand other foxes. But I have made him my friend, and now he is unique in all the world. . . . You are beautiful, but you are empty," he went on. "One could not die for you. To be sure, an ordinary passerby would think that my rose looked just like you—the rose that belongs to me. But in herself alone she is more important than all the hundreds of you other roses: because it is she that I have watered; because it is she that I have put under the glass globe; because it is she that I have sheltered behind the screen . . . because it is she that I have listened to when she grumbled, or boasted, or even sometimes when she said nothing. Because she is *my* rose."[134]

Aesthetic rebirth equips one with eyes to discern within the ordinary the penumbra of the extraordinary. There is a reopening of one's porosity to what is other to oneself. When the boy returns, the fox shares a secret: "It is only with the heart that one can see rightly; what is essential is invisible to the eye." This rebirth graces those to whom it is granted a second sight, an ability to perceive reality's hitherto concealed depths.

Aesthetic rebirth leads us to experience what Duns Scotus called *haecceitas*, the "thisness," of each finite being. Being is not neutrally present, mutely there, but is an active presencing that announces itself. Thus the "self" is not a discrete monad but communicative center of being. "To be a self," Desmond writes, "is to be a distinctive center of the original power of being."[135] He continues: "This original power is not a static determination but evidences a process of determining, and hence in itself is more than any determination. In that respect we are not dealing with *static* substance. But we could call self a thing, if we remember that things are not static unities; they too are concretions of the original power of being; things are determinate wholes that carry the trace of the overdetermined origin, and hence are never closed in on themselves."[136]

Instead of speaking of "the self," Desmond riffs on the work of Gerard Manley Hopkins and refers to an ongoing process of "selving" to capture how beings intermediate with and communicate themselves to one another. Here he echoes a refrain found in the work of Norris Clarke: "To be fully is to be substance-in-relation."[137] Hopkins explores selving in poetic verse:

> Each mortal thing does one thing and the same:
> Deals out that being indoors each one dwells;
> Selves—goes itself; *myself* it speaks and spells,
> Crying *What I do is me: For that I came.*[138]

The sensuous manifestation of being calls out to each of us. Moreover, this is not "a being" in any type of autistic or solitary unity. Each being, each self, bespeaks and proclaims itself in many and various ways: in the cry of the child, the power of the hurricane, the delicate beauty of the dew-covered rose, the taste of rosé as one contemplates the purple-and-orange gloaming of a summer's evening. Aesthetic rebirth refocuses our attention not on the broad category of "beauty" but on instances of it. Instead of a broad sweep of Beauty we are provoked into beholding singular instances of it made manifest in individuals. We return to Kearney: "Transcendence in a thornbush. The Eucharist in a morsel of madeleine. The Kingdom in a cup of cold water. San Marco in a cobblestone. God in a street cry."[139] Posthumous mind discerns how each being's singularity—its *haecceity*—proclaims and points toward its origin in the Creator. To those graced with second sight, physical reality is sacramental; all of creation, to recharged and reborn eyes, discloses God's presence.

The Erotics of Selving

The "idiocy of being" and the "aesthetics of happening" are both hyperboles of being that focus on our apprehension of beings outside of ourselves, beings of what we have denominated exterior transcendence (T_1). Although we are finite beings, we are "infinitely self-surpassing"[140] in and through acts of self-transcendence (T_2). Our capacity for self-transcendence comes from the advent or address of what is exterior and transcendent to us. For Desmond, we are endowed "with transcending power, but we do not endow ourselves. The immeasurable passion of our being as self-exceeding exceeds also the selving we are. It witnesses to a more primal porosity to what exceeds us. This erotics of selving is hyperbolic to a *conatus essendi* that drives itself to its own most complete self-determination in immanence. The *passio essendi* is marked by a primal porosity to what exceeds all determination and our own self-transcending."[141]

As we have discussed, eros cannot be defined solely by any sense of thoroughgoing indigence or lack. The progeny of Poros and Penia, Eros is marked by an enriched poverty, bearing within itself a promissory note guaranteed by Poros's resources. Through the "return" we are made "intimate again with this gifted poverty, and in the elemental eros of our being. To become mindful of the porosity is to come closer to the primal ethos."[142] It is an archaeological endeavor, entering into our intimate depths to uncover fertile resources too easily concealed on account of the incessant grasping of the *conatus*.

The "return" unclogs and reawakens us to the porosity of being. One turns inward and is struck by what Desmond calls the urgency of ultimacy, an "absolute, infinite restlessness for the absolute or the ultimate that is not satisfied by any finite good."[143] Drawing attention to our restlessness, reborn erotic mindfulness resists the seductions of idolatry in its search for the object of its love. As we discern the inherent equivocity of being—the "crack"—we find, like Augustine, that no finite being can ever satisfy us.[144] But rather than give up in frustration, we peer through the "crack" and look toward the creative origin of all being. Our most intimate desire is animated by the presence of a superior transcendence whose advent or call piques our appetite for the infinite and catalyzes our quest for fulfillment.[145] Reborn eros, mindful of the *passio*, affirms each finite being yet continues to move beyond finite being in its quest for the infinite. Every affirmation of finite being is accompanied by a negation as though one were to say inwardly: "You are *a* being, yet you cannot sate my hunger for the infinite. I long for ultimacy." Desire's restlessness orients and directs us toward something more.

Revitalized eros does not forsake the *conatus*, but corrects and balances it by re-emphasizing the priority of the *passio*. Where contemporary notions of "the erotic" tend to accent the *libido dominandi*, or the drive toward sexual conquest, Desmond's sense of eros is possessed of no such impulse. For him, the erotic is an openness to being "wooed" and being "willing to wait in love."[146] He describes wooing as "a distension of eros that is true to the intimacy of the *passio essendi*. There is a kind of readiness for gift in this, as when we truly listen to music. We hope to be hearers because we are ready to be patient listeners. There is a kind of obedience in wooing, and the porosity asked of the attendant is again not unlike a kind of praying. . . . Wooing is the *passio*, faithful to the porosity of love, waiting in patient readiness for the surprise of the other, the gift of the secret beloved."[147]

Westphal's call for a "humble metaphysics, acknowledging that it rests on faith and not pretending to be the Voice of Pure Reason"[148] resounds. Prayer's woo cannot be regarded one's own accomplishment, as though we compel the Holy One to speak. On the contrary, Desmond writes, "prayer at heart is not something that we do. Prayer is something that we find ourselves in, something that comes to us as we find ourselves already opened to the divine as other to us and yet as an intimate communication with us."[149] Having passed beneath the Angel of Death's wings, unclogged Eros allows itself to be wooed by the intimate universal abiding in the deepest recesses of one's being: "When we cry 'Abba! Father!' it is that very Spirit bearing witness with our spirit that we are children of God" (Rom. 8:15–16).

Hopkins hauntingly explores the contours and tensions of eros in his poem-prayer "Nondum" (Latin for "not yet"). The poem's epigraph comes from Isaiah 45:15, "Verily Thou art a God that hidest Thyself." The twenty-two-year-old poet writes:

> We see the glories of the earth
> But not the hand that wrought them all:
> Night to a myriad worlds gives birth,
> Yet like a lighted empty hall
> Where stands no host at door or hearth
> Vacant creation's lamps appal.

We guess; we clothe Thee, unseen King,
With attributes we deem are meet;
Each in his own imagining
Sets up a shadow in Thy seat;
Yet know not how our gifts to bring,
Where seek Thee with unsandled feet.

In these verses, an unfulfilled longing for the *deus absconditus*, the "hidden God." Hopkins voices his ache and struggles to see creation pointing toward the Creator. Unable to endure the silence, mortals "clothe Thee, unseen King" according to our own image and likeness; God becomes *imago hominis*. The poem swells with grievous sorrow as the Divine refuses to break its alienating silence. Hopkins endures; he continues to traverse "life's tomb-decked way" and invokes "patience with her chastening wand." The final verse:

Speak! whisper to my watching heart
One word—as when a mother speaks
Soft, when she sees her infant start
Till dimpled joy steals o'er its cheeks
Then, to behold Thee as Thou art,
I'll wait till morn eternal breaks.[150]

In no way does this prayer seduce or compel God's disclosure. Hopkins waits, attentively, and endures a dark night. He effects the stance of a listener, a potential hearer, one who takes up the night watch for any sign of the Holy One's advent. Rahner captures this dynamic when he describes our anthropology: "We are the beings of receptive spirituality, who stand in freedom before the free God of a possible revelation, which, if it comes, happens in our history through the word. We are the ones who, in our history, listen for the word of the free God. Only thus are we what we should be."[151]

With the balance between the *passio* and *conatus essendi* restored, the eros reborn in the posthumous mind permits us to dwell within the community of transcendence anew. Nourished at the wellspring of the *passio* and mindful of being's porosity, the antinomy between autonomy and transcendence dissolves. Freedom *for* self-transcendence (T_2) is achieved not despite actual transcendence (T_3) but because of it. In embracing the equivocity of being, in pondering the "crack," we undergo "a negation not nihilistic."[152] Every negation affirms; each *no* to the finite acts as a silent *yes* to the infinite for which we reach. Eros, metaxologically chastened, refuses to settle on any idol falsely promising to fulfill our longing. Self-transcendence thus becomes an eccentric and ecstatic other-reaching, open and hospitable to the advent of the divine. Born-again eros, purged by passing through nihilism's night, discovers at its core a paradoxical empty fullness. It is here where the heart's deepest wound, the "crack" that provokes anxiety and mortal terror, opens and we are wooed into its depths. What, or Who, we often seek beyond ourselves is found now within our innermost recesses. Reborn eros leads us further along Desmond's Augustinian odyssey from the exterior to the interior where we encounter the God *interior intimo meo et superior summo meo*—"more interior (to me) than my most intimate intimacy and superior to my highest summit" (*Conf.* 3.6.11).

The Agapeics of Community

Just as the rebirth of eros leads one to recognize the intimate universal abiding in the depths of one's being, the resurrection of *agape* allows one to see all being as relational: "Nothing is alone, hence the idea of finitude as for itself alone, and nothing other, cannot be taken as the last word, or the first. The agapeics of community intimates a surplus generosity that makes itself available in an absolved porosity of the *passio esssendi* that ethically lives itself as a *compassio essendi*. This is a sign of something more than the ethical, since it incarnates the holy."[153] Astonishment does not permanently bowl one over, but it removes the scales from our eyes that so often prevent us from seeing ourselves as members of the *metaxu*. An unclogged *passio essendi* testifies against any autism of being. With purged and renewed senses, we read creation's givenness as a sign of *compassio essendi*. Creation is undergone by the whole community of the *metaxu*; we undergo God's givingness along with (cum-passion) every other being. Solidarity is not a stance or political position but the deepest ontological reality of existence. This is, for Desmond, a "graced patience" that undergirds and subtends all of our actions meant to further the good of others "even if it does little or nothing to serve the advancement of some agenda of the servant."[154]

Desmond does not regard *eros* and *agape* as contradictory. Like the *conatus* and the *passio*, they are twins. In our age, however, we tend to overstress the erotic at the expense of the agapeic.[155] Too easily do we forget that the movement of eros is a response to *agape*'s call. Eros is indeed a seeking, but its intentionality is directed by an anterior agapeic address. In this, eros "seeks more than itself in seeking itself because its energized striving is already empowered by a secret agapeic surplus to which it is (called) to remain true, though it is free to turn it away and turn itself awry."[156] An agapeic address catalyzes all erotic striving. Self-transcendence (T_2) does not blindly cast about but is animated and directed by the agapeic woo of actual transcendence (T_3). For those who remain true to this agapeic woo, they can roam about the *metaxu* in an endless pilgrimage in search of the One for whom their heart longs. For those who betray this call, those who grow deaf, they grasp *this* or *that* finite thing, convinced that it will satisfy their deepest hunger. The "return" seeks to destroy these idols and allow the agapeic summons to be heard once more and restart our spiritual pilgrimage.

In *Perplexity and Ultimacy*, Desmond asks, "Is there an agapeic mindfulness that transfigures the ugly?"[157] Faced with the loathsome, the abominable, or the grotesque, is there anything capable of stirring within us a response of love? Desmond takes St. Francis of Assisi as an exemplar of agapeic mindfulness. Paul Crowley expresses a similar sentiment when, drawing on Kazantzakis's *Saint Francis*, he describes how Francis "prays to God to ask what more God might be asking of him. He has already restored the church of San Damiano and given up everything else for God. Yet he is riddled with fear of contact with lepers. He confides to Brother Leo: "Even when I'm far away from them, just hearing the bells they wear to warn passers-by to keep their distance is enough to make me faint." God's response to Francis's prayer is precisely what he does not want to hear: he must face his fears and embrace the next leper he sees on the road. Soon he hears the dreaded clank of the leper's bell. Yet, Francis moves through his fears, embraces the leper, and even kisses his wounds."[158]

For Crowley, "it is only by driving into the reality of suffering, and not evading it, that one can find a pathway to hope and encounter with the sacred."[159] There is an overcoming of fear by undergoing what he fears most: in the leper's embrace, Francis submits himself to death and is born again to behold Christ's figure in each leper, the one who had neither "form nor comeliness" (Is. 53:2), the one who appeared in history marred and despised, the "stone the builders rejected" who is now the cornerstone (Ps. 118:22).

Francis's kissing of the leper hardly reflects sober calculation. And this is the point: the figure of Francis is hyperbolic, he provokes us into pondering what fuels his actions by "throwing us over" ordinary logic. For Christians, Francis is an embodied testimony to agapeic hyperbole; he enacted the love received from God, and in and through his life, he testified to a new logic, a theo-logic, that vexed his father and inspired generations of followers. Viewed with posthumous mind, we see how *agape* cannot ever admit of a logical mean or calculation. As Aquinas observes, "Never can we love God as much as He ought to be loved, nor believe and hope in him as much as we should. Much less therefore can there be excess in such things. Accordingly, the good of such [theological] virtues does not consist in a mean, but increases the more we approach to the summit."[160] Posthumous mind remains attuned to this excess and is energized by it. So, too, Taylor writes: "What has always been stressed in Christian agape is the way in which it can take us beyond the bounds of any already existing solidarity."[161] *Agape*, he continues, "moves outward from the guts; the New Testament word for 'taking pity,' *splangnizesthai*, places the response in the bowels."[162] The woo of *agape* loosens the grasping hands of the *conatus* and relaxes them into the open receptivity of the *passio*. Francis kisses the leper not out of self-loathing but as an act of other-affirmation; in embracing the leprous other he discovers, beneath disfigured flesh, the face of a transfigured brother.

Let us contrast Francis's diurnal encounter with the leper with Zarathustra's "Night Song." Francis undergoes a dark grace when, moved by an agapeic *compassio essendi*, he embraces the leper. He awakens to a porosity empowering his movement through fear into a new way of beholding: moved by *agape* he embraces the figure of death and, through *agape*, he is reborn. Nietzsche, too, sings porosity but in a nocturnal key. *Das Nachtlied*, for Desmond, "is perhaps one of the most beautiful things Nietzsche has written, and yet for all its energy of self-affirmation, it is full of a nameless sadness, of something missing or missed."[163] For rather

than an agapeic embrace of alterity, it is a hymn sung in praise of absolute autonomy:

> Light am I: ah, that I were night! But this is my solitude, that I am
> girded round with light.
> Ah, that I were dark and obscure! How I would suck at the breasts
> of light!
> And I should bless you, little sparkling stars and glowworms
> above!—and be happy in your gifts of light.
> But I live in my own light, I drink back into myself the flames that
> break from me.
> I do not know the joy of the receiver; and I have often dreamed that
> stealing must be more blessed that receiving.
> It is my poverty that my hand never rests from giving; it is my envy
> that I see expectant eyes and illumined nights of desire.[164]

Zarathustra's song performs a parodic absolution. Whereas Francis's
prayer leads him into communion with the leper, the *Nachtlied* absolves
him from community. The contrast is stark: Francis's porosity is a freedom *for* relationship; Zarathustra extols his freedom *from* it. Francis's
prayerful openness to God (T_3) transforms how he dwells in the *metaxu*.
Such a deep weaving into the *metaxu* is not available to Zarathustra, for
he regards himself a mediator, a giver, and in no way as receiver. The
Holy Fool faces fear and finds agape; touched by the *compassio essendi*, he
is made a lover of all. The Ultimate Man hungers for wickedness as
"spite wells from my solitude" yet no draught slackens his thirst "which
yearns after your thirst."[165] Zarathustra's song incarnates utter absolution
(*ab-solvo*): from himself and by himself, alone.

To be reborn into the agapeics of community is to find oneself
porous to the divine intermediations at play within the *metaxu*. Renée
Köhler-Ryan beautifully expresses this: "In our elemental attentiveness,
we should become like beggars at the table of divine fullness: confident
in the riches of divine communication; and humble and sincere enough
to recognize and request them."[166] We are far from voyeurs peeping into
the *metaxu*; we are, on the contrary, active participants in its community. Unclogged through the "return," we regard ourselves not as being's masters and possessors of being but as "gifted beggars" who receive

everything as a gift. To know ourselves as graced is to know the *compassio essendi* that inverts the will to the power: instead of self-assertion, the *compassio essendi* ethically empowers its recipients to will and work toward the good of the other. And, in solidarity with the created order, we can be struck by the agapeic love of community and inquire into the ground that gives rise to such generosity and empowers acts of self-sacrificing love and devotion. In recognizing the agapeics of community, we see how the *metaxu* shimmers with signs pointing beyond "the between" toward God.

A SUBTLER EXERCISE: THE POETICS OF THE BETWEEN

The reader will not have missed my references to and engagement with poetry. This is deliberate: there are times when poetry, or music, or art communicate more than prose. Indeed, metaxology requires us to speak of being between, of the *metaxu*, with many voices. There are times when abstract language may be appropriate; other times require a defter touch. Sometimes a concept must be allowed to sing; elsewhere, one must feel fully the gravity of thought. Poetry demands intentionality: one must linger on the words and allow the meaning of the verse to unfold. Verses must be savored, stewed over, and meditated upon. To draw this chapter to a close, let me cite Desmond's poem that begins a chapter entitled "Beyond Godlessness":

> We have looked too low
> The ground beneath us
> Falls away
> & joy leaps up in us
> Out of nothing
> Leaps out of itself
> & the elemental world is there
> Again
>
> In the leap
> Joy looks up

As well as out
We dare no longer
Look too low
We look for more
Again

The poem recounts a double rebirth. First, there is the rebirth of the "elemental world" arising through the sudden surge of joy. Recall the image of the furrowed brow: the curious-minded person is hunched over and fixated on a determinate *this*. Then the ground gives way and what was secure is destabilized; one is caught off guard as "joy leaps up" as one unbidden yet not unwelcome. Rocked back, we behold the world again as we stand, anew, amidst (*meta*) beings with senses purged and open by an agapeic force beyond (*meta*) being.

This joy is our joy yet not ours; familiar yet foreign; intimate yet strange. Joy buoys our gaze, granting it an outward view over being and an upward view beyond (*meta*) being. Suddenly, one is extricated from the sediment and freed to roam again. The wound of joy disallows us to remain fixed in place and thwarts complacency. We are no longer permitted to look "too low," so our expectant eyes scan the horizon and sit vigil as one awaits patiently, attentively, the advent of the one who has stirred us from our slumber and bid us to sit the night watch. We sing as we keep vigil.

Desmond's poem guides the reader through two rebirths and expresses in poetically compressed form the trajectory of Desmond's entire chapter. The reader, to borrow the title of a collection of essays honoring Desmond's thought, is led to occupy a space between system and poetics. Within this space, one can learn the grammar of metaxology. Being tutored in the grammar of metaphysics, however, is not enough. It must be practiced. As Desmond observes, "The metaxological space of the intimate universal is always a communal setting for conversion, for *metanoia*. There is a metanoetics of the metaxological: being born again, a second birth in the dimension of the hyperbolic."[167] Metaphysics, rightly approached, can become a disciplined mindfulness open to the very goodness of the "to be" of existence.

Drawing on Pierre Hadot's work, I argued for approaching Desmond's thought as a form of "spiritual exercise." The nonnegotiable *terminus a quo* for this approach is "a real desire to dialogue."[168] As with any spiritual exercise, one must embark on it with a willingness to undergo the transformation of one's life. This spiritual exercise is a pilgrimage, a journey of seeking and finding aimed at transforming the one who sets out on it. Whereas a tourist follows a preplanned itinerary, moving from defined point to defined point, the pilgrim's route is shrouded in mystery. For the *terminus ad quem* of spiritual exercise is not a physical destination but a reorientation of one's life and a transformation of one's vision. One sets out from the workaday world upon a quest not to conquer but to encounter, not solely to be informed but to be gradually formed and re-formed as one opens oneself to the divine.

I tested my wager by reading Desmond's "return to zero" as an exercise in death. This is an exercise where one lives the shattering of nihilism and experiences, paradoxically, a graced nihilism: "a nihilating of despair in despair."[169] As Renée Köhler-Ryan observes, this experience of nothingness places Desmond in the company of Augustine and Aquinas: "Augustine's *nihilne plus* and Thomas's *videtur mihi ut palea* each speak to Desmond of the nothingness which is the 'return to zero' without which knowledge of God and of self, as sources of transcendence in intimate relationship to each other, are impossible."[170] Read as an exercise, the "return" unclogs our primal porosity as idols erected by the *conatus essendi* crumble under the *nihil*'s weight. Amidst the rubble we are struck into astonishment at being's gratuity: *being is!*—yet need not be. Posthumous mind is a graced affliction, an unwanted wisdom: by exposing the paltriness of finitude, it reminds us that no thing within the *metaxu* will ever satisfy desire. Yet, now that we see the "crack" in everything, we discern within the hyperboles of being a glimmer of hope. Signs encountered within the *metaxu* direct us—albeit indirectly—toward the origin and ultimate fulfillment of our restless longing.

Reading Desmond in this way allows his poetic metaphysics to led us subtly into a renewed awareness of the *poiesis* of being. In fact, Desmond's exercises contour and finesse the way we perceive and respond to the happening of the between; metaxological *aesthesis* enables us to recognize ever more deeply a metaxological *poiesis*. This is needful because, as Taylor notes of our era, "the constitutive, revelatory power of language is totally sidelined and ignored, or even denied. This understanding of language-use is correlative with a stance in which we treat things, and even each other, in purely instrumental terms."[171] Our language has been bewitched into the sleep of finitude and needs to be awakened. Herein lies the promise of poetic speech: because it "doesn't already rely on already recognized structures"[172] it can provoke readers to see things in a new way. Poetry requires us to pause, to ponder, and to probe the world in the text's light. Poetry, Taylor continues, "opens new paths, 'sets free' new realities, but only for those for whom it resonates."[173] Desmond's poetics opens new paths and, as we shall consider, reopens old ones. Metaxological poetics revitalizes our appreciation for the depth of language and, by attuning us to the hyperbole of being, transforms how we perceive the *metaxu*. Reborn *aesthesis* perceives more deeply the *poiesis* of the between, and this *poiesis* continues to influence our *aesthesis*. To draw once more on Taylor, metaxological poetics is less designative, neutrally pointing toward the happening, than constitutive.[174] Metaxology's attentiveness to the poetic "gives us a picture of language as making possible new purposes, new levels of behavior, new meanings."[175] In this way, it is a capacitating language enabling those tutored not to perceive a different world but to be attentive to the poetics of reality in a new and different manner.

If posthumous mind enables us to recognize the hyperboles of being and to discern the presence of the "crack" in everything, then we must explore how we might read these signs not only as being open to transcendence (T_3) but as serving as passageways or itineraries leading those who embark upon them toward an encounter with God. A metaxological approach to the hyperboles reveals pathways capable of leading seekers through a mystagogical process that renders them increasingly aware of the mystical element present in, and disclosed through, the *metaxu*.

FOUR

Exercising Transcendence

Indirect Ways to God

One must lose oneself in a state devoid of particular form or measure,
a state of darkness in which all contemplatives blissfully lose their
way and are never again able to find themselves in a creaturely way.
In the abyss of this darkness in which the loving spirit has died to
itself, God's revelation and eternal life have their origin, for in this
darkness an incomprehensible light is born and shines forth.
　　　　　　　　—John Ruusbroec, *The Spiritual Espousals*

When approached as a spiritual exercise, Desmond's "return to zero"
shifts how we perceive the world. Stated in a more traditional idiom, the
"return" guides us along a *via purgativa* and, by bringing us *to* and *through*
the nothing, renews our sense of creation's nonnecessity and gratuity. It
is, though it need not be. The "crack" in everything, beheld with purged
eyes, is read as a sign of creation's gratuity. The "return" acts as an *askesis*
of what Desmond calls "agapeic nihilism." To ponder the crack, to be
stunned by creation's existence, is to ruminate on the fact that God cre-

ates for no reason, creates out of no selfish need. Yet this "*nihil* is not any negating or destructive *nihil*. God does nothing for Himself; everything is done for the other. There is a sense in which nothing is *for* God. God lets be, since everything given by God is for that thing, given for that thing itself."[1] We undergo the throes of this *nihil* yet experience in the darkness not annihilation but gracious recreation as we discern in being's fragility the sign of a Creator who gives for no other reason than the good of being itself.

In this chapter, I show how metaxology opens or reopens four "indirections" to God. For Desmond, we have "no direct univocal pathway to God" but only "indirections directing human transcending."[2] First I discuss why there can be no univocal "proofs" and explore how we must speak, poetically and indirectly, of "ways" to God. Then I explore how the hyperboles of being—idiotic, aesthetic, erotic, agapeic—open up four indirections or itineraries leading us toward a renewed sense of God, and I indicate throughout how metaxology contributes to Christian theology and enriches Taylor's map of our age. Guided by Hopkins's "Hurrahing in Harvest," I conclude by showing how metaxology performs and attunes readers to disclosures, to epiphanies, of the divine. I emphasize performance because metaxology is not just the "philosophical discipline that examines and evaluates categories and arguments for their rational cogency; not just the philosophical interpretation of the ethos as reconfigured in light of the fundamental presuppositions and enabling (re) sources of intelligibility and value of a particular era, or people, or particular way of life; deeper than these, it seeks to open a pathway of philosophical mindfulness concerning the primal ethos of being."[3]

Metaxological *askesis* informs and transforms how one reflects on, lives within, and beholds reality. These exercises can render us attentive to discerning, even in a secular age, "signs in immanence of what transcends immanence and that cannot be fully determined in immanent terms."[4] We can be tutored to recognize in the hyperboles of being signs of a God "more inward than my most inward part and higher than the highest element within me."[5] I want to explore how metaxology can assist us to "exercise transcendence" and reawaken practitioners to the primal ethos of being. These practices can, I believe, contribute by "epiphanically attuning" those who undertake them to the signs of the Creator disclosed within the *metaxu*.

NO UNIVOCAL WAY TO GOD: THE SUBTLER
LANGUAGE OF INDIRECTION

There can be no univocal "proof" of God because univocity "contracts the ontological charge of the aesthetics of happening, makes too determinate the porosity of our being, fixes the urgency of ultimacy on objectified beings, and overall enfeebles the feel for transcendence as non-objectifiable."[6] Univocal proofs seek apodictic certainty but, as we have seen, univocity alone cannot account for the dynamic happening of the *metaxu*. But in an ethos reconfigured according to *l'esprit de géometrie*, it is hardly surprising that we find the likes of Richard Dawkins who dismiss Aquinas's first three "proofs" because they "rely upon the idea of a regress and invoke God to terminate it. They make the entirely unwarranted assumption that God himself is immune to the regress. Even if we allow the dubious luxury of arbitrarily conjuring up a terminator to an infinite regress and giving it a name, simply because we need one, there is absolutely no reason to endow that terminator with any of the properties normally ascribed to God."[7]

Dawkins assumes modernity's *mathesis* of being: the only beings that count are those that can be counted. Anything in excess of the canon of human rationality, anything that fails to fit within our conceptual schema, is rejected. And Dawkins would be correct *if* the God of Aquinas, or Desmond, were the god of ontotheology, a being amidst other beings. For if God is a member of a system, then the much-beloved question of high school sophomores can be posed: If God created everything, then who or what created God?

To respond to accusations such as Dawkins's, Desmond distinguishes between modern "theory" and premodern *theōria*. For him, modern theory "offers a general hypothesis or model, that itself is as mathematically precise as possible, and that is to be determined as true, verified, in terms of evidence from sense experience or experimental data . . . [it] is an abstraction of mind from being as given, with a view to ordering the given, and perhaps to gain control over it."[8] Earlier practices of metaphysics, by contrast, possessed a mindfulness rooted in *theōria*:

> The *theōroi* were religious delegates sent by the city states to the [Panhellenic] games, which were themselves religious festivals,

celebrations of the largess of being, largess evident in the great performances and deeds of outstanding humans. *Theōroi* were sent to enjoy the agape of being as ritualized in religious festivals. There is a watching here, a being spectatorial, but it is a joyful vigilance; it is an entirely active mindfulness . . . to the extent that a metaphysician is a *theōros*, he too is called to this essentially joyful vigilance, this celebrating mindfulness of the ultimate powers, at play in the between.[9]

Metaxology refuses to be abstracted from the *metaxu* and remains faithful to reality's flux. In place of an indifferent stance, it enjoins a "joyful vigilance" and recommends a celebratory spirit as one finds oneself a witness to the dynamism of being. Rather than an exhaustive system, metaxology enjoins a contemplative mindfulness, one attentive to the "crack" in everything and responsive to signs and disclosures of being's overdeterminacy. The metaxologically mindful subject stands with the *theōroi* and celebrates the astonishing gift of being. To accept the vocation as a *theōros* is to abjure the false promises of univocal proofs, proofs that ignore being's too-muchness, and to promote a mode of reflection that reflects *l'esprit de finesse*. Firmly ensconced in the *metaxu*, we do not need abstract arguments but ways or passages capable of leading us back to God.

Fidelity to the equivocity of the between requires a subtler philosophical language, one employing a discourse "tentative and open, suggestive of what is elusive, rather than dogmatically assertive with regard to some reality supposedly mastered."[10] Metaxology has recourse to four indirect ways of speaking about, or figuring, God: metaphoric, analogic, symbolic, and hyperbolic. Though these modes of indirect speech may be familiar, it seems prudent to show how they function within Desmond's philosophy.

As any writer knows, a good *metaphor* "has the power to surprise and open our receptivity to unexpected otherness."[11] Because our language about God drifts toward univocity, because our concepts of God can become reified and idolatrous, metaxology resists this "fixation" by retaining a sense of how metaphors function. True to the double meaning of *meta*, a metaphor arises from amidst beings—"my son is a lion"—but points to a reality in excess of the finite image: "Well, my son is not literally a lion, but he is strong and courageous." A good metaphor strikes the reader or hearer and causes one to cogitate on how the invoked image is, and is not, to be applied. It is periphrastic, communicating not linearly but in an asymptotic or oblique manner. In its indirect conveyance, a metaphor adverts attention to something mysterious and enigmatic that the image cannot exhaust. We experienced a periphrastic itinerary in our chapter 1 when we considered how Charles Taylor's metaphors—the moral corral, the ethical field, and the sacred forest—oriented and guided us along the terrain he maps throughout *A Secular Age*. A metaphor should not seek to satisfy thought because it works best by provoking the imagination into pondering and moving deeper into the meaning it discloses.

Theologians should be familiar with how metaphors arise from our being amidst beings and how they can point toward a God beyond being and a God beyond the constraint of speech. Scripture is a fecund field for the metaphorical imagination. A few illustrations:

Psalm 23:1—"The Lord is my shepherd."
Isaiah 64:8—"We are the clay, and you are our potter"
John 18:12—"I am the light of the world."
1 Corinthians 13:1—"If I speak in the tongues of mortals and angels, but do not have love, I am a noisy gong or a clanging cymbal."

We know God is not literally a shepherd who patrols the empyrean with a staff, nor is the Holy One a resplendent version of Patrick Swayze's character in *Ghost* who imposes form on the clay. But the metaphors are suggestive; they unfetter the mind to ponder God's fidelity and steadfast protection, to muse on God's intimate relatedness to creation. We cannot assign a wattage to Jesus, and we have no way of ascertaining the pitch of Paul's "noisy gong or clanging cymbal," but that is not the point. Metaphors activate the imagination and induce it to consider things in a new way. A good metaphor causes us to stumble and reconsider the relationship between the *sign* and the *signified*. For instance, God "is" my rock, God "is" my stronghold. The copula "is" points to an intimate link between the *metaxu* and God, but this linkage is hardly a univocal identity. Metaphor kick-starts the imagination and challenges it to detect the hidden connections and allusions encoded within the "is." The "is" of metaphor is not an equal sign (A = A) but a poetic portal conjoining two otherwise seemingly disjointed entities or ideas. And, if we limit ourselves to scripture, there would appear to be no limit to the potential metaphors for God: from leavening yeast to the gracious host of an eternal banquet, from a rock to the Father of all, these metaphors conjoin the finite with the infinite and provoke the imagination to ponder the various ways the finite is porous to and communicative of the infinite and the divine.

The use of metaphor, however, is not without peril. It is possible to be tempted into univocity: when "God is Father of all" is taken to mean God is a male with X and Y chromosomes, we vitiate the metaphor. Dennis Auweele observes: "Metaphors carry the danger that we are ferried (*pherein*) so far beyond (*meta*) the difference that we identify the sign with God: we conflate the sign for what it designates."[12] The "is" of metaphor can be seduced into forgetting difference and can be tempted to accent sameness, thereby denuding a metaphor of its communicate power. A domesticated metaphor, too insistent on the identity of terms, loses its bite and is robbed of its power to astonish and provoke the imagination. The salutary critique raised by feminist theologians over the images and language used to speak of God serves as a reminder of how metaphors can be misused and abused. The lesson: the *is* of metaphor must not be ossified into univocal sameness.

To avoid such domestication, metaxology has recourse to analogy. Analogical language accents difference-in-togetherness and foregrounds the interval between the *is* of affirmation and the *not* of negation. Analogy, as Desmond notes, "is a relation of likeness, and likening clearly keeps open the space of difference. Hence, if univocity is not absolutized, neither is equivocity."[13] Analogy retains a sense of unity-in-difference and is attentive to the "constitutive ambiguity to all our speaking about the ultimate."[14] Hence speech about God requires a proper chastening: whatever we say of God never exhausts or fixes determinately God's being. Like metaphor, analogical speech about God employs concepts and words drawn from the *metaxu* but recognizes the inherent fragility of such speech.

Taken together, metaphor and analogy permit us to speak of God using concepts drawn from the *metaxu*, even though no concept can ever capture fully the divine mystery.

Analogy draws its power from what Desmond considers the "*constitutive ambiguity* to all our speaking about the ultimate."[15] No word or concept can express fully or exhaustively the overdeterminacy of being. Rather than regarding our speaking's constitutive ambiguity as a disabling equivocity, he regards it as potentially fertile. He offers the following example of an analogy: "God is like (as) the joy of the morning." What does this mean?

It is both the joy of the morning and the being of God. There is an "is like (as)" that is complexly qualified by a sense of intricate, elusive, and subtle community. What joy there is in the morning is like God, though God is not the morning or not just this joy. The analogy borders on the equivocal, but if we have entered with purer mindfulness into the joy of the morning, the sweetness of its sheer being puts us in mind of the ultimate as ever freshly good: eternal joy in being, being eternal joy.[16]

Analogy taps into the fertile equivocity of speech that catches us in its undertow, pulling us beneath the surface of language into its roiling depths. Analogical language opens up passageways transporting us "to another dimension beyond objective determination and our own self-determination."[17] The "joy of the morning" conveys but a hint, a fleeting taste, of what it is to be transported into the presence of the divine.

Of course, analogical predication is not without potential pitfalls. Intended to preserve a sense of dynamic equivocity, it can also be "fixed" into a mathematical relation due to "its root in mathematical proportion, and in that respect one is also inclined to a kind of univocity: the difference of the between and ultimate transcendence is mapped as a ration on a quasi-univocal grid of relations. Such a grid easily freezes into a two-tiered system of otherwise unrelated terms, and hence risk the dualistic opposition between 'here' and 'beyond,' between immanence and transcendence as other that it is the greater power of analogy to circumvent."[18]

Dennis Auweele names the risk: if we "fix" our relationship to the divine through an analogy too closely modeled on mathematics, it "recedes then to become our 'relation' to the divine and not our self-transcending 'relating' as infused with marvel."[19] A fixed or quantitatively proportionate analogy (a:b as c:d) overstresses similarity. In keeping with the teaching of Lateran IV (1215), metaxology can insist that "between the creator and creature there can be noted no similarity so great that a greater dissimilarity cannot be seen between them."[20] When we claim that God creates "humankind in our image, according to our likeness" (Gen. 1:26), analogy insists we temper our claimed likeness to God with an awareness of the greater disproportionality between us. Invoking analogy does not "settle" the matter but involves one in a ceaseless process of qualifying and purifying our concepts about the nature of the relationship.

For Desmond, symbolic language builds upon and develops further analogy's difference-in-togetherness. The symbol, he writes, "is a throwing together (*sumballein*) of the differents; it is the sign of a 'being with,' a *sun-ousia*. A broken ring is divided and shared by two lovers, each half a token of their original togetherness and in their separation a sign of their promised and renewed togetherness"[21] In a religious symbol, the immanent and transcendent conjoin in "equivocal promiscuity."[22] Symbols point from immanence toward transcendence or, in a countermove, downward from above: "Suppose we take the erotic absolute as a symbol of God. . . . This symbol is one major way of trying to name the involvement of the divine with immanence. God is in love with creation, passionate for its good, zealous for the realization of its promise and integral wholeness. Is God then dependent on that immanent wholeness for God's own fulfillment?"[23]

Here we find the nub of Desmond's concern with Kearney's God. Given the tendency to emphasize Eros's *penia*, "lack," the symbol of an "erotic" God risks portraying the divine as needing humans. Desmond is rightly leery of any hint of Hegel *redivivus*, but Kearney's divine eros does not render God a "counterfeit double."[24] Desmond's caution is warranted, for, as Ricoeur observes, "symbols have roots. Symbols plunge us into the shadowy experience of power."[25] The metaxological symbol extends into the primal ethos and allows the natural to comingle with the supernatural. Attuned to the surplus of the ethos, symbolism works by directing our minds toward an "*immanent disproportion*, or *disproportion in immanence* irreducible to any univocal or dialectical concept."[26] The believer's "amen" uttered when receiving the consecrated host at each Eucharistic celebration is an assent to symbol-as-sacrament wherein one encounters the "infinite immanent in the finite, passing *incognito* in its festivity and travail, intimating the willingness of the ultimate to be involved with the ultimate in negation—the nothing of death."[27] For the metaxologically astute, one discerns within symbols more than meets the eye.

Our fourth and final mode of indirect speech is the *hyperbolic*. Where the symbol stresses togetherness, the hyperbolic figure accents overdeterminacy and excessiveness by giving "us a figure of the overde-terminate in the determinate and the self-determined, the overdetermi-nate that cannot be exhausted by determinacy or self-determination, the 'beyond' of immanence in immanence. The symbolic throws together, but stuns us with disproportion *in* immanence; the hyperbolic 'throws us above' (*huper-ballein*) in the disproportion *between* immanence and tran-scendence, just out of that being stunned with excess of being here."[28]

For Desmond, recourse to hyperbolic language is essential both for informing readers about the dynamism of the *metaxu* and for transform-ing how they regard dwelling within it. He deliberately tries to throw our mindfulness beyond the *metaxu* toward its transcendent and possibiliz-ing source. Hyperbole in this way is rigorously metaphysical speech. Thrust beyond finite concepts and categories, metaxological hyperbole necessitates we speak and sing of what is above and beyond being in a plurality of ways.

Hyperbole builds on, preserves, and maximizes the potencies of metaphor, analogy, and symbol. Metaxological metaphysics intends for us to be carried away and "thrown over" the *metaxu* as we celebrate the breakdown of univocal categories and seize the chance to explore newly opened indirections toward the divine. In effect, the incapacitation of univocity capacitates our return to God by opening hitherto concealed paths. Hence my advocacy for approaching metaxology as an *askesis*: it is not enough to "go over" the text because it must be undergone. We must allow ourselves to be implicated in the text's rhythm and moved by its beat. We must, in other words, risk ourselves in exercising transcendence if we wish to find God once more.

In Desmond's philosophy we find several "exercises in transcen-dence." These are indirect approaches that do not tell us about God but that invite us to set out with Desmond on a quest for the divine. It should be stated clearly: his "indirections" are not neutral arguments. They are, rather, practices intended to reawaken practitioners to a new, or renewed, sense of God. To be sure, suggesting that Desmond's texts not be "gone over" but "undergone" is not customary today. In our age—and here Desmond and Hadot concur—many of us have been weaned on a thin gruel of philosophical speculation where we learn about phi-losophy without ever doing or living it. By placing metaxology within the tradition of spiritual exercises and approaching it as a way of life, I hope to convince readers that metaxology can capacitate new ways of thinking philosophically and theologically. Metaxology, I believe, gets the gist of Martin Buber's tale of a rabbi,

> whose grandfather had been a disciple of the Baal Shem, [who] was asked to tell a story. "A story," he said, "must be told in such a way that it constitutes help in itself." And he told: "My grandfather was lame. Once they asked him to tell a story about his teacher. And he related how the holy Baal Shem used to hop and dance while he prayed. My grandfather rose as he spoke, and he was so swept away by his story that he himself began to hop and dance to show how the master had done. From that hour on he was cured of his lameness. That's the way to tell a story!"[29]

Metaxology, as an exercise in transcendence, can likewise cure spiritual lameness by rekindling the question of God and uncovering paths that return seekers to the sacred.

A FIRST INDIRECTION: THE IDIOCY OF BEING

Even students new to the study of philosophy and theology are familiar with "proofs" for God's existence. Some, such as Aquinas's "Five Ways," are a posteriori and probe the happening of the exterior world for signs of the divine; others, such as Anselm's "ontological" argument, are a priori and appeal to nothing other than reason itself. But think of how these "proofs" tend to be presented in textbooks, usually as stand-alone arguments to be read, analyzed, and evaluated. "A common view of the arguments for God's existence," Desmond observes, "sees them as neutral uses of reason that are purportedly convincing, or not, on the basis of a reason separate from any religious claims of revelation or faith."[30] Yet, he continues, "we do an injustice to the 'proofs' if we abstract them from the ontological context in which they are formulated."[31] His metaxological reformulation of traditional proofs, consequently, requires us to remain attentive to the interplay between each "way" and its originary ethos.

Earlier, I suggested the "return to zero" as a propaedeutic for one desiring to undertake Desmond's indirections. He would concur: "I do not think we can fully appreciate these hyperboles without genuine meta-physical mindfulness of the primal ethos of being."[32] Hence the need to pass through the purgative night of godlessness and to experience the shattering of coming to nothing: all comes *from* nothing, all returns *to* nothing, yet now *it is*. By reawakening to the primal ethos, we are struck by the hyperbolic idiocy of being. Shocked by its nonnecessity, we face a choice: take being "for granted as the final surd, just senseless idiocy" or meditate on it "as granted, though as disquieting us with its radical am-biguity, and in that ambiguity tantalizing with a light that is not its own light."[33] Our first indirection is guided by this idiotic light.

Let me offer a composition of place by drawing on Desmond's un-derstanding of the difference between "becoming" and "coming to be." Within the *metaxu* we must notice how the

> primal givenness of the "that it is" is not a matter of the "becom-ing" or "self-becoming" of beings. There is a "coming to be" prior to "becoming." The latter presupposes a prior "that it is," even grant-ing that this "that it is" is given with an open promise, and not as a static and completed fact. Granted, there is the openness of (self-) becoming, but there is granted a "being opened" to be, prior to de-terminate becoming. This is idiotic, since all determinate sense pre-supposes it, and no determinate sense can exhaust it. This "being opened" is the primal giving of the porosity of being, the between as enabling an astonishing diversity of becomings, self-becomings, and together-becomings.[34]

Roused from the slumber of postulatory finitism, the posthumous-minded subject is doubly struck. First, one is stirred to recognize that before one can take a stand on oneself, before any exercise of the *conatus essendi*, one must first be given to be through the *passio essendi*: there is a "coming to be" prior to any self-directed act of becoming. Second, post-humous mind is struck by the bivalent meaning of "being opened." On one level, "being opened" testifies to our own condition of being *opened* by the advent of transcendence. On another level, posthumous mind is given to marvel at *being* opened, that is, being as fundamentally porous. So opened, we mindfully occupy the *metaxu* as porous participants im-plicated in the rhythm of being. All around us hums a symphonic interplay of coming to be, of becoming, and passing away. We take our place in this cosmic chorus and tremble, for we sense its fragility as all being dangles precariously above the abyss of nothingness.

Our exercise begins by acknowledging ourselves as participants in the *metaxu* of creation, which we may regard as a "suspended middle" (*schwebende Mitte*) hovering between being and nothingness.[35] One is stirred into astonishment at being's idiocy, that finite being "shows a sheer 'that it is' which shines with an intimate strangeness. It happens to be without inherent necessity, and it might be called a surplus surd, but it is not absurd. The surplus givenness makes all finite intelligibilities possible, but it is presupposed by all and is not itself a finite intelligibility. Its surplus stuns us into mindfulness about what gives it to be at all, since it does not give itself to be, or explain itself."[36]

Rekindled astonishment does not prove God's existence. But by unclogging our porosity, it can purge our senses and permit us to perceive a halo of gratuity surrounding finite being. So, in place of a logical demonstration, this approach encourages a meditative consideration of creation. Desmond's indirect method recomposes readers in the ethos and invites us to consider once more the whole of the cosmos. As beings come into being and pass away, our notion of the "contingency of being" ceases to be a philosophical category. Mindful of the "crack," we know everything that is has come into being and will pass away. No entity needs to be, yet entities are. With Desmond's help, we can probe the "crack" in everything and discover in the mortal wound of finitude an opening to the creative giver and sustainer of existence.

Readers may here recognize echoes of Aquinas's Third Way[37] or cosmological argument. Desmond summarizes this way as: "If all being is possible being, ultimately all possible being is impossible."[38] Metaxologically reconstructed:

The finite world is contingent: things come into being and pass out of being. In the endlessness of becoming, there is one possibility that would be realized at some point: namely, that there would be no contingent being. After all, everything finite might not be; and at some time, in the infinite time of endless becoming, the possibility of everything *not being* will be. If this possibility of everything *not being* is possible, then nothing could ever come to be; for nothing comes from nothing; hence nothing could *now* exist. Thus, if everything is contingent, not even contingent existence now is possible. This is absurd, because the world of contingency is actually given. There must be another being, not contingent, to make contingency intelligible, possible, actual.[39]

Essentially, the equivocity of being communicates a common origin and destiny in the *nihil*: beings come from nothing and return to this nothing. Herein we confront the potential surd: In a world of becoming, why should we even raise the question *Why anything at all?* or *Why did being come to be?* in the first place? Is the whole of being little more than "senseless idiocy" or, in the enigma of it being at all, does it testify to a creative origin who gives it to be?

For Desmond, this surd is not absurd. On the contrary, it entices us to dwell more intensively within and upon the mystery at the heart of being. By immersing ourselves in the happening of the *metaxu*, by pondering how beings come to be and pass away, we can be stirred or provoked into a mindfulness of "an Other that *is* not through another, or does not *become* through another, but through whom all others *come to be*. One might call this an other origin, hyperbolically necessary. This origin is necessary in a sense that has neither come to be, nor become; rather it is the reserved source of all coming to be and becoming. This other origin, the ultimate necessary being exists—that is, God."[40]

As an exercise in transcendence, willingly immersing oneself in the flux renders one susceptible to the "bite of otherness"[41] that stirs an awareness of being's intimate strangeness. All beings share in existence, yet no being, or the totality of beings, exhausts existence. Or, as Brendan Sammon writes, "beings are constituted not only by their unique univocal identity but also by an otherness that is bound up with that identity."[42] The "bite" provokes contemplation of being's overdeterminacy and leads us to contemplate *why anything at all?* and "throws us" hyperbolically beyond finite and provokes within us the thought of a God who gives being to be.

This first hyperbolic indirection invites us to abide within the *metaxu* and risk being struck by being's givenness. The text "works," it enacts its metaphysical *poiesis* that transforms *aesthesis*, only by being implicated in the text's performance. This can occur by approaching the text not as a disengaged report about the *metaxu* but as a spiritual exercise or what Ludwig Heyde called an "experience of thought" that invites one to contemplate how "the contingent is not what it is in a necessary manner. Its being appears to be a sort of *suspension* of the hegemony of nothingness. Every moment of its existence it hangs, as it were, above the abyss of nothingness."[43] Metaxologically exercising the Third Way directs the reader's attention to and through the "crack," bids us to peer into the primal ethos, and allows the contingency of creation to direct our mindfulness toward the thought of a Creator.

The result, you might say, is an agapeic agnosticism much in keeping with Aquinas. The Dominican scholar Victor White describes Aquinas's agnosticism: "St. Thomas's position differs from that of modern agnostics because while modern agnosticism says simply, 'We do not know, and the universe is a mysterious riddle,' a Thomist says, 'We do not know what the answer is, but we do know that there is a mystery behind it all which we do not know, and if there were not, there would not even be a riddle. This Unknown we call *God*. If there were no God, there would be no universe to be mysterious, and nobody to be mystified.'"[44] Metaxologically reconfigured, the Third Way's quest leads not to mute mystery but to a presentiment of the mystery as generative and agapeically creative.

This first meditation is no ontotheological quest for a God who fits neatly in any conceptual schema. It is, instead, a periphrastic meditation asking us to notice how creation is hemmed in by nothingness or, in Desmond's articulation, how creation is "a radical origination that is bound by nothing."[45] As periphrastic, it requires us to abide within the *metaxu*, not to flee from it into abstractions, and to acknowledge being's contingency and nonnecessity. We swoon before this givenness; we grapple with the "metaxological asymmetry between being and nothing in which the affirmation of being has absolute priority."[46] We exclaim *being is* not as a tautology but as an astonished proclamation: *being is*, yet need not be. The metaphysical question—*Why something rather than nothing?*—is reraised, and our mind turns from what is given and ponders the question of a giver; being is not simply given but vibrates with an ongoing *givingness* whose rhythm appears to sing of, and to, God.

When the Third Way ceases to be a locus for meditation, when it is uprooted from the *metaxu* and turned into a syllogism or objective proof, it loses its power. Aquinas sought less to *inform* his readers than to *form* them to perceive that the "crack" in everything leads not to nihilistic despondency but opens outwards and upwards toward God. He indirects his students: instead of an abstract argument, he insists we remain in the *metaxu* and ponder the flux. In the rhythm of coming-to-be and passing-away we become mindful of creation as the *poiesis* of a creative origin. We are indirected into the flux where we come to hear the divine woo within the "crack" in everything; the "crack," so meditated upon, becomes the portal through which we delve deeper into the mystery of creation itself.

Before considering how metaxology overlaps with and contributes to theology, it might be helpful to recall our five commandments:

1. Thou shalt not index the divine to human reason
2. Thou shalt not be faithless to the flux
3. Thou shalt not produce counterfeit gods
4. Thou shalt be attuned and attentive to everyday disclosures
5. Be still and know: Metaphysics is a vocation

If this indirection awakens a mindfulness of the divine, it does so by drawing attention to the overdeterminacy of being. Whatever "God" is, it is not one more being within the system, nor is it Kant's *ens realissimum* who is "completely determined through its own concept."[47] If this is not ontotheology's God, neither is it a deity encountered by infidelity to the flux. As it turns out, it is through our intensive dwelling within the flux that gives rise to our awakened sense of God. At this news, Caputo can relax. Metaxology makes no claim to possess "the Truth" because what it calls "God" is not a determinate *something* but the least worst way to name to the intimate and inexhaustible mystery at the heart of existence. "God" is not a neutral word but an exclamation—God!—to the advent of the One who comes unbidden and whose arrival overwhelms our finite and idolatrous concepts. Kearney, too, is allayed: the quotidian announces the too-muchness of the Creator, disclosing in the ordinary the extraordinary generosity of the divine. Finally, metaxology is a response, a venturing forth impelled by the presentiment that our searching is a consequence of our first having been sought. The happening of the *metaxu* does not confront us with a God-shaped hole but awakens us to a mystery that is neither a surd nor absurd but solicitous and invitatory.

If metaxology has not violated our five commandments, let me make a connection with the Christian doctrine of *creatio ex nihilo*. In his "Undergoing Something from Nothing: The Doctrine of Creation as Contemplative Insight," Brian Robinette approaches the doctrine as a site for the prayerful contemplation of the sheer contingency and gratuity of our being. Like Desmond, he recognizes that God does not create to achieve a selfish purpose; there is no determinate why or reason for God's creativity. But lacking a determinate reason does render God's creative act irrational. Pondering *creatio ex nihilo* and taking seriously the *nothing* from whence being arises can hyperbolically "throw" one's mindfulness toward the thought of a Creator. To Robinette's question—*Why create at all?*—Desmond offers the following response:

> Creation is not arbitrary fiat, modeled on the capricious finger snap of some oriental despot. The metaphor of originative speaking is suggestive. God says "Let there be . . . and there was . . ." Creation is an original speaking letting be. Speaking brings the word to existence. The word, speaking, lets being be. A word is not a roar. The roar would be more like the diktat of the despotic divinity. The word, spoken originatively, is the expression of communicative being. The originating word issues from the goodness of generosity. The word is the creative expression of being as agapeic and as communicative transcending. Word brings a world to be, word communicates a world, lets it issue into a space of sharing with others. . . . Wording the between: a sung world—a song not only sung, but a song giving rise to new singers. The originative word would be the primordial "yes" that gives coming to be, a word that is also a blessing with being. We know this elementally in our own being given to be, lived as an affirmation of being that first lives us before we live it. The agapeic "yes" not only blesses with being, it blesses being: It is good to be.[48]

Robinette muses: "I find this passage astounding, worthy of reading aloud, worthy of rumination, worthy of singing, indistinguishable from prayer. What it communicates can only be 'beheld.' It does not translate into a hypothesis, even if it provides endless pasture for thought. Indeed, one might go so far as to say that our beholding is to share in God's own beholding."[49]

These insights have deep roots, not least in Aquinas's treatment of creation. Aquinas poses the question this way: "Whether creatures need to be kept in being by God?" Stated otherwise, is creation a one-off act or an event of ongoing preservation? His answer presages Desmond's metaxological response: "A thing is said to preserve another per se and directly, namely, when what is preserved depends on the preserver in such a way that it cannot exist without it. In this manner all creatures need to be preserved by God. For the being of every creature depends on God, so that not for a moment could it subsist, but would fall into nothingness were it not kept in being by the operation of the Divine power."[50]

Herbert McCabe employs a musical metaphor: "God must be at the heart of every being, acting in every action (whether determined or free), continually sustaining her creation over against nothing as a singer sustains her song over against silence—and that too is only a feeble metaphor, for even silence presupposes being."[51]

Nevertheless, it is instructive to consider Katherine Keller's critique of *creatio ex nihilo*. Theology, she contends, has trained the West "to shun the *depths* of the creation. Christianity established as unquestionable the truth that everything is created *not* from some formless and bottomless something but from nothing: an omnipotent God could have created the world only *ex nihilo*. This dogma of origin has exercised immense productive force. It became common sense. . . . Christian theology, I argue, created this *ex nihilo* at the cost of its own depth. It systematically and symbolically sought to erase the chaos of creation."[52]

Keller sounds a Caputo-like chord her suspicion, as Robinette observes, that "*creatio ex nihilo* represents the 'dream of metaphysical theology' enthralled by the idea of God's absolute dominion over creation and nonbeing, and thus a God who excludes and expels all that evinces liminality, ambiguity, and process."[53] Christian belief in a God who creates *ex nihilo* enshrined "dogmas of omnipotence: not just of the biblical lord of great if somewhat unpredictable power, but an immutable, unilateral All-Power clothed in the attributes of a single male Person (or two; or . . .)."[54] Embedded in this belief is a fear of the chaos of the deep, "a fear of whatever shadows our light, whatever transgresses boundaries, leaks across categories, sneaks out of closets, whatever she-sea might suddenly flood our fragile confidence. Fear of the 'female thing.' Of all things too deep and too fluid: we may call this fear 'tehomophobia.'"[55]

Tehomophobia—a fear of the primordial chaos (*tehom*)—is reflected in the binary logic of *creatio ex nihilo* according to which "one is either good or evil, corporeal or incorporeal, eternal or temporal, almighty or power-less, propertied or inferior."[56] *Creatio ex nihilo* serves not to awaken as-tonishment at creation's gratuity but, more sinisterly, to bless efforts to control and constrain chaos.

Even the word "creator," for Keller, comes "barnacled with stereo-types: of a great supernatural surge of father-power, a world appearing-zap-out of the void; a mankind ruling the world in our manly creator's image; a gift soon spoiled by its creatures' ingratitude."[57] Such stereotypes are symptomatic of *tehomophobia*. Though she admits that "one need not argue that this grid of dualisms *necessarily* accompanies the *ex nihilo* argument—only that historically it has done so."[58] This admission makes Robinette's intervention needful: rather than casting *creatio ex nihilo* aside, he recasts it as a site of transformative encounter. Reading the doc-trine contemplatively, as a *lectio divina*, is an exercise able to inform and form those undertaking it. Such prayerful consideration can allow one to perceive how God's creative action records no act of dominative "power over" but is, in actuality, an act of agapeic empowerment as God lets "finite creation be as irreducibly other."[59] Or, as Desmond describes it,

> the scandal of absolute power is that it communicates itself in an enabling *letting*: it lets the finite being be as other, it lets it be power—and the letting forces nothing, constrains nothing, coerces nothing; it simply releases into the goodness of free power itself. The scandal of divine (over)all-power is that it is the ultimate pa-tience: it is manifest in giving, in giving away from itself, not giving such that the recipient is forced to recognize the good of the giver, for the pure giving is for the good of the receiver, who may not comprehend he, she, or it is the recipient.[60]

In *God and the Between*, Desmond dedicates two chapters—"God of the Whole" and "God beyond the Whole" to a rigorous and sympathetic view of the God of Creation. Learned and informative as they are, one would be shortchanged if one did not heed their transformative potency. At the center of the poem prefacing "God beyond the Whole" we find the following stanzas, Desmond's poetry enacts a metaphysical *poiesis*:

Between nothing
& something
What happens
Is the pure surprise
Of everything
That is

Intimate to the between
Never captive to the between
The beyond
Springs surprise[61]

Creatio ex nihilo is not an arid statement of fact but a condensed exclamation of wonder at being at all. It is a statement encapsulating a sense of surprise and astonishment. Instead of a knockdown objectifying proof, it is a passage, a mystagogical opening, enticing us into a rekindled sense of awe. This is not poetry as adornment, but a solicitation to a new mode of attention. Thus, a contemplative approach to reading *creatio ex nihilo* with metaxological eyes performs by opening us to dwelling on the enigma *that anything is at all* and allowing us to be transformed as we prayerfully "inhabit that mystery through a long 'letting go.'"[62]

A SECOND INDIRECTION: THE AESTHETICS OF HAPPENING

Desmond's second indirection approaches God by way of the "aesthetics of happening." This approach dwells intensively on the *haecceity* of each being: *this* is. Creation as a dynamic event "shines forth with its own intimate radiance, coming to manifest its own marvelous intricacy of order."[63] Aesthetic happening, then, indicates a "sensuous figuration or figuring forth of the ontological potencies of the primal ethos."[64] If the modern ethos has left creation "seared with trade; bleared, smeared with toil," posthumous mind perceives the presence of "the dearest freshness deep down things."[65] To exercise the aesthetics of happening is not to formulate a theory about beauty but to risk being drawn in by beauty's call and becoming one of the *theōroi* whose mindfulness is alive to and enlivened by signs of the Creator perceived within "the glory of creation—offered both in given beauty and sublimity, and in what we ourselves create."[66] If our first indirection led us to consider how the "crack" of contingency directs our gaze from the finite realm toward the infinite Creator, this second indirection invites us to dwell on what Desmond calls the aesthetic infinite: "The sensuous manifestation of the surpassing power of being that cannot be reduced to merely finite proportions."[67]

We return to the *metaxu*, now with an eye to how beauty might be illuminated with the "finesse of religious poetics."[68] We experience beauty in many ways: the music of Bach's Cello Suite seeps into the heart; Picasso's *Guernica* seizes the spectator with its savage beauty and draws one into contemplation; the gloaming of a summer's eve as day cedes to night and the sky is dappled with heathery purple and streaked with red and orange. Desmond recounts an autumn evening when he climbed *Dún an Óir*, "Fort of Gold": "The climb was through boggy earth, watery on the hillside. . . . The height hovered in the air between earth and sea and sky, their conjunction in a massive rock. The late sun spilled over the height as we ascended, but the shadow was increasing on this side of land and harbor. Just before attaining the top we were wrapped for a time in sober shadow."[69]

This ascent is "aesthetic" (*to aesthētikon*) in the broadest way, for Desmond is not thinking his way up the mountain but physically climbing. Allusions to "sun spilled" and being "wrapped . . . in sober shadow" point to the physicality of this ascent. In a single step, he emerges from the shadow to find himself "in a reversed world—a golden world at almost the furthest reaches of the Western world."[70]

The sun was a revelation, but we were not given this gift without some call on us. On the height and on the side of the sun, the cliff was sheer. Gulls and crows hung there in the silence, a thousand feet above the silent wash against the wall of rock below. More used to the level plan, to us this vantage was vertigo. The gut knots at this height, but holding itself together the spirit exults. . . . Sky and sea merged, the water itself becoming a golden liquid. The air too, empty of obstruction, was a liquid gold . . . to stand was impossible on the rim of this cliff, and to lie down was almost to bow in reverence.[71]

At dusk he begins his descent, "the sun being obstructed, and me bearing down, like a priest with a monstrance, the memory of the other side."[72]

Without mentioning "God," Desmond recollects how the experience of beauty, or of the sublime, points toward something beyond the immanent order. In the happening at *Dún an Óir*, "something *beyond wholeness* is intimated in the showing there. There is a *saturated* equivocity to the aesthetics of happening."[73] A sensuous occurrence: the advent or "call" of the sublime is a rupture that somehow releases. Beauty's in-breaking unclogs porosity, rekindles a sense of the *passio essendi*, and breaks us free from the stale confines of the enclosed self. To encounter beauty, to undergo the rupture of the sublime, is to be afflicted with a dark grace. For the wound it leaves, the "crack" it exposes, renders flesh into a monstrance, a fragile and finite sign that points toward the infinite and ineffable. We must learn to recognize and read the "crack" in a metaxological manner.[74] Thus, whether opened with a glimpse of fugitive beauty or in being shattered by the sublime, Desmond's aesthetic indirections reorient how we behold the *metaxu* and challenge us to marvel at and bow before the surplus beauty of creation.

Although he does not offer an extended reformulation of it, Desmond does refer to Aquinas's Fifth Way as an indirection leading us to marvel at the intelligibility of finite creation. Aquinas's way unfolds as follows:

> For we see that some things that lack intelligence (i.e., material objects in nature) act for the sake of an end. This is clear from the fact that they always, or usually, act in the same way so as to achieve what is best (and therefore tend to a goal and do not reach it by chance). But things lacking intelligence tend to a goal only as directed by one with knowledge and understanding. Arrows, for instance, need archers. So, there is a being with intelligence who directs all natural things to an end, and we call this being "God."[75]

This way, John Wippel observes, "begins with something which Thomas regards as evident to us from the world of everyday experience. Natural bodies, that is to say, things which are equipped with their own natures but lack the power of cognition, act for the sake of an end."[76]

Within the *metaxu*, the observant eye detects something of an "unconscious teleology of nature."[77] Natural beings seem to act purposively, and the natural order itself can appear to be orchestrated as an ecological concert. Lyrics from *The Lion King* capture nature's symphony:

> From the day we arrive on the planet
> And blinking, step into the sun
> There is more to see than can ever be seen
> More to do than can ever be done
>
> There's far too much to take in here
> More to find than can ever be found
> But the sun rolling high
> Through the sapphire sky
> Keeps the great and small on the endless round[78]

The movie opens at dawn; all creation stirs as music guides bird and beast on their journey to behold a new lion king. Nature and its denizens, if only for a moment, stand in balance. We suspend disbelief: lions and hyenas and elephants bowing in unison is a scene more Isaiah 11:6 ("The wolf shall be a guest of the lamb") than Animal Planet! Let us see, though, if these lyrics speak more truly, more subtly, than we realize.

Desmond wants us to dwell on Aquinas's claim that "certain things act for an end." So we slow down and fix our attention on the world of exterior becoming. Things lacking in intelligence seem, often marvelously, to act harmoniously and in concert with the rest of creation to "achieve what is best." Aquinas, Brian Davies suggests, asks us to reflect on the created order and consider its intelligibility. How often, after all, do we stop to consider "the fact that female cats regularly and instinctively suckle their newborn kittens and thereby help them to become healthy cats? Or what about the fact that my heart regularly functions so as to circulate my blood and, accordingly, keep me alive? . . . In instances like these, he perceives goal-directed activity, but not activity that is goal-directed because a human being is at work."[79]

One can be seized by the beauty and orderliness of the *metaxu*. Just as a single rose may evoke wonder, so also can one be astonished at the cosmos. One can try to take it all in, yet a surplus remains. Sir Elton John sang rightly, there is "more to find than can ever be found." The created order is not a mute "thereness" but an epiphanic work of art. The beholder's eye does not rest on creation as it would on an idol but is directed *through* the finite realm from the *poiesis* of creation to its transcendent origin. The gaze passes from finite *poiesis* to the infinite Poet.

Instead of a univocal proof[80] this indirection reads the aesthetic happening of the *metaxu* as suggestive, prompting us to be attentive to the hyperbolic sign of a divine artist, whose "art"

> would not just be the technical imposition of form upon matter, but a more radical bringing to be from which both the elemental good of matter and form are themselves derived. Its *poiesis* would originate a coming to be: not just a self-becoming or selving of beings, not a mechanical ordering, not just a "forming" or self-forming, not just an organismic self-organizing, not a work of art giving birth to itself. Given this likening, this origination would be *unlike* any artistry we could adequately conceptualize, since our artistry always operates in the context of the givenness of being. This other art is hyperbolic to our artistry. We make something; we do not create it in the hyperbolic sense of bringing things to be.[81]

Desmond here draws attention to an analogical likeness between art and creation. Just as a work of art indicates the presence of a designer, so too does the intelligibility of creation point beyond itself to a creative artisan. In place of a formulation, where a:b as c:d, this indirection spurs us to consider the enigma of intelligibility: *Is the intelligibility of finite intelligibility itself intelligible in finite terms?*[82] Is intelligibility reducible to a fixed and static relationship between finite beings or does intelligibility require something, or in the case of the knower *someone*, who exceeds or transcends the finite? Desmond raises this issue: "Does it require reference to a source of intelligibility beyond itself that gives rise to the determinate intelligibles? This suggests a variation of the argument from *coming to be*: intelligibility as determinate is there as having come to be, and cannot make its own intelligibility intelligible; to make intelligible the intelligible means to appeal to a further determining source; since this cannot be our intelligence, relative to the cosmos as the aesthetics of happenings, it must be other."[83]

Desmond's take on Aquinas's Fifth Way is, again, no objectifying proof concluding with a triumphant QED. Metaxologically transposed and undertaken as an exercise, it is more finessed. It enjoins attentiveness to the exterior world where we find, in its intelligibility and beauty, a logic or *logos* we did not impose. Our musings lead us to consider a logic beyond human intelligence, a *"huperintelligible"* logic, that endows creation with intelligibility.[84] For Desmond, recognizing *"that beings are intelligible at all* rouses astonishment and perplexity that cannot be answered in terms of a determinate intelligibility."[85] We contemplate the givenness and restless beauty of creation, muse on the intelligibility of the tiniest particle and cosmos, and we are indirected toward an originative source or God "who not only thinks but loves, or whose thinking, as agapeic minding, is love of singulars, or living communities, love of the intimate universal not just of the abstract."[86] Jesus's hyperbolic depiction of a God who numbers the hairs on our head (Luke 12:7)[87] is, considered in this light, hardly inapt.

The impatient reader groans. Desmond hastens a reply: "There is nothing univocally clear about this, nor could there ever be. . . . Because this is an aesthetics, it is always equivocal to some degree, and always will be."[88] Indeed, the only way for us to interpret the "crack" in everything is by venturing outward to confront the equivocity, not to control it but to allow it to point us beyond the finite toward the infinite. What is true of great works of art is true of anything or anyone worthy of love: we embrace mystery. The surplus of meaning behind a text, a painting, a person invites us into ongoing engagement. Hence the need for spiritual exercises to train one to abide fruitfully with the enigmatic. This second indirection may not tie a bow around a discrete object called "God," but, for those traversing it, it can lead the pilgrim into a clearing where one may contemplate the arresting beauty and intelligibility of creation and discern, in the order, traces of the Creator. This periphrastic itinerary leads us not to a panoptic summit where we behold all things at once but guides us, as an experienced docent leads a tour through a museum, to behold each finite being as a work of epiphanic art.

This aesthetic itinerary suggests four areas where metaxology and theology can converge. Each could be treated at length, but I want only to gesture to places where a fruitful engagement might occur. In keeping with Desmond's own ascent of *Dún an Óir*, I begin with the theme of mystical ascent as found in Bonaventure's *The Journey of the Mind to God*.

Our first step in our ascent requires "setting the whole visible world before us as a mirror through which we may pass over to God, the Supreme Creator."[89] We are not called from the world but offered a chance to behold it aright, attentive to how "the supreme power, wisdom, and goodness of the Creator shine forth in created things."[90] Bonaventure's itinerary facilitates a grace-led transformation of one's vision:

1. First way of seeing: observer considers things in themselves and sees in them weight, number, and measure. (T_1)
2. Second way of seeing: the way of faith, believer considers world in its origin, development, and end. (T_2)
3. Third way of seeing: follow the created order toward Creator. (T_3)[91]

The movement: from the exterior to the interior, from the inferior to the superior. In at least two areas do *The Journey* and metaxology converge. Both are progressive, for each requires ongoing discernment within creation, and perfective, for each attunes one to perceive the over-determinacy, or perhaps the graced dynamism, of the between.

A second locus would be a metaxological consideration of the icon. Consider the saturated equivocity of praying before an icon. Is one beholding or beheld, or both? Icons do not call for a glance but solicit the gaze; as one's eyes traverse the space between, one senses oneself as being drawn or invited deeper. What to the onlooker appears a finite portrait becomes, in prayer, a portal to the infinite. Nicholas of Cusa expresses the icon's overdeterminacy:

> I behold as in a mirror in an icon, in a riddle, life eternal, for that is naught other than that blessed regard wherewith Thou never ceasest most lovingly to behold me, yea, even the secret places of my soul. With Thee, to behold is to give life; 'tis unceasingly to impart sweetest love of Thee; 'tis to inflame me to love of Thee by love's imparting, and to feed me by inflaming, and by feeding to kindle my yearning, and by kindling to make me drink of the dew of gladness, and by drinking to infuse in me a fountain of life, and by infusing to make it increase and endure.[92]

Sensuous imagery overflows as the interplay between beholding and being beheld erupts in spiritual frenzy. The proliferation of images and metaphors conveys the too-muchness into which one is drawn. The iconic gaze mediates, in metaxological parlance, its own hyperbolic indirection throwing us beyond the immanent realm toward the transcendent realm.

Lest one think all "ways" are somehow passive or contemplative, one may interpret the aesthetics of happening to be inclusive of active indirections. One might, therefore, consult Pascal or Dostoevsky for embodied practices leading to transcendence. Belief in God does not require one to think differently but to comport oneself in a new way. Pascal advises someone struggling with belief: "You want to be cured of unbelief and you ask for the remedy: learn from those who were once bound like you and who now wager all they have . . . follow the way by which they began. They behaved just as if they did believe, taking holy water, having masses said, and so on. That will make you believe quite naturally, and will make you more docile."[93]

As in ancient exercises, so here: one must desire some form of transformation and then apprentice oneself to those who have learned the way. Similarly, the Elder Zosima rejects logical proofs for God, but suggests another way to be convinced: "By the experience of active love. Try to love your neighbors actively and tirelessly. The more you succeed in loving, the more you'll be convinced of the existence of God and the immortality of your soul. And if you reach complete selflessness in the love of your neighbor, then undoubtedly you will believe, and no doubt will even be able to enter your soul. This has been tested. It is certain."[94]

Kearney nods. The Kingdom is found not in dusty tomes or syllogisms but in a cold cup of water offered to the thirsty stranger and the morsel of bread extended to the hungry beggar. But not only in the cup. In the cry of the poor, in the face of the widow and orphan, in an act of amnesty for the alien: each and every summons to pour oneself out in loving service to others can tap into the infinite wellspring of the Creator's agape and gradually reform us to be women and men of agapeic minds. Any event of aesthetic happening bears the potential of leading us, or hyperbolically throwing us over, toward the threshold of the sacred where we can encounter again, or even for the first time, the Holy One.

A final point of convergence comes from Joseph Ratzinger.[95] His argument begins by noting how the act of professing belief in God "implies opting for the view that the *logos* . . . stands not merely at the end but also at the beginning, that it is the originating and encompassing power of being."[96] The *logos* encompasses the whole of creation, reaching "mightily from one end of the earth to the other" (Wis. 8:1). He then turns to consider the scientific inquiry of nature. Scientists, he observes, also presuppose a logic within nature, otherwise their inquiries would be guideless. But where does this logic come from? This logic cannot have been "projected" by humans: nature's *logos* is discovered, not implanted, by humans. Thus, he proposes viewing nature's intelligibility as "the impression and expression of subjective mind and that the intellectual structure that being possesses and that we can *re*-think is the expression of a creative *pre*-meditation, to which they owe their existence."[97]

Ratzinger cites Einstein, for whom, in nature's laws, "an intelligence so superior is revealed that in comparison all the significance of human thinking and human arrangements is a completely worthless reflection."[98] But Einstein erects a wall between an impersonal god of mathematics and a personal god of revelation. For Ratzinger, this is not surprising: in Desmond's terms, it is symptomatic of modernity's postulatory finitism. Hence Ratzinger's question: "Can the mathematician who looks at the world mathematically find anything else but mathematics in the universe?"[99] Does a mathematical framework, in other words, give a sufficiently thick account of nature? Hans Jonas amplifies this question when he identifies the aporia resulting from Descartes's sundering of creation into the realms of *res extensa* and *res cogitans*. If the focus of scientific inquiry is limited to *res extensa*, that which can be measured and controlled, there then "ensues the paradox that reason itself has become an irrational entity, intelligence entirely unintelligible within the intellectual scheme of the scientifically knowable: in other words, the knower himself is among his objects, that is, the world, the unknowable par excellence."[100] If only what can be counted counts, then beauty and sublimity are counted out. Jonas resists this and decries its postulatory finitism: "Happening to be living material things ourselves, we have in our self-experience, as it were, peepholes into the inwardness of substance, thereby having an idea (or the possibility of an idea) not only of how reality is spread and interacts in extensity, but of how it *is* to *be* real and to act and to be acted upon. And we can still contrive, by certain acts of abstraction, to be *also* mathematicians and mathematical physicists: 'also'—to be 'nothing but' a mathematical physicist is plain absurdity."[101]

Neither Ratzinger nor Jonas jettison math; they reject, though, any remainderless reduction of biology to mathematics. Such a reduction cannot account, as Jonas notes, for our "self-experiences" or for the many and various "peepholes" that we peer into and glimpse not only the mechanics but also the *meaning* of being. It is precisely this feature of existence, its *meaning* as uncovered and explored by the *res cogitans*, that a mathematical god cannot sustain.

Ratzinger gazes through the "peephole" of aesthetic happening and is led to posit nature's intelligibility as a sign of its being-thought by a creator. Such hyperbolic "thinking" is a creative release of "what has been thought into the freedom of its own, independent existence."[102] Nature's *logos* points beyond the natural order toward a creative mind who creates not out of compulsion, or because of lack, but solely out of love. Consequently: "If the supreme point in the world's design is a freedom that upholds, wills, knows, and loves the whole world as freedom, then this means that together with freedom the incalculability implicit in it is an essential part of the world. Incalculability is an implication of freedom; the world can never—if this is the position—be completely reduced to mathematical logic."[103]

Desmond agrees: "Mindfulness of the signs is not the same as a mathematics of design."[104] These "ways" do not guide us to a univocal conclusion; they perform, rather, hyperbolically to induce a mindfulness of the too-muchness of the *metaxu* and "throw us over" toward God. We undertake Aquinas's Third and Fifth Ways, or think along with Ratzinger, and are struck by the overdeterminacy of being. These ways lead to oases for thought where one may seek refuge from the driving sands of the desert of atheism, refresh oneself in meditative waters, and be struck by beauty and order into a mindfulness of a God who creates agapeically.

A THIRD INDIRECTION: THE EROTICS OF SELVING

Whereas the idiocy of being and the aesthetics of happening indicate hyperbolic indirections discerned within the world of exterior transcendence (T_1), the itinerary probed in the erotics of selving follows a course set by self-transcendence (T_2). This indirection requires us to turn inward and to explore the inner dynamism of human desire. "The human being," Desmond observes, "is intimately hyperbolic as both finite and yet infinitely self-surpassing. We are endowed with transcending power, but we do not endow ourselves."[105] Continuing our Augustinian odyssey, we move from the exterior to the interior where, even in the depths of apparent solitude, we are stirred to recognize that we are not alone but always already in the presence of the Agapeic Creator and Sustainer.

I focus in this section on Desmond's reformulation of Anselm's ontological argument as an exercise to awaken the hyperbolic thought of God. I then address the viability of this indirection vis-à-vis Anselm's interlocutor, his fellow monk Gaunilo, and Immanuel Kant, both of whom offered critiques of the ontological argument. I conclude by drawing a connection between metaxology and prayer.

One of the fruits of exercising the "return" was a rekindled sense of the *passio essendi*. Beneath the conative "will to power," Desmond discerns the presence of the more primordial power that gives being to be *at all*. In an interview with Richard Kearney, Desmond asserts, "I've tried to talk about the *passio essendi* as more primordial than *conatus essendi*. Our endeavor to be is subtended by our being given to be. Our self-affirming will to be emerges out of a more primal being given to be."[106] The emphasis on the *passio*, as D. C. Schindler observes, has implications for the way in which we understand reason: "Reason does not first set itself in motion, in order thus to achieve itself, but is rather at its core moved by what is other than it (even if this 'being moved' is not a dead passivity). Reason is therefore primordially receptive in its structure, and its most basic act is affirmation and assent, even if it goes on at a later moment to doubt or take a critical distance. Reason first 'lets be.'"[107]

Desmond, similarly, speaks of reason's vocation as its summons to ponder what is in excess of and cannot be contained within the bounds of human rationality. Reason is called not to fix on *this* or *that* but to stand before the threshold of the finite and the infinite, to occupy the region between philosophy and religion. Human reason is self-transcending; it is both eccentric and ecstatic. It responds eccentrically to the advent of the other who elicits and orients its ecstatic other-reaching. Provoked by the call of the intimate universal, self-transcendence directs us outward toward exterior becoming (T_1) and inward into our own abyssal depths (T_2) where the echo of this call resounds.

When he offers his reformulation of the ontological argument, Desmond reminds us of the need to remain attentive to the ethos from which the argument springs. Anselm did not argue according to the canons of univocal logic or geometry; his milieu was a monastery and the generative ground was a life disciplined by prayer and meditation. Too often, Desmond observes, "the argument is treated as a kind of logical puzzle: in question is the logical validity of the deduction from the concept of God to God's existence, purely on the basis of the concept alone. This is more the neutral universality of reason than the living intimacy of the soul."[108] Kant's critique of the argument misses the mark inasmuch as it fails to implant Anselm's meditation within its originative ethos: the sap of life cannot reach a severed branch. I address this shortly.

This reformulation invites philosophical meditation. We begin by recollecting how, after traversing the "return," posthumous mind beholds the world. We know creation's fragility, we feel acutely our own contingency, and we savor anew existence's gratuity. We ponder the overdeterminacy of being as our imaginations range across creation. We gaze inward, venture downward, and probe our depths. Desmond: "Suppose thought thinks itself, and explores the inner abyss of itself, what does it come upon? The thought of what is in excess of all excesses. In the exploration of thought thinking itself the thought of what is other to thought emerges. The overdeterminate thought of what is radically other to determinate thought emerges in the immanent self-exploration, even self-determination, of thought itself."[109]

This passage must be read meditatively. This is no argument moving from premise to conclusion. It is an exercise, a performance of thought, pushing reason to its limits. Thought confronts what is "in excess of excess" and this excess cannot be determined or objectified. In its overdeterminacy, it eludes expression in word or concept. Our foray into meditative thinking does not bring us mastery over our depths; to the contrary, it chastens us through an encounter with the fathomless mystery that it is human reason's vocation to discern.

This is consonant with Anselm, who in *Proslogion* 2 describes God as "something than which nothing greater can be thought" (*aliquid quo maius nihil cogitari potest*).[110] Ludwig Heyde regards this formulation as more of a "*rule* for thought (whosoever wishes to think God must follow the rule that nothing greater than God can be thought) than a positive content of thought (what is then the content of this being greater than which nothing can be thought?)."[111] Anselm's definition of God, paradoxically, succeeds because of its failure as a definition: it fails to point to or indicate any determinate *thing* or *being* we might call God. God, per Anselm's definition, cannot be picked out of a lineup of deities because God is not the sort of thing that can be counted or ordered or identified as being-among-other-beings. Read metaxologically, Anselm offers a hyperbolic definition of God, one we need to meditate upon. If we are vexed by ambiguity, this is a healthy uneasiness, a salutary dis-ease. Why? Because it is an indication that "Anselm's acid" is dissolving conceptual idols and freeing us to move beyond self-constructed deities and toward a God beyond conceptual constraint, the God of whom Augustine so rightly said: *Si comprehendis non est Deus.*

Desmond is, in effect, asking us to read Anselm in a metaxological register. Instead of analyzing it from a disengaged stance and imposing our logic on it, he wants readers to allow the text to speak on its terms. He does not ask readers to bracket their experiences or suspend an awareness of being in the *metaxu*. But he does expect us to ponder the ethos from whence Anselm's argument arises. This exercise in transcendence works, consequently, only by allowing oneself to be implicated within it. Desmond points to the ironic effect of practicing Anselm's way: "The ontological proof, just in its truth, shatters the illusion of 'proof,' whether determinate or self-determining, whether univocal or dialectical. It brings us into the company of the incontrovertibility of the divine excess, an incontrovertibility that is never the outcome of any proof because it is the *incognito* necessity that precedes and exceeds every proof."[112]

Instead of an ironclad "proof," this way "probes" and explores our inwardness and renews the hidden porosity of being that flows through us. Indeed, this way can be approached more as a "probe" or a way to explore "go with the flow" of the argument and are struck by its vector: *ab inferioribus ad superiora.* We are humbled by our inferiority, astonished by the disproportion between fragile finitude and the Absolute. But before we despair there occurs a flash of insight as we realize that "we could not erotically seek at all, were not the effective urgence of the other transcendence already wooing in selving, calling to selving, and bringing back selving to transcendence itself, itself that never left and that always was available for us as other to it."[113] If posthumous mind renders us attentive to the "crack" within ourselves, this exercise enables us to dwell in the space of rupture. The hyperbolic thought of the God encountered via the ontological argument *"shatters in immanence itself the illusion of self-contained immanence."*[114] This shattering does not leave us destitute but enriches our sense of communion with the Agapeic Creator.

An aside: I once taught Anselm to high school seniors. In place of Gaunilo's "Lost Island" one student proposed a "Lost Cupcake." This would be, he proposed, the most perfect cupcake ever and for a few moments I countenanced the back-and-forth about flavors, size, and types of sprinkles before ending the debate. The students, like Gaunilo, seem to have been caught off guard by Anselm's hyperbole. Instead of reading Anselm's "way" as "throwing us above" and adverting attention to the transcendent, they interpreted him as saying that God is "bigger" than other things. At times, Gaunilo misquotes Anselm and writes of "that which is greater than everything."[115] Gaunilo, like my students, misread Anselm by positing a contrastive definition of God, as though God were one among a series. Of course, it takes finesse not to think of God as a *thing*. This is a peril of our language, as our facility with metaphor, analogy, and symbol can easily mislead us into thinking we know *what* we are talking about when we speak of God. Anselm and Aquinas would aver, "We do not." This metaxological exercise, by requiring us to remain attentive to hyperbole, works through a method of dislocation: it jostles us out of our conceptual ruts and returns us to the original ethos out of which Anselm's way emerged: his own encounter, in prayer, with a God *beyond* concept.

Rather than going into a detailed analysis of Kant's critique of the ontological proof—or of the cosmological and physico-theological proofs—we can take a shortcut by homing in on Desmond's challenge to Kant. "Kant's formulations," he writes, "mirror the modern reconfiguration of the ethos, hence they are heir to the univocalization of being consistent with Newtonian mechanism."[116] Absent from Kant's philosophy is any sense of existence as "redolent with the fullness of being, or the astonishing fact 'that it is at all,' or the glorious good of the 'to be.'"[117] The *Proslogion* begins with, and unfolds as, a sustained prayer to God; of prayer, Kant writes, "kneeling down or groveling on the ground, even to express your reverence for heavenly things, is contrary to human dignity."[118] Even had Kant read Anselm's argument—Desmond believes Kant was working with arguments inherited from Christian Wolff and René Descartes—it seems unlikely that his critical evaluation would have changed. Uprooted from its originary ethos, any "proof" or "way" cannot but limp along anemically. Even if Kant had Anselm's text in hand, it is hard to imagine how, rerooted in Kantian soil, Anselm's argument could thrive. Kant's reconfigured ethos, the ethos of modernity, would have proved too inhospitable.

Recent commentators on Desmond's work have likewise noticed how easily and often Anselm has been misread. Of Anselm's "way," Joseph Gordon and D. Stephen Long observe: "Anselm is not an analytic philosopher providing an irrefutable logical argument; he prays, and in his prayers he becomes astonished by what 'importunes him.' A way is opened, but it is not the univocal way of the modern ethos."[119] They are correct: the "way" is not a direct path or a stepwise argument leading a dispassionate inquirer to a conclusion. Hewing to a metaxological approach, any way to God must follow an indirection returning to and being renewed in the primal ethos. This, though, necessitates a subtler approach to philosophical reflection. One cannot approach Anselm's *Proslogion* and expect to be convinced of God's existence merely by going over the text. It can perform only if approached with a vulnerability and an openness to enter a dialogue by which one is informed[120] and potentially transformed. As Hadot observes, "Every spiritual exercise is a dialogue, insofar as it is an exercise of authentic presence, to oneself and to others."[121] This is especially true in the *Proslogion*, where we are allowed to eavesdrop on Anselm's prayer where thought and prayer intermingle. One can, of course, play the role of the voyeur who peers in from the outside, looking in without being looked at. Or one can kneel next to Anselm and make his prayer one's own: "I do not try, Lord, to attain Your lofty heights, because my understanding is in no way equal to it. But I do desire to understand Your truth a little, that truth that my heart believes and loves. For I do not seek to understand so that I may believe; but I believe so that I may understand. For I believe this also, that 'unless I believe, I shall not understand.'"[122]

Let me conclude by suggesting how this "way" contributes to and enriches our understanding of prayer. In but a few lines, Desmond encapsulates beautifully the dynamics at play within the erotics of selving and in Christian spirituality:

> Prayer is waking up to the already effective communication of the divine in passage: not just our communication with the divine, but our being already in that divine communication, within which we participate, now in sleep, now more mindfully awake. Prayer is awakening to the passing communication of the divine in the finite *metaxu*. We do not produce it; it is not the result of our determination or self-determination; we are "determined," or better, released into the middle where we can sink deeper into ontological sleep, or begin to awake more fully to what communicates us to be at all.[123]

If we interpret Anselm as offering not a "proof" but a "way" of prayerful probing, I think the hyperbolic nature of his understanding of God comes into focus. For Desmond, prayer is not an action of the *conatus* but is an awakening to something anterior and prior, something more primordial: the *passio essendi*. In our reconfigured ethos, many have fallen into the sleep of finitude, but a fitful sleep. Our days, too, are fitful. In our workaday world, where anxiety and depression are common, how are we just getting by? Addicts, before they hit rock bottom, are convinced that the next role of the dice, the next shot, the next hit of heroin will be the last. But it is never "the last." Suddenly, everything collapses. One sinks to one's knees and prays in a voice not one's own and in ancient, almost wordless, words. Breakdown possibilizes breakthrough; a light pierces the darkness and a new way is possible; a new life, a new spiritual day, dawns.

This Anselmian indirection seeks, in the self's innermost recesses, to commune with this source. Prayer, Robinette writes, is a "long letting go" in which we discover ourselves caught up in and carried away by a rhythm not of our making. Anselm's way capacitates a "letting go" at our most intimate level where we can respond to the "communication of the incognito God, in the deepest ontological porosity of one's soul, so deep that it seems like nothing, since too the porosity is itself no thing—the open space in which communication of the power to be is given and different selving take determinate form. One is not alone, even when one is alone."[124]

The hyperbolic God encountered as "something than which nothing greater can be thought" chastens the *conatus* and blunts its attempts to control the divine. One is aroused to a finessed sense of God, *Deus semper maior*, whose summons possibilizes our response. In prayer, we watch the antinomy of autonomy and transcendence collapse as we realize how we are made for the infinite. Divine power is, ultimately, empowering, freeing us to respond to the source of life who gives us to be out of love. We open our hands and hearts in prayer and receive what we have always been offered and what is ever present: the divine life coursing through us, sustaining us, loving us, and knitting us into one body, one agapeic community.

A FOURTH INDIRECTION: THE AGAPEICS OF COMMUNITY

With each way, Desmond asks us to remain attentive to signs of overdeterminacy in the finite order; he wants us to dwell contemplatively on the "crack" as a passageway leading back to creation's source. As spiritual exercises, these meditations have not simply informed us about the "crack" but have formed us to be mindful of it. We now pursue a fourth indirection, the "agapeics of community," wherein we explore how "our being is in receiving and in giving."[125] Whereas the erotics of selving accents the *conatus essendi* and acts of self-assertion, this indirection probes the fundamental relatedness of all beings and considers how the primordial *passio essendi* intimates our participation in an agapeic community. I conclude this section by suggesting how this exercise uncovers resources to complement Taylor's map.

I begin by once more recalling Pierre Hadot's conviction that philosophy was meant as "a concrete act which changed our perception of the world, and our life: not the construction of a system. It is a life, not a discourse."[126] Desmond aligns with Hadot: "Philosophy is not only a metaxological way of thinking about being, but a metaxological way of being according to thought."[127] As with the other indirections, this exercise transforms how we behold and live within the *metaxu*. This one, though, foregrounds the communal nature of our existence.

Our composition of place begins by reflecting on how we live in the *metaxu*, not as isolated monads, but as participants in the wider community of creation. The metaxological sense of being, Desmond observes, "articulates being in the between as a community of the plurality of open integrities of self-transcending being. The community is not a formation, after the fact, of beings first given to be as fully for themselves. They are given to be for themselves, but the first giving is a communication of being, and from the first giving they are communicative beings, and hence in immediate rapport with beings other than themselves."[128]

As an anthropological claim, this rejects a depiction of community as an outcome of a social contract: humans do not constitute community but are constituted by it. Desmond's point, though, is not limited to human communities. To be at all is to participate within being's community. Moreover, "beings are not monadic but communicative; their selvings are self-transcending and embody communicative power, more or less extensive and intensive, depending on ontological endowment."[129] The *haecceity* of each being is not mute but self-disclosing. Hopkins poetically observes this self-utterance: "Selves—goes its self; *myself* it speaks and spells, / Crying *What I do is me; for that I came.*"[130] Likewise, Psalm 19:1 contributes to the thought of both Augustine and Aquinas: "The heavens are telling the glory of God; and the firmament proclaims his handiwork." Creation has a vital pulse and dynamism. Its rhythm draws us into itself, coaxes us to lend our voices to its song, and we rejoice as we find ourselves sinking into the "surplus of the good."[131] In commending ourselves to the flux, we discern the presence of a radical ecology—a *logos* of our *oikos*, "home"—and we are stirred to wonder if the "togetherness of the community of immanent being reveals a primal porosity to the communication of an origin or good hyperbolic to the immanent 'whole.'"[132]

We are probing how the "intimate strangeness of being" connects all beings with one another and with God who makes all things to be and sustains them in their being. Let us begin, then, by recalling our third indirection, inspired by Anselm, and reflect on what light it can shed on what it means for us to be in community. Desmond suggests: "The power of the ontological way is just *its dwelling on a consummate relation, or an ultimate togetherness*: the ultimate togetherness of God with the mindfulness that comes to wakefulness in human selving. It is the being of the human to be communicative, but its communicative being finds itself in an inescapable community with ultimate communicative being. We come to the community in the ontological intimacy of human being, community given in the intimate soul but calling us beyond ourselves, above ourselves."[133]

Desmond returns to Anselm's ontological way and extends its implications. If this indirection leads us to encounter God in the abyssal depths of our being, this encounter does not lead us to solipsism or self-enclosure. On the contrary, it awakens our self of porosity not only to the Holy One but also to the whole of being. What, or rather Who, we discover in meditation is the intimate universal. The mystery I come to know at the heart of "my" being rests at the heart of all beings; it is, simultaneously, intimate and universal, which means we are constitutively and inescapably in community with one another and with God. *To be* at all is to be in communion with the rest of creation and the Creator.

The ontological way opens up "a way of immanence, but this *immanence itself turns out to offer us an intimate symbol/hyperbole of transcendence as other to our own self-transcendence*."[134] It is an archaeological way, probing our depths wherein we confront a presence somehow in excess of our depths. Heyde notes the way's eccentricity: "The Other is the source of our ownmost I. The Absolute does not lie outside ourselves as a strange reality, but is '*ours*' as the '*Other*' that constitutes our own being. This also implies that what is most essentially and personally 'ours,' is not a secure possession. We have received it."[135]

It is eccentric because it destabilizes the centrality and feigned independence of the "I." The "I" does not set the terms for the Absolute's arrival, but we need the ontological way to enact a "metaxological rumination and anamnesis"[136] to remember, or make present again, our awareness of the Absolute's priority. I am, and We are, because God gives us to be and sustains our being. We traverse this indirection and discover there is no self *apart* from the *metaxu* and its Creator but only *as* a part of it. Once again: to be a self, to be *at all*, is to be in relation.

Our invitation is to meditate upon what it means to be within the community of being. Awakened to and enlivened by the intimate strangeness of being, our exercise cultivates "a very different mindfulness of being in the between: an intimation of inexpressible good breaks through, inexpressible because overdeterminate, as beyond specific determination and our self-determination. Beyond this and that good, beyond our self-determination, the overdeterminate good of being shines in the fittingness of the community that is the metaxological between."[137] We must consider how we are capacitated to respond to this goodness in lives lived in ethical service. A word, then, about Desmond's approach to ethics.

Now, Desmond does not seek to found a school of ethics that can rival utilitarianism or deontology. He takes, instead, "a kind of 'step back' from this or that ethical theory, to address the ethos within which ethical theories come to articulation, as well as the different ethical potencies that are diversely formed by different ethical practices, and expressed reflectively by a variety of ethical theories."[138] His is a search for the surplus source that makes it possible to be good, and not just to do good. If theses ethics allow for a step back, they allow ascent and descent throughout the ethos, for instead of telling *what* to do, they orient us to *how*, and *who*, we ought to be. This is ethics not as strictures but as capacitating the adventure of selving as we respond to the intimations of the good disclosed in and through the *metaxu*. At the risk of overwhelming the reader, give Desmond the floor:

> Metaxological ethics names the ethos as the space wherein the ultimate good intimates itself in the idiotic, aesthetic, dianoetic, transcendental, eudaimonistic, and transcending concretions of life in the finite between. This good is communicated into the between, opening its finite otherness, and through this, opening to the self-becomings of different beings, each becoming towards what is good for it. We are pointed to a community of the good beyond self-determination, a community already there from the start, enabling the powers of self to be determining of itself, giving it to be itself, giving also the ethos of possibility wherein that power can be more fully realized.[139]

The point: within the *metaxu*, we confront a plurality of potencies (idiotic, aesthetic, dianoetic, transcendental, eudaimonistic, and transcending), each intimating the surplus goodness of being itself. Each potency is a portal through which the good of the "to be" is disclosed and whose threshold we are invited to cross in our quest for the good.

These portals, or passages, conduct us back toward "a community already there from the start," the community of the primal ethos. We become fully ourselves, not apart from this ethos, but only as part of it. This form of ethical reflection, rather than deriving commands, intends "to keep our living in the ethos open to the call of *transcendence itself*—not just our self-transcendence but transcendence itself as the ultimate power that possibilizes all transcending, indeed all being, and possibilizes it because transcendence itself is good. The best word in ordinary language for transcendence itself is the extraordinary word, God."[140]

Ethics and religion, for Desmond, cannot be sealed off from one another. The roots of both extend into the primal ethos and reflect our fundamental porosity to other finite beings and also to the infinite source of creation. In this, ethics and religion enjoin us to "read" and "discern" the potencies of the *metaxu* as signposts directing our ascent toward God and informing our descent as we return to the *metaxu* after having encountered God. A periphrastic ethics: we wander amidst beings (*meta*) and are indirected by the potencies beyond beings (*meta*) and then, renewed by an encounter with God, we descend once more. Our itinerary is not a straight ascent to an Archimedean point but an indirect journey through the *metaxu* in response to the "good" of being and the God disclosed epiphanically in all things.

Of course, the daily practice of ethics in search of what it means to be and to become good is not without challenges. The theologically attuned ear hears strains of original sin when Desmond describes how ethical practice "is mediated by a mindfulness, just as mindfulness is shaped in its openness by ethical integrity, and just as the integrity of both openness and mindfulness is nourished by living fidelity to the original patience of our being. A corruption of one infects the other."[141] One need not look far for evidence of corruption. Consider our ongoing ecological and humanitarian crises. Both attest to what he calls an attitude of "serviceable disposability" according to which, "things must serve us, be serviceable for us, but once they have served their use for us, they are disposable. Used, they are used up. Persons are also liable to be treated as disposable items."[142] The elemental goodness of the "to be" is relativized and judged based on "its goodness for me." We confront the scars of this daily: deforestation, polluted seas, oil spills, food shortages, and the widening gap of global income inequality.

Desmond's indirections, returning us to the sources of mindfulness, serve as a remediation of this corruption. By renewing our sense of participating with the community of the *metaxu*, he piques our mindfulness of how *"there is an ontological solidarity that is not neutral but ethical."*[143] This solidarity is grounded in and nourished by the intimate universal abiding at the heart of all beings: "We are opened to each other, before we come to ourselves. Here we live the porosity of our being between as ethically qualified, not only relative to the good of the 'to be,' but the good of the being of the other, and indeed of selving. This communication of the good of the 'to be' is not dominated by the *conatus essendi* but, rather, derives from fidelity to the more original *compassio essendi*."[144]

St. Francis embodies the *compassio essendi*, for his heart was moved in a moment of "graced patience" to recognize in the leper not a figure of disease but a beloved brother. This *compassio essendi* is not an abstract theory about being but is an embodied way of life. The past century, to be sure, has no shortage of women and men who provide similar testimony to a power beyond will to power: in the figures of Mother Teresa, Oscar Romero, and Dietrich Bonhoeffer we find examples of a *compassio essendi* that empowers the service of others even at great cost to oneself. Not long before her death, Ita Ford wrote the following as a tragic testament to the empowering *compassio essendi*:

> Yesterday I stood looking down at a 16-year-old who had been killed a few hours earlier. I know a lot of kids even younger who are dead. This is a terrible time in El Salvador for youth. A lot of idealism and commitment is getting snuffed out here now. The reasons why so many people are being killed are quite complicated, yet there are some clear, simple strands. One is that many people have found a meaning to life, to sacrifice, to struggle, and even to death. And whether their life span is 16 years, 60 or 90, for them, their life has had a purpose. In many ways, they are fortunate people.
>
> What I'm saying is, I hope you come to find that which gives life a deep meaning for you . . . something worth living for, maybe even worth dying for . . . something that energizes you, enthuses you, enables you to keep moving ahead. I can't tell you what it might be—that's for you to find, to choose, to love. I can just encourage you to start looking, and support you in the search. Maybe this

sounds weird and off-the-wall, and maybe, no one else will talk to you like this, but then, too, I'm seeing and living things that others around you aren't.[145]

Ford remained elusive: whatever, or whoever, empowered her to stay amidst the people could not be pointed to or argued toward, but only sought in, and as, love. The *compassio essendi* is not an achievement; instead, it is better likened to being a vocation or a calling to be and to enact what one has received. We are called by *agape* to be agapeic. In martyrs such as Ita Ford, we find incarnate exemplars of the agapeic nihilism that duplicates, in and through one's body, the divine givingness of the Creator.

As a way of life, the agapeics of community provides a hyperbolic sign pointing to the Agapeic Creator. We look to examples set by other women and men and are moved to muse on how their lives testify to the Creator and sustainer of all being. Indeed, this can be read as a truly catholic exercise because it requires us to consider not only the examples of well-known martyrs—Etty Hillesum, Gandhi, Martin Luther King Jr.—but also the lives of countless others who witnessed, in various ways, to the elemental goodness of being through lives of service to others. We gaze upon those who have shown us how to live because the community of agapeic service incarnates "a hyperbolic sign of transcendent good. Our participation in agapeic transcending is our fullest self-transcendence: our love, in transcending self, transcends to transcendence itself. We find ourselves in a love that not only passes beyond self, but more ultimately passes *between* ourselves and transcendence itself."[146]

Agapeic service "is not a matter of possessing power but of being empowered and being able to empower—but not with one's own power but within the energy of the divine in which it is one's privilege to participate."[147] Such lives of service testify to a hospitality to the God who universally holds all of creation in being and who intimately dwells within the center of each being. Indeed, for Christians, the martyrs themselves bear a Christomorphic shape. This is to be expected because the *compassio essendi* "reaches its absolute form in the God of Christ—absolute porosity, absolving porosity, passing into and through the mortal agony of the human and its *passio*—absolute passion become a *compassio essendi*."[148]

I link these ideas with Charles Taylor. I do this, first, because we now have metaxological resources to make good on my pledge to show how Desmond's thought augments Taylor's narrative of secularity. Second, Taylor also recognizes the hyperbolic nature of the "Kingdom of God." Without using the language of hyperbole, he reminds us "not to become totally invested in the code, even the best code of a peace-loving, egalitarian liberalism. We should find the center of our spiritual lives beyond the code, deeper than the code, in networks of living concern, which are not to be sacrificed to the code, which must even from time to time subvert it."[149] We betray God's Kingdom when we mummify it in codes and mute its anarchic potential. We need to recover, for Desmond and Taylor, its apocalyptic "sting" and embrace anew its revolutionary call. With the Kingdom's anarchic arrival, in the upheaval it inflicts on the status quo, we catch sight of the primal ethos and the divine *arche* that makes it possible to live agapeically.

"At the heart of orthodox Christianity, seen in terms of communion," Taylor writes, "is the coming of God through Christ into a personal relation with disciples, and beyond them to others, eventually ramifying through Christianity to humanity. God establishes the new relationship with us by loving us, in a way we cannot unaided love each other."[150] The ecclesiological implication cannot be ignored: the Church is called into being by and placed at the service of *agape*; *agape* is the lifeblood of its mission and the source of its missionary outreach. The Church's raison d'être, moreover, was a radical summons to catalyze a new network of relations grounded not in ethnicity or race or kinship, but solely on the divine gift of God's divine love. Alas, the ideal hardly ever achieves status as the real. As Taylor observes, "the church lamentably and spectacularly fails to live up to this model; but this is the kind of society it is meant to be."[151] Western Catholicism knows well this betrayal. How many of us were taught to live our lives *ad majorem Dei gloriam* but found, too often, ecclesial leaders who twisted it to read *ad majorem Mei gloriam*? The ecclesial service of divine love became caught up in self-preservation and self-love, and many, sadly, have suffered from this betrayal.

Following Ivan Illich, Taylor interprets the Good Samaritan as a parable tapping into abiding anarchic potential of the agapeic network (Luke 10:29–37).[152] Moved by the wounded man, the Samaritan defies cultural and religious proscriptions to assist him. This action creates a new kind of fittingness, belonging together, between Samaritan and wounded Jew. They are fitted together in a dissymmetric proportionality which comes from God, which is that of agape, and which became possible because God became flesh. The enfleshment of God extends outward, through such new links as the Samaritan makes with the Jew, into a network, which we call the Church. But this is a network, not a categorical grouping; that is, it is a skein of relations which link particular, unique, enfleshed people to each other, rather than a grouping of people together on the grounds of their sharing some important property.[153]

Herein rests the anarchic potential: the network of *agape* is based in and draws its strength from a divine source and can unfold irrespective of extant commitments and allegiances. *Agape* is irruptive, breaking in to overthrow old orders as it inaugurates the Kingdom here and now, in this place and time. Nor is *agape* indexed to any metaphor, analogy, or symbol. Jesus's parables possess multiples images, not because he lacked the skill to make a clear point, but because the Kingdom cannot be exhaustively expressed in images or words. The parables are hyperbolic, not meant to inform hearers but to form them as Kingdom-dwellers.

The corruption of the network of *agape* occurs when "it falls back into something more 'normal' in worldly terms."[154] We keep the practices but lose their originary spirit:

> The network of agape involves a kind of fidelity to the new relations; and because we can all too easily fall away from this (which falling away we call "sin"), we are led to shore up these relations; we institutionalize them, introduce rules, divide responsibilities. In this way, we keep the hungry fed, the homeless housed, the naked clothed; but we are now living caricatures of the network life. We have lost some of the communion, the "conspiratio," which is at the heart of the Eucharist. The spirit is strangled.[155]

Modernity, Taylor and Illich fear, domesticates the transformative anarchy of *agape*. Eric Gregory and Leah Hunt-Hendrix capture its bureaucratization when they write: "When a homeless shelter is built down the road, Christians put away the candle and extra mattress that they had always kept ready for the stranger who might appear, in need of a bed for the night. Now, when the Christian opens the door, she gestures in the direction of the hostel down the street and washes her hands of the need to engage personally with the visitor in need."[156] This does not deny the importance of the institutional structures that facilitate charitable engagement. It is, though, to observe only how easy it is to domesticate the anarchic potential of charity—a love that breaks boundaries and reconfigures the ethos—by codifying it.

How, then, should an agapeic community expend itself? Imagine that Desmond unfolds Taylor's map and puts it in front of us. He studies it, his finger following several different paths. Some of these paths appear to be modern highways, others are long-abandoned pilgrimage routes. He clears his throat and speaks. "Come here to me and look. Do you see this region? From up above, it looks denuded and lifeless. Not much grows there any longer." He gestures to a few sites. "Do you have the courage to venture into this urban desert, this suburban void, to see if spiritual life might be renewed?" So, members of the community set out to serve the needs of others. Much to their surprise, they find even in the bleakest of spiritual wastelands hints of an abiding thirst for life-giving waters. The voice of an unexpected prophet cries out, "Life is a banquet, and most poor sons of bitches are *starving* to death. Live!"[157] True, Auntie Mame is more of a celluloid prophetess, but she vividly recalls us to our deepest spiritual longings, a hunger easily ignored because its pangs are always with us. So the agapeic community commits itself to sinking new wells, even in the unlikeliest and most arid of places, in the hope of offering to others the life-giving water that sustains them. They know their communal call, their vocation, is to give as has been given to them. In an act of solidarity with their spiritual sisters and brothers, they become companions who wish to share the *agape* they have received.

The exercises here envisioned are suitable, I believe, for individuals and institutions. Perhaps the Church most of all, for it is where Christians undergo the *compassio essendi* in communion with one another. We eat from the same plate and drink from the same chalice as we gather around the same table. Desmond offers no new code but issues an invitation to reconsider how we live together in community. Together, we dig into the hidden depths of the *metaxu* and under his guidance expose the agapeic network at its core. *Agape* is not a lagniappe or "additional something" added to creation; it is, on the contrary, creation's innermost core. If Taylor furnishes the map of a secular age and its deserts, Desmond brings the metaxological dowsing rod to divine the presence of life-giving streams. With Desmond as our guide, we come to understand how there is no point on the map—ourselves included—not somehow rooted in and nourished by these agapeic streams. Taylor's map gives us the breadth of our secular age. Desmond uncovers its agapeic depths.

Exposing the hidden metaphysical depths of Taylor's map reconfigures our understanding of what it means to participate in the *metaxu's* community. All of creation, rooted in the agapeic generosity of the Creator, is transformed into a common home. Taylor's map, metaxologically conceived, provides us with a sense of how the intimate strangeness of being inscribes all of creation into a shared *oikos*. The *logos* of this *oikos* is *agape*, and what Desmond gives us to understand is the metaphysical depths of an authentic ecology. In coming to know ourselves as subjects of divine mystery, as participants in the act of creation, our response to one another and to the natural world must be one of agapeic service. This, perhaps, roots Pope Francis's understanding of the "integral ecology" described in *Laudato Sí*. Pope Francis cites St. Francis as the exemplar "of care for the vulnerable and of an integral ecology lived out joyfully and authentically. He is the patron saint of all who study and work in the area of ecology, and he is also much loved by non-Christians. He was particularly concerned for God's creation and for the poor and outcast. . . . He shows us just how inseparable the bond is between concern for nature, justice for the poor, commitment to society, and interior peace."[158]

The pope's integral ecology, galvanized at its core by *agape*, is effectively an integrating ecology summoning its participants to work for the good of our shared home. What Desmond helps us to see is how, on Taylor's map, there is no neutral ground on which we may feel unconstrained by the call to agapeic service because there is no point on the map outside of God's reach. Every point, above and below the map, bears the trace of God on it. To senses attuned by metaxological *askesis*, what had appeared to be God's gloaming comes to be seen, not as the encroachment of night, but as the prelude to a new dawn. By dawn's light, we perceive how we are interwoven into the agapeic network and discover how "simple daily gestures which break with the logic of violence, exploitation and selfishness"[159] contribute to the common good of creation. In leading us into creation's primordial depths, metaxology encourages us to sing with St. Francis a canticle to Brother Sun, Sister Moon, and take our place in our common home.

In the hyperbole of the agapeics of community, we find ourselves drawn into the ceaseless give-and-take of the *metaxu*. We are finite yet discern within finitude signs of the infinite exterior to ourselves, interior within ourselves, superior to ourselves. This porosity reminds us how "our being is in receiving and giving. We are receptive to the gift of the other, and we are free to give beyond ourselves to others, and in some instances, simply for the good of the other as other."[160] Read through a metaxological lens, Taylor's map becomes a living tableau that proclaims God as present in and disclosed through all beings. We call to mind exemplars of lived-out generosity, saints known and unknown. Words attributed to St. Ignatius of Loyola spring to mind: "Lord, teach me to be generous. Teach me to serve you as you deserve. To give and not to count the cost." Agapeic giving, a kenotic generosity, a "good measure, pressed down and overflowing" (Luke 6:38). Not just words, but incarnate expressions of the Agapeic Origin. A sense of astonishment "throws us over" toward the God encountered as the vitalizing force of the *compassio essendi* that endows us with courage to love others as we have been loved. Metaxological indirection leads us into the depths of Taylor's map where we hear the call, and are empowered to respond, to the challenge to "go and do likewise."

EXERCISING TRANSCENDENCE: HURRAHING IN THE *METAXU*

Companioned by Gerard Manley Hopkins, I conclude by suggesting how Desmond's metaphysics offers a resource for those who wish to encounter God anew. Simply stated: undertaken as a spiritual exercise, metaxology enables practitioners to reopen the question of God and ennobles us by giving us to behold how we are inscribed into the *metaxu*, not as isolated monads, but as participants in a community given to be, and sustained in its being, by an Agapeic Creator. Metaxology is not only an exercise in thinking but also, and more vitally, a transformative attunement into a way of metaphysical beholding and an awakening to one's own being beheld.

In 1878, Hopkins described "Hurrahing in Harvest" as "the outcome of half an hour of extreme enthusiasm as I walked home alone one day from fishing in the Elwy."[161] The sonnet captures a rekindling of astonishment that, read with metaxological eyes, encapsulates the "poetics of the between" and subtly weaves together the four indirections we have explored:

> SUMMER ends now; now, barbarous in beauty, the stooks arise
> Around; up above, what wind-walks! what lovely behaviour
> Of silk-sack clouds! Has wilder, willful-wavier
> Meal-drift moulded ever and melted across skies?
> I walk, I lift up, I lift up heart, eyes,
> Down all that glory in the heavens to glean our Saviour;
> And, éyes, heárt, what looks, what lips yet gave you a
> Rapturous love's greeting of realer, of rounder replies?
> And the azurous hung hills are his world-wielding shoulder
> Majestic—as a stallion stalwart, very-violet-sweet!—
> These things, these things were here and but the beholder
> Wanting; which two when they once meet,
> The heart rears wings bold and bolder
> And hurls for him, O half hurls earth for him off under his feet.[162]

The end of summer harvest in north Wales affords Hopkins his own unexpected reaping. Around him, "stooks," sheaves of grain, have been gathered and stacked; in the sky above, the "wind-walks" as tumbling clouds form and re-form themselves as they drift along. As he walks, it is as though he hears nature's wordless call to prayer; he lifts up his heart and his eyes, taking part now in creation's liturgy. The allusion to Ruth 2:3 is deliberate, for just as Ruth met her future husband, Boaz, while "gleaning" in the field behind the harvesters, Hopkins "gleans" in creation hints and intimations of the Savior's presence in all things. As Kevin Hart writes, "What was at first the gathering of the *vestigia dei* has suddenly become something more whole and more real than could have been anticipated. The gleaning has resulted in a rich harvest: Christ greets Hopkins in a manner that could not be 'realer' or 'rounder.'"[163]

Christ's advent reverses our understanding of divine communication because, as Desmond observes, "communication is from what is other to us first, and then from ourselves toward that otherness as other. The first initiative does not lie with us, and yet something is initiated. As initiating, we are always seconds."[164] This sonnet does not conjure Christ into creation but offers a poetic response to the epiphany of the *Logos* who reveals the divine life from within the *metaxu*.

This brings us to the sonnet's key line: "These things, these things were here but the beholder / Wanting." The doubling of "these things" is a redoubling, a stuttering intensification of his sudden awareness of creation's overdeterminacy. It is not Hopkins who imposes order and beauty upon nature, but he is awakened, as if out of a deep sleep, and given to behold creation with new eyes. Newly roused, he wipes the rheum of postulatory finitism from his eyes and is given to perceive that it is he who has been "wanting," that it is he who has been blind to creation's splendor. His poetic metaphor works, literally and literarily, to "carry us beyond" the terrestrial toward the Holy One as the "heart rears wings bolder and bolder" and bears him aloft in rapturous ascent. Hopkins awakens to being beheld by his Savior and, in knowing himself as beheld, is given to behold things anew. Creation is not an inert substrate awaiting our imprint. Instead, it communicates itself as an unsurpassable moment of "rapturous love's greeting."

"Hurrahing in Harvest" can be read as a poetic concretization of Desmond's indirections. For it is Hopkins who is moved idiotically to raise his entire self—"I lift up, I lift up heart, eyes"—toward "all that glory in the heavens." What had been, just lines before, the "skies" transmute into the "heavens" and he beholds Christ in creation. Sensuous aesthetic imagery communicates, furthermore, the surfeit of beauty and the rupture of the sublime as it paradoxically captivates the poet and liberates his heart to approach the Holy One. The "hurrah" of the harvest comes as he gleans the presence of Christ, the creative *Logos*, mysteriously present, not in a distant empyrean, but as the sustaining presence glimpsed in "azurous hung hills." As an erotic indirection, the beholder's "wanting" is not grudgingly acknowledged but ecstatically celebrated, for this "wanting" releases the beholder to follow the heart's longing toward the one for whom it most longs. Finally, we have a profound sense of the agapeics of community: the heart takes wing and "hurls for him, O half hurls earth." Why only "half hurls"? Because Christ is present within creation, not hovering in the ether but concretely "under his feet." For those with eyes to see and ears to hear, we are given to behold how all created beings are always "together with" in community with the *Logos*.

Hopkins's "hurrahing the harvest" proves simultaneously enabling and ennobling. It enables Hopkins to peer beneath nature's taken-for-granted surface and to perceive within creation signs pointing beyond the immanent order. The end-of-season harvest is transfigured as he finds himself drawn into a harvest that is never out of season: the harvest of Christ himself, who plays, as Hopkins notes elsewhere, in "ten thousand places." For the Christian, moreover, the poem proves ennobling. For instead of telling the reader what to think about, the sonnet draws the reader into an event of disclosure as the created order reveals its hidden depths, thereby allowing Hopkins—and perhaps his accompanying readers—to dwell within creation attuned to being called by, and englobed within, the divine presence.

Undertaken as exercises, Desmond's metaxological indirections empower us to "exercise transcendence" and help us to search within the immanent order for signs of God. One can, of course, select any one of the indirections and contemplate *that being is*, the intelligibility of nature, the intimate strangeness of being encountered in prayer, or the way our communities can be reconfigured according to an agapeic logic. Each one can stir us into contemplation. But if we take these indirections as a way of life, as a way of beholding, then we can see how each of them intermediate with one another. As we get caught up in the interplay of these ways, we can find our way of being in the *metaxu* undergoing a transformation. Like Irish musicians in a *seisiún*, each "way" contributes to and enhances the way we stand in the between, gradually attuning us to the rhythmic interplay of voices. Rightly attuned to the "crack," we find ourselves dwelling in, and overcome by, the "good *craic*" of creation. Desmond's ways are not dispassionate inquiries but exercises in attunement aimed at getting us to detect the rhythm and take our place within the symphonic composition of creation.

In metaxology we find a nuanced and exciting response to Taylor's call for "new and unprecedented itineraries" to the sacred. As a response, Desmond offers us four indirections beginning in the here-and-now that attempt to make sense of our experience of being within the *metaxu*.

Rather than abstract logical arguments, Desmond's ways are performative: they invite us to consider things mindfully from a metaxological vantage point in order to see if this new way of beholding makes better sense of our experience. For those weaned on the thin gruel of univocity, Desmond's recourse to subtle poetics cannot, at least at first, but be maddening. But by undergoing these "ways" as exercises, we begin to detect within the finite realm intimations of creation's overdeterminacy. Desmond's itineraries do not take us into new realms of Taylor's map but uncover the map's depths. Instead of directing us elsewhere, Desmond brings us on an exploration of the *metaxu* to uncover clogged and concealed springs whose water might renew our sense of God.

In a way, Desmond's innovative itineraries are no more than recuperations or repristinations of a venerable tradition. For, as we saw, his "ways" are efforts to return to the originary ethos of older arguments for God's existence. He would agree, at least in part, when Taylor observes that our goal "is not to return to an earlier formula, inspiring as many of these will undoubtedly be."[165] Desmond's task, however, is not an atavistic retrieval aimed at preserving the "older arguments" just as he finds them. We saw this in his reformulation of Anselm's argument. Instead of articulating it as a logical proof, he returns Anselm's way to its origins in prayer and meditation. This "way" is not meant to be read over but must be undergone as a practice. The same can be said of Aquinas's Third and Fifth Ways regarded not as artifacts but as still-viable "ways" to approach the divine. Each offers an opportunity to "exercise transcendence" as one pauses within the *metaxu* and gives oneself over to philosophical contemplation or, perhaps, prayer. If metaxology unclogs porosity and reawakens the *passio essendi*, this creates a space for a fruitful rapprochement between theology (*fides quaerens intellectum*) and philosophy (*intellectus quaerens fidem*).[166] I explore this further in chapter 5.

By leading us through a series of meditations aimed at returning us to the primal ethos, Desmond seeks to rekindle astonishment or, with Hopkins, to induce a "hurrahing" in the *metaxu*. We cannot compel our own astonishment; yet, by approaching metaxology as a form of spiritual exercise, it certainly seems possible to prime the pump, so to speak, by raising the question of God in new ways. These "ways" act as preambles of faith (*praeambula fidei*). We can read metaxology not as giving us "the answer" or as possessing "the Truth" but as a theater of encounter where the texts' poetics reorients our gaze and permits us to consider the *metaxu* anew. Each of the ways loosens our conceptual grasp on being, and allows us to relax and begin a process of inhabiting the mystery through a process of letting go. This letting go of our concepts, of our striving to master and control, need not precipitate an internal crisis. Indeed, the opposite is the case as the revitalized *passio* communicates a sense of being beheld. Before we can behold, we are beheld by a source beyond our control.

As beholders in and of the *metaxu*, we are "wanting." We are "wanting" in a way Augustine knew well: the heart is restless, its hunger can be sated by no finite being. We are wanting, too, because we have not yet realized fully what it means to be a beholder. Desmond points out that "we tend to think of beholding as a movement from us to something other to us. Beholding something seems to put the perceiver in a position of active superiority to the being beheld as other. My beholding seems to confer on me the preeminence: the other beheld may be marvelous but my beholding seems to be the privileged glory. This kind of beholding, I would say, is too full of itself, and hence lacks the fertile emptiness that is filled with openness."[167] One of Desmond's great contributions, I believe, is to drive home the nature of this "wanting." The quest begun in the "return to zero" leads back to the "fertile emptiness" of the *nihil* and then, through each of the indirections, allows our posthumous mind to consider creation in a new way. The purgative process of agapeic nihilism clears away the debris of self-assertion, demolishes idols erected by the *conatus*, and stirs within us a sense that before we behold we are first beheld lovingly by the Agapeic Creator. With purged senses, we scan the *metaxu* and discover many openings, many ways, capable of leading back to God.

Metaxology performs to the extent it is allowed to disorient and gradually reorient how one stands in the between. It does not allow us to impose ourselves or our frameworks upon creation. Rather, it makes possible a subtler way, one that allows us to hear and enter the rhythm of creation. Metaxology uncovers the opening that allows us to enter its ancient song. Metaxological metaphysics is a calling or vocation leading us into a refreshed sense of and relationship with God. Indeed, by leading to the porous threshold between philosophy and religion, between reason and faith, metaxology endows practitioners with what Keats called a "negative capability" enabling one to abide in "uncertainties, mysteries, doubts, without any irritable reaching after fact and reason."[168] Desmond equips his fellow travelers with the conceptual tools necessary to negotiate the "cracks" uncovered in the *metaxu*. My task now is to suggest how metaxology capacitates this "negative capability" by inculcating what I call *orthoaesthesis*, or, less barbarously, "epiphanic attunement."

FIVE

Epiphanic Attunement

> We are the beings of receptive spirituality, who stand in freedom
> before the free God of a possible revelation, which, if it comes,
> happens in our history through the word. We are the ones who, in
> our history, listen for the word of the free God. Only thus are we
> what we should be.
>
> —Karl Rahner, *Hearer of the Word*

Readers familiar with *The Lion, the Witch and the Wardrobe* may recall the
scene when Aslan offers to exchange his life for Edmund Pevensie's. Per
the law of the "Deep Magic," the White Witch had a claim on the life
of every traitor in Narnia, and Edmund, having betrayed his siblings, was
a traitor. During their negotiations, Aslan challenges the depth of the
Witch's knowledge of the law. She responds with fiery indignation: "Tell
you what is written on that very Table of Stone which stands beside us?
Tell you what is written in letters deep as a spear is long on the firestones
on the Secret Hill? Tell you what is engraved on the scepter of the
Emperor-beyond-the-Sea? You at least know the Magic which the Emperor put into Narnia at the very beginning. You know that every traitor
belongs to me as my lawful prey and that for every treachery I have a
right to kill."[1]

The Beaver minces no words: "So that's how you came to imagine yourself a queen—because you were the Emperor's hangman. I see." The power she exerts over life and death is not her own but parasitic; it is seized and grasped, not granted. Metaxologically stated, her reign bears the mark of a dominative *conatus essendi* severed from the endowing *passio essendi*. If we were to compare the White Witch and Aslan as archetypes of desire, she would be emblematic of a tyrannical *eros turannos*, he of a celestial *eros ouranios*.

As the night of Aslan's sacrificial death cedes to dawn, Lucy and Susan hear "a great cracking, deafening noise as if a giant had broken a giant's plate." They return to the Stone Table to find it broken and Aslan's body missing. In this moment of the ancient Table's breakdown, the children, and the reader, are astonished by a sudden breakthrough: there, "shining in the sunrise, larger than they had seen him before, shaking his mane (for it had apparently grown again) stood Aslan himself." Aslan reinterprets the events, for although the White Witch "knew the Deep Magic, there is a magic deeper still which she did not know: Her knowledge goes back only to the dawn of time. But if she could have looked a little further back, into the stillness and the darkness before Time dawned, she would have read there a different incantation. She would have known that when a willing victim who had committed no treachery was killed in a traitor's stead, the Table would crack and Death itself would start working backwards."[2]

Otherwise expressed: the White Witch's way of self-assertive grasping failed to root itself in the law. Her knowledge of the Law was severed from its originary ethos and had become a univocal rule subtending her claim to dominion. Aslan knew, however, its enigmatic origins; he knew the "way" of the Law was not the way of domination but a nondisabling vulnerability to an ancient power stronger even than Death. In Aslan's appearance amidst the Table's rubble, we glimpse what Kearney identifies as the "epiphanic paradigm of descent into darkness (*kenosis*) and ascent into light (*anabasis*)."[3] His sacrifice subverts the regnant order and, by breaking it down, possibilizes the breakthrough of a new order. In Narnia's darkest hour, when hope seems lost, his return is epiphanic, an "irruption of light in opacity,"[4] a manifestation revealing the Deep Magic's power and unleashing a countermovement of good against evil.

In this chapter, I explore how "exercising" metaxology might transform perception through a process of "epiphanic attunement." The itinerary of our exercises follows Kearney's paradigm: we endure the breakdown of the "return" and, with death-purged eyes, posthumous mind renders us attentive to signs of the infinite within the finite. We see, in short, divine light shining through the "crack" in everything. A restored sense of the *passio essendi* allows us to assume a new stance toward reality: we open ourselves in a gesture of hospitality and vigilantly listen in silence for the Agapeic One to speak. We are beings of perpetual expectancy who abide in an endless season of Advent; we are those who, with the whole of our being, listen within history for a revelatory word addressed to us by the Holy One. Epiphanic attunement describes how we are made able to recognize, and to respond, to events of divine disclosure. Metaxology transforms how we perceive the *metaxu* by giving us to behold all things with renewed senses.

First, I retrieve from Husserl a concept of orthoaesthesis (right perception) and transpose this concept into metaxological register. This transposition allows me next to explore the dynamics of epiphanic attunement in two narratives describing a process of "coming to perceive rightly" as a response to what Desmond calls "godsends." Then I suggest how the road to Emmaus narrative offers a palmary example of epiphanic attunement, and I gesture toward areas where the concept may be developed fruitfully in the future. I conclude by considering the relationship between metaphysics and theology and indicate how metaxology exposes the "crack" and porosity between them. Metaxology does not force a choice between them because it shows how both ways of thought are rooted in and are responses to the mystery of being and its disclosures. By leading us back into this primordial mystery, we will come to recognize and better appreciate metaxology's mystagogical impulse.

ORTHOAESTHESIS: FROM *STATUS QUO* TO SALUTARY BREAKDOWN

"Edmund Husserl blazed a path toward a phenomenology of the flesh," Richard Kearney writes, "when he broached the crucial theme of the living body (*Leib*)."[5] This emphasis on the role of the living body emerges explicitly in Husserl's *Ideas II*,[6] a text written in 1912, rewritten in 1915, and continually revised until he abandoned it in 1928. Husserl's assistants Edith Stein and Ludwig Landgrebe published the text posthumously, in 1952, after still further redaction.[7] At its core, *Ideas II* "concentrates on the unity of the self as person and on the self as an embodied, spatially oriented, and temporally located subject, thus providing a corrective to the rather disembodied idealist standpoint" of his earlier philosophy.[8] If his earlier work emphasized a disembodied transcendental ego, this work restored to the ego a body of living flesh.

To show why this restoration is important, let me offer a quick point of contrast between Descartes and Husserl. In the "Sixth Meditation" Descartes considers how

> the fact that I know that I exist, and that at the same time I judge that obviously nothing else belongs to my nature or essence except that I am a thinking thing, I rightly conclude that my essence consists entirely in my being a thinking thing. And although perhaps (or rather, as I shall soon say, assuredly) I have a body that is very closely joined to me, nevertheless, as I am merely a thinking thing and not an extended thing, and because on the other hand I have a distinct idea of a body, insofar as it is merely an extended thing and not a thinking thing, it is certain that I am really distinct from my body, and can exist without it.[9]

The body, for Descartes, hindered attainment of clear and distinct ideas. I am essentially a "thinking thing," *res cogitans*, for whom it is vital to bracket out the misleading information conveyed by the senses. In *Ideas II*, Husserl mends what Descartes sundered: "The Body is, in the first place, the *medium of all perception*; it is the *organ of perception* and is *necessarily* involved in all perception."[10] Rather than an impediment to knowledge, Husserl's body (*Leib*) is the means by which we apprehend and constitute the world we perceive. We do not "float" above the flux because, as embodied, we are immersed within it. The body, thus, is "the bearer of the zero point of orientation, the bearer of the here and the now, out of which the pure Ego intuits space and the whole world of the senses."[11] Where Descartes sought to filter out the contribution of sense data, Husserl's turn to the body effects a medieval retrieval: *nihil est in intellectu quod non prius in sensu* (nothing is in the intellect that is not first in the senses).

For Husserl, the body is the "bearer of the zero point of orientation, the bearer of the here and the now, out of which the pure Ego intuits space and the whole world of the senses."[12] It is the *Nullpunkt* where the axes of space and time intersect in one's flesh. Yet it is seldom the case that we experience our bodies as this zero point. Drew Leder describes this phenomenon as the body's disappearance.[13] For Leder, "disappearance" does not mean the body vanishes; trading on the "dis-" as a prefix of negation, it is more the case that the body simply does not appear to consciousness. Think, for instance, of the countless bodily movements and adjustments needed just to get us from our beds to the shower each morning. The way we move throughout the day with ease belies the ongoing interplay taking place within the body. An example: I walk through the airport, excited to be off on a long-awaited vacation. I fantasize about snorkeling, sailing, and drinking wine. I can turn my imagination to these pleasant anticipations, however, only because I am not thinking about a host of sensations and stimuli affecting me. I move without much, if any, thought of the operations of my viscera as my body digests my lunch; I am not aware of the change in tile color as I pass through the concourse; over the loudspeaker gate changes and boarding processes are announced but, because they do not affect my travel, I ignore them. My body and the barrage of sensations besetting it "disappear" as I dodge suitcases and avoid tripping over service animals as I make my way to my gate.

Even now, as you are reading these words, you are (I hope) so engrossed that you are relatively unconscious of your body. How do your socks feel? Your underwear? Are you now attentive to areas of your body you were not previously thinking about? This makes sense: accustomed to wearing clothes, we have learned to "filter out" their weight and texture and we pay them little heed. Think about how we become engrossed in a good novel or a captivating movie, or how we get into "flow" states while we are playing a game or participating in an activity we love. During these peak moments, entire regions of our body "disappear" in what Leder calls *background disappearance*, moments when entire regions of our body "can disappear because they are *not* the focal origin of our sensorimotor engagements but are backgrounded in the corporeal gestalt: that is, they are for the moment relegated to a supportive role, involved in irrelevant movement, or simply put out of play."[14] Immersed in an activity, bodily regions "disappear" into the background. A master chef does not think, "Now I lift the knife, now I bring it down," nor does the pianist say, "Now this finger, now that." Nor does either one think much about bile ducts, pancreatic enzymes, or the gall bladder. As they go about their tasks, a host of biological and physiological processes go unnoticed; the body as a whole "disappears," and it is this disappearance that allows the agent to focus her attention wholly on the task at hand.

In *Ideas II*, Husserl describes this "background disappearance" with a neologism: orthoaesthesis. Etymologically, the word means "right perception" and suggests how the world *normally* appears, the way appearances typically "coalesce into the unity of one concordant experience."[15] In an orthoaesthetic system, there is harmony between the subject and her world, allowing her to operate in a relatively unobstructed manner. Everything "works" and the workflow proceeds unimpeded. Thus the chef regularly negotiates the kitchen by chopping, slicing, weighing, tasting, and such, without giving much attention to *doing* it. Martin Heidegger describes this way of everyday dealing as being *Zuhandenheit* (ready-to-hand):

> The ready-to-hand is not grasped theoretically at all, nor is it itself the sort of thing that circumspection takes proximally as a circumspective theme. The peculiarity of what is proximally ready-to-hand is that, in its readiness-to-hand, it must, as it were, withdraw [*zurückzuziehen*] in order to be ready-to-hand quite authentically. That with which our every-day dealings proximally dwell is not the tools themselves [*die Werkzeuge selbst*]. On the contrary, that with which we concern ourselves primarily is the work—that which is to be produced at the time; and this is accordingly ready-to-hand too. The work bears with it that referential totality within which the equipment is encountered.[16]

Heidegger's ready-to-hand is the external world's complement to Leder's internal "background disappearance." Both are instances of, and are subtended by, Husserl's orthoaesthesis: when everything functions as it ought, one needs to pay little heed either to routine physical tasks or physiological processes. An orthoaesthetic state, then, describes a "concordant experience," the way the world typically "shows up" for us as embodied subjects. And, so long as our bodies and their functions operate unobtrusively, we can go about business without paying much attention to them.

But what happens when there is a breach in the system, a sudden disruption to a harmonious flow? The chef grabs a hot pan from a hapless rookie and burns her hand. Blistered, it "feels" different and she now feels things differently. How so? She runs a finger across her skin and feels swollen flesh where it had been smooth. She picks up her favorite knife and it feels somewhat awkward in her wounded hand. Things feel different, but the change is not with the exterior world but in my apperception of it. Husserl writes: "The changed data of the field of touch are indeed still apperceived according to appearances but precisely as anomalies, versus the concordant appearances of normally functioning sensibility, in which the same things are given in relation to the equally concordant and normally appearing parts of the Body and in relation to the whole of the Body."[17]

Muttering under her breath, she continues cooking but favors her other hand. She works more deliberately, more cautiously, because the knife is no longer an extension of her body but a hard-to-wield tool in her nondominant hand. What had been recessed and disappeared after the injury now obtrudes and makes smooth functioning impossible. A routine task is made arduous because it demands cutting with an injured hand the nondominant and nonpracticed hand in an unaccustomed way. If given to self-reflection, she might marvel at how easily she takes for granted the seamless concordant flow of her usual practice.

Not surprisingly, we seldom recognize an orthoaesthetic or normally functioning system until *after* a rupture has taken place. Heidegger described this disruption as "a certain un-readiness-to-hand"[18] interrupting the flow: the hammer is too heavy to lift, a key part is missing and the project cannot be completed, a limb is damaged and can no longer be used. We rue our clumsiness when we cut a finger and finish peeling potatoes with the other hand. And a breach with more permanent consequences, such as losing a limb or one's vision, can necessitate a total reorganization of life: learning to walk with a prosthesis, or having to redesign the house, or to develop new strategies for executing tasks once easily accomplished. Regardless, the experience of disruption recalls a sense of prior harmony, how things worked together and flowed normally. For a sous chef a pile of unpeeled potatoes is a predinner chore; for a man, the steps leading upstairs are just a means of getting to one's bedroom. For a chef with a maimed hand, the potatoes become an obstacle to a complete dinner; for a paralytic, the steps seem an insurmountable feat. The collapse of the quotidian operation elicits a reaction: the chef pines for things to go back to normal, whereas the paralytic must reassess his life and find a way to establish a new normal.

As you may have noticed, this model of orthoaesthetic perception is based on pathology, on the breakdown of an organ whose malfunction or woundedness affects one's apprehension of the world. Yet the collapse cannot be total. To denominate an event as an occurrence of breakdown presumes the typical functioning of the other organs. A systemic failure of all would, after all, be death. A rupture in the orthoaesthetic does not destroy the system, but significantly interrupts it. Thus Husserl: "Anomalies as such can therefore occur only in this form, namely that the normal world remains constitutively preserved, i.e., experienced, by the rest of the perceptual organs, the ones which, functioning reciprocally for each other as such organs, continue to give us experiences in the normal way."[19]

What is true for organ systems holds, likewise, in instances of intersubjective disagreement. As I interact with others, I may recognize how extensive "complexes of assertions about things, which *I* made in earlier periods of time on the ground of earlier experiences, experiences which were perfectly concordant throughout, are *not corroborated* by my current companions, and this not because these experiences are simply lacking to them (after all, one does not need to have seen everything others have seen, and vice versa) but because they thoroughly conflict with what the others experience in experiences, we may suppose, that necessarily are harmonious and that go on being progressively confirmed."[20]

Through intersubjective experiences, the possibility of having misinterpreted a given state of affairs arises. We encounter resistance to our settled claims about "how things are in the world" by rubbing up against others. Indeed, it may turn out that as "I communicate to my companions my earlier lived experiences" they will realize "how much these [experiences] conflict with their world, constituted inter-subjectively and continuously exhibited by means of a harmonious exchange of experiences."[21] Intersubjective engagement requires we negotiate our claims within a shared social space where conflicts can and do arise. I have a cousin who was much chagrined when he went to school having mismatched his socks. To his (then undiagnosed) colorblind eyes, the socks appeared identical; to his fashion-conscious classmates, his attire appeared, at best, quaintly odd. Within the social nexus of a classroom, the fashion faux pas was made manifest, and he learned to get a second opinion on his clothing choices before leaving the house each day.

Let me transpose orthoaesthesis into a metaxological key. The dynamism of the *metaxu* and the intermediation of beings can welcome Husserl's sense of the embodied subject emplaced within a nexus of other bodies. His insight into the intersubjective mediation between beings echoes Desmond's sense of our fundamental porosity. For neither one are we solitary subjects. Not only are we the "porosity of being become mindful,"[22] but also, for Desmond, we are the porosity of being become flesh. This "is embodied as an aesthetic field. Aesthetic environment means the milieu of all that surrounds us, all that envelops us, and all that seeps into and invades us. We are in it, but it is also in us. The aesthetic environment is originally not a neutral objective outerness. It is a field saturated with equivocal significance."[23]

Like Husserl, Desmond understands our lives as lived in congress with other beings. But when it comes to Husserl's sense of "orthoaesthesis," Desmond has reason to demur. For Husserl, it seems we become aware of "perceiving rightly" only in the breach, only *after* we suffer a breakdown of concordance. We experience a descent or, better, a decline from the "normal" and need to work to restore previous balance. For Desmond, however, the opposite is the case: it is with the breakdown of normal modes of perception that a breakthrough into a new and transformed mode is possible. One risks the *katabasis*, "descent," into the darkness of the "return" so that one's *anabasis*, "ascent," may be guided by a posthumous mind attentive to the "crack" in everything. This breakdown is not *pathological*, but, in rekindling a sense of God, deeply *theological*. By inducing a sense of the intimate strangeness of being, a strangeness too easily embedded in the sediment of the quotidian, our exercises seek to penetrate the mantle of the taken-for-granted. In returning us to the primal ethos, we are given to discern in the *metaxu* intimations of the infinite disclosed through the finite.

Inscribed into a metaxological framework, orthoaesthesis need not refer nostalgically to a lost-and-lamented sense of the status quo. On the contrary, this "right perception" apprehends otherwise concealed depths and lets one behold the "qualitative charge of the 'to be' of aesthetic happening."[24] Our exercises have aimed, with each hyperbolic indirection, to jostle us from the status quo and to reawaken within us a sense of the Transcendent, to stir up an awareness of God. Desmond does not want readers to languish in a neutral *metaxu*, a reconfigured order lacking in value, so he coaxes us onto an indirect itinerary to renew ourselves in the primal ethos: "The value-saturation of the original elemental aesthetic field contradicts the abstract notion that we live in a neutral world. There is no neutral world. The neutral world is a neutralized world—neutralized of the charge of ontological worth already constitutive of the aesthetics of happening. The neutralization does not destroy the charge, only diminishes or deforms it."[25] Orthoaesthesis perceives beneath the purportedly neutral ethos its hitherto concealed depths. Just as the breaking of the Stone Table revealed the power of the Deep Magic, so too does breakdown induced by the "return to zero" disclose the hidden "crack" in everything that allows mystery's hoary light to break into our lives.

Before considering how orthoaesthesis attunes us to divine epiphanies, allow me to draw on David Bentley Hart's insight into the "gaze of love." This gaze permits the agent to behold

each thing's fortuity, its mystery, its constancy within a "transfinite" unity, its immediate particularity, its radiant inherence within its own "essence," its intelligibility, and its way of holding together in itself the diversity of its transcendental aspects as a realized unity amid, and in unity with, multiplicity and change. The gaze of love seeks the being of things in the abiding source in which they participate; it is a way of seeing that is acquainted with moments of enchantment, which awaken it, however briefly, to a recognition of the persistence of being's peaceful and sustaining light . . . and of this light's "gratuitous necessity"; and these moments, however fleeting or imperfect, compel thought to risk a conjecture toward the infinite.[26]

The gaze of love perceives being not as an inert "thereness" but as a dynamic happening. It penetrates each being's *haecceity* and is directed beyond its *thisness* toward its endowing source. No voyeuristic peeping, this gaze "sees being as an infinite font of manifestation, knowing itself in the existence and essence of things, kenotically allowing (and so without alienation from its own diffusive goodness) the arrival in itself of what is, in itself, nothing: the pure ontic ecstasy of contingent existence."[27] It is attracted by what our metaxological exercises seek, namely, being's overdeterminacy, its too-muchness encountered idiotically, aesthetically, erotically, and agapeically. We can be hyperbolically indirected toward God and, through a renewal of our porosity, fall silent in astonishment at creation's gratuity. In this astonished silence, we stand as vigilant listeners. Our very selves open outward in ecstatic anticipation of a word we cannot compel, a word we long to hear with the entirety of our selves. "Only thus," as Rahner observed above, "are we what we should be."

As I use it, orthoaesthesis or "right perception" describes a way of beholding the "crack" in everything as one to the rhythmic interplay of the *metaxu*. It is the fruit of contemplative practice and, by undertaking metaxology as an *askesis*, we can be transformed into one of the *theōroi*. Not every breakdown is pathological and, in fact, some are salutary breakthroughs. Our exercises probe our reconfigured ethos to find chinks exposing the primordial ethos. By restoring our sense of being's overdeterminacy, these practices tutor us to perceive with Hart's "gaze of love." The created order, behold orthoaesthically, points beyond itself because it is the locus of revelatory moments, divine epiphanies, or what Desmond calls "godsends."

ORTHOAESTHESIS AS EPIPHANIC ATTUNEMENT

I want to develop this idea of orthoaesthesis in a theological register by suggesting how it capacitates "epiphanic attunement." If, as Hadot writes, "attention (*prosoche*) is the fundamental Stoic spiritual attitude,"[28] I propose epiphanic attunement as the fundamental spiritual attitude of the metaxologically tutored subject. Through metaphysical *askesis*, one can join ranks with the *theōroi* who actively contemplate creation with joyful vigilance. Attentive to the hyperboles of being, creation is a communicative tableau rife with signs pointing toward God. When one perceives orthoaesthetically, one's whole self is attuned to any chink or "crack" through which divine light might enter and illuminate the *metaxu*. Ever on the lookout for such disclosures, one effects a post of vigilant hospitality, open and receptive to the address of the Holy One. Of course, as Rahner observed, such "listening does not necessarily imply any actual hearing (neither in fact nor for the content). Perceiving God's silence is also an answer that makes the listening meaningful. Under God's silence too we may become what we have to be at any rate: personal finite spirit before the personal infinite free God, with whom we necessarily have to deal, at least by being aware of God's silence."[29]

Although we cannot compel God to speak, we can ready ourselves should a revelatory word enter our history. We can, in our daily lives, open ourselves in expectant silence and pray with the Psalmist: "I wait for the Lord, my soul waits, and in his word I hope; my soul waits for the Lord more than those who watch for the morning" (Ps. 130:5–6). We watch and pray for a word to shatter the silence.

In an essay entitled "Godsends," Desmond offers a fascinating, if not unambiguous, reflection on the nature of revelation. This is a signal development, as it marks an engagement with a topic central to theology. Indeed, one might wonder if this is not written as a response to Simpson's suggestion that, perhaps, "Desmond would benefit from a more positive account of revealed, confessional theology. Indeed, Desmond might need to 'come out of the closet' as a theologian as well—to be able to give a more robust accounting (and so remedy a kind of incompleteness in his present accounting) of the indeed necessary relation between, not only philosophy and religion, but philosophy and theology."[30]

Now, one will not find in "Godsends" any reference to *Dei verbum*—Vatican II's document on divine revelation—or mention of Karl Barth, but Barth would laud Desmond's understanding of revelation's irruptive suddenness. "Godsends," though not confessional theology, is nevertheless about *being religious* and this in two ways. First, there is "being *religious*" to describe a person's actions and the way the person's actions reflect, or derogate from, one's espoused religious commitments. Desmond uses Flannery O'Connor's character Ruby Turpin to explore this first sense of being *religious*. But "being religious" can stress *being* as religious. In this case, one is asked to consider how being itself is saturated with a religious significance many of us have become blind to detecting. Sometimes it takes a shock to our system to jostle us from our usual patterns of perception to see things as though for the first time.

Godsends: A Word and an Idea

"Godsends" follows three steps, three corkscrew turns penetrating ever deeper as he treats the "godsend" as *word*, *idea*, and *story*. Each step or turn leads us deeper into the richness of the *word*, of the *idea*, and brings out fully the treasures of O'Connor's *story*. He begins with its *Oxford English Dictionary* definition and notes the word's amphiboly. True, a "godsend" normally refers to an unexpected boon or fortuitous turn: an anonymous benefactor pays the balance on all your layaway items in a store; in dire financial straits, an unexpected inheritance arrives in the mail. At the same time, godsends may not always be received, at least not initially, with joy. The loss of a job, or the diagnosis of a disease, creates an upheaval in one's life. Looking back on the event, given some time and perspective, one may eventually come to regard it as a salutary disruption. One sees it, in a sense, as a "dark grace," a painful yet beneficial breakdown leading to a positive change. My friend lost a six-figure job on Wall Street in 2008. At first stunned, then forlorn, as the shock wore off he began to see, in the rubble of his career, prospects for an unimagined trajectory. He sold his condo and earned a degree in education. Now teaching in a Detroit public school, he regards the collapse of his former life as a gift—a godsend—allowing him to discern and accept what he now recognizes as his vocation.

Thus "godsend" cannot, then, be taken to have a univocal meaning. Indeed, Desmond emphasizes its equivocity in defining a godsend as "an event or happening that befalls us, and that may open out the opportunity of a benefit or boon, or surprising gift; an event that might well be shadowed by something suffered, and suffered not just in the receipts of gifts, but also in the visiting on some of pain and disaster or death."[31] How Shakespearean: what seems fair can be foul and what seems foul can be fair! If my friend's lifestyle change is an instance of the latter, one may think of how winning the lottery can at times help and at other times ruin a family's life. The phrase "mixed blessing" comes to mind.

The word "godsend" also connotes the *idea* "of a sending, by the divine to us, perhaps, and hence the insinuation of a kind of revelation."[32] A godsend is not experienced as a random bit of luck, a happenstance, but as a moment of divine communication; the godsend appears as having been deliberately sent by the divine. It is received as a message, even though neither the godsend's meaning nor message is transparent or obvious. Desmond: "A godsend might be noted but often we do not know what the meaning communicated is. Ambiguity and mystery may attend that more painful sense of equivocity that comes with the disaster that is a curse to one and a blessing to another. In the word 'send' also there is the implication of being sent on a journey, being called on a mission. The godsend may be a sending that causes us to set off on a way in the name of a mysterious cause."[33] One must discern the godsend's meaning. It is one thing to hear one's name called in the darkness; it is another, as Samuel learned, to make oneself vulnerable by responding, "Speak, Lord, for your servant is listening" (1 Sam. 3:9). The godsend rouses us from somnolence and reveals otherwise unimagined possibilities.

For Desmond, the godsend arrives as a shocking and unsettling surprise whose arrival simultaneously threatens and promises to unclog our porosity. Cognizant of Taylor's "buffered self" and "immanent frame," Desmond describes how "a godsend comes and we are no longer within the buffered closure in which we previously were. A veil is drawn back— the literal meaning of apocalypse (apo-kalypsis). A chink or crack happens in the closure of the 'immanent frame,' to use Charles Taylor's phrase. We have to ponder the light that comes through the chink and wonder how far we might travel in its illumination."[34]

If the godsend's arrival catches us off guard, its disorientation can reorient us to behold things anew. The godsend, as it were, can burst open the bounds of the ordinary to reveal its divine depths. One might think here of Thomas Merton: "In Louisville, at the corner of Fourth and Walnut, in the center of the shopping district, I was suddenly overwhelmed with the realization that I loved all those people, that they were mine and I theirs, that we could not be alien to one another even though we were total strangers. It was like waking from a dream of separateness, of spurious self-isolation in a special world, the world of renunciation and supposed holiness. The whole illusion of a separate holy existence is a dream."[35]

Something within Merton gave way, a clog dissolved, and it was revealed how all of us are intimately, albeit strangely, connected. What had been understood as parallel tracks of the natural and the supernatural, the sacred and the profane, appeared in the godsend's wake to crisscross and interpenetrate. The godsend did not dispel mystery but opened for Merton a passageway into its depths and allowed him to experience his porosity to those around him. He awoke to his middle condition, discovered himself in the sacred *metaxu*, and saw all things charged with God's presence. Hopkins's "hurrahing" continued in Louisville.

A godsend, even if welcomed, cannot but leave the recipient with a wound or trace, a permanent reminder of what one has undergone. Although we often associate epiphanies or moments of divine disclosure with light and illumination, one can imagine an epiphany as enshrouding one's senses in a purgative darkness before any light is glimpsed. The godsend involves both *katabasis* and *anabasis*, a breaking down and a building-up. Its arrival, often enough, induces a breakdown before yielding a breakthrough: "We have to be divested of the shutters before the chink that opens to the light is felt—felt as suffering that breaks down the shutters. And perhaps it is not surprising that the surprise of the godsend is very often in the dawning of a destitution where we can no longer count on anything, and not on ourselves either. Beyond all possible determination or self-determination the godsend visits. Perhaps we have to become as nothing for it to communicate in the newly evacuated space of porosity."[36]

Hence my suggestion that, within the context of an increasingly secular age, we needed to embark upon an exercise or an *askesis* such as the "return to zero." By pushing nihilism to its limit, by meditating on the implications of standing beneath the Angel of Death's wings, we face the truth of existence: we come from, and return to, nothing. In the wreckage of monuments built to honor the *conatus*, we may yet be astonished to hear a whisper: *yet it is*. In a flash, the Angel's wing is haloed with light and we are astonished at being's gratuity. Having passed through the valley of death and crowned with posthumous mind, we return from our meditation and occupy the *metaxu* with purged senses. We see with new eyes and perceive orthoaesthetically that all creation is a gift. The whole cosmos sings of God's ongoing *givingness*. The wound inflicted through the "return" doubles as a grace. As a wound, it recalls our frailty and testifies *memento mori*, "remember you will die." As a grace, restored porosity renders us robustly metaphysical as we find our place amidst and in congress with other beings (*meta*), and this porosity remains open to and serves as a reminder of the creative origin beyond finite being (*meta*) on whose account there is something rather than nothing. Upon the *metaxu* one finds no single children: we are, all of us, kith and kin with one another and the creative Other.

At this point, one may share Simpson's worry over "a possible logic of dualism here, where philosophy on its own can perform such that theology is redundant, unnecessary, rejected."[37] Desmond allays this concern. For although it is true that the hyperboles perform by throwing us beyond the immanent order, our movement toward God is not and cannot be self-initiated. Desmond insists that, with the godsend, "the movement comes to us. The ball of the divine play is first thrown to us. There is the gift of receiving. There is something of a reversal—it is not we who are intentionally in search of something, but something finds us, finds us out, and unexpectedly to us. When it comes, there is a surprising consonance of what is sent with secret desire hardly known or perhaps denied by us; and it is we who are the beneficiaries."[38]

Desmond is not positing two disciplines—metaphysics and theology—separated by an impermeable barrier. On the contrary, the advent of the godsend not only reveals a permeable threshold between them but also recovers, as D. C. Schindler notes, "a certain priority of religion *over* philosophy."[39] Or, to hearken back to our earlier discussion, we find here a reaffirmation of our fifth commandment: *Be still and know: Metaphysics is a vocation.* We are capable of self-transcendence because we have been opened by the advent of actual transcendence, God. The initiative rests always with the divine, and our openness to its reception is, itself, a gift.

Let me try to make this clearer with a joke. When I was a kid, my grandfather told a story of a tourist in Ireland who stopped to ask a local for directions to Dublin. The reply: "Well, sir, if I were you, I wouldn't start from here." The joke: if you really want to get someplace, then it is better to start out nearer to where you want to arrive at. I never found it funny. But tweak it a bit. A spiritual seeker asks for "the" way or even "a" way to God. For the jokester, or the univocal philosopher, the punchline remains the same. For the metaxologically minded the punchline is inapt. For the answer is simple: one can be directed to God from *any* point within the *metaxu* because *all* points pulse with divine life. *Creatio ex nihilo* is not a formula but a festive song singing of the Creator's ongoing givingness; Anselm's way is an archaeological expedition into the self's recesses where one discovers how, even when alone, one is never alone. Whether discerned within the exterior world or one's interiority, we can come to perceive how the "crack" in everything reveals how the light illuminating the *metaxu* directs our gaze to an Agapeic Creator. Hence, for the epiphanically attuned, "everything that is is a godsend; and yet nothing that finitely is is the source that communicates and reveals itself in the godsend."[40] Or, as Schindler writes, "in every object there hides a dimension of the godsend; in every subject sleeps porosity to receiving the godsend before any activity of conceiving it."[41] This *idea* of the godsend is concretized in Desmond's discussion of O'Connor's *story* "Revelation."

Before we take the third turn, from "godsend" as *word* to *idea* to its *story*, I return to the "ambiguity" noted in Desmond's treatment of revelation. On the one hand, he is at his most finessed when probing how the "crack" discloses the Agapeic Origin. Rightly perceived, creation is the locus of "general revelation." The Psalmist: "The heavens declare the glory of God, the skies display his craftsmanship" (Ps. 19:1). John Scotus Eriugena: "The whole world is a theophany."[42] If I am correct, metaxological exercises inform us about metaphysics and form us to perceive these traces within the *metaxu*. We have been attuned to behold creation orthoaesthetically with epiphanically attuned senses. Those who have undertaken the "return" and traversed the indirections, have been re-formed to behold all of creation with epiphanic eyes. The godsend does not and cannot leave us unscathed. In being struck, we bear a wound of knowledge—a trace, a scar, a graced reminder of a divine ingress into our lives. As Frodo's scar alerted him to the approach of the Nazgûl or Ringwraiths, and as Harry Potter's scar burned when Voldemort drew near, so too does this wound sensitize us to the presence of the divine in all things and bids us to remain watchful for disclosures of the divine.

Nevertheless, Desmond does not advance an explicit treatment of special revelation. No engagement with *Dei Verbum*, no exegesis of conciliar documents, no Christology or Trinitarian theology. Although he insists on remaining a philosopher, and though he probes the *metaxu* for signs of the "crack" between the finite and the infinite, theologians may be concerned by his recourse to theological concepts and themes. We see inklings of this in "Godsends" when he invokes the prophets and Jesus, and refers to *kenosis* but does not develop them:

What of the special revelation claimed for Jesus Christ? Christ would be the absolute godsend—the singular absolute, absolutely intimate with the absolute sender, and yet absolute as sent; not a nothing intermediate, though a kenotic intermediary absolutely porous to the sending source; there is an absolute community of God and godsend (Father and Son) and yet the revealed godsend does not diminish the transcendent mystery of the source, even while revealed in absolute immanence. The prophets: singular godsends of the absolute? Christ: the absolved and absolving godsend?[43]

Simpson's eyebrows raise and we can imagine him exclaiming: "Desmond, you speak of intra-divine community and kenosis. Is your theological slip showing? Declare yourself or explain why you end, not with a *Credo*, but a question mark." Manoussakis, who finds himself vexed by Desmond's silence about "Christ, even when writing on God,"[44] voices this impatience: "So the majority of references to Christ in GB [*God and the Between*] are to a Christ that serves merely as an example—in a sense not different from the Christological exemplarism one meets in Kant's *Religion within the Boundaries of Mere Reason*. Desmond avoids assigning to Christ's role and place any uniqueness as the in-between par excellence, or if he alludes to such an exception this is done in Christianity's name while carefully avoiding any personal endorsement."[45]

Kearney is more sanguine: "While hinting at his own personal Christian commitment, Desmond retains his position as a philosopher of religion rather than a proponent of dogmatic theology in leaving us with Christ as a *question*."[46] Finally, Patrick Gardner observes, "Desmond, of course, stops short of taking up the mantel of Catholic theology, and we need not force him to abandon this sense of methodological integrity."[47]

Gardner and Kearney are correct: Desmond is not engaged in an explicit theology. He is, rather, intent on uncovering the religious dimension of the *metaxu*. He helps readers to reflect on "being religious," insofar as being itself is saturated with religious significance. Hardly confined to a "theological closet," he might better be seen as leading us into Taylor's "sacred forest" where we risk having an experience akin to Hazel Motes, who saw "Jesus move from tree to tree in the back of his mind, a wild ragged figure motioning him to turn around and come off into the dark where he was not sure of his footing, where he might be walking on the water and not know it and then suddenly know it and drown."[48] Christianity, indeed Christ, is everywhere and nowhere in Desmond's thought. This is not something he needs to apologize for, nor is Christ a spectral presence we should rush to exorcise through some secularizing ritual. True: Desmond does not offer a systematic considera- tion of Chalcedon or Nicaea. He might not publically confess Christ as *the* Way, but can we not see that Desmond finds in Jesus *a* way that leads beyond Nietzsche's will to power toward a life of agapeic service?[49] In his "Caesar with the Soul of Christ," he argues for the superiority of Christ over Caesar, the way of agapeic service as superior to the self-assertion of will to power. Rather than a theological treatise, his approach is more of an archaeological expedition. Indeed, Desmond capacitates us to think how the *logos* or, better, the *Logos* is at play in the *arche* (origin) of being itself. The *ethos* is not neutral to the presence of the divine because it is both a reflection of and the dwelling place for the *Logos*. This is beauti- fully captured in the final verses of his canto "God Being (Too) Good."[50]

> The killers know
> The secret streak of
> God's quietness
> & are not shamed
> The living forget its radiance
> The holy feel its flame
> & are branded with its blaze
>
> By the flaring of this fire
> We behold your face
> In the criminal innocence
> Of the saving one

Desmond does not set out two opposing types, say Dionysius versus the Crucified, as Nietzsche would have it, but leads us toward the fire. We, too, can draw near and feel the flame and see past the dancing flames the shadowy figure of one who stares back at us in "criminal innocence." Christ may be incognito, but it is hard to imagine that Desmond's un- derstanding of the primal ethos could have come from anywhere other than Christianity.

I mention this to highlight how metaxology does not require us to build, or to tear down, any wall separating Athens from Jerusalem. Desmond opens an innovative way of thinking about philosophical theology or theological philosophy. For he leads us on an archaeological quest to excavate and expose the religious nature of the primal ethos. "Being religious" is not an adjectival phrase to describe humans but a metaxological insight into the very structure of being itself: being is shot through with religious significance. It is this insight that allows us to probe further the potential relationship between metaxology and theology. For philosophy ("love of wisdom") and theology (receptive listening to the Word of God) are nourished by the same wellspring. A revelatory godsend would not, then, impose something alien upon reason but would expose reason's intimately mysterious depths. By guiding us toward and resurrecting our sense of mystery, metaxology opens a mystagogical path. Thus, our metaxological exercises work on two levels. Generally, for those seeking to return to a sense of the sacred in a secular age, they work to resurrect a sense of astonishment at being's givenness and lead us to a consideration of how the "crack" in everything serves to point toward an Agapeic Creator. For those reading it on a theological level, this approach could be described as the "Hopkins option" whereby one is given to behold from within the *metaxu* the many and various disclosures of Christ's presence. Hopkins poetically testifies to such a disclosure when he writes:

> I say more: the just man justices;
>> Keeps grace; that keeps all his goings graces;
> Acts in God's eye what in God's eye he is—
>> Christ. For Christ plays in ten thousand places,
> Lovely in limbs, and lovely in eyes not his
>> To the Father through the features of men's faces.[51]

Metaxology, in incrementally guiding us deeper into the mystery of being, reveals its mystagogical edge. Rather than an antinomy—reason *or* faith—this mystagogical element reveals how reason and faith are equally rooted in and nourished at the wellspring of mystery. There exists, at a most basic and primordial level, a porosity between them. If

Christ appears to play within Desmond's thought, it is because metaxology and theology are sourced in, even if they respond differently to, the mysterious presence of the *Logos*. Let us turn, then, to consider how the godsend-inflicted rupture exposes and guides us into these abyssal depths where we might probe the nature of the threshold separating metaphysics and theology to see if there might be a greater porosity between reason and faith than is realized. To probe this, we turn now from the *idea* of the godsend to its *story* as found in O'Connor's "Revelation."

Godsends: A Story

We now take Desmond's third step, the final turn of the screw, and consider Flannery O'Connor's *story* entitled "Revelation" to illustrate how the godsend's irruption transforms perception. The story illustrates how a godsend precipitates a revelatory event that "draws the curtain back" (*revelare*) and reveals what, to untutored eyes, had been hidden. Yet the godsend does not deliver its recipient—in this story, Ruby Turpin—from her metaxu. On the contrary, it refigures how she perceives and understands her place within it. By reflecting on "Revelation" as a *story* I hope to unpack Desmond's understanding of the godsend and show how the godsend clarifies *what* orthoaesthesis is and *how* it works to attune recipients to everyday epiphanies.

The story opens with Ruby's entrance into a crowded doctor's office. It is clear that her physical size does not reflect any such spiritual magnanimity. Her pusillanimity is on display as she banters with a "pleasant-looking" woman seated nearby and the reader is drawn into her harsh inner monologue. For around her she observes how "the well-dressed lady had on red and grey suede shoes to match her dress. Mrs. Turpin had on her good black patent leather pumps. The ugly girl had on Girl Scout shoes and heavy socks. The old woman had on tennis shoes and the white-trashy mother had on what appeared to be bedroom slippers, black straw with gold braid threaded through them—exactly what you expect her to have on."[52]

The "ugly girl" is Mary Grace, a student at Wellesley College, who broodingly reads a textbook entitled *Human Development*. Her face is "blue with acne and Mrs. Turpin thought how pitiful it was to have a face like that at that age. She gave the girl a friendly smile but the girl

only scowled the harder."[53] The tension between the characters builds
and it becomes apparent to the reader, if not to Ruby, that Mary Grace
sees through her façade. Indeed, the reader cannot help but to ponder:
Who *really* is the ugly character? Ruby fancies herself quite a connois-
seur when it comes to measuring and categorizing people based on outward appearances. Today's reader should be unnerved at her wanton
racism and bigotry when we read how, when she tried to fall asleep, she
denominated classes of people:

> On the bottom of the heap were most colored people, not the kind
> she would have been if she had been one, but most of them; then
> next to them—not above, just away from—were the white-trash;
> then above them were the home-owners, and above them the home-
> and-land owners, to which she and Claud belonged. Above she and
> Claud were people with a lot of money and much bigger houses and
> much more land. But here the complexity of it would begin to bear
> in on her, for some of the people with a lot of money were common
> and ought to be below she and Claud and some of the people who
> had good blood had lost their money and had to rent and then there
> were colored people who owned their homes and land as well. . . .
> Usually by the time she had fallen asleep all the classes of people
> were moiling and roiling around in her head, and she would dream
> they were being crammed together in a box car, being ridden off to
> be put in a gas oven.[54]

Such are the nocturnal musings of a woman who can, without any
sense of contradiction, muse upon images of the Holocaust while simultaneously professing her love of and gratitude to Jesus. In her mind she
occupies the happy middle, the Aristotelian mean, within the Great
Chain of Being. Her position—not too high, not too low—is, itself,
a gift:

> To help anybody out that needed it was her philosophy of life. She
> never spared herself when she found somebody in need, whether
> they were white or black, trash or decent. And of all she had to be
> thankful for, she was most thankful that this was so. If Jesus had
> said, "You can be high society and have all the money you want and

be thin and svelte-like, but you can't be a good woman with it," she would have had to say, "Well don't make me that then. Make me a good woman and it don't matter what else, how fat or how ugly or how poor!" Her heart rose. He had not made her a nigger or white-trash or ugly! He had made her herself and given her a little bit of everything. Jesus, thank you! she said. Thank you thank you thank you![55]

Clearly, Ruby never heeded the Delphic Oracle: Know Thyself! She is a benighted soul lacking in self-knowledge and blind to her hypocrisy. Although she may assure herself as having been made "a good woman," we pause. A medieval adage here proves illuminating: *agere sequitur esse* (acting follows on being). Or, as Matthew the Evangelist put it, "By their fruits you shall know them" (Matt. 7:16). Having peered into her soul and seen its darkness, one wonders just what sort of fruit she bears in the world. Rather than gospel music, Ruby's soul appears rooted in and nourished by the ethos that gave rise to Billie Holiday's "Strange Fruit."

Although Ruby is blind to her hypocrisy, Mary Grace clearly is not. Ruby, in fact, grows increasingly dis-eased as she gradually becomes cognizant of the girl's manifest hostility toward her. Gradually but steadily Ruby grows unsettled as she finds herself incapable of escaping Mary Grace's contemptuous gaze. Hostility gathers in the girl's blue eyes, which, to Ruby, "seemed lit all of a sudden with a peculiar light, an unnatural light like night road signs give."[56] The climax comes when, in a moment of self-indulgent revelry, Ruby inwardly bursts into a paean of gratitude to Jesus. We, who have been eavesdropping on her inner monologue, know only too well her hypocrisy:

> "When I think who all I could have been besides myself and what all I got, a little of everything, and a good disposition besides, I just feel like shouting, 'Thank you, Jesus, for making everything the way it is!' It could have been different!" For one thing, somebody else could have got Claud [her husband]. At the thought of this, she was flooded with gratitude and a terrible pang of joy rang through her. "Oh thank you, Jesus, Jesus, thank you!" she cried aloud.[57]

Her ecstasy is fleeting, for at that moment Mary Grace heaves her book and strikes Ruby over her left eye. She lunges at Ruby and digs her fingers into her neck. Once she has been pulled away and restrained, a dazed Ruby cannot keep from looking at her. The girl's eyes were now "bluer than before, as if a door that had been tightly closed behind them was now open to admit light and air."[58] Seduced by her eyes, Ruby realizes the girl somehow knows her deeply, personally, and she speaks directly to her, "'What you got to say to me?' she asked hoarsely and held her breath, waiting as for a revelation. The girl raised her head. Her gazed locked with Mrs. Turpin's. 'Go back to hell where you came from, you old wart hog,' she whispered."[59] These words have more of an effect upon her than the book. Her life has literally been ruptured by a sudden and violent encounter with a book bearing the ironic title of *Human Development*. For the very (Mary) Grace spurned by Ruby, through her violent interruption of Ruby's benighted revelries and illusions, creates the opening for growth and development. In O'Connor's prose, a glint of her Thomistic leanings: "grace does not destroy nature but perfects it."[60] No one ever claimed, however, that this grace-guided perfection was easy.

When she returns home, Ruby tries to rest but the "image of a razor-backed hog with warts on its face and horns coming out behind its ears" invades her imagination. There is no mistaking it: Ruby knows deep down that "she had been singled out for the message, though there was trash in the room to whom it might justly have been applied. . . . The message had been given to Ruby Turpin, a respectable, hard-working, church-going woman."[61] Unable to sleep, she makes her way to the pig parlor where she begins to hose down the hogs. Her anger at this unwelcomed godsend erupts and she rages at God, "'What do you send me a message like that for?' she said in a low fierce voice, barely above a whisper but with the force of a shout in its concentrated fury. 'How am I a hog and me both? How am I saved and from hell too?'"[62] Her baleful cry meets silence. The setting sun continues to sink into the horizon; night gathers and her bitterness intensifies. As she fumes, she enacts the ugliness Mary Grace saw. After reciting her litany of complaints against God, and in a "final surge of fury," she roars, "Who do you think you are?" and then "the color of everything, field and crimson sky, burned for a moment with a transparent intensity. The question carried over the pasture and across the highway and the cotton field and returned to her clearly like an answer from beyond the wood. She opened her mouth but no sound came out of it."[63]

Her Job-like challenge ricochets and puts *her* into question. Struck by her own jeremiad, she falls silent and remains so for the rest of the story.

Up until this point, these events could have been reported by any onlooker as a random act of violence perpetrated against a middle-aged woman by a petulant teenager. But Ruby, and the reader, see things in a different light. Mary Grace's message "hits her." The book, we realize, serves as an unwanted—if most direly needed—godsend sent to tear the scales from Ruby's eyes. Its arrival has proven irruptive and destabilizing and has begun to call into question her clear-cut, illusion-free view of the world. But if the godsend has thrown her off balance, if it has wreaked havoc within her life, there is a moment of breakthrough in the breakdown. Ruby turns to behold her pigs as though their pen were a monstrance: "Like a monumental statue coming to life, she bent her head slowly and gazed, as if through the very heart of mystery, down into the pig parlor and on the hogs. They had settled all in one corner around the old sow who was grunting softly. A red glow suffused them. They appeared to pant with a secret life."[64]

Head bowed, she finds herself implicated in something beyond herself. As day cedes to night, she remains transfixed by the hogs, her "gaze bent to them as if she were absorbing some abysmal life-giving knowledge."[65] In the rubble of her sense of self-righteousness categories and schema, in the ruins of her sense of what it meant to be religious, Ruby Turpin glimpses the religious dimension of being itself. Before her eyes, creation's depths are uncovered.

In this uncovering, through this revelation, Ruby begins to "perceive rightly" in what I have taken to calling epiphanic attunement. The godsend does not contribute new information but catalyzes a progressive transformation of the way Ruby perceives all things. For the godsend unclogs her porosity and reignites her sense of Desmond's "intimate universal" that binds all of creation into a community with one another and the Creator. In this, the conflict with Mary Grace metamorphoses into the renewal of communion. Grace's projectile "up-ends all the projects of Mrs. Turpin" and reveals "something prior to and beyond all projects."[66] Unbidden and unwanted, the breakdown makes breakthrough possible. The pig-pen epiphany does not inform Ruby but forms her to perceive within the hogs her share in a secret life. This is a rebirth leading, as found on Cardinal Newman's gravestone, *ex umbris et imaginibus in veritatem*, "out of shadow and phantasy into the truth."

If the first epiphany gives Ruby a glimpse of a mysterious presence pulsing within the heart of being—her hogs "panting with secret life"—then the second epiphany overturns her understanding of the status quo's propriety. Lifting her gaze from the pigs to the sky, she sees

> a purple streak in the sky, cutting through a field of crimson and leading, like an extension of the highway, into the descending dusk. She raised her hands from the side of the pen in a gesture hieratic and profound. A visionary light settled in her eyes. She saw the streak as a vast swinging bridge extending upward from the earth through a field of living fire. Upon it a vast horde of souls were rumbling toward heaven. There were whole companies of white-trash, clean for the first time in their lives, and bands of black niggers in white robes, and battalions of freaks and lunatics shouting and clapping and leaping like frogs. And bringing up the end of the procession was a tribe of people whom she recognized at once as those who, like herself and Claud, had always had a little of everything and the God-given wit to use it right. . . . They were marching behind the others with great dignity, accountable as they had always been for good order and common sense and respectable behavior. They alone were on key. Yet she could see by their shocked and altered faces that even their virtues were being burned away.[67]

Like the prodigal son who "comes to himself" amidst the pigs (Luke 15:17), Ruby comes to see her old life in a new light. The order according to which she had lived has been upended and refigured. The chink in Ruby's world lets new light flood in and the logic of the status quo is subverted: the first shall be last and the last shall be first (Matt. 20:16).

The reader wonders: Does Ruby's life change? We are not told, but we have a clue. The story ends with Ruby making "her slow way on the darkening path to the house. In the woods around her the invisible cricket choruses had struck up, but what she heard were the voices of the souls climbing upward into the starry field and shouting hallelujah."[68] Though the vision evanesces and disappears, she seems newly attuned to something she did not hear, and could not have heard, before this epiphany. She bears upon her flesh and within her soul the wound of this graced encounter. In granting her a renewed vision of creation, the god-send opens and makes possible for Ruby a new way of life. To be sure, the swelling above her left eye will eventually dissipate, but the expansion of her soul need not shrink back to its original proportions. She has been gifted, or afflicted, by a subversive theo-logic overturning her sense of righteousness: her ways are not God's. If there is a gossamer strand of hope for conversion, it is in her attunement to the crickets' melody. For if she hears now in nature the whoops and cheers of those blazing a path toward heaven, perhaps it is not too late for her to find her place within this motley crew.

Ruby moves triadically from life to a text and then back to life, but not the life she once knew. The breakdown of the status quo, for Ruby and reader alike, exposes our primal porosity and gives us to see how the intimate universal binds us to hogs and crickets and "battalions of freaks and lunatics." If we descended with her into darkness (*katabasis*), our upward ascent (*anabasis*) is guided by the chink of light opened by the godsend. We stand with her, taking our place between the hogs and heaven, and behold all things with renewed senses. We perceive a kinship with all of creation and are struck by the falsity of our hierarchies based on clean and unclean, redeemed and the damned. If Jesus is present in the story, it is not the Jesus who serves as the guarantor of the bourgeois status quo. It is, instead, the Misfit's Jesus who has "thrown everything off balance." For the epiphanically attuned, one may exercise the "Hopkins option" and find the face of Jesus present in ten thousand places within the heaven-bound horde's faces. We can only imagine how life might go on for Mrs. Turpin. Perhaps she succumbs to nostalgia and reverts to her old ways, regarding the godsend not as a gift but as a freak event. Or, I hope, her ears might be forever attuned to hearing in the crickets the shouts of hallelujah, and she will embark upon a new way of life animated by this revealed rhythm.

I hope this has not been an indulgent detour. Each turn guiding our investigation of the godsend as *word, idea, story* has, with increasing vibrancy, given us to consider the porosity between the aesthetic, ethical, and religious dimensions of being. "Revelation" forces us to consider how the godsend does not inflict or create porosity but, with its rupturing arrival, exposes and enlivens the intimate universal. In Ruby's case, its arrival makes possible a *transitus*, a crossing of a threshold, as she is led from a life configured according to one logic to a life refigured according to another. This crossing, though, cannot take place apart from the body or the *metaxu*. O'Connor writes: "The action of grace changes a character. Grace can't be experienced in itself. An example: when you go to Communion, you receive grace but you experience nothing; or if you do experience something, what you experience is not the grace but an emotion caused by it. Therefore in a story all you can do with grace is to show that it is changing the character."[69]

O'Connor never heard of metaxological metaphysics and probably had never heard of orthoaesthesis. Nevertheless, her story puts narrative flesh on the process of epiphanic attunement. If our spiritual exercises cultivate a general attentiveness to the "crack" in everything, what "Revelation" offers us is a sense of what takes place when we undergo grace. Ruby's encounter with Mary Grace refigured but did not impart new knowledge—at least not immediately—but it initiated a process of being re-formed or attuned in a new manner. Grace causes a breakdown and allows Ruby a grudging breakthrough into new layers of meaning. "All of my stories," O'Connor muses, "are about the action of grace on a character who is not very willing to support it."[70] Although not without noetic content, grace acts by initiating the slow, and sometimes painful, event of conversion as one comes not only to *think* differently but to *behold* all things anew. Reading "Revelation" with metaxological eyes, we see the potential for a fruitful intermingling between an "aesthetic theology"—in this case modeled by a literary text's appropriation of theological themes—and a "theological aesthetics," which prompts us to reflect upon our embodied and aesthetic experiences in light of theology.

"My Lord and My God": Beholding Christ's Graced Porosity

I now treat John 20, Thomas's encounter with the Risen Christ, as a scriptural instance of the godsend's arrival. Let me start by tweaking Wittgenstein's aphorism. Instead of his picture, I want to suggest that "A painting held us captive. And we could not get outside it, for it lay in our imagination and our imagination seemed to repeat it to us inexorably."[71] The painting to which I refer is Caravaggio's *The Incredulity of Saint Thomas* (*Incredulità di San Tommaso*), which depicts Thomas's encounter with the Risen Christ. Thomas, who had not been present at Jesus's first appearance (John 20:19–22), rejects the disciples' testimony when they tell him, "We have seen the Lord" (20:24). Rather than doubtful or skeptical, Thomas is better regarded as resolute in his unbelief (*apistos*), and he tells them, "Unless I see the mark of the nails in his hands, and put my finger in the mark of the nails and my hand in his side, I will not believe" (20:25). Thus it is Jesus's second appearance that Caravaggio depicts. Three disciples huddle around Jesus with Thomas at the forefront. Jesus serenely pulls back his robe and guides Thomas's right hand toward his pierced side. Thomas's finger slides into the wound and his face becomes an image of wonderment: eyes widen and astonishment ripples across his brow as, in this haptic happening, faith is born.

One problem: Caravaggio's painting has enframed or set the imaginative parameters on the way many read and interpret this text; it is the aesthetic complement to postulatory finitism, a "Pictionary finitism." For although Jesus does say to Thomas, "Put your finger here and see my hands. Reach out your hand and put it in my side. Do not be unbelieving [*apistos*] but believe" (20:27), there is no scriptural evidence for Thomas having done so. Brian Robinette observes: "Thomas's response is not to touch in a strictly empirical way—again, we are never told that Thomas does what he originally set out to do—but to make a bold acknowledgment only possible in faith."[72] Instead of physical contact, we have a confession of faith as Thomas exclaims: "My Lord and my God!" Robinette regards this as "among the clearest affirmations of Jesus as 'God' in the New Testament, and it comes as a response to an unanticipated upsurge of insight into the meaning of Jesus as the crucified-and-risen One. The theme of Jesus' unity with the Father is found throughout John's gospel . . . but here we have an affirmation from a disciple who discerns the reality of God in Jesus' crucified-and-risen 'form.' To 'see' this form is to 'see' the Father."[73]

If Caravaggio's painting would have us believe Thomas's faith comes as a result of touching Jesus's wounds, a close reading of the text gives us pause. In remonstrating Thomas, Jesus does not mention touching but only *seeing*, and indicates that sight is not essential for belief: "Have you believed because you have seen me? Blessed are those who have not seen and yet come to believe" (20:29). "In other words," Robinette writes, "blessed are those who enter into this structure of faith as a response to apostolic testimony: 'We have seen the Lord.'"[74]

I will return to Robinette but need first to retrieve an insight from Hilary of Poitiers. In *The Trinity*, he observes how, as a Jew, Thomas would have daily recited the Shema: "Hear, O Israel, the Lord your God is one Lord" (Deut. 6:4). Thomas, no doubt, would also have heard Jesus say things such as "I and the Father are one," "All things that the Father has are mine," and "I in the Father and the Father in me."[75] So, how is it that when Thomas exclaims, "My Lord and my God," he is not, as Hilary notes, "unmindful of the principal commandment"?[76] Is this not a betrayal of Jewish monotheism? The Shema would appear antithetical with Jesus's claims to unity with the Father. Yet, Robert Wilkens notes, "during Christ's lifetime these words apparently made little impact on [Thomas]. It was only when Thomas knew the resurrected Christ that he grasped the meaning of what Jesus had said earlier."[77] An *aporia*: How could Thomas profess God's unity yet, upon meeting the Risen Christ, identify him as Lord and God?

Although Wilkens appears seduced by Caravaggio's depiction, he manages to capture the incisiveness of Hilary's question:

> During Christ's lifetime [Jesus's] followers did not grasp fully who he was. Even though some of his sayings imply that he had a unique relation to God, and he performed miracles and revealed his heavenly glory to his most intimate followers at his Transfiguration on the mount, his disciples did not have eyes to see who he was. They had sound theological reasons for their opacity. They knew by heart the words of the Sh'ma, "Hear O Israel, the Lord your God is one Lord." Hence Hilary asks a question I am sure many other readers of the New Testament have asked themselves: How could a faithful Jew who had recited the Sh'ma since childhood, whose prayers were addressed to God the king of the universe, address Christ as God or Son of God, as the earliest Christians did? Hilary's answer is that the Resurrection of Christ transfigured everything. When Jesus came and stood among the disciples and put his finger in his side, Thomas said, "My Lord and my God!" When confronted by the risen Christ one does not say, "How interesting," but "My Lord and my God!"[78]

As Thomas peers into the wounds of the Risen One, the way he sees the world suddenly and irrevocably transforms. His gaze is, as it were, converted by Christ and he begins to see the world from another point of view and with eyes illuminated by faith. Jean-Luc Marion would identify this as a conversion from perceiving according to "the intentionality of the world" to perceiving according to "the intentionality which the Holy Spirit teaches to the gaze."[79] The ruptured flesh of Christ ruptures the structures of Thomas's understanding. This encounter does not add information to, or stack another proposition upon, faith's content (*fides quae*). It elicits, rather, the birth of an explicitly Christian mode of believing and perceiving (*fides qua*). For it is in this moment that Thomas perceives Jesus *as* the Christ and Son of God. This is not Thomas's self-wrought achievement but a grace. Thus, what Caravaggio depicts, what the gift of faith perpetuates, is what Marion describes as "an anamorphosis, a shifting of the witness's point of view on the *mystērion*, a crossing of the epistemological break that makes [one] see Jesus as the Christ, as the Son of God—that makes Christ show himself to [one] as Christ gives himself, as Son *from the Father's point of view*."[80] Christ's wounds are, for Thomas, a blessed porosity that enables him to perceive not a different reality, but reality differently. The infusion of charity, the gift of the Holy Spirit, does not inform him about *what* he sees but, with eyes opened in faith, transforms *how* he perceives everything.

Yet as Robinette pointed out above, future generations do not need to duplicate Thomas's experience to undergo a similar transformation of perception. The apostolic witness—enshrined in the gospel's preaching and expressed in the Church's ministry—is sufficient to mediate an encounter with the Risen Christ. Paul, in his Letter to the Romans, captures this: "Faith comes from what is heard" (10:17). Coming to faith is entering, or living into, an ongoing dialogue rooted in the experience of the apostles. We do not come to faith as a solo endeavor but only as members of a community. In a positivistic era convinced that only what can be counted can count, Sandra Schneiders throws down the gauntlet: as was the case with Mary Magdalene and Thomas, our "obsession with the historical-physical must give way to faith in the ecclesial-bodily presence of Jesus."[81] We come to belief in Christ not as monads, not apart from the Christian Church, but only as a part of the *ecclesia*. In an ideal world, one without hypocrisy and ecclesial scandal, it would be a bumper sticker slogan: "No Church, No Jesus. Know Church, Know Jesus."

Although it is not his word, Robinette would assent: what we find in Thomas's encounter with the Risen Christ is the grace-initiated and grace-guided process of orthoaesthesis. The Risen Christ's inbreaking into the upper room induces a breakdown for Thomas, but in the wounded body—a porosity glorified by the Resurrection—there is a breakthrough. Robinette: "The gospel of John imparts a knowledge of the risen One that requires something far more demanding than the assimilation of a piece of information within a pre-established framework of intelligibility. 'Jesus is risen' is not merely a proposition. It is something to be 'lived-into.' It entails a profound shift in perception, judgment, and action on the part of those who would be its witnesses. It requires a conversion to a new way of 'making sense.'"[82]

After his encounter with the Risen Christ, Thomas does not simply tuck a new discrete fact into his cognitive repertoire, he does not "fit" the Resurrection into any extant schema. For him to make sense of his encounter with Christ requires a wholesale revolution, a "living into" an entirely new understanding of reality governed by a logic in excess of our terrestrial categories. Robinette, drawing on Marion, regards the Resurrection as the "saturated phenomenon *par excellence*."[83] And, noting an overlap between the godsend and the saturated phenomenon, Desmond writes: "If there is an idea of the godsend, it is one exceeding our concepts, and the saturated phenomenon expressly exceeds the embrace of (conceptual) intentionality. It overflows what conceptual intentionality can contain within itself; indeed reverses its more normal direction as aimed at that with which it can be in (mutual) correlation. There is a kind of asymmetry communicated from the other side, so to say, which is not the other side of intentionality conceived as a subject-object relation."[84]

Here, a convergence between the metaphysician Desmond and the phenomenologist Marion. For Desmond, the godsend's interruption does not destitute creation but reveals its overdeterminacy; or, to use Marion's phrase, it reveals the world as "saturated" with divine presence. On our own, we cannot perceive this but, with eyes opened and attuned by the godsend, we may peer into creation's graced depths. We do this, though, not of our own volition but as a response to being addressed. It is a vocation. Standing before the porous threshold between ignorance and knowledge, between reason and faith, between unbelief and belief, we cross because we are summoned to enter the uncovered and revealed order. The proclamation "Jesus is risen," is not a gobbet of information to be fit in within our conceptual map. It is a hyperbolic claim, one that threatens to catapult its hearers from our terrestrial logic into a celestial or revealed theo-logic. "Jesus is risen" claims that the fabric of our known reality is unexpectedly porous; it is an anarchic claim that destabilizes our securities by insisting on an *arche* beyond our control. For, through the Resurrection, the will of the Creator is revealed as death itself is turned backward and a new way of life is made possible for those who, in hearing the apostolic testimony, are drawn into the community of faith where we meet, in ten thousand faces and places, the presence of the Risen Christ.

Desmond does not treat in depth the special revelation of Christ, but I believe my take on the godsend shows how the concept can accommodate and express the dynamism of coming to faith in the Risen Christ. I turn again to Robinette: "Resurrection belief cannot simply be apprehended. It is *given*. It *manifests itself*. It *presents itself* as a possibility through apostolic witness. It invites. It summons. Responding to it will entail some kind of self-dispossession, a leaving behind, but also a new welcoming and in-habitation. Faith comes *ex auditu*, as Gift."[85]

St. Paul agrees: "So faith comes from what is heard, and what is heard comes through the word of Christ" (Rom. 10:17). Rahner, too, assents: we are beings of a receptive spirituality. Faith is not our achievement, the result of conative striving, but is a gift we undergo. For Thomas, this receptivity took place in beholding the glorified wounds of the Risen One. He saw, and had to negotiate, the paradoxical occurrence of discontinuous continuity. There is a breakdown of his former pattern of perception but, rather than rendering him blind, there is a breakthrough of faith giving him to behold all things anew, and he surrenders to the logic revealed by the Crucified-and-Risen One. Peering into the wounds of his publicly executed friend, pierced flesh exposes the deathless mystery at creation's heart. To graced eyes, the rupture reveals a life, a logic, a *Logos*, that is unleashed through Christ's porous flesh and extended through word and sacrament to future generations. Two millennia later, we require neither haptic nor optic confirmation to prove or demonstrate the veracity of the Christian faith. Our faith is to be "lived into" as we respond with our whole selves to the Word proclaimed in and through the life of the Church. To encounter and confess the crucified and Risen

Christ as the deepest and abiding truth of all creation is not to undergo a change of mind but entails, fundamentally, being drawn into the movement and life of discipleship. As a Christian, to see the world orthoaesthetically is to see it from the Father's point of view and to see in Christ's iconic face, as well as in the wounds of his body, the hyperbolic sign of the God whose creative will conquers and transforms death itself.

DISCERNING PATTERNS OF PERCEPTION ON THE ROAD TO EMMAUS

Having explored the general dynamics of orthoaesthesis, I want to suggest how it might contribute to theological reflection. We now turn to accompany Jesus's disciples as they travel from Jerusalem to Emmaus (Luke 24:13–35). The story begins in the wake of a breakdown as the disciples' hopes in Jesus appear, at least to their eyes, to have been crucified with Jesus at Calvary. With grief-laden hearts, Cleopas and his companion are deep in conversation when they are joined by a third. Luke divulges the identity of this stranger, but the two companions do not recognize Jesus in their midst because "their eyes were kept from recognizing him" (24:16). The stranger breaks into their conversation and asks, "What are you discussing with each other while you walk along?" The disciples pause. Cleopas: "Are you the only stranger in Jerusalem who does not know the things that have taken place there in these days?" When the stranger asks, "What things?" the disciples retell the sad events surrounding Jesus of Nazareth.

Jean-Luc Marion offers an incisive take on their response, likening their renarration of recent events in Jerusalem to "a police report: that Jesus of Nazareth, 'a prophet mighty in deed and word before God and all the people' was condemned to death, then crucified by the authorities. Here is the accident, the incident, the 'event,' in short the fact guaranteed by an intuition offered to all, to the public, and to which an entire city (and what a city!) can testify."[86]

The disciples are, as it were, "facing the facts." They "had hoped he that he was the one to redeem Israel" (v. 20) but these hopes died along with Jesus. But, on account of the testimony of some women, the settled matter of Jesus's death has been disturbed. For, upon their visit to the tomb, they did not find his body but encountered angels. They, moreover, delivered to the other disciples an incredible message: Jesus is alive. Some members of the group, of course, rushed off to verify the women's testimony, and they, too, discovered an empty tomb, "but they did not see him" (v. 24). Of course they did not believe: the absence of something, even a body, does not necessarily translate into its presence elsewhere. For those first "witnesses," conventional logic demanded an explanation, it required some as yet unaccounted for "fact" to make sense of what had transpired. Constrained by their terrestrial logic, the disciples trod the road to Emmaus befuddled and confused. Thus, Marion points out, it is not the lack of evidence that prevents them from recognizing Jesus but, rather, the excess of evidence that overwhelms them and keeps them from "making sense" of it. They require not better data but a way of considering the preposterous claim "Jesus is risen" from a different angle. If the story does not fit into their schemas, it is because they need a new, graciously expanded, way of interpreting.

On that Easter morning, the disciples found themselves torn between two irreconcilable claims: Jesus is dead, Jesus is alive. They, like the rest of Jerusalem, are in the know about what has transpired. Dead is dead, just as $A = A$, and Jesus is dead. They saw firsthand the brutal efficiency of Rome's death apparatus, and the publicity of crucifixion left no ambiguity about Jesus's fate. Yet from the women in their group a new and wholly subversive take on events: Jesus was dead but is no longer dead. Terrestrial logic fails as $A = \text{not-}A$, dead is not-dead. How to make sense of this dissonance? They choose to extricate themselves from the equivocal flux of claims and head to safety. They seek to preserve the safety and integrity of their bodies as well as their psyches, for the women's claims are unbelievable. They do not yet have a framework capable of reconciling these claims. For Marion, the disciples are very much like us: "It is thus not the intuition of facts that they lack, but rather the intelligence (the concepts), as do we, today: well do they know, as do we, with scientific certainty, that Jesus died and that one does not come back from the dead; we can deplore this fact, especially in this case, but in the end that's how it is; we must stay reasonable and not lose our heads."[87]

The disciples are doubly beset. Not only have they endured the breakdown of their hopes, but the news born by the women threatens their understanding of the world. They mourn the loss of Jesus yet are constrained by and loath to give up their understanding of reality. They give embodied testimony to Wittgenstein's claim in the *Tractatus*: "The world is all that is the case" (§1). They are pragmatic realists, who, in the wake of their leader's ignominious death, flee in order to preserve their own lives. Even if they carry grief in their hearts, at least they can take comfort in their logic and realism: "The world is determined by the facts, and by there being *all* the facts" (§1.11),[88] and they know the facts.

The tension and strain placed on their concepts comes to a head with the stranger's inbreaking. Their recapitulation of the "facts" betrays the shallowness of their understanding, for although they have seen and are "the know," they clearly have not understood the meaning of these events. The stranger offers them not a word of consolation but a rebuke: "Oh, how foolish you are, and how slow of heart to believe all that the prophets have declared!" (v. 25). Their slowness of heart, their clinging to terrestrial logic and their refusal to accept the *logos* of the Kingdom prevents them from seeing rightly. Even as he walks among them, they remain blind. Why? Marion suggests:

> What concrete sign, what sensible perception, what intuition was lacking? None whatsoever, clearly. In fact, they kept themselves from recognizing him. Why were they denying the evidence? Not because it was deficient—it wasn't lacking in the slightest—but because it contradicts their entire comprehension (their miscomprehension, or at the least, their pre-comprehension) of a phenomenon that is nevertheless patently beneath their eyes, and in their ears. They do not recognize him because they cannot even imagine that this is really him, Him, who has rejoined them, so far do their poor, cobbled-together, honest-to-goodness concepts find themselves outstripped by "events" that leave them petrified within a matrix of irrefutable prejudices.[89]

Locked into a fixed and definite view of a world organized by "facts," all other testimony and evidence is deemed inadmissible. For the reader, the scene is akin to a Sherlock Holmes story where all the evidence is at hand yet cannot be seen by untrained eyes. Jesus's disciples, like Dr. Watson, see but do not perceive: their horizons are too narrow to get the

big picture. The disciples, in this way, are held captive by a sort of postulatory finitism where life is finite and cannot but be finite. Or, as Marion
writes, a world in which "the dead man is dead, period. Every other possibility finds itself completely excluded, not even considerable."[90]

What unfolds within this pericope is the dissolution of the disciples'
postulatory finitism, the breakdown of their old way of perception and
the inbreaking of a new mode of perception. The Risen Jesus does not
spring his identity on the disciples. Nor does he deploy an abstract argument. Instead, he resumes his role as teacher and, in a way reminiscent
of Socrates in the *Meno*, uncovers and brings to light what they could,
but would not, allow themselves to see. He calls them "foolish" because
they have not yet allowed the *idiocy* of the Easter proclamation, borne to
their ears by the women who found the tomb empty, to penetrate their
hearts. The Risen One, consequently, renarrates the events, not to give
them new evidence, but to allow them to behold the evidence anew: "Beginning with Moses and all the prophets, he interpreted to them the
things about himself in the scriptures" (Luke 24:27). The disciples undergo a moment of divine pedagogy or, as Charles Taylor puts it, they are
"starting to be educated by God."[91] Indeed, this is a moment of education
in its most literal and etymological sense: they are being "led out"
(*educere*) of one framework of understanding and drawn into a new way
of perceiving events. They are being offered a "better account" of what
happened. Rather than an apodictic argument for what they should see,
Jesus goes to them, ad hominem, and instructs them step-by-step. In the
retelling of the story and by expanding the narrative horizon, they are
capacitated to behold all things anew. As Aslan disclosed to the children
the meaning of what they had seen but not understood, so does the
Risen Jesus tutor his disciples into a new way of perceiving. This is a
grace-induced anamorphosis that shifts how they behold the world.

As the three approach a village, the stranger looks as though he
wishes to continue his journey. But they enjoin him: "Stay with us, because it is almost evening and the day is now nearly over" (Luke 24:29).
In the climax, having taken his place at the table, the stranger "took
bread, blessed and broke it, and gave it to them. Then their eyes were
opened, and they recognized him" (v. 30–31). Suddenly, they perceive
rightly. Everything clicks into place and they see Jesus in their midst,
not due to their efforts but because he makes himself known. In the

aftermath of this revelatory breakthrough, they become what they have received as they are transformed into godsends and are sent back to Jerusalem as bearers of good news: "The Lord has risen indeed" (v. 34).

Through the bread's breaking the disciples see, orthoaesthetically, Christ's presence. With grace-opened eyes, they receive not an anonymous theophany but a Christological epiphany. In the breaking, or cracking of the bread, the divine light of Christ bursts forth amidst creation as a sign of what is beyond creation. In this pericope we find the divine *poiesis* sacramentally transforming *aesthesis* that unfolds through a triple breaking:

1. An inbreaking of Christ in their midst who guides their understanding and shifts their stance (*anamorphosis*) to behold all things anew.
2. A breakdown of old categories and schemas as the stranger tutors them into a new mode of perceiving.
3. A breakthrough into a new mode of life, a new way of being in and beholding the world, animated by the proclamation: "The Lord has risen indeed."

Of course, we know this new mode of seeing is not the result of any grasping on the disciples' part. The narrative shows them as incapable of understanding what has happened by their own lights: they have seen but cannot interpret the evidence correctly. But if the disciples' coming to see rightly is not the achievement of the *conatus essendi*, it is not exactly the fruit of the *passio essendi*. For although this moment of divine pedagogy is something the disciples undergo, this undergoing does more than renew their sense of the intimate strangeness of being. As their hearts burn, as they are tutored to recognize the Risen One in their midst, they undergo what I call the *passio caritatis*, "undergoing of charity," endowing them with the grace not only to perceive the "crack" in everything but also to peer through the "crack" and detect the presence of the Crucified-and-Risen One.

The *passio caritatis* is a term not found in Desmond's oeuvre, but it resonates with what he calls the "sacred *passio essendi*: the receiving of our being as patient to the divine communication."[92] This coheres with Desmond's understanding of the agapeic (Latin: *caritas*) and accents a divine initiative and the "incognito generosity or surplus of affirmative 'to be' as good that is always at work"[93] in the *metaxu*. We are made patient to the gift of divine communication, to the invitation of the sacred *passio*, in many ways. Desmond writes of this:

> It can come to the child who un-self-consciously prays in adoration. It can come to the lover who cannot quite believe the chance encounter with the love of his or her life. It can come in the gift of inspiration that an artist will knead into a work of art speaking from depths beyond determinacy and hinting at mysteries beyond self-determination. It can come in the woo of mystical love. It can come in the liturgies of communion when the agape of the divine dying and rising is commemorated, coming to be again in the form of elements that sustain daily life.[94]

The sacred *passio* arouses us to the religious dimension of existence and bids us to open the self to what is beyond the self. We are awakened to the agapeics of the intimate universal expressed by Augustine: *interior intimo meo et superior summo meo* (more inward than my most inward part and higher than the highest element within me).[95] The call of the sacred admits of a wide spectrum and can be discerned variously: from a child's urge to pray, to an anonymous call to communion, to the theophany of a God made known in the humble species of bread and wine, a God sacramentally present within the immanent order.

As a theological expansion of Desmond's thought, the *passio caritatis* provides a way of thinking about God's grace, not as an "object," but as a transformative process of being drawn into and reconfigured through the Spirit's infusion charity. As I see it, the *passio caritatis* does not replace the sacred *passio* but deepens it and brings to the fore its theological content. Through the Spirit's *poiesis* in infusing charity, one's *aesthesis* is deepened and transformed. Through the *passio caritatis*, one begins to share in the divine life of the Trinity and can perceive the divine presence, the Risen Christ's presence, in the *metaxu*. It is here one is presented with what I described earlier as "Hopkins Option" and graced with perceiving Christ in all things. The way Desmond refers to the Emmaus suggests he would agree. For, although he does not develop its theological implications, he describes the story as recounting a profound dawning:

Before one did not see, but now one begins to see; begins to see because a light that one cannot command is coming up and going over one. One is being lighted; one is not enlightened, one is being enlightened. We are the recipients of something that we cannot entirely specify or pin down. It stuns us into silence. The seeds of a metanoetics are being sown. A new *noesis*: a new mindfulness that does not know what it knows, and yet it knows that the same things will no longer be the same. . . . It is more like a slow conversion, a turning, a kind of *periagōgē*, a being turned around.[96]

Indeed, for Cleopas and his companion, there is a radical turning: having glimpsed the Risen Christ, they turn around and go back to Jerusalem with senses made new. Robinette observes: "What they had not understood in 'real time' became respectively intelligible through the Easter experience. Their memory was slowly being reconfigured by the re-narration: They said to each other, 'Were not our hearts burning within us while he was talking to us on the road, while he was opening the scriptures to us?'" Christ, revealed in the breaking of bread, sends them back to Jerusalem not to resume an old life but to embark upon a new one reconfigured by the grace of knowing the Risen One. Once more, the triple pattern is on display: Christ's *inbreaking* destabilized extant schemas and in this *breakdown* of logic's categories there is a *breakthrough* into a life guided by the disclosed *Logos*.

What the *passio caritatis* offers is a way of reflecting on how the gift of charity transforms how one abides within the *metaxu*. If our exercises encourage us to contemplate the "crack" in everything, if Desmond leads us to the threshold between philosophy and religion, then the *passio caritatis* allows us to perceive Christ's presence through the "crack." Through the *passio caritatis* or "undergoing of charity," the metaxological becomes the mystagogical.

Paul Crowley is helpful here. Building on Karl Rahner, Crowley describes mystagogy as "guiding an initiate into the world of faith, into its depths as they are realized interpersonally in God."[97] Mystagogy draws one ever more deeply into the graced order of creation. If reflecting on the *passio essendi* awakens us to the mystery of creation, and if the sacred *passio* attunes us to creation's fundamental religiosity, then the *passio caritatis* graciously allows one to discern and respond to Christ's presence within this mystery. In this, the *passio caritatis* is a knowing and being known by the Holy One revealed by the Christ made visible by the Holy Spirit, the Christ who points beyond himself toward the Father. Undergoing charity makes possible not a new mode of thinking, but a new way of being. It is through the gift of charity we perceive the whole *metaxu*, all of creation, as saturated or overdetermined with charity.

Were I to write another chapter, I would develop *passio caritatis* at length. In keeping with our theme of spiritual exercises, this would require reading Jesus's parables as uncovering a series of "parabolic indirections." Jesus's parables, as is well known, often have an element of the hyperbolic within them as they struggle to use finite words to express the abundances of God's love and mercy. Parables, as Gerhard Lohfink observes, do more than communicate "the overflowing generosity of God."[98] They mean to exercise us, to vex us, and stir our imaginations to consider how a reality reconfigured according to the logic of God's Kingdom might appear. The parables do not only inform us about the Kingdom but form us to participate within it. If we see the whole of the Christian life as a *passio caritatis*, then we might approach the parables as theaters of encounter: we contemplate them with an openness to being addressed through them. By forming our imaginations through their imagery, parabolic indirections would capacitate Christians to perceive Christ at work in history and to discern how we are being called to participate in the work of the Kingdom. They would become, in effect, parabolic portals giving us to perceive in the *metaxu* the *poiesis* of being as manifesting here and now how God's Kingdom is breaking into and transforming our world.

What might it look like for Christians to be caught up in a parabolic indirection? Could they rest content with the status quo or would they find, in their friendship with the Risen Christ, an encouragement to allow the anarchic logic of God's Kingdom to challenge and subvert our human logic? Consider: the parable of the workers in the vineyard (Matt. 20:1–15) is more than a nice story about God's generosity. The story intends to create a fissure within our own order and to show how our terrestrial order could be reconfigured. Parables work by transforming our imaginations; they uncover the "crack" through which God's reign breaks into the world, a reign where "different rules apply. It is true that people work from morning to night here too. God's world is not a land of the lotus eaters. But here work has dignity, and no one need go home in the evening filled with worry and anxiety. No one is alone. Above all: it is possible to live without rivalry because there is now something greater and more expansive than all one's own desires: work for God's cause. Precisely this common cause desired by everyone creates a solidarity that makes it possible to suffer with the suffering of others and to join in others' joy."[99]

For those undergoing the *passio caritatis*, this parable reveals no utopia (literally "no place"), but a prolepsis of what could be. In quickening Christian faith (*fides qua*), the *passio caritatis* enables us to read and respond to parables not as fanciful ideals but as viable possibilities. They open up parabolic indirections in and through which the proclaimed Word of God takes flesh in each era and contributes to reconfiguring the *metaxu* according to its revealed logic: "For the wisdom of this world is foolishness with God" (1 Cor. 3:19). If the parables disrupt or disorient us, they do so in a salutary way by exposing another, graced, order according to which we might live our lives.

What would it mean to embody and enact in our daily lives the subversive grace of God's Kingdom? What would it be for our ethos or our lives to be reconfigured by the *passio caritatis*? If Hart's "gaze of love" appears too passive, too aligned with the *passio essendi*, perhaps we might turn to Johann Baptist Metz. If parabolic indirections simultaneously *inform* us about God's Kingdom and *form* us to detect its inbreaking presence, then perhaps instead of the "gaze of love" we could see ourselves as being offered the dark grace of a "mysticism of open eyes, which sees more and not less. It is a mysticism that especially makes visible all invisible and inconvenient suffering, and—convenient or not—pays attention to it and takes responsibility for it, for the sake of a God who is a friend to human beings."[100] Epiphanically attuned by grace, the Christian is hardly delivered from the quotidian flux. On the contrary, she is returned to the flux not *with* a mission but *as* a mission. The godsend opens us to perceive how, as David Tracy writes, "God reveals God-self in hiddenness: in cross and negativity, above all in the suffering of all those others whom the grand narrative of modernity has set aside as non-peoples, non-events, non-memories, non-history."[101] It is into dangerous spaces the godsend sends us as bearers of good news and empowers solidarity with the suffering and the forgotten. The Christ glimpsed through the "crack" bids us to bear glad tidings to the interstitial places in history. Perhaps here we have the foundations for a metaxologically informed political theology intent on discerning and reconfiguring the *metaxu* according to the logic of charity rather than human will to power.

THE ORTHOTIC FOURFOLD: THEOLOGICAL METHOD AND REORIENTATION IN THE *METAXU*

I would like to suggest how a metaxologically informed understanding of orthoaesthesis might contribute to theological method. Theologians, I trust, will be familiar with the "Wesleyan Quadrilateral" used to depict the four sources of Christian theology: scripture, tradition, reason, and experience. In what follows, I would like to develop a similar fourfold by adding the concept of orthoaesthesis to the triad of orthodoxy, orthopraxis, and orthopathy. What results, if I may be so bold as to offer a neologism, is an "orthotic fourfold" able to orient and guide philosophical and theological reflection in the *metaxu*. By "orthotic" I do not mean a shoe insert but a way of "straightening" or "aligning" the way we understand our emplacement within the world. An "orthotic" apparatus does not replace a functioning limb but supports, aligns, and corrects its functioning. Theologians have rightly and fruitfully drawn on orthodoxy/orthopathy/orthopraxis, but I believe the triad remains incomplete, and, as I hope to show, the addition of orthoaesthesis addresses a hitherto unrecognized lacuna.

Most readers will be aware of the reciprocal relationship between orthodoxy (right belief, right praise) and orthopraxis (right conduct). Johann Baptist Metz identifies their intimate relationship: "What the word 'orthopraxis' recalls first and foremost is the price to be paid for orthodoxy."[102] And David Tracy observes: "Without orthopraxis, orthodoxy is always in danger of becoming the shoddy shell of a once vital religion; without true orthodoxy, orthopraxis is always in danger of becoming a diffuse, confused, and confusing spirituality."[103] Missing from this dialectic, however, is the subject's affectivity: Does not emotion, or feeling, shape the way we perceive and respond to the world around us? Jon Sobrino, consequently, insists on adding a third category: orthopathy. For Christians, this would mean "the correct way of letting ourselves be affected by the reality of Christ."[104] More broadly, it describes how we are affected by objects of right belief and motivated to enact what has touched us.

An example might bring out the dynamics of this triad. Every year at the Easter Vigil, Christians hear once more the Exodus story. It is no small feat to make these familiar narratives come alive for a congregation. Sure, we know *what* they are about and even a half-decent preacher can suggest *how* we should live them out. But how to move the heart and stir up a passionate response? In 2018, the homilist read the following from Andrew Young's *An Easy Burden: The Civil Rights Movement and the Transformation of America.* The setting: Easter Sunday in Birmingham, Alabama, in 1964. Martin Luther King is in jail. A decision is made to march from the New Pilgrim Baptist Church to the jail after Easter services. When the march begins, almost 5,000 women and men dressed in their Sunday best have gathered:

> We marched from New Pilgrim until we arrived at a point about two blocks from the jail, where the police had set up barricades to block us. They were out in full force, Bull Connor barking orders with his foghorn voice. Fire trucks blocked the street, and the firemen were ready with hoses. . . . As we approached the barricades, marching slowly right up to them, Bull Connor shouted at us: "Y'all have to disperse this crowd. Turn this group around." But there were five thousand people behind us, and up ahead, two blocks away, were our people in jail who were surely watching what was happening from their tiny window cells.
>
> Wyatt Walker and I were leading the march. I can't say we knew what to do. I know I didn't want to turn the march around, whatever the consequences. So . . . I asked the people to get down on their knees and offer a prayer. The entire group dropped to their knees and began to pray. They were praying an old-fashioned kind of long-meter moan, mixed with singing . . .
>
> Suddenly, Rev. Charles Billups, one of the most faithful and fearless leaders . . . jumped up and hollered: "The Lord is with this movement! Off your knees. We're going on to the jail!" And everybody in the front rows—they had been praying now for about five minutes—got up and started right toward the barricades and the amassed police. Stunned at first, Bull Connor yelled, "Stop 'em, stop 'em!" But none of the police moved a muscle . . . they all just stood

there watching us as if they were transfixed. Even the police dogs that had been growling and straining at their leashes when we first marched up were now perfect calm. The firemen just stood there, holding their hoses. We were walking right past them and Bull Connor was yelling, "Turn on the hoses, turn on the hoses!" But the firemen didn't move either. I saw one fireman, tears in his eyes, just let the hose drop at his feet. Our people marched right between the red fire trucks, singing, "I want Jesus to walk with me." They were not rushing; it was a very slow, serious march. . . . It was quite a moment to witness: I'll never forget one old woman who became ecstatic when she marched through the barricades. As she passed through, she shouted, "Great God Almighty done parted the Red Sea one mo' time!"[105]

The congregation was electrified: many of us with moist eyes felt ourselves drawn into this most sacred night's events in a new way. Our hearts were set on fire as we saw how the narrative of the Exodus had been enacted in our own country and could, still, be given flesh in our lives. We were not told to *think* about the Exodus, we were not told to *act* according to some abstract precept. We were, rather, invited to take our role in the ongoing Exodus from death to life, from slavery to liberty, from darkness to light as disciples of Jesus Christ. This was not a preacher's emotional manipulation. It was a moment of grace as we were implicated in and animated by the rhythm of the scriptures. We felt ourselves affected by God's Word preached and enfleshed here and now. We heard not *a* story but *our* story and a call to allow the gospel's story, God's ongoing story, to form our lives.

I am quite certain that what so many of us experienced that evening could be recognized as *orthopathy*. Yet I cannot help but to feel that we "felt rightly" because we were perceiving rightly, because our own eyes were being opened to behold *orthoaesthetically*. One "feels rightly" as a consequence of "perceiving rightly." The two are ineluctably bound together, because if we do not perceive the world rightly, if prejudice and preconceptions blind us, then our subjective response—our affect—will be distorted. "Right feeling" as a response to reality requires "right perception." At the vigil, the homilist led us to see history through the scriptures and feel the Exodus and the Resurrection as operative within history. We did not "perceive rightly" because we were delivered from history or whisked away to a "view from nowhere." We were brought to perceive rightly because we saw precisely where we were: denizens of the *metaxu*, residents of an ethos saturated with surplus fullness. Aware of Detroit's racial unrest, not mention the long history of racism in the United States, we could not but be touched. We saw God's liberation at work, not in the past, but in the present. Our eyes were opened to see the injustice of our world not simply as a source of social outrage but, with eyes liturgically trained and hearts opened, as a "crack" through which grace could be seen.

A visual of this relationship can be seen in figure 1. The fourfold is composed of two dialectical pairings: orthodoxy/orthopraxis and orthopathy/orthoaesthesis. The more familiar dialectic, orthodoxy/ orthopraxis, I call the "what" poles: they indicate what we believe and what we do. The other dialectic has "how" poles: how we perceive and how we are affected by it. Each pairing has, moreover, an introverted and an extroverted polarity. Orthodoxy describes one's assent to and inward appropriation of the *fides qua* and *fides quae*. Orthopraxis is the price one pays for these beliefs inasmuch as they inform the way we are in the world. Orthopathy describes motivational content, the affective response one has to the world as it is disclosed. It is orthopathy that taps into the *fides qua*, as Charles Billups did by rising up from kneeling and encouraging his sisters and brothers to press onward. It is orthopathy that is moved by the cry of the poor, the face of the widow, the knock of the stranger at the door. It is how we are animated and sustained to persevere even in the face of opposition. Yet to have "right feeling" one must perceive aright. We need to perceive rightly if we are to have any hope of responding well.

Figure 1. The Orthotic Fourfold

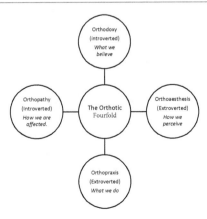

The Reverend Billups and the elderly woman in Young's story were attentive to and enlivened by this porosity. In the march's breakdown—facing an intractable oppressor who would not be reasoned with—they saw their people standing with Israel, pressed against the Red Sea, as Pharaoh charged toward them. They perceived, like Moses did, the divine presence as spurring them forward. They saw how the stories of the Exodus and the Resurrection were not bygone tales but were being recapitulated once again in 1964. They saw their story, their history, as an outworking and a continuation of God's providence. Their lives had been nourished by scripture—with Exodus 14 and 15 and the Resurrection narratives—and with Easter eyes they saw not reality as "cracked" and porous to God's grace at work. They sang out of exuberance at what they saw unfolding before them. The woman, a modern variant of the prophet Miriam who danced in joy (Ex. 15:20–21), could see and sing God's grace at work in history: Great God Almighty done parted the Red Sea one mo' time! In her, right belief (orthodoxy) and right action (orthopraxis) are inseparable from God's grace breaking through in history (orthoaesthesis) and her being moved by it (orthopathy).

With this schema in mind, let us return to the road to Emmaus to see how the *passio caritatis* transforms the disciples. Let me emend Tracy's observation: without orthoaesthesis, orthopathy is always in danger of becoming a solipsism concerned only with one's own feeling; without orthopathy, orthoaesthesis is always in danger of becoming a detached and aloof stance toward the world. As they journey toward Emmaus, the disciples undergo a fourfold transformation. The stranger interrupts their conversation and invites them to share their version of the story. Their plans are changed by his arrival, and rather than allow him to continue onward alone, they invite him to lodge with them and to break bread together. Wounded by grief, they extend an offer of hospitality to the alien (orthopraxis). For, as they have walked, they have experienced a shift in their understanding. What they have begun to feel, an inchoate sense of recognition, is expanding and reshaping the horizon of their understanding. They are undergoing a tutorial by the Risen One: the *Logos* is disclosing and attuning them to the ways of *Theos* (orthodoxy). The transformation climaxes in the liturgical gesture of taking, blessing, breaking, and giving. The affective fire of faith enkindled by the stranger's renarration and reframing of events (orthopathy) effects a conversion within their vision and the veil is lifted from their eyes. In the stranger's words and gestures, the disciples finally recognize in their midst the word and deed (Hebrew: *dabar*) of the Father. Now they perceive rightly (orthoaesthesis) what was before them, and they return to Jerusalem, bringing good news of the Lord they have encountered in the breaking of the bread.

The addition of orthoaesthesis makes possible a fourfold way of dwelling in the *metaxu*. Without gainsaying the importance of a knowing/doing dialectic, a more robust anthropology will be attentive to the dimension of perceiving/feeling. What we know and what we do need to be brought into conversation with how we perceive and how we respond. Who we are as selves arises at the intersection of the *what* dialectic (doxy/praxis) and the *how* dialectic (aesthesis/pathy). The fourfold offers a cruciform way of orienting philosophers and theologians as they abide within and reflect upon the *metaxu*. For we stand between all four poles and need to negotiate the consequences of a modification to any one of them: a shift or reconfiguration of one influences the functioning of the others. All must work together, symphonically, to keep attuned to and in tune with the graced happening of the *metaxu*.

A "CRACK" BETWEEN METAPHYSICS AND THEOLOGY

At the end of chapter 1, we considered Paul Janz's critique of Charles Taylor. As you will recall, Taylor believes that every era, every ethos, possess and strives toward achieving some vision of human flourishing. What Taylor wants to challenge, however, are those accounts that believe human flourishing possible without appeal to some sort of transcendence. It is here, though, that Janz intervenes by objecting to the ambiguous way Taylor uses the word "transcendence." Taylor, Janz charges, never provides an account for what the word means. Taylor needs to offer, accordingly, "some sort of critical or rationally demonstrative account, however indirect it might have to be, of what the meaningfully authoritative 'content' of the transcendent might be for human life."[106] Taylor may appeal to theological sources, may invoke agape, yet "these claims are not demonstrated, in any critically constructive way, to be attributable *uniquely* to transcendent or theistic sources."[107] This led us to ask, looking at the detailed map drawn by *A Secular Age*: Is there any *there* there?

In metaxological terms: Taylor is guilty of "postulatory theism," presuming what needs to be argued and demonstrated. Taylor may draw a compelling map, he may well exhort us to discover new itineraries to the sacred, but why should we bother looking? If we want to appease Janz, what we need is not a logical appeal to God but an ontological demonstration of it. *If* there is a God, how do we know? How, moreover, would God make itself known?

Can Desmond respond to Janz's request for a "rationally demonstrative account, however indirect it might have to be"? My answer: Yes, and he does so by providing a series of indirections that awaken us to and indirect us toward an encounter with God. These indirections do not gesture toward a disengaged reality "out there" in the empyrean but invite one on a mystagogical quest into the *metaxu's* innermost recesses. We have, in the West, fallen into a slumber and grown deaf to the woo of mystery. If Desmond's indirections lead us to the porous threshold and encourage us to put our ear to the "crack," the gift of charity may allow us to hear a voice wooing us to "come and see" (Jn. 1:39) and open our eyes to see Christ's presence in all things.

Metaxological metaphysics does not offer us a neutral "proof" of God but draws us along an itinerary where we are implicated in the happening of the *metaxu* and are invited to undergo a renewed sense of its goodness. Attuned to the poetics of the between, metaxology capacitates us to behold the "crack" in everything and provides a systematic way to reflect on how created beings are interrelated with one another and, more importantly, with creation's endowing source. If Janz insists on an ironclad demonstrative proof akin to a mathematical syllogism, we can gladly deny this request: God cannot be constrained by univocal logic. If he will be satisfied by a series of exercises rousing us anew to the mystery of God, then he will find in Desmond a most able guide. As a matter of fact, perhaps it is Desmond's great service not to try to settle "the God question" but to show that the question remains viable and deserves to be asked in every era.

Now to Janz's second point, how would God make Godself known? We have seen two ways of reflecting on this question. As exercises, each indirection required us to ponder the nature of the "crack" in everything. Each "way" sought to rock us back on our heels and to prompt us to ponder, from various angles, the primordial of metaphysical question: Why something rather than nothing? Desmond wants us to feel the weight of creation's gratuity, to swoon before its contingency, and to allow ourselves to be hyperbolically mindful of the Agapeic Origin who creates for no other reason than out of sheer goodness. As we saw with Victor White's interpretation of Aquinas, Desmond is trying to lead a skeptical generation back toward the mystery of existence to show how it is not something to be solved, or resolved, but celebrated. These philosophical indirections do not give us answers; rather, they bid us to listen, to open ourselves to something in excess of ourselves, and to wait patiently to see if the Creator and Originator might address us. Although we cannot compel revelation, orthoaesthetically attuned senses must remain vigilant for any divine epiphanies. Where we find openings between immanence and transcendence, there we may be struck by Desmond's indirections: the idiocy of being, the refulgence of beauty in the aesthetics of happening, the infinite yearning of the erotics of selving, the enabling power of the good found in communities. We are stirred to acknowledge the intimate strangeness of being, and we muse on how, if we take "being religious" at its etymological level (*religare* = to bind), the porosity of being bespeaks our primordial interconnectedness. To be is to be in relation, to be intimately related to all other beings, including the Creator who sustains all things. To be at all is to be religious.

If the Agapeic Origin does condescend to reveal the Divine Self, how might this happen? Well, Desmond has already gone some way in exploring this with his understanding of the godsend. Theological reflection is our response to the arrival of the godsend, our way of reflecting on its irruption into and its transformation of our world. What this will require, then, is the reception and evaluation of stories concerning how the godsend arrived, what effect it had, and how it has capacitated a new way of beholding the world around us. On Easter, Christians read Exodus beneath the Easter sun and find themselves rerooted in the ongoing history of salvation. Perhaps here my suggestion of the orthotic fourfold proves helpful, for it engages us in the ongoing task of assessing and reviewing who we are within the happening of the *metaxu*. Theology is not just an academic discourse but a way of life requiring us to discern over and again within the *metaxu* how the Holy One's presence abides within all things in general and, especially, how this divine presence has taken flesh—our flesh—in the incarnation of Jesus Christ. Christians look to Christ as the sign of the new creation who, through word and deed, proclaims and enacts God's Kingdom.

None of this entails a *duplex ordo* separating the natural from the supernatural order, nor any impervious wall separating philosophy from theology. But to be true to their origins, philosophy and theology both require an archaeological expedition in search of the *logos*, or *Logos*, at the origin (*arche*) of being itself. Desmond:

> We are enabled to seek the truth before we possess the truth, and this prior enabling is not determinate thought, nor determined through ourselves alone, hence it cannot be defined in the logic of autonomy. This prior enabling is just what allows us to be relatively autonomous at all. We would not be autonomous were not autonomy enabled by something prior to and other to autonomy. Self-determining thinking is released into its own freedom to think for itself by an enabling resource that is not self, a source not to be captured in terms of this or that determinate thought, or by thought's own determination by and for itself. There is more that allows thinking to be itself more than itself.[108]

Theology and philosophy are, each in its own way, responses to the call of the Transcendent (T_3), a call heard not only "out there" in the happening of exterior transcendence (T_1) but also in the very marrow of our selves (T_2). Theology is not a settled body of knowledge but a response and part of an ongoing dialogue: it is *fides quaerens intellectum*. So, too, philosophy: it is *intellectus quaerens fidem*. For a faith seeking understanding, a metaxologically awakened porosity serves to "remind theology that the task of coming to understand is never simply left behind, and truth is not something that can be grasped in a closed fist."[109] Caputo kicks up his heels and dances: the "Truth" is not something grasped, or dominated, but is approached asymptotically without any pretense of possessing it. Theology's gesture must be an open-armed gesture of receptivity and welcome to the One who cannot be encompassed. Likewise, a "seeking intelligence" is a response to a call; reason, like faith, has a vocation. Whereas the modern theorist affects a pose of cool and calculated indifference, Desmond exhorts philosophers to join ranks with the *theōroi*, who luxuriate in the ludic happening of the *metaxu*. Perhaps, he writes, "the vocation of reason is to ponder this exceeding. Perhaps it is to grant anew the porosity of philosophy and religion, closed in the interim of univocalizing modernity, now itself coming to a close. In the interim of new time, the secret enigma of being, the mysterious love of the divine, passes beyond that closure."[110]

Philosophy's vocation is not to take wing at dusk and survey what has transpired during the day. It is called, instead, within the *metaxu* where it can respond to its vocation to be a "lover of wisdom" by discerning "what is most important, and ultimate: what it means to be, to be true, to be good, to be a human person, what is or is not sacred, what God is."[111]

Let us dwell for a moment on philosophy as a vocation. It is nothing out of the ordinary to speak of theology as the vocation to reflect on the revealed content of faith. But, Desmond avers, the philosopher, too, has a vocation: "Since there is a call, there is a receiving more primal than any self-asserting. The receiving so qualifies the self-asserting, that all self-affirmation might undergo a *metanoia* in which our indebtedness to an endowing source beyond ourselves moves us in the direction of gratitude rather than self-glorification. There is reverence for what has been given rather than arrogance for what is claimed as one's own."[112]

As an activity, philosophy is elicited, not self-initiated. In this, it shares with theology the task of listening and then opening itself to what is Other to the self. As practices, philosophy and theology share a commitment: before speaking, or reflecting, they are open—because opened—and receptive. Both have roots extending deep into the primal ethos where the secret sap of divine Mystery flows into and enlivens each. Philosophy, enacted metaxologically, and Christian theology both discern, in the "crack" separating them, a shared sense of an abiding *logos*. For the philosopher, the *logos* sings an ancient and inchoate melody of creation; for the theologian having undergone the *passio caritatis*, scripture and tradition attune her ears to hear in this melody a word, the Word, and a call to discipleship. The philosopher's vocation begins in astonishment and wonder; the theologian's vocation takes shape as eyes opened by wonder begin, through charity, to recognize and respond to the Risen One.

The "crack" between a metaphysics and theology allows an intermediation between the disciplines at their most basic level. But the "crack"
is best seen as a poetic passage into a festive happening. Just as the Irish
speak of the "crack," there is a rhythmic interplay between philosophy
and theology, reason and faith, into which all can be drawn. What metaxology does is to show how we are always already caught up in this interplay, in the "crack" of being. Again, as Desmond observes, we start amidst
things and "we are open to things. We are open because we are already
opened. Before we come to ourselves as more reflectively thoughtful,
we already are in a porosity of being, and are ourselves this porosity of
being become mindful of itself. This ethos of being I call 'the between,'
and for me metaphysics is not an abstraction from this but a more deeply
mindful engagement with it. We are already enabled to be within the
between."[113]

If Taylor draws us a reliable map of our secular age, if he has shown
us how the desert of modern atheism has taken over once lush fields,
Desmond guides us to an oasis. For Desmond gives us, not a new map,
but the permit and the tools to begin excavating Taylor's map in order to
uncover wellsprings of life-giving water. As a response to Janz, Desmond
might say: the sources of human fullness do not hover above us but
reside deep within the earth. We do not need abstract arguments; we
need, instead, archaeological courage. As Desmond helps to clarify, the
godsend's irruption and unexpected does not deliver us over to a different or alternative reality. By inducing a breakdown, the inbreaking of
the Transcendent is a breakthrough transforming the way we perceive,
and dwell within, the *metaxu*.

So, does Desmond need to be ushered out of the theological closet?
This is not the best way to pose the question. No doubt, throughout his
writings he demonstrates an openness to and a familiarity with theology.
His treatment of the godsend, language of *kenosis*, and understanding of
creatio ex nihilo are all drawn from theological discourse. And this makes
sense for, as he observes, philosophical thinking is at its richest when it
is in "intermediation with its significant others, such as art and religion."[114] But rather than crossing the threshold and entering into theological territory, Desmond continues to sojourn in the *metaxu* between
philosophy and theology. Here, as he probes the space of the *metaxu*
searching for "cracks" and passageways between the immanent and tran-

scendent realms, he serves both philosophy and theology. For those who have ears to hear and eyes to see, the *logos* of metaxological philosophy may be recognized as the *Logos* of revealed theology.

In keeping with the *Chronicles of Narnia*, Desmond is more an owner of a wardrobe through which one finds secret and unexpected passages between modes of thought. What a speaker leaves unsaid does not mean it is unspeakable, and if Desmond has not set to working out the theological implications of his thought, then there is no reason for others not to come after him and take up the task. What Desmond has accomplished, though, is to show that there are yet passages between the immanent and the transcendent realms, that the question of God is still viable, and that there are ways we can undertake as indirections capable of renewing our sense of porosity to the Holy One. By uncovering the religious dimension of being, of being porous to and communicative of its divine origin, he has exposed a porosity allowing for communicative passage not only between philosophy and theology but also between other disciplines. Hence my own recourse to poetry, literature, and music: in the *metaxu*, all voices are welcome and can be balanced. Perhaps this, alone, is a reason to practice metaxology: it allows for ongoing and pluralized conversations, it fosters dynamic interchange and eschews fixity, it grows stronger by incorporating myriad viewpoints because it knows no one voice, no one view, can ever say or see it all. What Cardinal Walter Kasper says of Christology can be applied to metaxology. For the cardinal, Christology "inquires not just into this or that existent, but into existence in general. A Christian is so to speak compelled to become a metaphysician on account of his faith. . . . A pluralistic approach to philosophies and theologies is not only legitimate but necessary. But, fundamentally, Christology cannot be inserted into any predetermined philosophical system. And there is no question of applying predetermined philosophical categories within Christology. On the contrary, faith in Jesus Christ is a radical questioning of all closed systems of thought."[115]

Christ throws everything off balance and punctures any closed system into which he is introduced, not to destroy the system as an anarchist but to reveal the depths of being and return us again and again to the primordial ethos, the sacred origin or *arche* from whence we come. The *logos* of the *metaxu* and the *Logos* of Christology are not at all antithetical. To senses opened and attuned by grace, they are the same. If our quest to give an account of being between leads us to the "crack" where we open ourselves in astonished silence before the mystery of being itself, we may come to hear within the silence the stirring of a voice calling us to himself and inviting us onward in a new quest to "come and see" (John 1:39), to "taste and see" (Ps. 34:8), and to "take up your cross and follow me" (Matt. 16:24). For the journey through the *metaxu* is only ever just begun and, because sung and sustained in its being by a Creator "ever ancient, ever new,"[116] the song of being in which we are all participants may never be done.

THE END OF OUR PILGRIMAGE?

I entitled this chapter "Epiphanic Attunement" because I believe this to be the effect metaxology has on those who practice it as a mode of philosophical and theological reflection. As an *askesis*, it encourages us to see how extraordinary the ordinary is. As I have tried to show, metaxology opens a new mode of perception by bringing us to behold the "crack" or equivocity of being. This way of seeing runs counter to the normal mode of perception operative in our modern ethos. Consequently, we have needed to "exercise" ourselves to attune ourselves to detecting the "crack." Like any spiritual exercise, this *askesis* was not primarily directed at changing the way we think but at forming and transforming the way we perceive and abide in the *metaxu*. Metaxology, undertaken as a spiritual exercise, cultivates a mode of mindfulness and a concomitant way of life both receptive and response to disclosures of the divine in the everyday.

But, when Desmond introduces his idea of "godsends," he moves us closer to theology. Having developed a metaxological sense of ortho-aesthesis, I tested it by looking at Flannery O'Connor and two Gospel narratives. I wanted to demonstrate how not every breakdown is a loss. Paradoxically, instances of breakdown can be counted as a gain when they facilitate some form of transformative breakthrough. The breakdown/breakthrough dialectic undergone in the "return to zero" pulses within O'Connor's "Revelation" and the Gospels. To be implicated in this dialectic is to undergo a gradual attunement leading to a transformation of the *fides quae* and the *fides qua*. In the register of Christian theology, epiphanic attunement gradually tutors us to recognize not only general disclosures of God but, in scripture and tradition, the presence of the Risen Christ in the *ecclesia*. I then introduced the idea of the *passio caritatis* and suggested adding orthoaesthesis to the triad of orthodoxy, orthopraxis, and orthopathy to form what I called the orthotic fourfold. Both the *passio caritatis* and the quadrilateral remain in need of development, but I hope they suggest ways in which metaxology can be expanded and employed by theologians in the service of the life of faith.

Finally, I returned to Quebec in order to raise the question about the relationship between metaxology and theology. Rather than regarding them as impermeable to one another, Desmond helps us to see how both are nourished from the same wellspring. The *logos* of the *metaxu* and the *Logos* of theology can, when beheld with senses attuned through the passion of charity (*passio caritatis*), be seen as one and the same. There are not two *logoi* but one *Logos* perceived in two different ways. Unlike ontotheology, metaxology does not set the *a priori* conditions on which a god may arrive. Its openness to transcendence, its attunement to an Agapeic Origin, allow us to imagine that *if* the Origin should desire to reveal itself, it would do so not through any violent imposition but through a revelatory exposition. Through the gift of charity, one sees not another world but beholds the world otherwise. Metaxology capacitates one to interpret the "crack" as a sign of an Agapeic Creator. Those who have undergone the *passio caritatis* can discover within the "crack" the one in whom "were created all things in heaven and on earth, the visible and the invisible" (Col. 1:16). Through the Spirit's gift of charity, the *metaxu* becomes a monstrance disclosing the Christocentricity of creation.

The time has come: let us rise from Desmond's hearth, stretch our legs, and head out into the streets. We have come a long way and this stage of our quest draws to a close. Cork is known for good music, and somewhere a fiddler is rosining his bow: there will be music tonight. We pull our collars up, step out into the street and marvel. As day cedes to night, the gloaming's heather-and-purple-and-red sky saturates the horizon. Perhaps our day is not quite done and a trip to the pub is in order. We've worked up a mighty thirst, so let us invite William Desmond and Charles Taylor to join us for a pint as we reflect together on where we have been and where, should we set out once more tomorrow morning, our journey might yet take us.

In(con)clusion

If transcendence as other is vertical to time, cutting into it, cutting across it, we are asked to be ready for renewal in the interruptions of immanence. . . . The mystery is always there, seldom named, never dispelled. In ethical, religious, and philosophical service, beyond all determinate cognition, we live from agapeic astonishment, live in metaphysical perplexity before this mystery. In a mindfulness beyond determinate knowing, the Unequal comes toward us, offering over and over again, the unearned gift of the agape of being, singing to our deafness the unbearable music of the ultimate amen.

—William Desmond, *Being and the Between*

Charles Taylor and William Desmond place an order and select a table. They are in time: the musicians have gathered. An old man taps his fiddle bow on the table and the group comes to order. He begins to play, coaxing from his instrument a tune learned as a boy, a tune he has in turn taught to generations of students. Its provenance is unknown, its author long forgotten, but it lives on in an unbroken musical tradition. Flute and harp, whistle and pipes, accordion and fiddle spring to life: the *seisiún* begins. An ancient melody is born anew as instruments interweave and intermingle, each drawing on and contributing to each other. A pause and then a set of jigs led by a young woman, a fine whistle player. Desmond raises his glass to Taylor. Words seem inadequate and unneeded. They take in the atmosphere of the pub, relaxing into its *ethos*. The odor of turf perfumes the air, music englobes the listeners, laughter and chatter fill the pub: mighty *craic*, great *craic*. No determinate thing, the *craic* is the evening's happening, an overdeterminate event of being together. Too much for words, it must be undergone. All are implicated in and touched by it. Not even the world-weary can resist tapping their feet or giving in to the *craic*, the "crack," in everything. "In the wounds of being," Desmond muses over his glass, "mindfulness originates."[1] The "crack" is an openness that opens, a wound that blesses those it inflicts with a sense of being's too-muchness. Caught up in the *craic*, caught off guard by it, we surrender to the surplus. We give ourselves over to the rhythm and are set free to dance.

Taylor looks across the table. "William," he says, "I was reflecting on something you wrote in *Desire, Dialectic, and Otherness*. With your permission, let me quote you." You wrote: "If the givenness of being is thus overdetermined, there is a sense in which there are no absolutely univocal or literal facts. If the world is seen as the *poiēsis* of the power of being, its thereness is closer to a condition of poetry than of prose. This means that any metaphysical talk about the fact of being cannot itself be simply matter of fact. The world as an original image is more than the sum of finished determinate facts, and its thereness cannot be exhausted in univocal speech."[2]

"Metaxological metaphysics," Taylor continues, "is less a of Saying than Singing. The poetic is not epiphenomenal to your thought but essential. Prose, as it were, informs us but poetry performs by opening long-clogged passageways and restoring our sense of the intimate strangeness of being. Am I right in this?" Desmond nods. But how to reply? A pause in the music creates an opening. He makes eye contact with the *seisiún*'s leader, clears his throat, and contributes some verse to the evening's merriment:

Along the shore's edge
Bent into the gale
Blowing from out beyond
Struggling to stay in place
Almost at a standstill
Unable to go further
I am turned

& I turn
& am borne
On the way

In balance and quick
Running
Effortlessly
Home[3]

Appreciative silence broken by polite applause. Desmond acknowledges his listeners and the music resumes. Taylor winks: "Well, you sure aren't lingering on the shore of Dover Beach! In fact, in place of Arnold's 'melancholy, long, withdrawing roar' I hear the fanfare of a homecoming." Desmond's is a wan smile, but a smile nonetheless. He is no stranger to Dover Beach; indeed, many friends and colleagues are firmly ensconced there. Yet when the eclipse squelched the day's light, as the gale winds picked up speed, he sought no shelter. He faced the winds and was turned and set onto a new course, propelled and sustained by a force neither of his own conjuring and certainly not at his command. Now he sings of conversion and invites others to join him in this chorus. If we cannot speak univocally of such things, this does not condemn us to silence. It commends us to find new, innovative, and subtler ways of communicating what has been undergone. We need poetry to lead us back to the *poiesis* of being.

We have come quite a distance since meeting Charles Taylor in Quebec. The map he drew of our age prompted our quest, guiding us from the restrictive constraints of the moral corral out into the wider ethical field, and then, in a daring move, he bade us to enter the forest where we might risk encountering God once more. Yet, as Paul Janz trenchantly observed, a question lingers. Why should we trust this map? Tolkien drew detailed maps of Middle Earth, but the map is not the territory. There is no *there* there! Without some sort of "rationally demonstrative account, however indirect it might have to be, of what the meaningfully authoritative 'content' of the transcendent might be for human life,"[4] Taylor is susceptible of the charge of having committed the philosophical error of dogmatism, the "rationally unsustainable reification or hypostatization (into a putatively objectively authoritative or ontological source) of a 'transcendent' point of reference that is, in truth, only a linguistic (and negative) notion of the intellect."[5] Taylor's map, one might say, needs of some sort of metaphysical mooring lest his summons for new itineraries to the sacred be dismissed as little more than a snipe hunt.

In chapter 2, we made our way to Cork where we enjoined William Desmond to tutor us in metaxological metaphysics. Ours was a twofold hope. First, we wanted Desmond to uncover the metaphysical depths of Taylor's map in order to demonstrate to Janz its reliability. Second, as theologians we wanted to see how Desmond could also advance upon Taylor's project by responding to the latter's call for "new itineraries" capable of guiding seekers toward an encounter with God. I am aware: at the mention of metaphysics, philosophical noses crinkle. We began our pilgrimage, accordingly, by canvassing several prominent philosophers of religion—Heidegger, Caputo, Kearney, and Westphal—to find out how previous metaphysical undertakings had erred. We then compiled a list of "five commandments" a theologian would have to obey in order to draw fruitfully on metaphysics while also avoiding the error of ontotheology. The rest of the chapter sought to introduce readers to Desmond's philosophy. Without any pretense to being an all-encompassing "system," metaxology provides us with concepts and categories capable of describing what it means to be in "the between," or *metaxu*. Riffing on Emerson and Leonard Cohen, we saw how metaxology was especially attentive to the "crack" in everything. Metaxology capacitates us to perceive the "crack" in all things, not as a fatal flaw or mortal wound, but as the mark of being's porosity to what is beyond being. To be at all is to be in relation with the whole of creation and its Creator. The crack in everything, the "wound of being," is not a fatal flaw but a poetic passage through which the rhythm of primordial creation pours forth and enlivens the *metaxu*.

In chapter 3, we used the work of Pierre Hadot to frame Desmond's philosophy as a spiritual exercise. Here I showed how metaxology, as an *askesis* or discipline, "works." The poetics of the between not only inform but also, and more importantly, form the way the reader beholds the *metaxu*. Metaxological poetics "work" to communicate what it means to be in the between and to implicate the reader in the *metaxu*'s happening. One might see this as being capacitated with Keats's "negative capabilities"—the ability to stand within and withstand the darkness, ambiguity, mysteries, and doubts of existence. Following the "return to zero" we allowed Desmond to lead us beneath the crushing darkness of the *nihil* where we underwent the breakdown of our determinate categories and conceptual idols. However painful this purgative process was, its result was a sudden and irruptive breakthrough as we were brought to perceive all of being with a posthumous mind. We saw, with senses refined by passing through death, not a different reality but reality differently: what was taken *for* granted is, for the posthumous mind, suddenly was beheld *as* granted and gratuitously given. Being *is*, yet need not be.

Our initial practice of the "return" emboldened us, in chapter 4, to accompany Desmond on four "hyperbolic indirections" leading us to God. We traversed four such indirections—idiotic, aesthetic, erotic, and agapeic—and explored how metaxology not only rekindled our sense of God but also converged and contributed to Christian theology. Here we saw how adroitly Desmond responds to Taylor's call for new itineraries: not only does he suggest unique pathways (the agapeic), but he shows us how old ways (Aquinas's Third and Fifth Ways; Anselm's meditation) can be recharged by returning them to their originary ethos. We concluded by reading Hopkins's "Hurrahing in Harvest" as a metaxological performance through which one becomes attuned to epiphanies of the divine. Metaxology returns us to the primal ethos of being wherein, in and through exercises of transcendence, we become "epiphanically attuned" to detect within the *metaxu* signs of the Creator who sings and sustains creation into existence.

In chapter 5, I borrowed a term from Edmund Husserl—orthoaesthesis—and gave a metaxological sense of what "right perception" might mean. We moved from Ruby Turpin's pig parlor to the road to Emmaus and saw how the irruption of the godsend works to uncover the concealed depths and to reveal the secret life at the heart of being. The godsend is, in this way, less an imposition than a gracious exposition allowing creation's innermost reality to shine forth. Epiphanic attunement flowers into an abiding disposition, a vigilant patience as one awaits with one's entire being the advent of sacred. Such attunement, cultivated through the practice of *askesis*, cannot compel God to speak, but it maintains a stance of hospitality for God's arrival. Where others would see the unwanted and despised, the epiphanically attuned agent perceives not an alien Other but a sister and brother. If Gerard Manley Hopkins is right, if Christ does play in ten thousand places, then the whole of the Christian life can be seen as bristling with joyful anticipation as one can perceive Christ's presence in all persons and place. The Irish poet Patrick Kavanagh expresses this transformed mode of perception in "The Great Hunger":

He read the symbol too sharply and turned
From the five simple doors of sense
To the door whose combination lock has puzzled
Philosopher and priest and common dunce.
Men build their heavens as they build their circles
Of friends. God is in the bits and pieces of Everyday—
A kiss here and a laugh again, and sometimes tears,
A pearl necklace round the neck of poverty.[6]

The godsend arrives, reopens our senses, and through the rupture it inflicts one sees the world anew and as charged with God's presence. The epiphanically attuned subject occupies the *metaxu* with grace-touched senses and detects, as Kavanagh writes, how "in a crumb of bread the whole mystery is." We are graced and burdened of this mystery, which allows us to incarnate and enact what St. Paul exhorts: "Rejoice always, pray without ceasing, give thanks in all circumstances" (1 Thess. 5:16–17). Our lives become, when epiphanically attuned, an embodied eschatological petition: *Maranatha*, "Come, O Lord, Come!"

What, then, might be said of Desmond's achievements, philosophical and theological? Should Taylor take Janz's critique to heart, Desmond arrives as a welcome presence. Rather than extending the borders of Taylor's map, Desmond's archaeological endeavor penetrates deep into the soil to uncover hidden reservoirs of life-giving water. Even in the desert of modern atheism one can dig down and discover wellsprings sufficient to turn the parched desert into an oasis. Desmond has, in my estimation, aided Taylor in helping to firm up the metaphysical foundations of his map. There is, indeed, a *there* to be sought. This is no snipe hunt. And this *there* is not just at the borders but is, for those with eyes to see and ears to hear, everywhere. The Transcendent and Agapeic Other abides in the immanent; God is present in and can be sought through all things, so long as our senses are directed—or, in our case, indirected—aright.

In guiding us along a series of indirections, Desmond responds to Taylor's call for new itineraries leading toward an encounter with God. Some of these ways, we saw, repristinate formerly reliable ways. Rather than severing the "ways" from the ethos, Desmond allows the "ways" to reframe and transform the way we behold all of reality. He tutors us through these indirections to perceive the excessiveness and gratuity of creation. Just as a *seisiún* is more than the sum of musicians and instruments, so too there is more to creation than the totality of beings. The *craic* bespeaks this too-muchness, this overdeterminate happening. Music, like the *metaxu*, points beyond itself to an inexpressible surplus incapable of being pinned down or captured by concepts. The "crack" in everything is porous to another logic, the logic of a wholly, nay Holy, Other. Metaxology gives us to behold how living according to this logic is not a threat, *pace* Kant, to our autonomy. On the contrary, it is this absolving heteronomy that endows us with authentic autonomy: we are as we should be precisely because we have been given to be by this Origin. At the root of existence, all existence, is not the wanton exercise of power (will to power, an unfettered *conatus essendi*) but the agapeic creativity of the One who sings creation into being (*passio essendi*). The Christian, in turn, is one who has glimpsed by the light of the graced porosity of Christ's wounds the human face of this Agapeic Creator and knows oneself to have been sent on mission (*passio caritatis*).

One way of framing Desmond's contribution to theology is by reflecting on how each of the five commandments—five *pro*scriptions— have been transformed into five *pre*scriptions. If we set out wary of straying into the realm of ontotheology, now at the end of our travels we can read these commandments, not as erecting an insuperable wall between philosophy and theology, but as identifying the porosity between the two. Read prescriptively, our commandments can guide theologians in thinking through how they might undertake theological reflection in a metaxological key. Instead of a prohibitory "Thou shalt not," each becomes an encouraging "Thou shalt" allowing theologians to make full use of metaxology's hospitality to thinking across disciplinary thresholds. I take each commandment briefly in turn.

First commandment, with a bow to Heidegger: *Thou shalt not index the divine to human reason.* More positively rendered, we can now describe the metaxologically sensitive thinker as one who is attuned a God in excess of human reason. The inability of human reason to corral and constrain the Infinite is not to be lamented but celebrated. Yes: we desire to satisfy our desire to know. Fact: every answer piques a new question and our hunger grows with the more we know. True: there is a disproportion between our finite reach and our infinite longing. By giving us to sense the "crack" in everything, metaxology trains our gaze toward the

Infinite. We are not first the beholders because we are, foremost, the beheld: those who stand before the gaze of the Holy One: "You know when I sit down and when I rise up; you discern my thoughts from far away. You search out my path and my lying down, and are acquainted with all my ways" (Ps. 139:2–3). Before we give the measure, we are first measured. Our incapacity to index the Holy One to the canon of our reason is, paradoxically, a capacitation whereby we are freed to luxuriate in the too-muchness, the surplus power of the Agapeic One who bursts the limits of our terrestrial logic. Where ontotheology seeks to constrain God within the system, a metaxologically tutored theology rejoices in the God who is always "bigger" and in excess of any system we can concoct. This is the Holy One before whom we might dance.

Second commandment, with a salute to Caputo: *Thou shalt not be faithless to the flux*. If Desmond's indirections have succeeded in anything, it is in enjoining us to remain vigilant before the whole of being. Instead of fleeing from the flux, we have been bidden to stand within it and open ourselves to it. What first appears a cacophony of sounds, a welter of voices, reveals a secret rhythm and pulse. We do not encounter God, or hear God's woo, apart from the world's happening but only as a part of it. We are to be faithful to the flux; confident within it. *Con-fides*: "a confidence in which there is a 'faith with': a confiding. Something is confided to us, and we are given to be as confident."[7] Entrusted to us within the *metaxu* is a sense of the flux, not as anarchy, but a hierarchy that points beyond itself toward creation's endowing origin. Our summons is not to master the flux but to allow the flux to sing of its Creator and to find our place within the chorus. The prohibition now becomes an invitation to take our place within the metaxological symphony of Creation.

Third commandment, with a back slap to Caputo: *Thou shalt not produce counterfeit gods*. Long before Caputo or Desmond, Augustine knew: "You stir man to take pleasure in praising you, because you have made us for yourself, and our heart is restless until it rests in you." But how easily we are seduced to betray the depth of our desire by the false promise of a quick fix: drugs, sex, alcohol, riches, and honors. These become the shaky centers of our lives, the lodestars by which we orient ourselves. Idolatry is not too strong a word. Desmond suggests the "absorbing god" as the "principle of completion which, purporting to be absolute wholeness, subsumes all parts within itself and in this engulf-ment absorbs their distinctiveness."[8] We are made for more, for the in-finite, and any *thing* offering itself as the key to our wholeness as "the Answer" or "The Truth" must be rejected. If we have knowledge of the Absolute we cannot be seduced into thinking ourselves to have Absolute Knowledge. God comes not according to our terms but irruptively, often as an unexpected and even unwanted godsend, whose arrival precipitates a calamitous breakdown before inaugurating a transformative break-through. If we espy a golden calf or any other idol occupying space in the Temple, we should heed Nietzsche and take up our hammers—the *Götzen-Dämmerung*—and clear the altar.

Fourth commandment, with a wink to Kearney: *Thou shalt be at-tuned and attentive to everyday disclosures.* Already a positive prescription, here Kearney and Desmond agree that we need to cultivate a practice of attention to the micro-eschatologies announcing God's presence in all things. No small feat! The "Omni-God" rightly denounced by Kearney would announce itself in feats of power and might—the God for whom we are watchful, however, not as a Zeus-like figure, not as the All-Destroyer, but as an empowering Omnipotence, the Holy One who endows creation with existence solely out of the goodness of exis-tence itself:

> Empowering
> It does not overpower
> It is over all power
> The enabling origin
>
> It enables nothing for itself
> It enables everything for itself
> It has not need to insist
> Its reticence gives to exist[9]

In her Cambridge University office, Sarah Coakley rejoices to find a kindred spirit who intuits God's power as a "gentle omnipotence," a power-in-vulnerability.[10] As *kairos* ruptures and transforms *chronos*, divine *kenosis* interrupts and reconfigures our understanding of divine power. God's power is not manifested through dominion but through service; God's abiding presence is announced not in garish wonders but comes under the guise of the quotidian: the knock at the door, a request for cold water, the cry of a child at the border, the Sacred Presence under the appearance of bread and wine. Our epiphanic attunement, cultivated through metaxological *askesis*, has made us vigilant to these divine disclosures. The Kingdom's arrival takes place not with the implementation of an ideology but as an eschatological invitation to be enacted in and through our response to the One disclosed in "mustard seeds, grains of yeast, tiny pearls, cups of water."[11] The theologian's sensibility must be not only be informed well—orthodoxy and orthopraxis—but also well formed to perceive the sacred within the secular (orthoaesthesis) and to be affected accordingly (orthopathy).

Fifth commandment, with a high five to Westphal: *Be still and know: Metaphysics is a vocation*. Metaphysics, at least in its metaxological form, has been approached not as "the system" but as, in line with Pierre Hadot, a way of life. It is responsive to a call coming from outside of ourselves, a summons calling the addressee to marshal forth all of one's resources to probe into and reflect on the happening of the *metaxu*. Metaphysics is not the ground of faith but is part and parcel of faith's response. Westphal describes this sort of metaphysics capable of serving faith as "pragmatic," which means

> understanding that theory is and ought to be embedded in practice. Here that means that theology and its own proper metaphysics properly arise out of the practice of faith (and thus are not the "view from nowhere") and that they properly serve to guide and inspire these practices: private prayer, character formation, public worship, and service to others. Here metaphysics is to be embedded in a spirituality that is simultaneously an inward journey, and upward journey, and an outward journey. It is not a preamble to faith but a reflection that arises out of faith and seeks to serve the life of faith.[12]

Lest one be unnerved by the last sentence, I add: for Desmond, metaxology is not an independent philosophical discipline sealed off from the religious. The two are porous to one another, but in our reconfigured ethos these passages are often clogged. The religious is not, consequently, something superadded to the *metaxu*, but is its innermost dynamic core. To be stirred into mindfulness *at all* is to be, even if inchoately, in communion with the Transcendent. A pragmatic metaphysics, metaxology guides our descent (*katabasis*) into and renewed ascent from (*anabasis*) the *metaxu* and capacitates us to take our place in the *poiesis* of being. Metaxology is not, then, a *what*—a stand-alone system, a completed map, an exhausting and exhaustive account of every being—but a *way* of being mindful and responsive to the felt summons to inquire ever deeper into the whole of being.

As a theologian, I add with a wink: Desmond shows that metaphysics does, in fact, have a prayer. And this in two ways. First, in dubbing him the "Last Metaphysician," Manoussakis underestimates metaphysics' staying power. In Desmond we see yet another metaphysical awakening. After a long slumber and generations of desuetude, his metaxological approach to metaphysics offers one viable itinerary. Without pretense to articulating *the* way, metaxology offers *a* way. It is not a hegemonic attempt at grasping and controlling but is, instead, a vocation to give an account of what it means to be at all. It originates not in idle speculation or abstract reasoning but as a response to the astonishment of having been addressed by the advent of the Transcendent. One hazards to speak metaphysically because one recognizes oneself as having been bidden to do so.

As a discourse, metaxology serves the philosophical and theological life. In this way, metaxology has a prayer insofar as it leads its practitioners to assume a stance of vigilant listening. Attentive to the "crack" in everything, one listens patiently and contemplatively. One opens oneself to the silence and waits in longing. Is this prayer? Rahner: "Perceiving God's silence is also an answer that makes the listening meaningful. Under God's silence too we may become what we have to be at any rate: personal finite spirit before the personal infinite free God, with whom we necessarily have to deal, at least by being aware of God's silence."[13]

The caducity of discourse is the happy fault, the *felix culpa* of human reason: when our words are exhausted and our concepts shattered, then in the rubble one may hear in the silence the woo of the Holy One. A metaxological itinerary, guiding us through the "return to zero" traverses a mystagogical path whereby our senses are purged as we undergo the dark night of nihilism. The purgation of darkness unclogs our primal porosity and we cry with Samuel: Speak, Lord, your servant is listening! And, as night cedes to day, as our eyes peer through the dust and debris of our fallen idols, the dawn from on high breaks upon us. The dawn does not dispel or banish the Mystery into which we have been drawn but deepens it. We blink with orthoaesthetically attuned eyes and perceive how the *logos* of being is *agape*. The *Logos* is not a disengaged canon floating high in the sky like Plato's sun; it is, rather, incarnate and present in history. Thus Balthasar: "It is too good to be true: the mystery of being, revealed as absolute love, condescending to wash his creatures' feet, and even their souls, taking upon himself all the confusion of guilt, all the God-directed hatred, all the accusations showered upon him with cudgels, all the disbelief that arrogantly covers up what he had revealed, all the mocking hostility that once and for all nailed down his inconceivable movement of self-abasement—in order to pardon his creature, before himself and the world."[14]

For those with eyes to see, Christ "the power of God and the wisdom of God" (1 Cor. 1:24) is encountered as the core and essence of being itself. The scandal of Jesus's particularity is, for many, an utterly idiotic and impossible-to-believe claim. For those given the dark grace to experience how "God's foolishness is wiser than human wisdom, and God's weakness is stronger than human strength" (1 Cor. 1:25), the idiocy of Christianity's claim records the breakthrough into time and space of *agape* itself, as it works to reconfigure our ethos according to the logic of God's Kingdom. The Christian, consequently, is caught up in the pierced-yet-glorified grasp of the Agapeic One and invited to say nothing more and nothing less than "Amen" with one's being. This is the empowering power extended by the *passio caritatis*; a mixed grace indeed as it simultaneously threatens and promises to refigure our lives in a cruciform pattern. To assent to the *passio caritatis* is to risk enfleshing St. Clare of Assisi's prayer:

> We become what we love
> And who we love shapes what we become.
> If we love things, we become a thing.
> If we love nothing, we become nothing.
> Imitation is not a literal mimicking of Christ,
> Rather it means becoming the image of the beloved,
> An image disclosed through transformation.
> This means . . . we are to become vessels
> Of God's compassionate love for others.

The credibility of Christianity depends on this assent. We put our lives on the line, accepting the promise and the peril of being transformed by the *passio caritatis* into *idiots* for Christ who are moved by love to "go and do likewise" (Luke 10:37) in offering ourselves in agapeic service to the least of our sisters and brothers and to the exalted and Agapeic Other—our Father in heaven—modeled on Christ our brother.

Understood theologically, what I proposed as the "orthotic fourfold" allows us to dwell within the *metaxu* at the crossroads of four polarities: orthodoxy, orthopraxis, orthopathy, and orthoaesthesis. To have undergone the *passio caritatis*, to have been reconfigured according to the pattern of the Crucified One, allows us to perceive as Christ perceives, to love as Christ loves. The *passio caritatis* offers us a share in the divine life and renews our senses to behold and respond to the world with hands and eyes and ears—our whole selves—as bearing the trace of grace. This may be what St. Paul meant by having "the mind of Christ" (1 Cor. 2:16)—not an abstract *noesis* but an embodied *aesthesis*, or mode of perception. Indeed, the oft-debated meaning of the Greek *pistis Christou* (faith *in* Christ or faith *of* Christ?) may not need to be univocally decided: the orthoaesthetically attuned is one who perceives with the faith *of* Christ, one who detects Christ's presence in all things, because one hears the woo of the Risen One beckoning from the crack in everything. To the orthoaesthetically constituted, we do not need the security of a binary either/or. On the contrary, we luxuriate in the intermediation of the both/and because there we experience fully the surplus of divine presence in all things.

Would that I could now write "in conclusion" and bring this project to a close. Such resolution may sate an appetite for closure but would betray the spirit of the book. There can be no cut-and-dry resolution, no final sentence after which one might drop the mic and exit the stage. There is only an in(con)clusion. When the last order of the night is placed, when the musicians play the evening's last set, and as the barkeep washes glasses, there is but a temporary cessation of activity. Revelers will go their separate ways and the musicians will pack their instruments, but the *craic* is neither expunged nor exhausted. It lives on in memory and coaxes us into the future. Heraclitus: you never step into the same river twice. The *seisiún*: you never play the same tune twice because the living tradition refuses to be fixed and insists on growing and evolving.

Metaxology: speak of the between as much as you like, sing of it and commend it to verse, but there will always be too much to be said and sung. Metaxology bids us to stay faithful to the flux, to remain alert to the dynamism of the *metaxu*, and to allow ourselves to be drawn into and transformed by the intermediation of being. On the proscenium of the *metaxu*, there are no objective spectators: we are, all of us, a part of the ongoing performance.

To read Taylor's map with metaxological eyes is to see, even in the most unlikely places, openings to the Transcendent and new ways of reflecting on how the Holy One is disclosed in time and space. I have endeavored to show how metaxology can enter into fruitful and illuminating dialogue with poetic, musical, literary, and theological sources. I have indicated, furthermore, certain places where these insights might be further developed. How might metaxology be illuminated by, and reciprocally illuminate, the work of Ian McGilchrist in his *The Master and His Emissary* or of social psychologists such as Kenneth Gergen and Jonathan Haidt? How might Desmond be brought into conversation with theologians such as René Girard, Sarah Coakley, and Karl Rahner? I have suggested how one might develop something like the *passio caritatis* or offer a fourth dimension (orthoaesthesis) to the triad of orthodoxy, orthopathy, and orthopraxis. If we are sensitive to the dynamism of metaxology, what would it look like to reread, say, the Council of Chalcedon (451 CE)? Might we find in Chalcedon an anticipation of metaxology's unwillingness to "freeze the flux" as it tries to express the paradoxical fullness of Christ's humanity *and* divinity? Could our understanding of Christ's Real Presence in the Eucharist be enriched by a metaxological reframing? Might metaxology assist us in rethinking the relationship between theology and philosophy, and between theology and science?

To my mind, William Desmond's theological achievement is found in metaxology's ability to provide not just a way of thinking but, when undertaken as a form of spiritual exercise, a way of living. He raises the question of God and shows how the question can become an existential quest. Metaxology, so approached, concerns less *what* one perceives than *how* one does so. It makes possible what Paul Crowley has called a "mystagogy of believing" drawing one into the depths of the Mystery at the heart of all creation.[15] In a quest akin to Bonaventure's *The Journey of the Mind to God*, one is guided stepwise to perceive God's presence in all things. Led by grace along this itinerary, the wayfarer undergoes, like Francis, a *transitus* from slavery to freedom, from death to new life. We are plunged into the purgative darkness of divine Mystery and brought to behold, in time, the form of the Crucified One in whom we are called to sabbatical rest. By practicing metaxology as an *askesis*, by exercising transcendence in the *metaxu*, we begin to find ourselves rocked back on our heels: what had seemed the unstoppable eclipse of God, beheld with attuned eyes, appears a new day's dawn. As the darkened plain is touched by morning's light, one finds oneself stirred by an ancient melody. Foreign yet familiar—nay, intimately strange—the music passes into us, heals our deafness, and renews our porosity to the Holy One.

NOTES

Foreword

1. Augustine, *De trinitate* 14.5: *ab inferioribus ad superiora ascendentes uel ab exterioribus ad interiora ingredientes.*

Introduction

1. Dupré, *Religious Mystery and Rational Reflection*, 139.
2. Desmond, *God and the Between*, 338.
3. Taylor, *A Secular Age*, 25.
4. Rahner, "Christian Living Formerly and Today," 15.
5. Imhof and Biallowons, *Karl Rahner in Dialogue: Conversations and Interviews, 1965–1982*, 176.
6. Taylor, *A Secular Age*, 755.
7. Hume, *Enquiry concerning Human Understanding*, 114. All emphasis in quoted material in this book is original unless otherwise indicated.
8. Arnold, "Dover Beach," in *Dover Beach and Other Poems*, 86–87.
9. Desmond, *Philosophy and Its Others*, 41.
10. Dante Alighieri, *The Divine Comedy*, 47.
11. Desmond, *God and the Between*, xii.
12. Kearney, *Anatheism*, xi.
13. Elie, *The Life You Save Might Be Your Own*, x.

ONE   Beating the Bounds of *A Secular Age*

1. Taylor, *A Secular Age*, 307.
2. Ibid.
3. Pew Research Center, "U.S. Public Becoming Less Religious" (2015), http://www.pewforum.org/2015/11/03/u-s-public-becoming-less-religious/.
4. Louis Dupré, *Passage to Modernity*; Michael Allen Gillespie, *The Theological Origins of Modernity*; Hans Blumenberg, *The Legitimacy of the*

Modern Age; Mark Lilla, *The Stillborn God*; and Brad Gregory, *The Unintended Reformation.*

5. Nietzsche, *The Gay Science*, 180.

6. Dupré, *Religious Mystery and Rational Reflection*, 133.

7. Crowley, "Mystagogy and Mission: The Challenge of Nonbelief and the Task of Theology," 12.

8. Taylor, *The Ethics of Authenticity*, 11.

9. Ibid.

10. Taylor, *A Secular Age*, 592.

11. Ibid., 2–3. See also Ruth Abbey, "Theorizing Secularity 3," in Colorado and Klassen, ed., *Aspiring to Fullness in a Secular Age*, 98–124.

12. Taylor, *A Secular Age*, 20.

13. Epstein, *Good without God.*

14. Weber, "Science as a Vocation," 13–14.

15. Taylor, *A Secular Age*, 539.

16. Taylor, *A Secular Age*, 307.

17. Smith, *How (Not) to Be Secular*, 132.

18. Taylor, *A Secular Age*, 309.

19. Ibid.

20. Ibid., 311.

21. Taylor, "Iris Murdoch and Moral Philosophy," in *Dilemmas and Connections: Selected Essays*, 3–23.

22. See Jon Butler, "Disquieted History in *A Secular Age*," in Warner, VanAntwerpen, and Calhoun, eds., *Varieties of Secularism in a Secular Age*, 193–216. Butler writes that *A Secular Age* could have been "half its size, even a third, because fewer pages would almost inevitably have forced more focused arguments and clearer expositions" (197).

23. Taylor, "Explanation and Practical Reason," in *Philosophical Arguments*, 34–60.

24. This is not counted a gain by all readers. Although Taylor limits his scope to "Latin Christendom," some critics have resisted his meganarrative as insufficiently attentive to subaltern narratives. Saba Mahmood notes that "Latin Christendom" is hardly homogenous. Rather than "a" story, attention needs to be given to many stories. Because he neglects to account for subaltern narratives, Taylor's efforts might be seen as enclosing or constraining others by imposing a story not their own upon them. See Saba Mahmood, "Can Secularism Be Otherwise?," in Warner, VanAntwerpen, and Calhoun, eds., *Varieties of Secularism in a Secular Age*, 282–99.

25. Taylor, "Overcoming Epistemology," in *Philosophical Arguments*, 1–19; Taylor, "Engaged Agency and Background in Heidegger," in Guignon, ed., *The*

Cambridge Companion to Heidegger, 317–36; Dreyfus and Taylor, *Retrieving Realism*.

26. Dreyfus and Taylor, *Retrieving Realism*, 1.

27. Gordon, "The Place of the Sacred in the Absence of God: Charles Taylor's *A Secular Age*," 650.

28. Taylor, *Sources of the Self*, 72.

29. Taylor, "Explanation and Practical Reason," 36. Stephen Long similarly recognizes the importance of ad hominem reasoning in Taylor's *A Secular Age* in Long, "How to Read Charles Taylor: The Theological Significance of *A Secular Age*."

30. Taylor, *Sources of the Self*, 72.

31. Ibid., 39.

32. Taylor, *The Explanation of Behavior*.

33. Smith, *Charles Taylor: Meaning, Morals, and Modernity*, 42.

34. Taylor, "Peaceful Coexistence in Psychology," in *Human Agency and Language*, 117.

35. Smith, *Charles Taylor*, 42.

36. Abbey, *Charles Taylor*, 166–67.

37. Taylor, "Explanation and Practical Reason," 59.

38. Taylor, "What Is Human Agency?," in *Human Agency and Language*, 15.

39. Frankfurt, "Freedom of the Will and the Concept of a Person," 6.

40. Taylor, "What Is Human Agency?," 16.

41. Ibid., 17.

42. Ibid., 16.

43. Ibid., 24.

44. Ibid., 26. This is akin to Ricoeur's distinction between the *idem-* and *ipse-*identity. The *idem-*self is the perduring *who* announcing itself through *what* one is. They overlap, of course, but *who* one is—one's identity—is irreducible to any single *what* or amalgam of *whats*. See Paul Ricoeur, *Oneself as Another*, 120–21.

45. Taylor, "What Is Human Agency?," 43.

46. Ibid., 17.

47. Ibid., 26.

48. The gist: there is a prohibition on using technology to influence the course of another civilization. In the film, Spock regards it a violation of the Prime Directive to be seen by the aboriginal population of the planet they are trying to save. The "good" of the people, as encoded in the directive, trumps the "good" of his own life.

49. Taylor, "The Diversity of Goods," in *Philosophy and the Human Sciences*, 241.

50. Taylor, "Explanation and Practical Reason," 37.

51. Harris, *The Moral Landscape: How Science Can Determine Human Values*.

52. Dennett, *Breaking the Spell: Religion as a Natural Phenomenon*.

53. Taylor, "Explanation and Practical Reason," 59.

54. Ibid., 41.

55. Ibid., 54.

56. Ibid., 42.

57. There is a role for apodictic judgments: strike zones, tax codes, speed limits, exchange rates all appeal to an objective standard. The question is whether all disagreements—from debates about speed limits to debates about abortion—can appeal to a neutral premise to adjudicate the dispute in an apodictic and remainder-free manner.

58. Taylor, "Explanation and Practical Reason," 36. Otherwise stated: you need a hermeneutic of charity.

59. Taylor, "Explanation and Practical Reason," 51.

60. I borrow here from Zane Yi, "The Possibility of God: An Examination and Evaluation of Charles Taylor's Transcendental Critique of Closed Worlds," 19–20.

61. The transition from Aristotelian to Galilean theories of motion. In adopting the latter, scientists were able to make sense of "violent" motion in a way not possible to Aristotelian science. By adopting the standpoint Y (Galilean science), hitherto unclear or hazy elements of X are made clear.

62. Taylor refers to Foucault's *Discipline and Punish* and the execution of a man guilty of attempted regicide. This type of public spectacle is unthinkable to us, but it made sense in a former framework.

63. Taylor, "Explanation and Practical Reason," 51. The more therapeutic model, it involves one interlocutor helping the other to identify a contradiction and to transition, gradually, to another point of view.

64. Ibid., 54.

65. Ibid., cited by Taylor.

66. Blakely, "Returning to the Interpretive Turn: Charles Taylor and His Critics," 402.

67. Ibid.

68. Colin Jager, "Charles Taylor's Romanticism," in Warner, VanAntwerpen, and Calhoun, eds., *Varieties of Secularism in a Secular Age*, 191.

69. Ibid.

70. Taylor, *A Secular Age*, 728.

71. Ibid., 755.

72. Ibid., 25.

73. Desmond, *Being and the Between*, 210.

74. Taylor, "Iris Murdoch and Moral Philosophy," 3.

75. Taylor, *Sources of the Self*, 125.

76. Ibid.

77. Ibid., 5.

78. Illich, *Rivers North of the Future: The Testament of Ivan Illich as told to David Cayley*, 52–54.

79. Ibid., 197.

80. Taylor, "Iris Murdoch and Moral Philosophy," 5.

81. Taylor, *A Secular Age*, 179.

82. Ibid., 215.

83. Taylor, *Sources of the Self*, 224.

84. Taylor, *A Secular Age*, 221–24.

85. Ibid., 230.

86. Ibid., 5.

87. Taylor, *Modern Social Imaginaries*, 25.

88. Taylor, *A Secular Age*, 172.

89. Ibid.

90. Taylor, "Overcoming Epistemology," 4.

91. Ibid.

92. Dreyfus and Taylor, *Retrieving Realism*, 13–14.

93. Ibid., 25.

94. Taylor, "Iris Murdoch and Moral Philosophy," 6.

95. Taylor, "Overcoming Epistemology," in *Philosophical Arguments*, 7.

96. Murdoch, *The Sovereignty of the Good*, 8.

97. Taylor, *A Secular Age*, 542.

98. Ibid.

99. Ibid., 551.

100. Ibid.

101. Taylor, "Iris Murdoch and Moral Philosophy," 5.

102. Ibid., 8.

103. Smith, *How (Not) to Be Secular*, 24.

104. Taylor, "Afterword: Apologia pro Libro suo," in *Varieties of Secularism*, 303.

105. Ricoeur, *Time and Narrative*, 41.

106. Taylor, *A Secular Age*, 565.

107. Ibid., 10.

108. Ibid., 9.

109. Murdoch, *The Sovereignty of the Good*, 93.

110. Ibid., 12.

111. Murdoch, *The Sovereignty of the Good*, 93.

112. Taylor, "Iris Murdoch and Moral Philosophy," 12.

113. Taylor, "The Diversity of Goods," in *Philosophy and Human Sciences*, 2:243.

114. Ibid.

115. Taylor, *A Secular Age*, 835.

116. Taylor, "Iris Murdoch and Moral Philosophy," 14.

117. Taylor, *A Secular Age*, 597.

118. Ibid., 600.

119. Ibid., 595.

120. Taylor, "Iris Murdoch and Moral Philosophy," 15.

121. Taylor, *A Secular Age*, 325.

122. Ibid., 551.

123. Taylor, "Iris Murdoch and Moral Philosophy," 15.

124. Ibid.

125. Lewis, *The Lion, the Witch, and the Wardrobe*, 188.

126. Taylor, "Iris Murdoch and Moral Philosophy," 5.

127. Taylor, *A Secular Age*, 668–70.

128. Taylor, "Iris Murdoch and Moral Philosophy," 16.

129. Ibid., 17.

130. Taylor, *A Secular Age*, 15.

131. Ibid., 624.

132. Ibid., 635.

133. Taylor, "Iris Murdoch and Moral Philosophy," 19. In regard to (1), options (b) and (c) will differ on *how* this is understood and enacted, but they agree *that* this is the supreme good.

134. Taylor, *A Secular Age*, 637.

135. Ibid., 638.

136. Taylor, "Iris Murdoch and Moral Philosophy," 15.

137. Taylor, *A Secular Age*, 730.

138. Ibid., 731.

139. Faulkner, "The Bear," in *Go Down, Moses*, 198.

140. Taylor, *A Secular Age*, 769.

141. Ibid., 22.

142. Ibid., 574–75.

143. Taylor, *Sources of the Self*, 47.

144. 2 Samuel 12:1–14.

145. Luke 24:13–35. We return to the Emmaus narrative in chapter 5.

146. Taylor, *A Secular Age*, 149.

147. Paul Janz, "Transcendence, 'Spin,' and the Jamesian Open Space," in Colorado and Klassen, eds., *Aspiring to Fullness in a Secular Age*, 49.

148. Ibid.

149. Ibid.

150. Desmond, "The Porosity of Being: Towards a Catholic Agapeics," in Taylor, Casanova, McLean, and Vila-Chã, eds., *Renewing the Church in a Secular Age*, 287.

151. Desmond, *The Intimate Strangeness of Being*, xvi.

152. Hadot, *The Present Alone Is Our Happiness*, 87.

153. Desmond, *Desire, Dialectic and Otherness: An Essay on Origins*, 17.

154. Janz, "Transcendence, 'Spin,' and the Jamesian Open Space," 49.

TWO   A Crack in Everything

1. Desmond, *Perplexity and Ultimacy*, 2.

2. Kelly, introduction to *Between System and Poetics*, 1.

3. Simpson, *Religion, Metaphysics, and the Postmodern*; Simpson, ed., *The William Desmond Reader*.

4. Desmond's *Ethics and the Between* was the focus of *Ethical Perspectives* 8, no. 4 (2001): 231–331; *God and the Between* was addressed in *Louvain Studies* 36, no. 2-3 (2012): 219–317; *Hegel's God: A Counterfeit Double* was discussed in *The Owl of Minerva* 2 (2005): 91–200.

5. In addition to *Between System and Poetics*, there is Simpson and Sammon, eds., *William Desmond and Contemporary Theology*.

6. Kelly, introduction to *Between System and Poetics*, 3.

7. Desmond, "The Porosity of Being," in Vila-Chã, ed., *Renewing the Church in a Secular Age*, 287.

8. Richard Kearney, "Two Thinks at a Distance," in Simpson, ed., *The William Desmond Reader*, 237.

9. Desmond, *Being and the Between*, xvi.

10. Desmond, "The Porosity of Being," 287.

11. Ibid.

12. John Manoussakis, "The Silences of the Between," in Simpson and Sammon, eds., *William Desmond and Contemporary Theology*, 269.

13. Consider: Caputo, *Heidegger and Aquinas*; Mark A. Wrathall, ed., *Religion after Metaphysics*; Manoussakis, *God after Metaphysics*; Hector, *Theology without Metaphysics*.

14. Desmond, *The Intimate Strangeness of Being*, 101.

15. Desmond, *Between System and Poetics*, 20.

16. Desmond, *God and the Between*, 10.

17. Desmond, *The Intimate Strangeness of Being*, 13.

18. Thomson, "Ontotheology? Understanding Heidegger's *Destruktion* of Metaphysics," 297.

19. John Betz, "Overcoming the Forgetfulness of Metaphysics," in Simpson and Sammon, eds., *William Desmond and Contemporary Theology*, 67.

20. Ibid.

21. Heidegger, *Identity and Difference*, 55.

22. Ibid., 56 (emphasis added).

23. Ibid., 54.

24. Westphal, *Transcendence and Self-Transcendence*, 18.

25. Heidegger, *Identity and Difference*, 60.

26. Ibid., 72.

27. Ibid.

28. Schindler, *The Catholicity of Reason*, 237.

29. Westphal, *Overcoming Onto-Theology*, 257.

30. Westphal, "The Importance of Overcoming Metaphysics for the Life of Faith," 263.

31. Westphal, *Transcendence and Self-Transcendence*, 19.

32. Ibid.

33. Simpson, *Religion, Metaphysics, and the Postmodern*, 7.

34. Caputo, *Radical Hermeneutics*, 3.

35. Caputo, *The Insistence of God*, 113.

36. Ibid., 191.

37. Ibid., 192.

38. Caputo, *On Religion*, 113.

39. Caputo, *Radical Hermeneutics*, 1.

40. Caputo, *The Insistence of God*, 191.

41. Caputo, *Radical Hermeneutics*, 3.

42. Ibid., 189.

43. Caputo, *On Religion*, 140.

44. Ibid., 141.

45. Ibid., 139.

46. Ibid., 114.

47. Kearney, "Epiphanies of the Everyday: Toward a Micro-Eschatology," in John Manoussakis, ed., *After God*, 11.

48. Kearney, *The God Who May Be*, 24.

49. Ibid.

50. Kearney, *Anatheism*, 72–73.

51. Ibid., 73.

52. Ibid., 53.

53. Ibid.

54. Kearney, "Epiphanies of the Everyday," 4.

55. Kearney, *Anatheism*, 7.

56. Richard Kearney, "God after God," in Kearney and Zimmermann, eds., *Reimagining the Sacred*, 7.

57. Ibid., 9.

58. Kearney, *Anatheism*, 88–99.

59. Kearney, "Epiphanies of the Everyday," 11.

60. Kearney, *The God Who May Be*, 49–51.

61. Ibid., 51.

62. Ibid.

63. Ibid., 13.

64. Kearney, "Enabling God," in John Manoussakis, ed., *After God*, 46.

65. Westphal, *Overcoming Onto-Theology*, 87.

66. Westphal, "Hermeneutics and the God of Promise," in John Manoussakis, ed., *After God*, 85.

67. Westphal, "The Importance of Overcoming Metaphysics for the Life of Faith," 253.

68. Ibid., 259.

69. Ibid.

70. Ibid., 272.

71. Ibid.

72. Ibid.

73. Janicaud, *Phenomenology and the "Theological Turn,"* 50.

74. Ibid., 55.

75. Marion, *God without Being*, xxx.

76. Falque, *Crossing the Rubicon: The Borderlands of Philosophy and Theology*, 134.

77. Pickstock, "What Shines Between: The *Metaxu* of Light," in Kelly, ed., *Between System and Poetics*, 107.

78. Simpson, *Religion, Metaphysics, and the Postmodern*, 5.

79. Desmond, *Being and the Between*, 3.

80. Ibid., 16.

81. Ibid., 45.

82. William Desmond, "Wording the Between," in Simpson, ed., *The William Desmond Reader*, 195.

83. Kelly, introduction to *Between System and Poetics*, 3.

84. Desmond, *The Intimate Strangeness of Being*, xvii.

85. Desmond, *Being and the Between*, 5.

86. Desmond, "The Metaphysics of Modernity," in Adams, Pattison, and Ward, eds. *The Oxford Handbook of Theology and Modern European Thought*, 546.

87. Ibid., 545 (emphasis added).

88. Ibid., 547.

89. Ibid., 547–48.

90. William Desmond, "Idiot Wisdom and the Intimate Universal: On Immanence and Transcendence in an Intercultural Perspective," in Brown and Franke, eds., *Transcendence, Immanence, and Intercultural Philosophy*, 161.

91. Desmond, *The Intimate Strangeness of Being*, 5.

92. Plato, *Theaetetus* 155d3-4.

93. Desmond, *Being and the Between*, 8.

94. Desmond, *The Intimate Strangeness of Being*, 8.

95. Desmond, *Being and the Between*, 15.

96. Desmond, *Philosophy and Its Others*, 229.

97. Desmond, "Wording the Between," 196.

98. Desmond, "The Theater of the *Metaxu*: Staging the Between," 113.

99. Desmond, *Ethics and the Between*, 17.

100. Desmond, "Wording the Between," 212.

101. Taylor, *Modern Social Imaginaries*, 23.

102. Taylor, "Afterword," in *Varieties of Secularism in a Secular Age*, 308.

103. Desmond, *The Intimate Universal*, 166.

104. Taylor, *Modern Social Imaginaries*, 25.

105. Desmond, *The Intimate Universal*, 24.

106. Janz, "Transcendence, 'Spin,' and the Jamesian Open Space," 49.

107. Desmond, *The Intimate Universal*, 166.

108. Desmond, *Ethics and the Between*, 41.

109. Simpson, *Religion, Metaphysics, and the Postmodern*, 27. For a similar take, see Martin Heidegger, "The Question concerning Technology," to see how an instrumental stance—enframing or reconfiguring—renders the world a "standing reserve." Soil becomes a mineral deposit; tracts of land become coal fields; rivers become power sources.

110. Ibid.

111. Desmond, "*Autonomia Turannos*: On Some Dialectical Equivocities of Self-Determination," 235.

112. Merold Westphal explores this antimony in Westphal, *In Praise of Heteronomy: Making Room for Revelation*.

113. Desmond, *Beyond Hegel and Dialectic*, 287.

114. Desmond, *The Intimate Strangeness of Being*, 120.

115. Desmond, "On God and the Between," in Brabant and Boeve, eds., *Between Philosophy and Theology*, 102.

116. Desmond, *Is There a Sabbath for Thought?*, xi.

117. Hopkins, "The Grandeur of God," in *The Major Works*, 128.

118. Desmond, "The Theater of the *Metaxu*: Staging the Between," 113.

119. Desmond, *The Intimate Universal*, 167.

120. Ibid.

121. Ibid.

122. Desmond, *Being and the Between*, xiii.

123. Ibid.

124. Desmond, *The Intimate Universal*, 425.

125. Desmond, *The Intimate Strangeness of Being*, 36.

126. Desmond, *Being and the Between*, 49.

127. Ibid., 18.

128. Gladwin Hill, "For Want of Hyphen Venus Rocket Is Lost," *New York Times*, July 27, 1962.

129. Desmond, *The Gift of Beauty and the Passion of Being*, 99.

130. Desmond, *Being and the Between*, 50.

131. Andrew Ferguson, "The Heretic," *Weekly Standard*, March 25, 2013, http://www.weeklystandard.com/the-heretic/article/707692.

132. Nagel, *Mind and Cosmos*, 8.

133. Ibid., 12.

134. Desmond, *Being and the Between*, 82.

135. Ibid., 63.

136. Ibid., 19.

137. Plato, *Theaetetus* 150d-e.

138. Aristotle, *Metaphysics* 983a18–20.

139. Desmond, *The Intimate Strangeness of Being*, 7.

140. Desmond, *Being and the Between*, 17.

141. Ibid., 191.

142. Desmond, "Between System and Poetics," 17.

143. Desmond, *The Intimate Universal*, 421.

144. Desmond, *Being and the Between*, 87.

145. Ibid.

146. Desmond, "Flux-Gibberish: For and against Heraclitus," 478.

147. Aristotle, *Rhetoric* 3.5.1407b12.

148. Ibid., 3.5.1407b15–18.

149. Descartes, *Discourse on Method*, 11.

150. Pinkard, "Analytics, Continentals, and Modern Skepticism," 189.

151. Caputo, *What Would Jesus Deconstruct?*, 29.

152. Desmond, *Is There a Sabbath for Thought?*, 59.

153. Desmond, "Sticky Evil: On Macbeth and the Karma of the Equivocal," in *God, Literature, and Process Thought.*

154. Shakespeare, *Macbeth*, 2.4.10–17.

155. Desmond, *Desire, Dialectic, and Otherness*, 33.

156. Ibid., 22.

157. Ibid.

158. Ibid., 24.

159. See Desmond, *God and the Between*, chap. 2.

160. Plato, *Symposium* 192e.

161. Augustine, *Confessions* 1.1.

162. Aquinas, *Summa theologiae* Ia-IIae, q. 9 ad. 6.

163. Desmond, *Desire, Dialectic, and Otherness*, 177–78.

164. Ibid., 178.

165. Desmond, *Intimate Universal*, 421.

166. Ibid.

167. Desmond, *Being and the Between*, 131.

168. Ibid., 143.

169. Desmond, *The Intimate Strangeness of Being*, 17.

170. Taylor, *Hegel and Modern Society*, 55.

171. Ibid., 64. For Taylor, "hermeneutical dialectics" is an alternative to "strict dialectics." The latter takes its starting point from a position that is beyond contest and then traces how it unfolds. Taylor sees "strict dialectics" as riddled with flaws. So, whereas Hegel might not accept the distinction between strict and hermeneutical dialectics, Taylor sees the latter as preserving Hegel's accomplishment.

172. Desmond, *The Intimate Strangeness of Being*, 24.

173. Ibid.

174. Desmond, *Desire, Dialectic, and Otherness*, 142.

175. Hegel, *Phenomenology of Spirit*, 11.

176. Ibid., 18.

177. Ibid., 144.

178. Ibid., 19.

179. Ibid., 2.

180. Simpson, *God, Religion, and the Postmodern*, 31.

181. Desmond, *The Intimate Strangeness of Being*, 19.

182. Desmond, *Being and the Between*, 172.

183. Desmond, *Perplexity and Ultimacy*, 14.

184. Desmond, *Hegel's God: A Counterfeit Double?*

185. Hegel, *Hegel's Lectures on the History of Philosophy*, 1:xiii; quoted in Westphal, *Transcendence and Self-Transcendence*, 81.

186. Taylor, *Hegel and Modern Society*, 11.

187. Ibid., 29.

188. Desmond, *"Autonomia Turannos,"* 242.

189. Desmond, *Desire, Dialectic, and Otherness*, 179.

190. Ryan, "An Archaeological Ethics," in Kelly, ed., *Between System and Poetics*, 127.

191. Desmond, *Being and the Between*, 197.

192. Desmond, *The Intimate Strangeness of Being*, 11–12.

193. Desmond, *Art, Origins, Otherness*, 21.

194. Desmond, *The Intimate Strangeness of Being*, 36.

195. Surber, "Reading Desmond," in Kelly, ed., *Between System and Poetics*, 59.

196. Desmond, *Philosophy and Its Others*, 4.

197. Ibid., 5.

198. Desmond, *The Intimate Universal*, 164.

199. Desmond, "Wording the Between," 197.

200. Desmond, *The Intimate Universal*, 423.

201. Ibid.

202. Desmond, *Perplexity and Ultimacy*, 130.

203. Ibid.

204. Ibid.

205. Desmond, *The Intimate Universal*, 316.

206. Desmond, *Desire, Dialectic, and Otherness*, 179.

207. Desmond, *Being and the Between*, 44.

208. Ibid., 206.

209. Desmond, "The Theater of the *Metaxu*: Staging the Between," 114. We discuss Desmond's preference for metaxology over analogy later. He treats analogy in Desmond, "Analogy, Dialectic, and Divine Transcendence: Between St. Thomas and Hegel," in *The Intimate Strangeness of Being*, 231–59.

210. Clarke, *Explorations in Metaphysics*, 113.

211. Desmond, *Art, Origins, and the Absolute*, 268.

212. Simpson, *God, Religion, and the Postmodern*, 46.

213. Ibid., 90.

214. Desmond, *Being and the Between*, 206.

215. Hopkins, "As Kingfishers Catch Fire," 129.

216. Augustine, *Confessions* 10.6.

217. Desmond, *Hegel's God*, 3.

218. Ibid.

219. Desmond, *The Intimate Strangeness of Being*, 120.

220. Desmond, *Being and the Between*, 19.

221. Desmond, *Hegel's God*, 3.

222. Kearney, "Maybe Not, Maybe: William Desmond on God," in Kelly, ed. *Between System and Poetics*. Kearney cites Desmond's accent on possibilizing as making Desmond less sympathetic to Kearney's understanding of divine *posse*. Desmond's response to Kearney's *The God Who May Be* identifies six different senses of the word "possibility" and invites Kearney to specify precisely how he uses *posse*. Their exchange is a model of rigor and charity: each takes the other seriously as they try to understand their disagreements and find a way forward.

223. Westphal, "The Importance of Overcoming Metaphysics for the Life of Faith," 261.

224. Desmond, "Maybe, Maybe Not," 114.

225. Ibid.

226. Desmond, *Perplexity and Ultimacy*, 230.

227. Ibid., 230.

228. Desmond, *Desire, Dialectic, and Otherness*, 235.

229. Desmond, *Being and the Between*, 208.

230. Desmond, *Desire, Dialectic, and Otherness*, 235–36.

231. Kearney, *The God Who May Be*, 54.

232. Ibid.

233. Desmond, *The Intimate Strangeness of Being*, 10.

234. Ibid., 5.

235. Plato, *Theaetetus* 174a.

236. Desmond, *Being and the Between*, 8.

237. Desmond, *The Intimate Strangeness of Being*, 106.

238. Desmond, *Being and the Between*, 8.

239. Desmond, *The Intimate Strangeness of Being*, 106.

240. Ibid., 270.

241. Desmond, *The Intimate Universal*, 53.

242. Balthasar, "Movement toward God," in *Explorations in Theology*, Vol. 3, *Creator Spirit*, 15; quoted in D. C. Schindler, *The Catholicity of Reason*, 45.

243. Ibid., 16, quoted in Schindler, *The Catholicity of Reason*, 46.

244. Desmond, "Wording the Between," 201–2.

245. Ibid., 202.

246. Ibid.

247. Ibid., 203.

248. Desmond, "The Porosity of Being: Towards a Catholic Agapeics," 270.

249. Desmond, "Idiot Wisdom and the Intimate Universal," 163–64.

250. Desmond, *The Intimate Universal*, 270.

251. Desmond, *The Gift of Beauty and the Passion of Being*, 87.

252. Desmond, *The Intimate Strangeness of Being*, 11.

253. Ibid.

254. Desmond, *Perplexity and Ultimacy*, 104.

255. Desmond, *Being and the Between*, 188.

256. Simpson, *God, Religion, and the Postmodern*, 36.

257. Ibid.

258. Buckley, *Denying and Disclosing God*, 8.

259. Ibid., 23.

260. Ibid., 9.

261. Ibid., 15.

262. Ibid., 18.

263. Ibid.

264. Ibid., 19.

265. Ibid., 20.

266. Ibid., 37.

267. Desmond, *The Intimate Strangeness of Being*, 281.

268. Simpson, *God, Religion, and the Postmodern*, 38.

269. Desmond, *Ethics and the Between*, 41.

270. Desmond, *The Intimate Strangeness of Being*, 283.

271. Buckley, *Denying and Disclosing God*, 34.

272. Ibid., 34–35.

273. Ibid., 37.

274. Wittgenstein, *Philosophical Investigations*, 81.

275. Desmond, *The Intimate Strangeness of Being*, 288.

276. Desmond, *Art, Origins, and Otherness*, 271.

277. Desmond, *The Intimate Strangeness of Being*, 283.

278. Desmond, *The Intimate Universal*, 262–63.

279. Desmond, *Philosophy and Its Others*, 259.

280. Taylor, *A Secular Age*, 353–61, 755–61.

281. Ibid., 761.

282. O'Regan, "The Poetics of Ethos: William Desmond's Poetic Refiguration of Plato," 278.

283. O'Regan, "Repetition: Desmond's New Science," in Kelly, ed., *Between System and Poetics*, 69.

284. Hopkins, "Nondum," quoted in Taylor, *A Secular Age*, 763.

285. Emerson, "Compensation," in *Ralph Waldo Emerson: Essays & Lectures*, 292.

286. Desmond, *The Intimate Universal*, 49.

287. Wordsworth, "The Tables Turned," in *The Major Works*, 130–31.

THREE   The Poetics of the Between

1. Desmond, *God and the Between*, 10.

2. Desmond, "Between System and Poetics: On the Practices of Philosophy," 21.

3. Desmond, *God and the Between*, 248.

4. Ibid., 249.

5. Ibid., 26 (italics original).

6. Hadot, *Philosophy as a Way of Life*, 279.

7. Desmond, *God and the Between*, 31.

8. Ignatius of Loyola, *Spiritual Exercises*, no. 1.

9. Ibid., 148.

10. The *Spiritual Exercises* are not a do-it-yourself program. Undertaken as Ignatius envisioned, they are part of a living tradition because the *Exercises* are "handed over" from the director to the retreatant.

11. Hadot, *Philosophy as a Way of Life*, 126.

12. Ibid., 83.

13. Hadot, *The Inner Citadel*, 35.

14. Hadot, *The Present Alone Is Our Happiness*, 87.

15. Antonaccio, "Contemporary Forms of *Askesis* and the Return of Spiritual Exercises," 69.

16. Hadot, *Philosophy as a Way of Life*, 201.

17. Ibid., 202.

18. Ibid., 266.

19. Ibid., 267.

20. Ibid.

21. Kant: "Thoughts without content are empty, intuitions without concepts are blind" (*Critique of Pure Reason* A51/B76).

22. Hadot, *What Is Ancient Philosophy?*, 188.

23. Ibid.

24. Ibid., 189.

25. Hadot, *Philosophy as a Way of Life*, 84.

26. Ibid., 82.

27. Hadot, *The Present Alone Is Our Happiness*, 116.

28. Hadot, *Philosophy as a Way of Life*, 83.

29. Ibid.

30. Ibid.

31. Ibid.

32. Epictetus, *The Enchiridion*, 1.

33. Ibid. Compare Epictetus with Ignatius of Loyola's "Rules for Discernment" found in annotations nos. 313–36 or the "First Principle and Foundation" in no. 23.

34. Hadot, *Philosophy as a Way of Life*, 84.

35. Ibid.

36. Ibid., 85.

37. Murdoch, *The Sovereignty of the Good*, 89.

38. Weil, *Waiting for God*, 62.

39. Ibid.

40. Desmond, *Is There a Sabbath for Thought?*, 1.

41. Hadot, *Philosophy as a Way of Life*, 85.

42. Irvine, *A Guide to the Good Life*, 68.

43. Ibid., 69.

44. Hadot, *The Inner Citadel*, 105. Hadot also refers to this as the "method of decomposition."

45. Ibid.

46. Ibid., 133 (emphasis added).

47. Plato, *Phaedo* 64a, in *Complete Works*, ed. John M. Cooper.

48. Ibid., 67c–68c.

49. Hadot, *Philosophy as a Way of Life*, 94–95 (emphasis original).

50. Ibid., 95–96.

51. Hadot, *The Inner Citadel*, 135.

52. Lucian of Somosata, *Charon*, 437.

53. Hadot, *Philosophy as a Way of Life*, 96.

54. Hadot, *What Is Ancient Philosophy?*, 205.

55. Hadot, *The Inner Citadel*, 135.

56. Marcus Aurelius, *Meditations* 7.9.

57. Hadot, *The Present Alone Is Our Happiness*, 173.

58. Hadot, *Philosophy as a Way of Life*, 97.

59. Pascal, *Pensées*, 53.

60. Ilsetraut Hadot, "The Spiritual Guide," in Armstrong and Armstrong, eds., *Classical Mediterranean Spirituality*, 445.

61. Ibid.

62. Hadot, *The Present Alone Is Our Happiness*, 91.

63. Schneiders, "The Study of Christian Spirituality," 52.

64. Coakley, "Silence, Prayer and Desire in Pedagogical Practices: A Conversation with Sarah Coakley," 49.

65. Hadot, *Philosophy as a Way of Life*, 109.

66. Desmond, "Between System and Poetics," 25.

67. Desmond, *Is There a Sabbath for Thought?*, 17.

68. Ibid., 105.

69. Hadot, *The Present Alone Is Our Happiness*, 104.

70. Taylor, *Philosophy and the Human Sciences*, 104.

71. Ibid., 113.

72. *Being and the Between* in 1995 and *Ethics and the Between* in 2001. Throughout his oeuvre, Desmond recurs to the fourfold. There is a monomaniacal dimension to Desmond's thought such that the fourfold remains consistent throughout, even while it is developed and extended.

73. LeClercq, *The Love of Learning and the Desire for God*, 101.

74. Ibid., 218.

75. Garret Barden explores Desmond's ethics and Ignatian discernment. He shows how metaxology can contribute to a way of life directed by the discerned good in Barden, "Ethics and the Discernment of Spirits," 254–67.

76. Ignatius, *Spiritual Exercises*, no. 46.

77. Ivens, *Understanding the Spiritual Exercises*, 47.

78. Desmond, *God and the Between*, 20.

79. Charles Taylor, *A Secular Age*, 365.

80. Desmond, *God and the Between*, 20.

81. Buckley, *At the Origins of Modern Atheism*, 349–50.

82. Desmond, *God and the Between*, 21.

83. Desmond, *Being and the Between*, 508.

84. Feuerbach, *The Essence of Christianity*, 26.

85. Nietzsche, *Thus Spoke Zarathustra*, 297.

86. Ibid., 110.

87. Dupré, *Religious Mystery and Rational Reflection*, 142.

88. Desmond, *God and the Between*, 23.

89. Ibid., 28.

90. Pope Francis, *The Joy of the Gospel: Evangelii Gaudium*, 27 (§53).

91. Nietzsche, *The Will to Power*, 550.

92. Nietzsche, *The Gay Science*, 181.

93. Desmond, *God and the Between*, 28.

94. Dennis Auweele argues Nietzsche evades Desmond's critique. Although he gives a compelling reading of Zarathustra's "Other Dance Song," he misses Desmond's point: Nietzsche may well offer an existential "no" to the divine origin, but can he follow through on the implications of this utterance?

(Auweele, "Metaxological 'Yes' and Existential 'No': William Desmond and Atheism," 649–54).

95. Aristotle, *Metaphysics* 993b6-7.

96. Desmond, *God and the Between*, 29.

97. Ibid.

98. Ibid.

99. Arnold, "Dover Beach."

100. Desmond, *God and the Between*, 29.

101. Shelley, "Ozymandias," in *The Major Works*, 198.

102. Rahner, *The Need and the Blessing of Prayer*, 5.

103. Ibid., 8.

104. Ibid.

105. Desmond, *Being and the Between*, 203.

106. Hadot, *The Inner Citadel*, 135.

107. Desmond, *God and the Between*, 31.

108. Ibid., 31–32.

109. Taylor, *A Secular Age*, 5.

110. Desmond, *God and the Between*, 338.

111. Desmond, *Is There a Sabbath for Thought?*, 13.

112. Ibid.

113. Desmond, *God and the Between*, 32.

114. Ibid., 32.

115. Desmond, *Philosophy and Its Others*, 278.

116. Ibid.

117. Hadot, *The Present Alone Is Our Happiness*, 90.

118. Hadot, *Philosophy as a Way of Life*, 97.

119. Desmond, *God and the Between*, 33.

120. Ibid., 4. We will return to this point in the next chapter.

121. Desmond, *Being and the Between*, 25.

122. Desmond, *Is There a Sabbath for Thought?*, 25.

123. Desmond, *God and the Between*, 2.

124. Desmond, *Is There a Sabbath for Thought?*, 65.

125. Desmond, *Philosophy and Its Others*, 361.

126. Desmond, *God and the Between*, 11.

127. Ibid., 36.

128. Wittgenstein, *Tractatus Logico-Philosophicus*, 5.

129. Ibid., 88–89.

130. Ibid., 89.

131. Levertov, "Primary Wonder," in *The Stream & the Sapphire*, 33.

132. Desmond, "Wording the Between," 225.

133. Desmond, *God and the Between*, 38. In chapter 5 I will explore the concept of what I call *orthoaesthesis*, "right perception," as a consequence of metaxological attunement.

134. Saint-Exupéry, *The Little Prince*, 79.

135. Desmond, *Being and the Between*, 380.

136. Ibid. One might consult Norris W. Clarke, "To Be Is to Be Substance-in-Relation," to explore a Thomistic understanding of substance as "dynamic self-identity expressing itself in action"; see Clarke, *Explorations in Metaphysics*, 102–22.

137. Clarke, *Person and Being*, 14.

138. Hopkins, "As Kingfishers Catch Fire," 129.

139. Kearney, "Epiphanies of the Everyday: Toward a Micro-Eschatology," 3.

140. Desmond, *God and the Between*, 12.

141. Desmond, "Wording the Between," 225.

142. Desmond, *God and the Between*, 41.

143. Simpson, *Religion, Metaphysics, and the Postmodern*, 100.

144. Augustine, *Confessions* 1.1.

145. One might explore connections between Desmond's erotics of selving and Rahner's *Vorgriff auf esse*, or "pre-apprehension of being." The *Vorgriff* is "the dynamic movement of the spirit toward the absolute range of all possible object[s]. In this movement, the single objects are grasped as single stages of this finality; thus they are known as profiled against the absolute range of all the knowable" (Rahner, *Hearer of the Word*, 47).

146. Desmond, *The Intimate Universal*, 325.

147. Ibid.

148. Westphal, "The Importance of Overcoming Metaphysics for the Life of Faith," 272.

149. Desmond, "Idiot Wisdom and the Intimate Universal," 166.

150. Hopkins, "Nondum," 82–83.

151. Rahner, *Hearer of the Word*, 142.

152. Desmond, *God and the Between*, 41.

153. Desmond, *God and the Between*, 12.

154. Desmond, *The Intimate Strangeness of Being*, 201.

155. Nygren, *Agape and Eros*. Kearney notes the danger of reducing eros to *agape* or *agape* to eros and suggests teasing out "a very specific modality of eros, *agapeic eros*, which would be suitable to God" (see Kearney, "William Desmond on God," 195).

156. Desmond, *The Intimate Universal*, 360.

157. Desmond, *Perplexity and Ultimacy*, 162.

158. Paul Crowley, *Unwanted Wisdom*, 85. Though it lacks the same panache, one might also consult Bonaventure's "Life of St. Francis" for his version of this encounter.

159. Ibid., 86.

160. Aquinas, *Summa theologiae* Ia-IIae, q. 64, a. 4.

161. Taylor, *A Secular Age*, 246.

162. Ibid., 741.

163. Desmond, *Is There a Sabbath for Thought?*, 227.

164. Nietzsche, *Thus Spoke Zarathustra*, 129.

165. Ibid.

166. Köhler-Ryan, "Gifted Beggars in the *Metaxu*: A Study of the Platonic and Augustinian Resonances of *Porosity* in *God and the Between*," 256.

167. Desmond, *The Intimate Universal*, 54.

168. Hadot, *Philosophy as a Way of Life*, 93.

169. Desmond, *God and the Between*, 31. For a patristic iteration of this exercise, one might consult Evagrius Ponticus in Ward, ed., *The Sayings of the Desert Fathers*, 63–64. Ignatius of Loyola also has a death-bed meditation in the *Spiritual Exercises* (no. 187).

170. Köhler-Ryan, "Thinking Transcendence, Transgressing the Mask," in Simpson and Sammon, eds., *William Desmond and Contemporary Theology*, 195.

171. Taylor, *A Secular Age*, 758.

172. Ibid.

173. Ibid.

174. Taylor, *The Language Animal*, 3–50.

175. Ibid., 4.

FOUR   Exercising Transcendence

1. Desmond, *Perplexity and Ultimacy*, 231.

2. Desmond, *God and the Between*, 122.

3. Desmond, "On God and the Between," 106.

4. Ibid., 108.

5. Augustine, *Confessions* 3.7.

6. Desmond, *God and the Between*, 122.

7. Dawkins, *The God Delusion*, 101.

8. Desmond, *Being and the Between*, 42.

9. Ibid.

10. Desmond, *Desire, Dialectic, and Otherness*, 214.

11. Desmond, *God and the Between*, 123.

12. Auweele, "The Poverty of Philosophy: Desmond's Hyperbolic Gifts and Caputo's Events," 419.

13. Desmond, *God and the Between*, 123–24.

14. Ibid., 124.

15. Ibid.

16. Ibid.

17. Ibid.

18. Ibid.

19. Auweele, "The Poverty of Philosophy," 419.

20. Heinrich Denzinger, *Enchiridion symbolorum definitionum et declarationum de rebus fidei et morum: Compendium of Creeds, Definitions and Declarations on Matters of Faith and Morals*, ed. Peter Hünnermann, 806.

21. Desmond, *God and the Between*, 125.

22. Ibid., 126.

23. Ibid.

24. Kearney, "William Desmond on God," 195. Here he suggests a middle position: an agapeic eros. Taylor, *Hegel and Modern Society*, notes God's "need" for and dependence on humanity to be God.

25. Ricoeur, *Interpretation Theory*, 69.

26. Desmond, *God and the Between*, 126.

27. Ibid.

28. Ibid.

29. Buber, *Tales of the Hasidim*, 17–18.

30. Desmond, "God, Ethos, Ways," 13.

31. Ibid., 14.

32. Desmond, "Wording the Between," 224.

33. Desmond, *God and the Between*, 130.

34. Ibid.

35. Patrick Gardner discusses the "suspended middle" in Gardner, "God and the Between: Desmond, Przywara, and Catholic Metaphysics," in Simpson and Sammon, eds., *William Desmond and Contemporary Theology*, 167–72.

36. Desmond, "Wording the Between," 225.

37. *Summa theologiae* Ia, q. 1, a. 2, 3.

38. Desmond, *God and the Between*, 132.

39. Ibid.

40. Ibid.

41. Ibid., 133.

42. Sammon, "The Reawakening of the Between," in Simpson and Sammon, eds., *William Desmond and Contemporary Theology*, 47.

43. Heyde, *The Weight of Finitude*, 40.

44. White, *God the Unknown*, 18.

45. Desmond, *Desire, Dialectic, and Otherness*, 217.

46. Ibid., 225.

47. Kant, *Critique of Pure Reason*, A606, B634.

48. Desmond, *God and the Between*, 253.

49. Robinette, *The Difference Nothing Makes*, forthcoming.

50. *Summa theologiae* Ia. q. 104 ad. 1.

51. McCabe, *God Matters*, 59–60.

52. Keller, *The Face of the Deep: A Theology of Becoming*, xvi.

53. Robinette, "The Difference Nothing Makes: *Creatio Ex Nihilo*, Resurrection, and Divine Gratuity," 525.

54. Keller, *The Face of the Deep*, 16.

55. Keller, *On the Mystery: Discerning Divinity in Process*, 58.

56. Ibid., 49.

57. Keller, *The Face of the Deep*, 6.

58. Ibid., 49 (emphasis added).

59. Desmond, *God and the Between*, 283.

60. Ibid., 320.

61. Ibid., 241.

62. Robinette, "Undergoing Something from Nothing: The Doctrine of Creation as Contemplative Insight," in Laird and Hidden, eds., *The Practice of the Presence of God: Theology as a Way of Life*, 24.

63. Desmond, *God and the Between*, 134.

64. Ibid.

65. Hopkins, "God's Grandeur," 128.

66. Desmond, *God and the Between*, 135.

67. Desmond, *Desire, Dialectic, and Otherness*, 186.

68. Ibid., 137.

69. Desmond, *Philosophy and Its Others*, 268.

70. Ibid.

71. Ibid.

72. Ibid., 269.

73. Desmond, *God and the Between*, 135.

74. I think of *Jaws* when Hooper and Quint compare scars, each body a palimpsest of experience. But it is the barely still visible trace—Quint's removed tattoo—that exposes his *pathos* or, better, his *passio*. Quint's monologue articulates how he has been "given to be" after the sinking of the *Indianapolis*.

75. Aquinas, *Summa theologiae* Ia, q. 2, a. 3, quoted in Brian Davies, *Thomas Aquinas's "Summa Theologiae,"* 46.

76. Wippel, "The Five Ways," in Davies, ed., *Thomas Aquinas: Contemporary Philosophical Perspectives*, 187.

77. Desmond, *God and the Between*, 137.

78. *The Lion King*, DVD, Walt Disney Studies Home Entertainment, 2017.

79. Davies, *Thomas Aquinas's "Summa Theologiae,"* 47.

80. Desmond, in *God and the Between*, writes: "'Proof' is the misplaced demand for a univocity that betrays what is most powerful and suggestive in that aesthetics of happening, what keeps open the space of transcendence, whether that of nature as other, or our own self-surpassing, or that of the ultimate transcendence as other to us. . . . Instead of seeking an inappropriate univocity, we need mindfully to read the signs," 140.

81. Ibid., 137.

82. Ibid., 138.

83. Ibid., 138–39 (emphasis original).

84. Ibid., 139. Consult Nagel, *Mind and Cosmos*, for a nontheistic view of teleological laws.

85. Desmond, *God and the Between*, 139.

86. Ibid.

87. A task made easier on the Holy One by some of us who have less to count.

88. Ibid.

89. Bonaventure, *Journey of the Mind to God*, 8.

90. Ibid.

91. Ibid. Bonaventure, of course, did not index his three forms of sight to Desmond's three transcendences.

92. Nicholas of Cusa, *The Vision of God*, 17.

93. Pascal, *Pensées*, 125.

94. Dostoevsky, *The Brothers Karamazov*, 56.

95. Ratzinger, *Introduction to Christianity*.

96. Ibid., 152.

97. Ibid.

98. Ibid., 153.

99. Ibid., 154.

100. Jonas, *The Phenomenon of Life*, 73–74.

101. Ratzinger, *Introduction to Christianity*, 91.

102. Ibid., 157.

103. Ibid., 160.

104. Desmond, *God and the Between*, 140.

105. Desmond, "Wording the Between," 225.

106. Kearney and Desmond, "Two Thinks at a Distance," in Simpson, ed., *The William Desmond Reader*, 243.

107. D. C. Schindler, "The Positivity of Philosophy," in Simpson and Sammon, eds., *William Desmond and Contemporary Theology*, 126.

108. Desmond, *Is There a Sabbath for Thought?*, 10.

109. Desmond, *God and the Between*, 144.

110. Anselm of Canterbury, *Proslogion*, in *The Major Works*, chap. 2, 87.

111. Heyde, *The Weight of Finitude*, 47.

112. Desmond, *God and the Between*, 144.

113. Ibid., 143.

114. Ibid., 144.

115. Anselm of Canterbury, *Proslogion*, chap. 26.

116. Desmond, *God and the Between*, 94.

117. Ibid., 95.

118. Kant, *Metaphysical Principles of Virtue*, 99.

119. Gordon and Long, "Way(s) to God," in Simpson and Sammon, eds., *William Desmond and Contemporary Theology*, 144.

120. Davies, "Anselm and the Ontological Argument," in Davies and Leftow, eds., *The Cambridge Companion to Anselm*, 157–78.

121. Hadot, *Philosophy as a Way of Life*, 90.

122. Anselm, *Proslogion*, chap. 2.

123. Desmond, *Is There a Sabbath for Thought?*, 130.

124. Desmond, *The Intimate Universal*, 49.

125. Desmond, *God and the Between*, 12.

126. Hadot, *Philosophy as a Way of Life*, 279.

127. Desmond, *Philosophy and Its Others*, 21.

128. Desmond, *God and the Between*, 151.

129. Ibid.

130. Hopkins, "As Kingfishers Catch Fire," 129.

131. Desmond, *Ethics and the Between*, 10.

132. Ibid., 152.

133. Ibid.

134. Ibid., 153 (emphasis original).

135. Heyde, *The Weight of Finitude*, 58.

136. Desmond, *God and the Between*, 153.

137. Ibid., 154.

138. Desmond, "Finding Measure in Exceeding Measure: On *Ethics and the Between*," *Ethical Perspectives*, 320.

139. Desmond, *Ethics and the Between*, 12.

140. Ibid.

141. Desmond, *God and the Between*, 146.

142. Desmond, *The Intimate Universal*, 425.

143. Desmond, *God and the Between*, 155 (emphasis original).

144. Ibid.

145. Ford, *"Here I Am Lord": The Letters and Writings of Ita Ford*, 195.

146. Desmond, *God and the Between*, 156.

147. Desmond, "Consecrated Thought: Between the Priest and the Philosopher," 106.

148. Desmond, *The Intimate Universal*, 115.

149. Taylor, *A Secular Age*, 743.

150. Ibid., 282.

151. Ibid.

152. For more on Illich's influence on Taylor, see Eric Gregory and Leah Hunt-Hendrix, "Enfleshment and the Time of Ethics," in Colorado and Klassen, eds., *Aspiring to Fullness in a Secular Age*, 217–39.

153. Taylor, *A Secular Age*, 739.

154. Ibid.

155. Ibid.

156. Gregory and Hunt-Hendrix, "Enfleshment and the Time of Ethics," 226–27.

157. Dennis, *Auntie Mame*, 298.

158. Pope Francis, *Laudato Sí: On Care for Our Common Home*, no. 10.

159. Ibid., no. 230.

160. Desmond, *Is There a Sabbath for Thought?*, 68.

161. Hopkins, *The Letters of Gerard Manley Hopkins to Robert Bridges*, 56.

162. Hopkins, "Hurrahing in Harvest," in *Major Works*, 134.

163. David Bentley Hart, "For the Life Was Manifested," in Stallings, Asensi, and Good, eds., *Material Spirit: Religion and Literature Intranscendent*, 86.

164. Desmond, *The Intimate Strangeness of Being*, 266. Desmond uses Wordsworth's "Tintern Abbey" to explore the interplay between beholding and being beheld.

165. Taylor, *A Secular Age*, 755.

166. Desmond, *Is There a Sabbath for Thought?*, 19.

167. Desmond, *The Intimate Strangeness of Being*, 266.

168. Keats, *The Complete Poetical Works and Letters of John Keats*, 277.

FIVE   Epiphanic Attunement

1. Lewis, *The Lion, the Witch and the Wardrobe*, 141.

2. Ibid., 163.

3. Kearney, "Secular Epiphanies: The Anatheistic Hermeneutics of Gerard Manley Hopkins," 369.

4. Ibid.

5. Kearney, *Anatheism*, 87.

6. Husserl, *Ideas Pertaining to a Pure Phenomenology and to a Phenomeno-logical Philosophy.*

7. Moran, *Introduction to Phenomenology*, 172.

8. Ibid., 172.

9. Descartes, *Meditations on First Philosophy*, 96.

10. Husserl, *Ideas II*, 61. Edith Stein, *On the Problem of Empathy*, makes the same observation (43).

11. Ibid.

12. Husserl, *Ideas II*, 61.

13. Leder, *The Absent Body*, 26–27.

14. Ibid., 26.

15. Husserl, *Ideas II*, 71.

16. Heidegger, *Being and Time*, 99.

17. Husserl, *Ideas II*, 72.

18. Heidegger, *Being and Time*, 103.

19. Ibid., 77.

20. Ibid., 84–85 (emphasis original).

21. Ibid., 85.

22. Desmond, "Wording the Between," 203.

23. Desmond, *The Intimate Universal*, 253.

24. Ibid., 254.

25. Ibid.

26. Hart, *The Hidden and the Manifest*, 35.

27. Ibid.

28. Hadot, *Philosophy as a Way of Life*, 84.

29. Rahner, *Hearer of the Word*, 151.

30. Simpson, *Religion, Metaphysics, and the Postmodern*, 94.

31. Desmond, "Godsends: On the Surprise of Revelation," 10.

32. Ibid.

33. Ibid.

34. Ibid., 11.

35. Merton, *Conjectures of a Guilty Bystander*, 153.

36. Desmond, "Godsends," 21.

37. Simpson, *Religion, Metaphysics, and the Postmodern*, 94.

38. Ibid., 23.

39. Schindler, "The Positivity of Philosophy," 134.

40. Ibid., 12.

41. Ibid., 22.

42. Ibid., 12.

43. Desmond, "Godsends," 13.

44. Manoussakis, "The Silences of the Between," 270.

45. Ibid., 284.

46. Kearney, "The Gift of Creation," 281.

47. Gardner, "God Beyond and Between," 182.

48. O'Connor, *Wise Blood*, 16.

49. Desmond, *Is There a Sabbath for Thought?*, 217.

50. Desmond, *God and the Between*, 327.

51. Hopkins, "As Kingfishers Catch Fire," 129.

52. O'Connor, "Revelation," in *Collected Works*, 635.

53. Ibid.

54. Ibid., 636.

55. Ibid., 642.

56. Ibid., 637.

57. Ibid., 644.

58. Ibid., 645.

59. Ibid., 646.

60. *Summa theologiae* Ia, q. 8 r. 2.

61. O'Connor, "Revelation," 647–48.

62. Ibid., 652.

63. Ibid., 653.

64. Ibid.

65. Ibid.

66. Ibid., 26.

67. O'Connor, "Revelation," 654.

68. Ibid.

69. O'Connor, "To *A.*," in *Collected Works*, 1067.

70. Ibid.

71. In Wittgenstein, *Philosophical Investigations*, §115: "A *picture* held us captive. And we could not get outside it, for it lay in our language and language seemed to repeat it to us inexorably."

72. Robinette, *Grammars of Resurrection*, 102.

73. Ibid.

74. Ibid.

75. Hilary of Poitiers, *The Trinity* 7.12.

76. Ibid., 235–36.

77. Wilken, *The Spirit of Early Christian Thought*, 90.

78. Ibid., 90–91.

79. Marion, *Givenness and Revelation*, 68.

80. Ibid., 82.

81. Schneiders, *Jesus Risen in Our Midst*, xviii.

82. Robinette, *Grammars of Resurrection*, 102.

83. Ibid., 110.

84. Desmond, "Godsends," 22.

85. Robinette, *Grammars of Resurrection*, 113.

86. Marion, "They Recognized Him; and He Became Invisible to Them," 146.

87. Ibid., 147.

88. Wittgenstein, *Tractatus Logico-Philosophicus*, 5.

89. Marion, "They Recognized Him; and He Became Invisible to Them," 147.

90. Ibid.

91. Taylor, *A Secular Age*, 668.

92. Desmond, *The Intimate Universal*, 402.

93. Ibid., 361.

94. Ibid., 402–3.

95. Augustine, *Confessions* 3.6.

96. Desmond, "Godsends," 28.

97. Crowley, "Mystagogy and Mission: The Challenge of Nonbelief and the Task of Theology," 12.

98. Lohfink, *Jesus of Nazareth: What He Wanted, Who He Was*, 113.

99. Ibid.

100. Metz, *A Passion for God: The Mystical-Political Dimension of Christianity*, 163.

101. Tracy, *On Naming the Present: God, Hermeneutics, and Church*, 43.

102. Metz, *Faith in History and Society*, 136.

103. Tracy, "A Hermeneutics of Orthodoxy," 72.

104. Sobrino, *Christ the Liberator: A View from the Victims*, 210.

105. Young, *An Easy Burden: The Civil Rights Movement and the Transformation of America*, 222–23.

106. Ibid., 49.

107. Ibid.

108. Desmond, *The Intimate Strangeness of Being*, 217.

109. Schindler, "The Positivity of Philosophy," 132.

110. Desmond, "Analogy and the Fate of Reason," 16.

111. Desmond, "Consecrated Thought: Between the Priest and the Philosopher," 97.

112. Ibid., 98.

113. Desmond, "Wording the Between," 196.

114. Desmond, in "Responses" observes of *God and the Between*: "The last part of the book is so explicitly theological as to make me wonder who among philosophers might hear what it is trying to do, just because it is theological, and who among theologians is willing to think through the suggestions made, because of their undisguised commitment to metaphysical thinking in the metaxological mode," 302.

115. Kasper, *Jesus the Christ*, 9.

116. Augustine, *Confessions* 10.23.

In(con)clusion

1. Desmond, *Philosophy and Its Others*, 221.

2. Desmond, *Desire, Dialectic, and Otherness*, 219.

3. Desmond, *God and the Between*, 159.

4. Janz, "Transcendence, 'Spin,' and the Jamesian Open Space," 49.

5. Ibid.

6. Kavanagh, "The Great Hunger," in *Collected Poems*, 41–42.

7. Desmond, *Is There a Sabbath for Thought?*, 156.

8. Desmond, *Desire, Dialectic, and Otherness*, 35.

9. Desmond, *God and the Between*, 314.

10. Coakley, *Powers and Submissions*, 37.

11. Richard Kearney, "Enabling God," in Manoussakis, ed., *After God*, 46.

12. Westphal, "The Importance of Overcoming Metaphysics for the Life of Faith," 277.

13. Rahner, *Hearer of the Word*, 151.

14. Balthasar, *Love Alone Is Credible*, 102.

15. Crowley, "Mystagogy and Mission: The Challenge of Nonbelief and the Task of Theology," 24.

BIBLIOGRAPHY

Abbey, Ruth. *Charles Taylor*. Princeton, NJ: Princeton University Press, 2014.

Adams, Nicholas, George Pattison, and Graham Ward, eds. *The Oxford Handbook of Theology and Modern European Thought*. Oxford: Oxford University Press, 2013.

Alighieri, Dante. *The Divine Comedy*. Edited by David H. Higgins. Translated by C. H. Sisson. New York: Oxford University Press, 1998.

Alison, James. *The Joy of Being Wrong: Original Sin through Easter Eyes*. New York: Crossroad, 1998.

Anselm of Canterbury. *The Major Works*. Edited by Brian Davies and G. R. Evans. New York: Oxford, 2008.

Antonaccio, Maria. "Contemporary Forms of Askesis and the Return of Spiritual Exercises." *The Annual of the Society of Christian Ethics* 18 (1998): 69–92.

Aquinas, Thomas. *Summa Theologiae*. Translated by Laurence Shapcote. Lander, WY: The Aquinas Institute for the Study of Sacred Doctrine, 2012.

Armstrong, Arthur Hilary, and A. A. Armstrong, eds. *Classical Mediterranean Spirituality: Egyptian, Greek, Roman*. New York: Herder, 1986.

Arnold, Matthew. *Dover Beach and Other Poems*. New York: Dover, 1994.

Augustine. *Confessions*. Translated by Henry Chadwick. New York: Oxford University Press, 1998.

Auweele, Dennis. "Metaxological 'Yes' and Existential 'No': William Desmond and Atheism." *Sophia* 52, no. 4 (2013a): 637–55.

———. "The Poverty of Philosophy: Desmond's Hyperbolic Gifts and Caputo's Events." *American Catholic Philosophical Quarterly* 87, no. 3 (2013c): 411–32.

Ayres, Lewis, and Medi Ann Volpe, eds. *The Oxford Handbook of Catholic Theology*. Oxford: Oxford University Press, 2015.

Balthasar, Hans Urs von. *Love Alone Is Credible*. Translated by D. C. Schindler. San Francisco: Ignatius Press, 2004.

Blakely, Jason. "Returning to the Interpretive Turn: Charles Taylor and His Critics." *The Review of Politics* 75, no. 3 (2013): 383–406.

Bonaventure. *The Journey of the Mind to God*. Translated by P. Boehner. Indianapolis: Hackett, 1993.

Brabant, Christophe, and Lieven Boeve, eds. *Between Philosophy and Theology: Contemporary Interpretations of Christianity*. Farnham: Ashgate, 2013.

Brown, Nahum, and William Franke, eds. *Transcendence, Immanence, and Intercultural Philosophy*. Basingstoke: Palgrave Macmillan, 2017.

Buber, Martin. *Tales of the Hasidim*. Toronto: Schocken, 1991.

Buckley, Michael. *At the Origins of Modern Atheism*. New Haven, CT: Yale University Press, 1990.

———. *Denying and Disclosing God: The Ambiguous Progress of Modern Atheism*. New Haven, CT: Yale University Press, 2004.

Caputo, John. *Heidegger and Aquinas: An Essay on Overcoming Metaphysics*. New York: Fordham University Press, 2009.

———. *The Insistence of God: A Theology of Perhaps*. Indianapolis: Indiana University Press, 2013.

———. *On Religion*. New York: Routledge, 2001.

———. *Radical Hermeneutics: Repetition, Deconstruction, and the Hermeneutic Project*. Indianapolis: Indiana University Press, 1988.

———. *What Would Jesus Deconstruct? The Good News of Postmodernism for the Church*. Grand Rapids, MI: Baker, 2007.

Clarke, W. Norris. *Explorations in Metaphysics*. Notre Dame, IN: Notre Dame University Press, 1994.

Colorado, Carlos D., and Justin D. Klassen, eds. *Aspiring to Fullness in a Secular Age: Essays on Religion and Theology in the Work of Charles Taylor*. Notre Dame, IN: University of Notre Dame, 2014.

Comte, Auguste. *Introduction to Positive Philosophy*. Indianapolis: Hackett, 1988

Crowley, Paul. "Mystagogy and Mission: The Challenge of Nonbelief and the Task of Theology." *Theological Studies* 76, no. 1 (2015): 7–28.

———. *Unwanted Wisdom: Suffering, the Cross, and Hope*. New York: Continuum, 2005.

Cusa, Nicholas. *The Vision of God*. Translated by Emma Gurney Salter. Escondido, CA: Book Tree, 1999.

Davies, Brian. *Thomas Aquinas's "Summa Theologiae": A Guide and Commentary*. Oxford: Oxford University Press, 2014.

————, ed. *Thomas Aquinas: Contemporary Philosophical Perspectives*. New York: Oxford University Press, 2002.

Davies, Brian, and Brian Leftow, eds. *The Cambridge Companion to Anselm*. Cambridge: Cambridge University Press, 2006.

Dawkins, Richard. *The God Delusion*. New York: Random House, 2016.

Dennett, Daniel Clement. *Breaking the Spell: Religion as a Natural Phenomenon*. New York: Penguin, 2006.

Dennis, Patrick. *Auntie Mame (an irreverent escapade)*. New York: Broadway Books, 2001.

Denzinger, Heinrich. *Enchiridion symbolorum definitionum et declarationum de rebus fidei et morum: Compendium of Creeds, Definitions and Declarations on Matters of Faith and Morals*. 43rd ed. Edited by Peter Hünermann. San Francisco: Ignatius Press, 2012.

Descartes, René. *Discourse on Method and Meditations on First Philosophy*. Translated by Donald Cress. Indianapolis: Hackett, 2010.

Desmond, William. *Art, Origins, Otherness: Between Philosophy and Art*. Albany: SUNY Press, 2003.

————. *"Autonomia Turannos*: On Some Dialectical Equivocities of Self-Determination." *Ethical Perspectives* 5, no. 4 (1998): 233–53.

————. *Being and the Between*. Albany: SUNY Press, 1995.

————. *Being Between: Conditions of Irish Thought*. Galway: Arlen House, 2008.

————. *Beyond Hegel and Dialectic: Speculation, Cult, and Comedy*. Albany: SUNY Press, 1992.

————. "Consecrated Thought: Between the Priest and the Philosopher." *Louvain Studies* 30, no. 1-2 (2005): 92–106.

————. *Desire, Dialectic, and Otherness: An Essay on Origins*. Eugene, OR: Cascade, 2013.

————. *Ethics and the Between*. Albany: SUNY Press, 2001.

————. "Finding Measure in Exceeding Measure: On Ethics and the Between." *Ethical Perspectives* 8, no. 4 (2001): 319–31.

————. "Flux-Gibberish: For and against Heraclitus." *The Review of Metaphysics* 70, no. 3 (2017): 473–505.

————. *The Gift of Beauty and the Passion of Being*. Eugene, OR: Cascade, 2018.

————. *God and the Between*. Malden, MA: Blackwell, 2008.

————. "God, Ethos, Ways." *International Journal for Philosophy of Religion* 45, no. 1 (1999): 13–30.

————. "Godsends." *Ephemerides Theologicae Lovanienses* 92, no. 1 (2016b): 7–28.

———. *Hegel's God: A Counterfeit Double?* Burlington, VT: Ashgate, 2003.

———. *The Intimate Strangeness of Being: Metaphysics after Dialectic.* Washington, DC: Catholic University of America Press, 2012.

———. *The Intimate Universal: The Hidden Porosity among Religion, Art, Philosophy, and Politics.* New York: Columbia University Press, 2016.

———. *Is There a Sabbath for Thought? Between Religion and Philosophy.* New York: Fordham University Press, 2005.

———. "The Metaphysics of Modernity." In *The Oxford Handbook of Theology and Modern European Thought*, edited by Nicholas Adams, George Pattison, and Graham Ward, 543–63. Oxford: Oxford University Press, 2013.

———. "Neither Deconstruction nor Reconstruction: Metaphysics and the Intimate Strangeness of Being." *International Philosophical Quarterly* 40, no. 1 (2000): 37–49.

———. *Perplexity and Ultimacy: Metaphysical Thoughts from the Middle.* Albany: SUNY Press, 1995.

———. *Philosophy and Its Others: Ways of Being and Mind.* Albany: SUNY Press, 1990.

———. "Responses." *Louvain Studies* 36 (2012): 302–15.

———. "Schopenhauer's Philosophy of the Dark Origin." In *A Companion to Schopenhauer*, edited by Bart Vandenabeele, 89–104. Malden, MA: Blackwell, 2012.

———. "Sticky Evil: On Macbeth and the Karma of the Equivocal." In *God, Literature, and Process Thought*, edited by Darren Middleton. New York: Routledge, 2002.

———. "The Theater of the Metaxu: Staging the Between." *Topoi* 30, no. 2 (2011): 113–24.

Dreyfus, Hubert, and Charles Taylor. *Retrieving Realism.* Cambridge, MA: Harvard University Press, 2015.

Dupré, Louis. *Passage to Modernity: An Essay in the Hermeneutics of Nature and Culture.* New Haven, CT: Yale University Press, 1995.

———. *Religion and the Rise of Modern Culture.* Notre Dame, IN: University of Notre Dame Press, 2008.

———. *Transcendent Selfhood: The Loss and Rediscovery of the Inner Life.* New York: Seabury, 1976.

Elie, Paul. *The Life You Save Might Be Your Own.* New York: Farrar, Straus and Giroux, 2004.

Emerson, Ralph Waldo. "Compensation." In *Ralph Waldo Emerson: Essays & Lectures*, edited by Joel Porte. Boone, IA: Library of America, 1983.

Epictetus. *The Enchiridion.* Translated by George Long. Mineola, NY: Dover Publications, 2004.

Epstein, Greg. *Good without God: What a Billion Nonreligious People Do Believe.* New York: Harper, 2010.

Falque, Emmanuel. *Crossing the Rubicon: The Borderlands of Philosophy and Theology.* Translated by Reuben Shank. New York: Fordham University Press, 2016.

Faulkner, William. *Go Down, Moses.* New York: Vintage, 2011.

Feuerbach, Ludwig. *The Essence of Christianity.* Translated by George Eliot. Amherst, NY: Prometheus, 2004.

Ford, Ita. *"Here I Am Lord": The Letters and Writings of Ita Ford.* Edited by Jeanne Evans. New York: Orbis, 2005.

Francis, Pope. *The Joy of the Gospel: Evangelii Gaudium.* Washington, DC: United States Conference of Catholic Bishops, 2014.

———. *Laudato Sí: On Care for Our Common Home.* Huntington, IN: Our Sunday Visitor, 2016.

Frankfurt, Harry G. "Freedom of the Will and the Concept of a Person." *The Journal of Philosophy* 68, no.1 (1971): 5–20.

Girard, René. *Deceit, Desire, and the Novel.* Translated by Yvonne Freccero. Baltimore: Johns Hopkins University Press, 1965.

Gordon, Peter E. "The Place of the Sacred in the Absence of God: Charles Taylor's *A Secular Age.*" *Journal of the History of Ideas* 69, no. 4 (2008): 647–73.

Griffioen, Sander. "Towards a Philosophy of God: A Study in William Desmond's Thought." *Philosophia Reformata* 75, no. 2 (2010): 117–40.

Guignon, Charles. *The Cambridge Companion to Heidegger.* Cambridge: Cambridge University Press, 2011.

Hadot, Pierre. *The Inner Citadel: The Meditations of Marcus Aurelius.* Translated by Michael Chase. Cambridge, MA: Harvard University Press, 1998.

———. *Philosophy as a Way of Life: Spiritual Exercises from Socrates to Foucault.* Translated by Arnold Davidson. Oxford: Blackwell, 2011.

———. *The Present Alone Is Our Happiness: Conversations with Jeannie Carlier and Arnold Davidson.* Stanford, CA: Stanford University Press, 2001.

———. *What Is Ancient Philosophy?* Translated by Michael Chase. Cambridge, MA: Belknap, 2004.

Harris, Sam. *The Moral Landscape: How Science Can Determine Human Values.* New York: Simon and Schuster, 2011.

Hart, David Bentley. *The Hidden and the Manifest: Essays in Theology and Metaphysics.* Grand Rapids, MI: Eerdmans, 2017.

Heaney, Seamus. *The Redress of Poetry.* Oxford: Clarendon, 1990.

Hector, Kevin. *Theology without Metaphysics: God, Language, and the Spirit of Recognition.* Cambridge: Cambridge University Press, 2011.

Hegel, Georg Wilhelm Friedrich. *Hegel's Lectures on the History of Philosophy.* Translated by T. M. Knox and Arnold Miller. Oxford: Clarendon, 2003.

———. *Phenomenology of Spirit.* Translated by A. V. Miller. Oxford: Oxford University Press, 2013.

Heidegger, Martin. *Identity and Difference.* Translated by Joan Stambaugh. Chicago: University of Chicago Press, 2002.

———. "The Question Concerning Technology." In *Basic Writings*, translated by David Krell. London: Routledge, 2010.

Heyde, Ludwig. *The Weight of Finitude: On the Philosophical Question of God.* Translated by Alexander Harmsen. Albany: SUNY Press, 1999.

Hilary of Poitiers. *The Trinity.* Translated by Stephen McKenna. Baltimore: Catholic University of America Press, 2010.

Hill, Gladwin. "For Want of Hyphen Venus Rocket Is Lost." *New York Times*, July 27, 1962.

Hopkins, Gerard Manley. *The Letters of Gerard Manley Hopkins to Robert Bridges.* Oxford: Oxford University Press, 1955.

———. *The Major Works.* Edited by Catherine Phillips. Oxford: Oxford University Press, 2009.

Husserl, Edmund. *Ideas Pertaining to a Pure Phenomenology and to a Phenomenological Philosophy. Second Book: Studies in the Phenomenology of Constitution.* Boston: Kluwer, 1989.

Illich, Ivan. *The Rivers North of the Future: The Testament of Ivan Illich as Told to David Cayley.* New York: House of Anansi, 2011.

Irvine, William B. *A Guide to the Good Life: The Ancient Art of Stoic Joy.* Oxford: Oxford University Press, 2008.

Ivens, Michael. *Understanding the Spiritual Exercises: Text and Commentary.* Leominster: Gracewing Publishing, 1998.

Janicaud, Dominique. *Phenomenology and the "Theological Turn."* Translated by Bernard Prusak. New York: Fordham University Press, 2000.

Kant, Immanuel. *Critique of Pure Reason.* Rev. 2nd ed. Translated by Norman Kemp Smith. New York: Palgrave Macmillan, 2007.

———. *Ethical Philosophy: The Complete Texts of Grounding for the Metaphysics of Morals, and Metaphysical Principles of Virtue, Part II of the Metaphysics of Morals, with on a Supposed Right to Lie because of Philanthropic Concerns.* Translated by James Ellington. Indianapolis: Hackett, 1994.

Kasper, Walter. *Jesus the Christ.* New York: Continuum, 2011.

Kavanagh, Patrick. *Collected Poems.* New York: Norton, 1964.

Kearney, Richard. *Anatheism: Returning to God after God.* New York: Columbia University Press, 2011.

———. "The Gift of Creation." In *William Desmond's Philosophy between Metaphysics, Religion, Ethics, and Aesthetics*, edited by D. Vanden Auweele, 217–84. Cham, Switzerland: Palgrave Macmillan, 2018.

———. *The God Who May Be: A Hermeneutics of Religion*. Indianapolis: Indiana University Press, 2001.

———. *On Paul Ricoeur: The Owl of Minerva*. London: Taylor & Francis, 2017.

———. *On Stories*. London: Routledge, 2002.

———. *Paul Ricoeur: The Hermeneutics of Action*. London: Sage, 1996.

———. "Secular Epiphanies: The Anatheistic Hermeneutics of Gerard Manley Hopkins." *Dialog* 54, no. 4 (2015): 367–74.

Kearney, Richard, and Jens Zimmermann, eds. *Reimagining the Sacred: Richard Kearney Debates God*. New York: Columbia University Press, 2015.

Keats, John. *The Complete Poetical Works and Letters of John Keats*. Boston: Houghton Mifflin, 1958.

Keller, Catherine. *The Face of the Deep: A Theology of Becoming*. New York: Routledge, 2003.

———. *On the Mystery: Discerning Divinity in Process*. Minneapolis: Fortress Press, 2007.

Kelly, Thomas A. F., ed. *Between System and Poetics: William Desmond and Philosophy after Dialectic*. New York: Routledge, 2016.

Laird, Martin, and Sheelah Trefle Hidden, eds. *The Practice of the Presence of God: Theology as a Way of Life*. London: Taylor & Francis, 2016.

Leclercq, Jean. *The Love of Learning and the Desire for God: A Study of Monastic Culture*. Translated by Catharine Misrahi. New York: Fordham University Press, 1982.

Leder, Drew. *The Absent Body*. Chicago: University of Chicago Press, 1990.

Levertov, Denise. *The Stream & the Sapphire*. New York: New Directions, 1997.

Lewis, Clive Staples. *The Lion, the Witch and the Wardrobe*. London: HarperCollins, 2000.

Lohfink, Gerhard. *Jesus of Nazareth: What He Wanted, Who He Was*. Translated by Linda M. Maloney. Collegeville, MN: Liturgical Press, 2012.

Long, Steven. "How to Read Charles Taylor: The Theological Significance of *A Secular Age*." *Pro Ecclesia* 27, no. 1 (2009): 93–107.

Lucian of Somosata. *Charon*. In *Lucian*, Vol. 2, translated by A. M. Harmon. Cambridge, MA: Harvard University Press, 1915.

Manoussakis, John, ed. *After God: Richard Kearney and the Religious Turn in Continental Philosophy*. New York: Fordham University Press, 2006.

———. *God after Metaphysics: A Theological Aesthetic*. Bloomington: Indiana University Press, 2007.

Marion, Jean-Luc. *God without Being.* Translated by Thomas Carlson. Chicago: University of Chicago Press, 2012.

———. "They Recognized Him; and He Became Invisible to Them." *Modern Theology* 18, no. 2 (2002): 145–52.

McCabe, Herbert. *God Matters.* New York: Continuum, 2012.

Merton, Thomas. *Conjectures of a Guilty Bystander.* New York: Image Books, 1968.

Metz, Johann Baptist. *A Passion for God: The Mystical-Political Dimension of Christianity.* Translated by Matthew Ashley. New York: Paulist Press, 1998.

Middleton, Darren, ed. *God, Evil, and Process Thought.* Burlington, VT: Ashgate, 2002.

Milbank, John. *Theology and Social Theory: Beyond Secular Reason.* Malden, MA: Blackwell, 2013.

Moran, Dermot. *Introduction to Phenomenology.* Oxford: Taylor and Francis, 2014.

Murdoch, Iris. *The Sovereignty of the Good.* London: Routledge, 1970.

Nagel, Thomas. *Mind and Cosmos: Why the Materialist Neo-Darwinian Conception of Nature Is Almost Certainly False.* New York: Oxford University Press, 2012.

Nietzsche, Friedrich. *The Gay Science: With a Prelude in Rhymes and an Appendix of Songs.* Translated by Walter Kaufmann. New York: Vintage, 2010.

———. *Thus Spoke Zarathustra.* Translated by R. J. Hollingdale. New York: Penguin, 1969.

———. *The Will to Power.* Translated by R. J. Hollingdale. New York: Vintage, 1968.

Nygren, Anders. *Agape and Eros.* Translated by Philip Watson. London: S.P.C.K., 1953.

O'Connor, Flannery. "Revelation." In *Collected Works*, 633–54. New York: Library of America, 1988.

O'Regan, Cyril. "The Poetics of Ethos: William Desmond's Poetic Refiguration of Plato." *Ethical Perspectives* 8, no. 4 (2001): 272–306.

———. "What Theology Can Learn from a Philosophy Daring to Speak the Unspeakable." *Irish Theological Quarterly* 73, no. 3-4 (2008): 243–62.

Pascal, Blaise. *Pensées.* Translated by A. J. Krailsheimer. New York: Penguin Books, 1995.

Pfau, Thomas. *Minding the Modern: Human Agency, Intellectual Traditions, and Responsible Knowledge.* Notre Dame, IN: University of Notre Dame Press, 2015.

Pinkard, Terry. "Analytics, Continentals, and Modern Skepticism." *The Monist* 82, no. 2 (1999): 189–217.

Plato. *Complete Works*. Edited by John M. Cooper. Indianapolis: Hackett, 1997.

Rahner, Karl. *Faith in a Wintry Season*. Translation by Harvey Egan. New York: Crossroad, 1990.

———. *Hearer of the Word*. Translated by Joseph Donceel. New York: Continuum, 1944.

———. *Karl Rahner in Dialogue: Conversations and Interviews*. Edited by Paul Imhof and Hubert Biallowons. New York: Crossroad, 1986.

———. *The Need and the Blessing of Prayer*. Translated by Bruce Gillette. Collegeville, MN: Liturgical Press, 1997.

Ratzinger, Joseph. *Introduction to Christianity*. Translated by J. R. Foster. San Francisco: Ignatius Press, 2004.

Ricoeur, Paul. *From Text to Action*. Translated by Kathleen Blamey and John Thompson. Evanston, IL: Northwestern University Press, 2007.

———. *Interpretation Theory: Discourse and the Surplus of Meaning*. Fort Worth: Texas Christian University Press, 1976.

———. *Oneself as Another*. Translated by Kathleen Blamey. Chicago: University of Chicago Press, 1992.

———. *Time and Narrative*. Translated by Kathleen McLaughlin and David Pellauer. Chicago: University of Chicago Press, 2010.

Robinette, Brian D. "The Difference Nothing Makes: Creatio Ex Nihilo, Resurrection, and Divine Gratuity." *Theological Studies* 72, no. 3 (2011): 525–57.

———. *The Difference Nothing Makes: Creation, Christ, Contemplation*. Forthcoming.

———. *Grammars of Resurrection: A Christian Theology of Presence and Absence*. New York: Crossroad, 2009.

Ruusbroec, John. *"The Spiritual Espousals" and Other Works*. Translated by James Wiseman. New York: Paulist Press, 1985.

Saint-Exupéry, Antoine de. *The Little Prince*. Translated by Richard Howard. New York: Harcourt, 1998.

Schindler, D. C. *The Catholicity of Reason*. Grand Rapids, MI: Eerdmans, 2013.

Schneiders, Sandra Marie. *Jesus Risen in Our Midst: The Bodily Resurrection of Jesus in the Fourth Gospel*. Collegeville, MN: Liturgical Press, 2013.

———. "The Study of Christian Spirituality: Contours and Dynamics of a Discipline." *Christian Spirituality Bulletin* 8, no. 1 (1998): 1–12.

Shearin, W. H., and Brooke Holmes, eds. *Dynamic Reading: Studies in the Reception of Epicureanism*. New York: Oxford, 2012.

Shelley, Percy Bysshe. *The Major Works*. Edited by Zachary Leader and Michel O'Neill. New York: Oxford University Press, 2009.

Simpson, Christopher Ben. *Religion, Metaphysics, and the Postmodern: William Desmond and John D. Caputo.* Indianapolis: Indiana University Press, 2009.

——. "Theology, Philosophy, God and the Between." *Louvain Studies* 36 (2012): 226–38.

——, ed. *The William Desmond Reader.* Albany: SUNY Press, 2012.

Simpson, Christopher Ben, and Brendan Thomas Sammon, eds. *William Desmond and Contemporary Theology.* Notre Dame, IN: University of Notre Dame Press, 2017.

Smith, James K. A. *How (Not) to Be Secular: Reading Charles Taylor.* Grand Rapids, MI: Eerdmans, 2014.

Smith, Nicholas H. *Charles Taylor: Meaning, Morals and Modernity.* Malden, MA: Blackwell, 2002.

Sobrino, Jon. *Christ the Liberator: A View from the Victims.* Translated by Paul Burns. New York: Orbis, 2001.

Stallings, Gregory C., Manuel Asensi, and Carl Good, eds. *Material Spirit: Religion and Literature Intranscendent.* New York: Fordham University Press, 2013.

Stephen, James Fitzjames. *Liberty, Equality, Fraternity: And Three Brief Essays.* Chicago: University of Chicago Press, 1991.

Taylor, Charles. *Dilemmas and Connections: Selected Essays.* Cambridge, MA: Belknap, 2011.

——. *The Ethics of Authenticity.* Cambridge, MA: Harvard University Press, 1991.

——. *Hegel and Modern Society.* Cambridge: Cambridge University Press, 1980.

——. *Human Agency and Language.* Vol. 1 of *Philosophical Papers.* Cambridge: Cambridge University Press, 1985.

——. *The Language Animal.* Cambridge, MA: Belknap Press, 2016.

——. *Modern Social Imaginaries.* Durham, NC: Duke University Press, 2004.

——. *Philosophical Arguments.* Cambridge, MA: Harvard University Press, 1995.

——. *Philosophy and the Human Sciences.* Vol. 2 of *Philosophical Papers.* Cambridge: Cambridge University Press, 1985.

——. *A Secular Age.* Cambridge, MA: Belknap Press, 2007.

——. *Sources of the Self: The Making of the Modern Identity.* Cambridge, MA: Harvard University Press, 1989.

——. *Varieties of Religion Today: William James Revisited.* Cambridge, MA: Harvard University Press, 2003.

Thomson, Iain. "Ontotheology? Understanding Heidegger's *Destruktion* of Metaphysics." *International Journal of Philosophical Studies* 8, no. 3 (2000): 297–327.

Tracy, David. "A Hermeneutics of Orthodoxy." *Concilium* 2 (2014): 71–81.

———. *On Naming the Present: Reflections on God, Hermeneutics, and Church.* Maryknoll, NY: Orbis, 1994.

Vila-Chã, João, ed. *Renewing the Church in a Secular Age: Holistic Dialogue and Kenotic Vision.* Washington, DC: Council for Research in Values and Philosophy, 2016.

Warner, Michael, Jonathan VanAntwerpen, and Craig J. Calhoun. *Varieties of Secularism in a Secular Age.* Cambridge, MA: Harvard University Press, 2010.

Westphal, Merold. "The Importance of Overcoming Metaphysics for the Life of Faith." *Modern Theology* 23, no. 2 (2007): 253–78.

———. *Overcoming Onto-Theology: Toward a Postmodern Christian Faith.* New York: Fordham, 2001.

———. *Transcendence and Self-Transcendence: On God and the Soul.* Indianapolis: Indiana University Press, 2004.

White, Victor. *God the Unknown and Other Essays.* New York: Harper, 1956.

Wilken, Robert Louis. *The Spirit of Early Christian Thought: Seeking the Face of God.* New Haven, CT: Yale University Press, 2003.

Wittgenstein, Ludwig. *Philosophical Investigations.* Translated by G. E. M. Anscombe. Malden, MA: Blackwell, 2008.

———. *Tractatus Logico-Philosophicus.* Translated by D. F. Pears and B. F. McGuinness. New York: Routledge, 2006.

Wordsworth, William. *The Major Works.* Edited by Stephen Gill. New York: Oxford, 2008.

Wrathall, Mark. *Religion after Metaphysics.* Cambridge: Cambridge University Press, 2004.

Yi, Zane G. "The Possibility of God: An Examination and Evaluation of Charles Taylor's Transcendental Critique of Closed Worlds." PhD diss., Fordham University, 2013.

INDEX

Abbey, Ruth, 10

Absolute, 60, 210, 216, 296

absolute original, 105

actual transcendence (T$_3$). *See* transcendence itself (T$_3$)

ad hominem reasoning, 8–9, 14–15, 16, 18

aesthetic experience, 199–200, 259

aesthetic rebirth, 166, 167, 168

aesthetics of happening, 165–68, 198–207

affirmation of ordinary life, 22–23

agape, 172, 173, 174, 221, 222, 223–24

Agapeic Creator, 105, 220, 225, 230, 248, 251, 281, 287, 294

agapeic mind, 114, 173, 203, 205

agapeic nihilism, 180, 220, 230

Agapeic Other, 293, 300

agapeic service, 220, 224, 250, 300

agapeics of community, 172–76, 214–25

agnosticism, 193

analogy, 185–86, 187

anatheism, 62

Anselm of Canterbury, Saint: critique of, 211, 213; ontological argument of, 208, 210–11, 216,

229; *Proslogion*, 209, 211; understanding of God, 209–10, 213

Antonaccio, Maria, 132

apodictic reasoning, 8, 9–14, 15, 18, 26, 306n57

Aquinas. *See* Thomas Aquinas, Saint

Aristotle: comparison to Plato, 81, 82; critique of Heraclitus, 83; on geometry in philosophical inquiry, 82; *Nichomachean Ethics*, 14; observation of being, 68, 79; view of equivocity, 83

Armstrong, Karen: *The Case for God*, 19

Arnold, Matthew: "Dover Beach," xix, 152–53, 290

askesis (practice of philosophical exercise), 52, 133, 153

astonished silence, 242

astonishment: agapeic, 114; consideration of creation and, 191; description of, 108–9; metaphysical thinking as, 70, 108, 157; metaxology and experience of, 109, 113

atheism, xvii, 2, 4, 70, 120, 153

attention (*prosoche*), 134, 136–37, 139, 142, 148, 242, 296

Ryan G. Duns, SJ,
is assistant professor of theology at Marquette University.

9 780268 108137